CREAM
A PEOPLE'S HISTORY

Richard Houghton

First published in 2021 by Spenwood Books Ltd,
2 College Street, Higham Ferrers, NN10 8DZ.

All rights reserved
© Richard Houghton, 2021

The right of Richard Houghton to be identified as author of this work has been asserted in accordance with Section 77 of the Copyright, Design and Patents Act 1988.

A CIP record for this book is available from the British Library.

ISBN 978-1-9168896-0-6

Printed and bound by Sound Performance Ltd,
3 Greenwich Quay, Clarence Road, Greenwich, London, SE8 3EY.

Design by Bruce Graham, The Night Owl.
Photo copyrights: As captioned.

BY THE SAME AUTHOR

You Had To Be There: The Rolling Stones 1962 - 69

The Beatles - I Was There

The Who - I Was There

Pink Floyd - I Was There

The Rolling Stones - I Was There

Jimi Hendrix - The Day I Was There

Led Zeppelin - The Day I Was There

The Smiths - The Day I Was There

The Jam - The Day I Was There (with Neil Cossar)

Black Sabbath - The Day I Was There

Rush - The Day I Was There

The Wedding Present - Sometimes These Words Just Don't Have To Be Said (with David Gedge)

Orchestral Manoeuvres in the Dark - Pretending To See The Future

Simple Minds - Heart of the Crowd

Shaun Ryder's Book of Mumbo Jumbo

CONTENTS

INTRODUCTION 06

BEGINNINGS 07

1966 13

1967 77

1968 183

2005 328

EXTENDED PLAY 375

AFTERWORD 381

INTRODUCTION

CREAM'S TIME TOGETHER as a working band was less than three years, but the impact they had on modern music, bridging the gap from the British blues explosion through psychedelia and into progressive rock, cannot be under estimated. The accounts of over 500 previously unpublished eyewitness accounts I have collected together here are testimony to that.

It is sometimes difficult to confirm the dates and venues on which and at which Cream performed. As one contributor to this book recalls, Eric Clapton told him he never knew where the band would be playing the following day. For several of the shows remembered in this book, there is conflicting information online and in previously printed documents as to when and where they took place.

Christopher Hjort's book, *Strange Brew: Eric Clapton & The British Blues Boom 1965-1970*, was an excellent and absorbing guide through those times, but the information in that occasionally differed both from whereseric.com and jackbruce.com. I also had reference to *Cream: The World's First Supergroup* by Dave Thompson, Eric Clapton's *The Autobiography*, *Hellraiser* by Ginger Baker with Ginette Baker, and *Cream - The Legendary Sixties Supergroup* by Chris Welch.

Where I have not been able to verify the dates using existing sources, I have gone with the recollections of the contributor unless there is compelling evidence that the show did not take place. If anyone has information about Cream shows, I'd love to hear from them at iwasatthatgig@gmail.com.

I am indebted to my many contributors for sharing their memories with me. I'd also like to thank the many local newspaper editors who published my original appeal for fans to come forward, and to Mark Zuckerberg for inventing Facebook. Without it, tracking down fans who saw some of these performances would have been so much harder.

Finally, I'd like to thank: Geoff Sell; Howard Johnson; Mike Kelsey; Geraint Catling; Paul Burke; John Tomlinson and web wizard Bruce Koziarski.

And especially Bruce Graham for his design expertise, and Kate Sullivan for her continued domestic goddessness and willingness to let me disappear off to my computer for hours on end.

Richard Houghton,
Manchester, UK.
July 2021

BEGINNINGS

Eric Clapton, Peter 'Ginger' Baker and Jack Bruce were all active on the British music scene before coming together to form Cream.

CAMBRIDGE UNIVERSITY MAY BALL
MAY 1962, CAMBRIDGE, UK

GINGER, A MEMBER of Blues Incorporated, plays a side gig with fellow Blues Incorporated member Dick Heckstall-Smith and others at Cambridge University. Jack joins the group to jam on stage. It is Jack and Ginger's first meeting.

BBC RADIO'S JAZZ CLUB
12 JULY 1962, LONDON, UK

JACK, HAVING QUIT the jazz band he was playing in, joins Blues Incorporated.

NOVEMBER 1962, LONDON, UK

GRAHAM BOND JOINS Blues Incorporated. The offshoot Graham Bond Trio (featuring Bond, Bruce and Baker) begin playing the odd show together.

FLAMINGO CLUB
LATE FEBRUARY 1963, LONDON, UK

JACK, GINGER AND Graham Bond leave Blues Incorporated and branch out on their own as the Graham Bond Trio.

EARLY 1963

ERIC CLAPTON JOINS his first band, Rhode Island Red and the Roosters.

MARQUEE CLUB
APRIL 1963, LONDON, UK

THE GRAHAM BOND Trio briefly becomes a quartet with the temporary addition of John McLaughlin. Dick Heckstall-Smith is then recruited and the Graham Bond Organisation (featuring Jack and Ginger) is born.

CIVIC HALL
SEPTEMBER 1963, MACCLESFIELD, UK

THE ROOSTERS FOLD. Eric joins Casey Jones & The Engineers, playing his first show in Macclesfield.

STUDIO 51
18 OCTOBER 1963, LONDON, UK

ERIC IS RECRUITED to the Yardbirds, appearing with them for the first time at Studio 51.

Our entire reason for existence was to honour the tradition of the blues.
Eric Clapton

CRAWDADDY CLUB, RICHMOND ATHLETIC ASSOCIATION GROUNDS
3 NOVEMBER 1963,
RICHMOND-UPON-THAMES, UK

I WAS THERE: VALERIE DUNN
I USED TO regularly go to the Crawdaddy Club in Richmond to see the Yardbirds. I was quite friendly with them. I'd chat to them and they gave me all their old harmonicas when they were slightly clapped out, because I played blues harmonica. I used to get up and play maracas with them. If one of the guitarist's strings would go, they'd stop to put a new string on and they used to throw the maracas down to me to play while they were changing the strings on the guitar. I made them a lucky mascot out of chamois leather. I embroidered 'Yardbird' on it and Eric managed to attach it to the end of his guitar when he was playing on the set. He was really pleased with it. That was quite nice. I'll never forget that. I was really chuffed. Good old Eric. He was a Mod back then.

RHODES CENTRE
11 JULY 1964, BISHOP'S STORTFORD, UK

I WAS THERE: AUSTIN REEVE
I USED TO listen to Elvis and the early rockers on Radio Luxembourg every night, even before I was a teenager, and occasionally went to the local jazz club on a Saturday night. My earliest rock gigs were at local venues such as the Saturday Scene at the Corn Exchange, Chelmsford and at the Rhodes Centre in Bishops Stortford. One of the first gigs that I went to was to see the Yardbirds at Rhodes in mid-1964. They had appeared on Ready Steady Go on TV the night before and I was really impressed with their sound, especially the lead guitarist - the then virtually unknown Eric Clapton.

My girlfriend at the time had seen them at the Ricky Tick Club in Windsor and raved about them. I was blown away by their music live, especially as the support group for that night didn't turn up, so the Yardbirds played two long sets to fill in. Eric pulled out all the stops that night. My girlfriend had met the band at Windsor and she chatted to them in the interval but I was too timid to say much. I saw the Yardbirds several more times, with Eric and later with Jeff Beck and Jimmy Page, but that night at Rhodes was the best.

4TH NATIONAL JAZZ & BLUES FESTIVAL, RICHMOND ATHLETIC ASSOCIATION GROUNDS
9 AUGUST 1964, RICHMOND-UPON-THAMES, UK

GINGER AND JACK are amongst the 'friends' the Yardbirds invite to join them on stage.

Eric was with the Yardbirds at the time, and Ginger and me were with Graham Bond Organisation. That's the first time I'd heard Eric at all and, of course, I was impressed. There were other people playing with us, too, but I think the three of us stood out. **Jack Bruce**

KING MOJO CLUB
9 APRIL 1965, SHEFFIELD, UK

AFTER 18 MONTHS as a Yardbird, Eric joins John Mayall's Bluesbreakers, appearing with them for the first time in Sheffield.

KLOOK'S KLEEK, RAILWAY HOTEL
25 MAY 1965, WEST HAMPSTEAD, UK

I WAS THERE: VALERIE DUNN
WE USED TO see Eric there when he was with John Mayall and we'd buy him a drink at the bar.

IL RONDO
23 JULY 1965, LEICESTER, UK

I WAS THERE: GRAHAM AUCOTT

I SAW CREAM twice at the George Ballroom in Hinckley. It was 17 shillings (85p) to get in. Family were the same price. But the first time I saw Eric was when he played with the Bluesbreakers at the Il Rondo on Silver Street in Leicester. He opened up with the Tommy Tucker classic, 'Hi-Heel Sneakers', and a good night was had by all.

AUGUST 1965, LONDON, UK

JACK IS FIRED from the Graham Bond Organisation.

BLACK PRINCE
30 AUGUST 1965, BEXLEY, UK

ERIC, HAVING DECIDED to leave, plays his 'last' show with the Bluesbreakers. John Mayall agrees to hold Eric's job for him should he return.

BLUESVILLE MANOR HOUSE BALLROOM
11 OCTOBER 1965, IPSWICH, UK

JACK JOINS JOHN Mayall's Bluesbreakers.

BLUE TRIANGLE CLUB
4 NOVEMBER 1965, EALING, LONDON, UK

ERIC RETURNS TO the Bluesbreakers after his so-called 'Greek adventure'. He and Jack play the first of 13 shows together.

RED CROSS HALL
21 NOVEMBER 1965, SUTTON, UK

HAVING RECEIVED A better financial offer from Manfred Mann, Jack plays his final gig with the Bluesbreakers.

1966
UNKNOWN VENUE
MARCH 1966, OXFORD, UK

GINGER HAS DECIDED to form his own group. He drops in on a Bluesbreakers gig to enlist Eric as guitarist. Eric agrees to join provided Jack is on bass.

BRAEMAR AVENUE, NEASDEN
APRIL 1966, LONDON, UK

ERIC, JACK AND Ginger jam together at Ginger's home.

ST ANN'S TOWN HALL, BRONDESBURY
MAY 1966, LONDON, UK

ERIC, JACK AND Ginger begin rehearsing.

Musically, we didn't really have a plan. **Eric Clapton**

THE TWISTED WHEEL
30 JULY 1966, MANCHESTER, UK

I WAS THERE: BOB GARBUTT

THE BLOKE I was with asked me if I wanted to meet some friends in a pub. I was then introduced to each one and Ginger Baker looked like the Wild Man of Borneo. After a couple of drinks we left and went into the Twisted Wheel. Cream played that night. Brilliant.

I WAS THERE: ROB HOLLAND, AGE 17

AS A 17-year-old I would travel up to Manchester from South Cheshire with my older brother and his mate in his mate's Mini Cooper. We'd strut around Manchester Piccadilly for a while in our Mod suits. There was a clothing factory in Crewe where staff could 'acquire' suit lengths of fabric which you could get made up as a cash job in someone's front room. As darkness gathered the strolling crowds would drift to the clubs, and for us that meant the Twisted Wheel for the 'all-nighters'.

I'm afraid I remember little of the Cream night itself. I do recall getting Eric Clapton's autograph on an advert flyer and expected

Rob Holland was at The Twisted Wheel for the sounds of Motown and not to see the genesis of the fabled new supergroup Cream

to find it tucked away somewhere in my late mum's house over 40 years later when we cleared it - but no such luck. My claims to have been there have, in later years, been met with scepticism, so I bought Eric Clapton's autobiography to convince others, and perhaps myself, that the gig actually took place as many said that the first Cream performance was at the Reading Festival. And there it is - 29 July 1966, the day before the famous World Cup final.

I have to say the pull to the Twisted Wheel was more the Motown and soul-type acts - you can't really dance well to Ginger Baker's lengthy drum solos! - so Cream was a big difference to me, but the memory stuck with me.

6TH NATIONAL JAZZ & BLUES FESTIVAL, ROYAL WINDSOR RACECOURSE
31 JULY 1966, WINDSOR, UK

I WAS THERE: JEFF RICHARDS, AGE 16

THE EXPLOSION OF music in the Sixties away from skiffle and jazz was manna from heaven for young teenagers. I'd seen Eric Clapton in the Yardbirds and followed his music with John Mayall, and to be perfectly honest, I didn't take much notice of the line up for the Windsor and Reading Jazz and Blues Festival. I knew Jack Bruce had played with Manfred Mann, but wasn't aware of what a brilliant bass player he was. So the day England won the World Cup at football, Jimmy James and the Vagabonds and The Who played their set at Windsor. Yeah, I didn't have much tolerance to alcohol, but you had to celebrate. Consequently I had a hangover the next day, which luckily wore off by the evening when Cream played. Holy crap - blown away doesn't cover it. If I recall correctly they repeated a couple of numbers because they didn't have a big set list. What a way to close a festival.

Jeff Richards had shaken off his World Cup hangover by the time Cream appeared at the Windsor Festival

I WAS THERE: AUSTIN REEVE

I FOLLOWED ERIC'S progress to John Mayall's Bluesbreakers during the 'Clapton is God' era and saw the band a couple of time locally. Eric seemed to get better every time I saw him and he had a tremendous following by that time. The Bluesbreakers' line-up was always changing and before long, Eric was off again, being replaced by the great Peter Green. I managed to catch up with Eric again at the National Jazz and Blues Festival at Windsor in July 1966 - my first major rock festival. The programme listed a band that had no name at that time and was simply called 'Eric Clapton - Jack Bruce - Ginger Baker'. This was the band's first major gig, having only done a warm-up at the Twisted Wheel in Manchester a couple of nights before. I had seen Jack and Ginger before in Graham Bond's Organisation and knew we were in for something special.

The band were timetabled to play last on the Sunday night and it was pouring with rain. I remember walking down to the stage in the downpour, following Eric who was being sheltered from the deluge by a multi-coloured golf umbrella carried by a gorgeous blonde. The weather kept a lot of people away but the performance was worth getting wet for. I can't remember what numbers were played but I was totally bowled over by their sound and their combined musical skill. They hadn't rehearsed many numbers, so the set was fairly short and the announcer at the end had to tell the audience that there were no more numbers for an encore. It was really a night to remember. England had won the World Cup the previous afternoon but I always remember the Cream debut more fondly - as I was there!

I WAS THERE: GIZZY GILLESPIE
THE FIRST TIME I saw Clapton was with the Cream at the 1966 Jazz and Blues Festival at Windsor. They only did three songs but it was enough to have the crowd going mad. It could have been their first public performance. Then they got a residency at the Marquee Club on a Tuesday night. You had to get there early as the queue was all the way down Wardour Street. The Ship is a pub on Wardour Street. When the Cream were playing it would be rammed with people - some quite famous and, like me, looking like they had just jumped off the sleeve of Sgt. Pepper.

I WAS THERE: EDDIE SPECKMAN
I SAW ERIC Clapton with the Yardbirds at the Atalanta, and I saw Jack Bruce and Ginger Baker there with Graham Bond. I didn't see Cream at the Atta, but I saw them at the Windsor Festival. Eric had a perm, and a very frilly cream shirt.

I WAS THERE: RICHARD LUETCHFORD
I SAW THEM on three occasions, the first being the Windsor Jazz and Blues Festival where they topped the bill. They were not listed as Cream but under their individual names. Windsor was a prestigious gig in front of an audience of 15,000. In those days that was a big festival

and it was still quite jazz-based, with mostly British jazz in the afternoon and the blues rock bands in the evening. It was a showery day with some good acts to see, including Reg Dwight (aka Elton John) playing in the Marquee with Bluesology. Georgie Fame was a great crossover act for loyal jazzers and pop fans alike. There was also The Action, an underrated Mod band. Cream were the last act of the day and the heavens opened just as they started! Clapton was in an ironic gold lamé jacket and white flares, Bruce playing his Fender six string bass with a harmonica harness and Baker with his double bass drum kit. They were loud, and got a great reception from the crowd. The set was short but the band had rehearsed only a few songs which they stretched out with solos. We were left wanting more but I had to get the train back to Clapham Junction where I lived, and so the festival ended.

I WAS THERE: STEVE MEW

MY INTEREST IN music started when The Beatles arrived like a shot in the arm of the British pop music scene. Then the Stones arrived and their first single 'Come On' raised the hairs on the back of my neck and started my first love of rhythm and blues. I was 15.

I initially became aware of Eric Clapton through the excellent and innovative Yardbirds, almost wearing out their Five Live Yardbirds LP. In 1965 the Blue Moon Club in Cheltenham opened, hosting many exciting bands such as The Action, The Who, Small Faces - and Cream twice. I visited frequently, always trying to go if John Mayall was on. To me, it was this band that really allowed Eric's style to develop; fiery like the three kings - Freddie, Albert and BB - but on steroids, with his Gibson through his Marshall Bluesbreaker 18 watt amplifier, but also very delicate at times, as he was almost like a butterfly touching the strings.

I got friendly with John McVie, who would take my mate and self to the pub (The Continental, I think) and buy us a half in the break. Eric didn't join us, but just nodded his hello in recognition. I think he was actually a bit shy. John was really worried that Eric was leaving the Bluesbreakers. Because of his huge presence in the band, we tried to reassure John that although Eric would be a big loss, John Mayall would always come up trumps with a replacement and this proved to be so with the very special Peter Green, who it could be argued was more BB King than BB.

Appearing in other bands (mainly the Graham Bond Organisation) Jack Bruce and Ginger Baker appeared at the club, and so I started to appreciate their obvious talents. Being a budding bass player myself I was not quite so taken with Jack as he played a fender six string bass which I didn't really like. However, he played a stunning solo in one number that left me awestruck. Now, as for Ginger - what a drummer! A force of nature, and always smiling as I recall.

So there it was that the three of them - advertised initially as Bruce, Baker and Clapton and not as 'Cream' - came together in July 1966 to form what to me was one of the best groups on the planet. The end of July 1966 saw myself and a couple of mates at the Windsor Jazz and Blues Festival at Balloon Meadow on the Royal Windsor racecourse. As I recall it was pretty wet. I shared an umbrella - and she my huge PVC coat - with a young lady (unknown) as we anticipated their appearance. She smelt lovely - and I didn't!

They came on stage to tremendous applause with good-humoured banter from and with the crowd. One fan shouted, 'Everything but the kitchen sink, Ginger!' Ginger was busy amusing us with his juggling skills with his sticks, bouncing them off his drums and catching them. His kit was pretty minimal by today's standards. Not that he needed much - he was a monster player. To my mind he always played with the song and the music to add to the tune, not to detract from it.

One fan shouted, 'Everything but the kitchen sink, Ginger!'

Their performance was electrifying, with not many numbers and extensive improvisation of great quality and interesting. They only played for about 40 minutes as I recall. We were pretty close to the stage and the sound quality was very good. Both Jack and Eric using double Marshall 100 stacks. I'm not sure if Ginger was miked but, blimey, he didn't need it. His drum solo in 'Toad' was so impressive it brought the crowd to their feet. They truly deserved the title of 'supergroup'. Cream had arrived.

I WAS THERE: STEWART WATKINS, AGE 18

I WAS A raw, naïve 18-year-old from the Welsh valleys on his first trip away from home. I remember not being very impressed. Perhaps I'd expected too much after being a big Yardbirds and John Mayall fan, although living in South Wales I hadn't seen either play live. I think I was hoping for a kind of bigger, better Bluesbreakers but of course they were actually more sophisticated than that, and I don't think I was ready for that. But I loved Eric's playing - and still do - and knew of Jack Bruce's bass playing, especially since he used a Fender VI six string bass.

It was the culmination of a musical, and life, journey that had started five or six years earlier. I had enjoyed the music of the Fifties with Elvis, Cliff and others but when the Shadows hit with 'Apache' I knew I was going to be a bass guitarist just like Jet Harris. I loved the whole Fender look and sound and, to a 13-year-old, this was it! But then Jet took it to a whole new level by going solo and playing his legendary Fender VI, a six string sunburst bass guitar that looked like a guitar but made the most fantastic bass sounds, especially when being played by a blond-quiffed, leather-jacketed god.

In 1962 or '63, I had acquired my first bass and was playing in a local band, in pubs and working mens' clubs, the latter only catching up very slowly with modern music trends including increasingly long hair. Through The Beatles and the Stones we became aware of black musicians and their music and began incorporating numbers such as 'Walking the Dog', 'Got My Mojo Working' and even 'Hoochie Coochie Man' into our sets, much to the consternation of local club entertainment secretaries. By 1964, even at the top of the Welsh valleys, we were well aware of the Downliner Sect, the Pretty Things and all the others, including the Graham Bond Organisation and the Yardbirds. We bought the LPs and played them to death, trying to learn every lick and nuance, speeding them up and slowing them down to try to catch the intricacies of the guitarists. I still believe that *Five Live Yardbirds* is one of the finest live recordings of a band in its prime, and it took us to alternatives of 'Smokestack Lightning' and 'I'm a Man'.

Then - shock, horror - Eric Clapton left the Yardbirds and joined John Mayall and recorded the legendary *Beano* album. This was British blues being played at its finest and I was in love. Why the British version of American blues had such an effect on so many of us I've never really understood but it obviously resonated right through us. Perhaps it was the working class, underdog feel that reverberated so very strongly. Modern American jazz also made its mark, especially that of John Coltrane, Miles Davies, Thelonius Monk, Charles Mingus and others. It was mean, moody, frantic music influencing bands like Graham Bond Organisation. Although the GBO were on my radar, my music was guitar-driven. Nonetheless, we all knew about Ginger Baker and Jack Bruce.

And then Eric joined up with Jack and Ginger to form the first 'supergroup', The Cream. (The 'the' was later dropped). Three of the finest blues players in the country together in one band. By now I had been working on the shop floor of the Hot Strip Mill at Ebbw Vale steelworks for two years, had a little money and when it was advertised that The Cream would be playing at Windsor, me and my friend Phil said 'we're going!'

We got a local bus from Ebbw Vale to Newport, and then on to London's Victoria Coach Station. We didn't know how to get to Windsor but somehow we did. I remember joyously walking with many other similarly minded young people, getting in with our prepaid tickets and pitching our tent. Then, joy of joys, we were in amongst the whole festival experience, out of the valleys and into Windsor Great Park and the racecourse. I remember the fabulous Move, the Small Faces getting pennies thrown at them and The Nice, featuring Keith Emerson with his whips and knives and rocking his Hammond back and forth.

Eventually, the mighty Cream took the stage

Eventually, the mighty Cream took the stage. I don't remember a great deal of it; perhaps I had drunk too much beer. I Remember being impressed but not overwhelmed. Perhaps we had expected too much, perhaps they wanted to surprise us too much, perhaps the long drum solo didn't impress. But I do remember Jack standing there with his Fender VI bass. I'm not sure that they played many blues numbers. I believe it may also have rained.

Finally, it all came to a close and we had to somehow find our way back into London. With no transport, we just began walking. It was very cold, so we walked, found shelter, rested, shivered, started moving and slept briefly in underpasses. Somehow we got back into central London and I remember watching the city coming to life in a very early dawn. As we walked past Marble Arch and on through Hyde Park, we suddenly came across Cassius Clay, as he was then, jogging through the park with three or four trainers accompanying him. He was there to fight Brian London - he won with a knock out in the third round. I still have his autograph from that day.

By now we were grumpy and tired from lack of sleep and sleeping rough. When Phil saw a small hotel he said 'we're going in there' and in we went, to my first ever hotel stay. I don't know what it cost but it was worth it!

The next day, I bought the *Paul Butterfield Blues Band* LP (a rarity in Ebbw Vale) and then it was back to Victoria and homeward bound to Newport and Ebbw Vale, full of stories of derring do and music 'like you've never heard before', and to tell everyone we'd seen Cream.

I WAS THERE: TOM CRAWFORD

I WAS A teenager and a full-blown Mod with a Lambretta SX 200 scooter. I was into all sorts of music at the time - Northern Soul, jazz, blues, etc. - and I have always been a Clapton fan, so being at the first official concert of Cream was a dream come true. My best friend and I travelled down to Windsor on our scooters and slept rough for the days at the festival as we had little money. I was helping to clear the grounds for the three days of the festival and was on the front row when Cream came on around midnight. They played into the early night and with it being a calm atmosphere I am sure it would have been heard in the next county. Each member had an individual spot and both Ginger Baker and Clapton took full advantage of it. I'll never forget it.

I WAS THERE: WILLIAM RICHARDSON

William Richardson was at Windsor

I AM A Durham miner's son, brought up in the North East of England. From the age of 16 to 18 years of age I became aware of blues music. My first heroes were The Animals from Newcastle who, like other bands, played a lot of American blues covers. Unfortunately, I never saw them live until they reformed in the Seventies. I was also keen on the Rolling Stones and my schoolmate obtained tickets for a gig of theirs at Sunderland. We went along and did not hear a note they played as they were drowned out by the girls screaming. It took two hours before my ears returned to normal!

In September 1965 I went to Coventry University to study chemistry. The students' union put on regular gigs every Saturday so I went to lot of them. Another ex-schoolmate who was a student in London invited me down for the weekend with a promise of a gig at Chelsea Art College. There I saw the Graham Bond Organisation. What a performance it was, and guess who his sidemen were? Jack Bruce and Ginger Baker! I had never seen a drummer perform like that.

Life continued at college and fellow students mentioned a rising guitar player called Eric Clapton. I listened to his playing with John Mayall and the Bluesbreakers on a fellow student's LP and was amazed at Eric's blues playing. A few months later they were booked to play at our university and I bought a ticket, only to discover when I turned up that Eric had left the band. However, I still had a great night as Eric's replacement was Peter Green. What a marvellous show they put on. I was also persuaded to watch a gig at the local ballroom. Manfred Mann were performing and Paul Jones had just left. Jack Bruce was on bass guitar and vocals. He had left Graham Bond and was standing in with the Manfreds before forming Cream.

My friends and I went to the Windsor Jazz and Blues Festival. We heard that Cream had been formed and were making their official debut. It was an outdoors gig so not as loud as it could have been. I think they played a short set that afternoon. I recall Jack Bruce saying they had not had a lot of time to rehearse and write songs. As an encore they played one they had played already. Nobody minded.

TOWN HALL
6 AUGUST 1966, TORQUAY, UK

I PROMOTED THEM: LIONEL DIGBY

I BOOKED CREAM for their first major indoor show. Their fee was £75.

In 1953 I had joined the Household Cavalry Life Guards. I was stationed at Knightsbridge in London and used to go to the skiffle and jazz clubs. By 1956 rock'n'roll was coming in and the cellar of the 2i's coffee bar was where it was all happening. It used to be packed. You

Lionel Digby promoted Cream's first big indoor show

had the likes of Cliff Richard, Adam Faith, Screaming Lord Sutch and Joe Brown all going down there and singing for £1 and a free Coke. Tom Littlewood ran it.

When I was demobbed in December 1956 I came home to Torquay and it was dead. It was still the Dark Ages as far as the British economy was concerned, with no street lighting and us still on rations. There were just a few youth clubs playing records - mostly American apart from one or two by Cliff Richard and Wee Willie Harris - and *Six-Five Special* on television. It was still the big band era. The village halls were still playing dance hall stuff and the only band that came to Torquay was Ted Heath once a year.

Lionel Digby booked Cream at Torquay Town Hall for £75

I met up with a chappie called Johnny Harris who, like me, had just come out of the army. He put a little band together with no guitars - just piano, bass, drums and vibes. The vibes did the guitar work. They'd play the latest things from America but had nowhere to play. Torquay's Co-op Hall had things like Women's Institute meetings and tombola clubs going on, while regular dance nights were Friday and Saturday, but it was free on Tuesday nights so I booked it. We opened it up on the second Tuesday in February in 1957 and it was a massive success. We ran every Tuesday. It was the only rock'n'roll venue in the south west. Kids were coming down from Exeter and Plymouth, 20 to 30 miles away. Then Saturday night became available and we did Saturday nights.

Within a fortnight of opening the Co-op Hall, we went and played at the Badminton Hall, Paignton, and started doing regular dances in Paignton, Brixham, Totnes, Newton Abbott and Exeter. And then

I started bringing down the early people like Ricky Vallance (of 'Tell Laura I Love Her' fame), Screaming Lord Sutch and Tommy Bruce, all these people that were coming out of the 2i's. Most of them didn't have a band to back them so I had a skiffle group which played the Co-op Hall back them.

In 1960, I was an assistant manager at my family's hotel but chucked it all in to go full time as a promoter. Torquay Town Hall became the major venue in the west country. I could get 2,000 people in there, and I had a series of dance halls - the Johnson Hall in Yeovil, the Queen's Hall in Barnstaple, the Civic Hall and St George's Hall in Exeter, a hall in Plymouth and the Flamingo down in Cornwall. I started to get known in London and managers would ring me for their bands to go on.

Rock and roll was new but all the agents were old timers doing dance bands and big bands and cabaret acts. Young lads who had worked in London came into the promoting business and branched out on their own. I was in on the ground floor and started it all in the south west. All over the country this was happening, with small promoters dividing up the country between them. Len Canham had the south coast, Bob Potter had Camberley and all round London, the Kennedy brothers had Manchester and John Mills did Bristol. Agents in London would know who to go to.

Robert Stigwood said they wanted to do a major gig away from London

---

And promoters would swap bands with each other. Some of my bands would have a week's holiday up north and a northern band would come down here and do a week in the west country. Everybody went to Devon and Cornwall for their holidays then. The coal mines shut down for a fortnight, the steel works shut down, you'd have the Sheffield fortnight and so on. You'd have four girls staying in one twin-bedded room, and four boys in another. Torquay, Newquay and Looe and everywhere used to heave. I'd book a small hall in somewhere like Newquay that held several hundred and put something on for the holidaymakers. I'd pay the bands £100 a week whether they were a three piece or a six piece. They'd travel down and pay for their own petrol and accommodation. A lot of them would sleep in the van, or they'd pick up girls and sleep with them in their holiday chalets. Bands wanted to come down to the west country.

We all knew about Cream because they were quite big because of the bands they'd played in beforehand, and there was so much stuff on 'Slowhand' Clapton, as everybody knew him, and it was in all the music papers about this first supergroup with Eric and Ginger Baker and Jack Bruce. But they had no record out.

The Robert Stigwood Organisation was managing Cream. I knew Bob Stigwood. He rang me up one day, said they'd been rehearsing, and that he wanted to do a major gig away from London and away from the press. The week before that they appeared in a small club up north somewhere. But Torquay Town Hall was the first major event they did, and it was packed.

What amazed me was how nervous they were about the reaction they were going to get, because this was their first major gig with 2,000 kids in a packed ballroom. That for a band without a record was quite amazing. How many other bands without a hit record could do that, outside of London?

Ginger was the only one that was really into the drugs heavily. Ginger used to be high when he went on. Eric Clapton wasn't. Ginger I think had a bottle of whisky. I can't remember what Jack Bruce was drinking. All Eric wanted was Coca-Cola.

I WAS THERE: MAUREEN BROWNING

MY LATE SISTER and I were on two weeks' holiday at Pontins South Devon Holiday Camp in Paignton in August 1966. We saw the posters for Cream at Torquay Town Hall on Saturday 6th August and got tickets. The holiday camp was on the bus route running around Torbay between Torquay and Brixham, with Paignton in the middle. We went out to catch the bus, saw it coming and rushed to get on it, not realising we got on the one going in the wrong direction. We were halfway to Brixham before we realised and had jump off at the next stop and get one going the other way, making it to Torquay Town Hall just in time.

Maureen Browning saw the Torquay Town Hall show, but only just

What a fabulous evening it was. The place was buzzing, the music incredible - and the bus ride back uneventful! We later worked as Bluecoats at this holiday camp, and needless to say we learnt all the bus routes!

I WAS THERE: PAUL ARCHER, AGE 14

I SAW CREAM on what I believe to have been only their third ever gig together. I probably only paid about five or six shillings and I remember the announcer introducing them individually. They only played for about an hour, mainly numbers from what would have been their first album, *Fresh Cream*. I only saw them the once, although I later saw Jack Bruce live in Blackpool doing a lot of Cream numbers and he was fantastic. I've also been to many Eric Clapton concerts over the years.

FLAMINGO BALLROOM
7 AUGUST 1966, POOL, REDRUTH, UK

I PROMOTED THEM: LIONEL DIGBY

THE NEXT DAY they went down and did the Flamingo Ballroom down in Redruth, Cornwall.

BROMLEY COURT HOTEL
12 AUGUST 1966, LONDON, UK

I WAS THERE: DENNIS BOUNDY, AGE 18

I SAW CREAM twice at the Bromel Club at the Bromley Court Hotel. One time Long John Baldry was there too, propping up the bar with a bottle of whisky. There was only a small crowd as they were not very well known then. They performed on a low stage at one end of the room. I remember it cost seven shillings and six pence in old money to get in, or 37.5p now.

I WAS THERE: DOUG VIEWEG

THE ONLY MEMORY I have is of Ginger Baker breaking his drum sticks and throwing them into the audience.

I WAS THERE: GEORGEANA BIRD

I AM NOT keen on solos and I thought, 'If that man is not going to stop twanging that guitar I am leaving.' Whoops!

I WAS THERE: RICHARD SEARLES, AGE 14

I WAS AT Bromley Court Hotel with my school friends, and we were really close to Eric Clapton's amp stack. It was bloody loud and my ears were ringing for some time afterwards. In fact, I've had tinnitus in my left ear for many years since. I'm a guitarist myself so that doesn't help!

I WAS THERE: MICK MURPHY

Mick Murphy remembers Eric's amp dying

MY FIRST EXPERIENCE of watching Cream was at the Bromley Court Hotel in Bromley, formerly the Bromel Club. At one gig, when it came to Baker's drum solo, Eric and Jack went to the bar for a drink and to mingle. After a while they went back to the stage to plug in and start again. But Ginger showed no signs of slowing down so they unplugged and went back to the bar. This happened a couple of times, before it seemed Ginger realised they were about to join in again. The 'Toad' solo must have been nearing over 15 minutes long. As we were leaving we could see blue lights flashing through the glass and when we got outside we could see it was an ambulance. Not being quite sure what had happened, we asked one of the doormen. 'Oh,' he said, 'the drummer has collapsed. We think it was exhaustion.' It was not a big stage and the low ceiling was dripping with water, or sweat.

Another time I recall some of the audience were sort of psychedelic dancing or 'trancing'. Someone must have got a bit carried away and bumped into the speaker which had Eric's amp on top and - crash! - it fell off, killing his sound. The gig was stopped for around 20 minutes whilst the techy tried to fix it. I think a valve had gone. He got it fixed about the normal closing time, Eric Clapton then announced over the mic, 'We are sorry for the delay but we would now like to play on to make up for it...' but the last part of his sentence was cut short as the PA and some lights were turned off because it was the usual closing time. Eric then shouted into the mic, 'Who the fucking hell turned the PA off?' But just as he started to shout the words the mic came on again, leaving the crowd in hysterics. They did play on and played some of the best they had all night.

My brother Brian is a few years older than me and, being older, he and I never really stood together. He recalls Cream being nearly two hours late for one gig and, when they did finally arrive, he overheard a massive row between Jack and Ginger. Eric must have had enough as he came onstage by himself, plugged in (maxed up) and aggressively hit the first few chords of 'I'm So Glad'. He was quickly joined by the other two members!

Cream played the Bromley Court Hotel in Peyton Place, Bromley four times in total, also appearing there on 14 and 21 December 1966 and again on 22 February 1967.

BLUE MOON CLUB
13 AUGUST 1966, CHELTENHAM, UK

I WAS THERE: ROD GAY

I'D SEEN CLAPTON years before. A mate and I went up to London at Christmas time to see my mate's family. We were going to go to Trafalgar Square for the New Year but didn't get there as we were both ill - something we ate. We walked across Hammersmith Bridge and we saw that The Beatles' Christmas show was on at Hammersmith Odeon. They were in a residency over Christmas, and the Yardbirds were a support act. You couldn't hear The Beatles because of all the screaming - it was bedlam - but I remember coming away and saying how great the Yardbirds were.

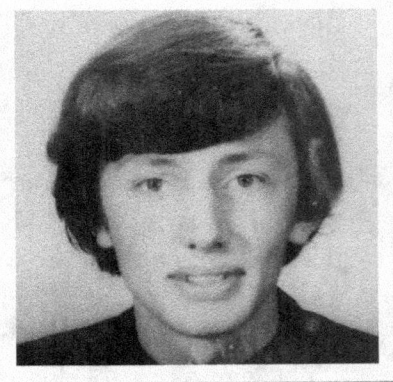
Rod Gay remembers a funny sort of atmosphere at the Blue Moon

My brother Tom and I were keen on blues as a progression from the Stones - people like Muddy Waters, Howlin' Wolf, Buddy Guy. Tom was a real blues man. He was the one with the shoulder length hair. I'm from a small town in the Cotswolds so we weren't exactly handy for many gigs. But I went with some mates to the Reading Jazz and Blues Festival in '65. Georgie Fame was on the bill, and The Who.

Some people had the album that showed Clapton reading *The Beano* on the Bluesbreakers album cover. When I went up to university in Hull, I remember seeing John Mayall up there but by that time Clapton had left. Peter Green was playing guitar. It was my first winter at university when *Fresh Cream* came out. I knew it was coming out and I'd been anticipating it quite keenly, thinking that this was going to be something new and exciting. And I remember being somewhat disappointed when they released the single 'Wrapping Paper'. I thought 'that's a bit weak.' But clearly it was just meant to try and pander to the *Top of the Pops* brigade. Everybody ended up on there just to get known.

The gig was notable for its energy

I went to the Blue Moon with Tom and a mate. We weren't regulars at the Blue Moon but we knew they were on and we knew we had to see them. We were keen. We were enthusiastic. We were the sort of people who went to dances and spent the whole night standing there watching the band. Tom was a real blues man with shoulder length hair but the mate we went with was a very dapper Mod-type character. We came in on the bus. Living 20 miles outside of Cheltenham you had to suffer for your entertainment and had to be prepared to get home late.

It was a funny sort of atmosphere. The evening light was coming in through the window and it had more of the atmosphere of a church hall than a night club. There weren't many people there. It felt like one of those gigs where bands still have contractual obligations to small venues even though they are becoming famous.

The gig was notable for its energy. They had an interval and Ginger Baker's shirt was soaked in sweat. The venue was playing some music in the lead up to the band performing and Jack Bruce picked up his bass and immediately began playing along with a Motown song. It whetted your appetite and made you think you were going to see something good. It wasn't full. We ended up standing on a bench down the side to get a better view. We always wanted to look at people's fingering and get some sense of the detail of what they were doing. It was a weird atmosphere. I'd seen John Mayall at Smiths Industries Social Club Christmas do in Bishops Cleeve and it was steaming, but this was like being at one of their rehearsals. You almost got the impression they were playing for themselves, not for who was out there in front of them. You were just there with them, as close as you wanted to be. They played two sets. There was an interval. I just remember standing there and taking it in, with this wall of sound hitting us.

It felt like we were watching a blues band, rather than the Jack Bruce-penned numbers and the psychedelic stuff that came later. I remember listening to those albums and thinking there'd been a change, a shift in what they were doing. Cream coming along represented a whole wider transition from the poppy, rock 'n' rolly stuff into the more psychedelic and drug-infused rock. It was dope, it was acid. The cover of *Disraeli Gears* shouted acid rock to you. I've got *Cream's Greatest Hits* on CD and I don't even know if I like some of the stuff on it any more. At the time you were getting into the spirit of the thing but I'm not sure that some of their stuff has stood the test of time.

In 1968 I left university early and went off to India. And when I came back that November, Cream were on the television in their farewell concert. Something had happened in the six months I was away and they'd broken up.

I WAS THERE: BILL WHITE

I SAW CREAM live at the Blue Moon in Cheltenham twice. I remember there was music press excitement at the formation of the group and that the venue was full. I'd seen Bruce and Baker with Graham Bond and Clapton with John Mayall at the same venue. Being a Mod, I was actually more into seeing The Action at the time - and Spencer Davis and the Steampacket. I certainly remember Clapton at the Blue Moon in a non-playing capacity; he was seeing a girl from Cheltenham at the time and was wearing a pair of brown and white brogues with no socks!

I WAS THERE: NIGEL SOUTHGATE

THEY GOT PAID about £35 for the gig. Tickets were 10 shillings (50p) each. There was a tiny stage in the corner with room for about three musicians next to a glass enclosure where the disco was. Clapton had bell bottoms on with the fringed hair and long sideboards. The music was great, and mainly off the *Fresh Cream* album. I also saw Hendrix there.

He got paid £45 as 'Hey Joe' had just gone into the charts. Both he and Cream used Marshall stacks as amps. Cream's kit arrived in a green Austin A30 estate. Hendrix arrived by train.

I WAS THERE: MIKE WILLIAMS

I SAW CREAM perform twice at the Blue Moon Club. The place was packed to capacity. There was no air conditioning at venues in those days and the condensation dripped from the ceiling and down the walls. As smoking was allowed in those days, the cloudy atmosphere resembled a London street in Victorian times. It was a great gig though, and the three piece group excelled with a real authentic grinding blues rock sound. Ginger Baker's drum work was tight and the thudding bass of Jack Bruce was hypnotising. Of course, the whole thing was held together by the mesmerising guitar skills of Eric Clapton. To see them once was amazing but to see them twice inside three months was simply awesome.

MY DAD WAS THERE: STEPHEN REID

CREAM PLAYED THE Blue Moon Club twice, on 13 August and 19 November 1966. I know this because my father Bill was one of the owners

The ledger from the Blue Moon showing the returns on putting on a Cream show and I still have the ledgers and accounts for the club. In August 1966, the club had an attendance of 389 people and took £176, including just over £14 on the coffee bar and four pounds and five shillings on the cloakroom. The group's fee was £92, so after other costs were deducted that was a return of over £50.

In November, they had 522 people through the door and took almost £239, with four pounds, twelve shillings and threepence taken by the cloakroom. But the group's fee had increased to £200 so despite the bigger attendance the profit after other expenses on the second show was less than £20.

My father loved Ginger Baker and thought he was a proper jazz drummer, although he thought a fellow called Lennie Hastings was better! A 17 or 18-year-old Ginger was in the Terry Lightfoot Band, with my father on double bass. The albums they made are still on sale on bloody Amazon - we do not get a penny from sales. When my father was in his later years, suffering from vascular dementia, he would watch three programmes on repeat: a Ginger Baker documentary called *Beware of Mr Baker*, the Keith Richards *Origin of the Species* progamme - and *Minder*!

MARQUEE CLUB
16 AUGUST 1966, LONDON, UK

I WAS THERE: ALEXANDER VALENTINE

GROWING UP AS a teenager through the Fifties and Sixties was a fantastic time. The introduction of rock 'n' roll from America came first, with stars like Little Richard, Fats Domino, and Bill Haley and the Comets. This progressively evolved into the terrific Blues era, as so many youngsters were taking up playing a selection of instruments, the main one of course being the electric guitar. Blues bands sprang up everywhere and the musicians kept changing from one group to

Alexander Valentine saw Cream at the Marquee

another as personalities and playing styles caused break ups, but it was all to the good, as throughout these changes musicians gained experience and new skills to create great music. Among these were two of my favourite players at the time - Eric Clapton and Ginger Baker.

Eric seemed to radiate talent. He was a natural and continually improved over the years to become an international superstar; Ginger Baker was a fun drummer. Ginger played good drums but he was also a comedian and I remember one of his favourite ploys was to be featured in a drum solo occasionally, where he played his heart out and used tremendous physical effort, after which he would stage a noisy collapse over his drum kit to create a dramatic effect. Crazy guy! I followed the blues bands around most of the great live music venues of those days such as the Richmond Hotel, Eel Pie Island, the Ealing Broadway Cellar Club and, of course, the internationally famous Marquee Club in Soho. Long live the blues.

I WAS THERE: TONY LOFTUS

Tony Loftus was at the Marquee

IT ALL STARTED when I was at Exeter Tech College. I was at college with a friend called Julian Piper who was a very good guitarist. He used to buy the music press, read about a gig coming up at Exeter University and said 'why don't we go along?' It was the Graham Bond Organisation - Graham Bond, Jack Bruce, Ginger Baker and Dick Heckstall-Smith. It was absolutely amazing and they blew me away. And I thought 'this is for me'. I had a chat with Jack Bruce in the urinal. That's my claim to fame!

I moved to London in 1966. I went to the Marquee Club on quite a regular basis. I saw Jimi Hendrix there. I think Clapton was actually in the audience that night, along with Mick Jagger and Marianne Faithfull and about 30 people altogether. Cream played there several times on a Tuesday. You'd just turn up and pay your half a crown (12.5p) on the door. It was unbelievable really. They always had brilliant supporting bands like Family and Amen Corner.

I was surprised to see how hippy-looking Cream were. It was that sort of time in London. They were all wearing tights - and bandanas! As well as their music, they were pushing their sexuality on stage. The music was really vibrant. I bought the albums and I loved the first one. We saw them quite a few times. They were just a band we used to go and see but they were a band that I would want to go and see. Apart from John Mayall and Peter Green, there weren't many others that caught my imagination quite like them.

I WAS THERE: PETE CLARKE

I SAW THEM twice, once at the Marquee and the second time at the Royal Albert Hall. My main memory of the Marquee is Ginger Baker tapping me on the shoulder and saying 'skooze me, mate' as he took to the stage, followed by Jack and Eric.

ORFORD CELLAR CLUB
17 AUGUST 1966, NORWICH, UK

I WAS THERE: JOHN BAILEY

IN THE MID-Sixties I visited all the music venues in Norwich at one time or another. My favourite was the Orford Arms run by Douro Potter, with the Cellar Club run mainly by Howard Platt. It was the area of the Mods and musical tastes were fickle. The Cellar was a platform for bands to up the ante. The biggest name I saw there was the Jimi Hendrix Experience, but I also saw Cream there. The Orford Cellar was painted matt black, with Batman and Robin characters in luminous paint lit up by ultraviolet tubes. Upstairs in the bar, pride of place was taken by the jukebox which was really bassy and loud. Most of the records were the latest soul releases from the US which were brought into the pub by the American airmen at USAF Mildenhall and which were otherwise unavailable in Britain at the time.

I WAS THERE: HELEN DAVENPORT, AGE 15

IT WAS BEFORE ID was needed. Me and my friend Nan were a couple of hippie chicks, and I was wearing a skirt made out a yellow parachute and a cheese cloth shirt. I was probably stinking of patchouli oil and a gentler aroma of cannabis. I was always barefoot so it was quite dodgy in the dark and very smoky nights down in the Orford Cellar. I also remember not being able to afford 10 shillings (50p) to see Jimi Hendrix play at Dereham Village Hall!

I WAS THERE: TONY RICHARDSON

THE CELLAR WAS just that - a regular cellar, probably about 15 to 20 feet square with a small bar in the far corner and a steep set of stairs for the entrance and exit. The place was packed, with people standing shoulder to shoulder, and you could hardly get your drink up to your mouth to drink it. I shudder to think what would have happened if there had been a fire. We were diehard Eric Clapton fans. He appeared regularly down the Cellar with John Mayall's Bluesbreakers and then with Cream. I remember seeing Hendrix there and he was excellent, but I considered him just a flashy player and not as good as Clapton. Clapton is God as far as I am concerned.

I WAS THERE: VICKI REYNOLDS

MY LATE HUSBAND saw the band at the Orford Cellar. After the gig they were all in the bar upstairs and he got their autographs on a card which he thought was from where they stayed whilst in Norwich. The card was one of his prized possessions.

Cream played the Orford Cellar Club again on 12 October 1966.

EEL PIE HOTEL
24 AUGUST 1966, TWICKENHAM, UK

I WAS THERE: STUART DIENN

I WAS ABOUT 15 years old and most Saturdays went to Eel Pie Island in Twickenham to listen to the live music. I lived in Teddington so Twickenham for me was just a hop, skip and a jump. I'd get on my bike or I'd walk or get a bus. A bus was tuppence (1p) and it was a 27 bus from Waldegrave Road to Twickenham Junction. At the time my father was on Radio London 266 as DJ Earl Richmond. He would give me all the EPs, singles and LPs. And when I saw this Cream one, I thought, 'Hmmm, that's not going to be very good, is it?' But I played it and nearly busted the bloody record player. I played it and played it and played it and I just could not get the tunes out of my head. When I heard that Cream were playing at Eel Pie Island I was there like a shot. It was fantastic to hear live and listened to every note and the words sung. When Cream were playing, there wasn't a sound. Nobody was cheering. They were just listening because it was that good.

Clapton did a couple of solos and they went into a couple of songs off the LP and all of a suden Clapton took himself off the stage and left Ginger Baker to do a 20 minute solo. It was absolutely phenomenal. People stood there just agog. Their chins were on the floor. It got a bit boring in the end because he did repeat several riffs about three times but even so, Ginger Baker is one of the best drummers I've ever seen.

It was a bit surreal. I was very young. I wasn't into the drug scene but a lot of people were. The only thing you could drink on Eel Pie Island was Newcastle Brown, in the big pint bottles. The floor of the Eel Pie Hotel was sprung. If somebody went down along the bar, people on the other side of the room started going up and down. And I thought, 'Are they all that drunk or is it just me?' I wondered if the drugs that were being smoked in the area were starting to affect me. But it was the floor.

There was an audience of about 300 for Cream and still more wanting to get in

---

It held about 250 to 300 people. And if people really wanted to see somebody it would be 400 to 500 and it would be really crowded. But a lot of people used to stand outside and have a drink in the summer because it was that loud you could hear it outside. And inside it was so warm from the amount of people and the body heat they generated that on two occasions, women were being carried out because of the heat.

There was an audience of about 300 for Cream and still more wanting to get in. I can't remember how much it cost to get in, probably 7/6 (37p) or 10 bob (50p), depending on what band it was. When the Stones were there it was 10 bob. That was my week's pocket money up the spout. There used to be so many bands turning up there and you'd think 'what's a band of that calibre doing here?' because it wasn't a really clean venue. It was a bit grotty. And the sound system was about 16 feet above the stage, so how they got the soundchecks right I'll never know.

There was only one way of getting there, over the bridge on foot, and if they caught you on the bridge you had to pay your entrance fee. But sometimes I'd get a mate of mine who owned a motorboat to bring me on the river side of the hotel. He'd come alongside, cut his engine and we'd drift out, come into the jetty, I'd jump off and he'd drift off and then start his engine further down river and I'd just walk up to the venue.

A lot of the people who lived on the island really started getting up in arms about having to pay the entrance fee on the bridge because these security guys wouldn't let them on the island even though they lived there. So they were kicked out and they had to have security on the entrance on the door instead.

IL RONDO
26 AUGUST 1966, LEICESTER, UK

I WAS THERE: STEVE BOTT, AGE 16

I ATTENDED THE two gigs that Cream played at the Il Rondo. Unfortunately, the second one didn't take place due to the non-arrival of their equipment. The Il Rondo was a small nightclub on Silver Street in the centre of town. I was a Mod, and if you were a Leicester Mod then Friday night at the Il Rondo was the place to be. There was always a live band on. A couple of mates had asked if I fancied going down to the Il Rondo to see Cream. This would be my first visit to a nightclub.

Steve Bott was at the Il Rondo, which was the place to be

It must have been quite a scoop for the nightclub owner to land Cream, as Clapton was very high profile and had already picked up the 'Clapton is God' tag during his stint with John Mayall. But it seems they played loads of small venues even after the release of *Fresh Cream*. I remember having my first vodka and lime and my first rum and black. Someone must have got them for me as I was only 16. I can't recall the entire set list but I do remember them playing 'Spoonful', 'I'm So Glad' and 'Crossroads' - and Ginger's 20 minute drum solo. I managed to bag a spot about 10 feet in front of Eric, which was brilliant.

I managed to bag a spot about 10 feet in front of Eric

Back in the day I was probably as big a fan of clothes as I was of music. Eric was wearing a red satin-look shirt with long rounded collar (called a dog ear collar apparently, and subsequently available in some ridiculous lengths). I hadn't seen this style before - tab collars, pinned or button downs were the norm for the well-respected Mod in Leicester. I was so impressed I bought some fabric and had one made in gold satin. Very tasteful! This period was a sort of turning point as far as fashion was concerned. In six months it would be all paisley patterns and perms.

I WAS THERE: BRIAN JORDAN
THEY HADN'T BEEN formed long and, as I understood it, were doing a series of smallish gigs to knock the set and songs into shape. We were all Clapton fanatics from his Yardbirds and *Beano* album days, and knew of Baker and Bruce but not so much. Memories of the gig were Clapton's introduction to a song written by Ginger Baker, 'and aptly named 'The Toad'!', and their last song - that Clapton said they hadn't performed live before - as they launched into 'I Feel Free'. We weren't quite sure what to expect from the band, but being Clapton blues fans we were surprised by the music. Not that we disliked it. It was also the first time I'd heard a drum roll on two bass drums.

I also saw them at the Arts Ball gig at Granby Halls in 1968, the year they eventually broke up. They were heavily into the rambling solo phase by now which was quite tedious. We liked listening to all their well-known songs but they really tried your patience. I saw Eric Clapton sort of apologise for this phase on TV some years ago. And I have a vague memory of seeing them somewhere else but it's lost in the mists of time!

I WAS THERE: MICK PINI
THE CREAM PLAYED three times at Il Rondo. The first two gigs happened (they also played there on 28 October 1966) but the third was cancelled because their gear had been stolen. The Cream were wandering around at that third gig and I remember Eric, Ginger and Jack coming outside the club looking for their gear. It never turned up.

I WAS THERE: PETER WALKER
I HAD THE pleasure of seeing them at several venues, including the Il Rondo. I'll always remember walking past Jack Bruce's speaker and being blasted from the power from his six string bass.

I WAS THERE: MIKE PRUDEN

I REMEMBER THEM playing the Il Rondo twice - August 26th and October 28th 1966 - and I also saw them at the Arts Ball at Granby Halls in Leicester on February 9th 1968. At one of their appearances, I had a short chat with Clapton which consisted of me asking him how he managed to play as loud as he did in a recording studio situation. I had some recording experience myself and knew you could not go above a certain level, to which his answer was 'tell them to fuck off'! We talked about the Rickenbacker guitar that he had tried but disliked. I also mentioned the Chicago blues man Magic Sam who he acknowledged liking. Not the same can be said of his opinion on various other sidemen from the Yardbirds or Bluesbreakers (I will mention no names). I also told him I'd seen him play his last gig with John Mayall at Blaises in Kensington, where he continually turned his back on the audience. This might have been the point at which he got up and walked to the stage. I also remember thanking him.

Fashion-wise, he was wearing a Guardsman's jacket which was a look taken from The Beatles. And the Gibson Les Paul he was known to use had recently been stolen and he was playing another Les Paul, a very early 1952 model with a trapeze tailpiece which he said he was trying out.

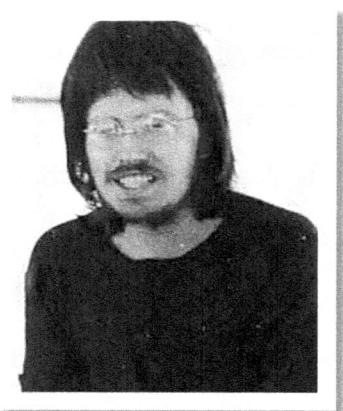

Mike Pruden chatted with Eric

RAM JAM CLUB
27 AUGUST 1966, LONDON, UK

I WAS THERE: JACK REES, AGE 16

I WAS LIVING in Brockley. I had worked for a year as a messenger in Fleet Street where a work mate turned me on to the Marquee Club in Wardour Street, just off of Oxford Street. I used to go there often and saw bands like The Who, The Kinks and the Spencer Davis Group. Someone then told me about the Ram Jam Club in Brixton. I started going there because I loved soul and Tamla Motown, and Geno Washington and the Ram Jam Band - after which the club was named - would do decent cover versions of those songs and I could always ask a girl to dance!

I showed up one night and instead of the Ram Jam Band it was Cream. My only experience of blues music at that time was the Rolling Stones. When I heard Cream start to play I thought, 'What the fuck is this?' and after three songs I thought, 'Wow, this is kinda noisy, it's not very melodic and how can I ask a girl to dance to this?'

When I heard Cream start to play I thought, 'What the fuck is this?'

During the following months I looked at the Rolling Stones songs on my LP and who wrote them, as I did with all the LPs I bought. I backtracked and started listening to the original artists they covered and my liking for the blues grew. Several months later, I first heard, 'I Feel Free' by Cream. I really liked it and went and to listen to a Cream album at the local record store. Although not obviously bluesy by now, my ears were a little better trained and I could hear the influence of the blues. From then on I was a convert.

After performing at the Ram Jam Club, Cream went on to play a post-midnight 'All Night Rave' at the Flamingo Club in London. Cream were to return and play the Ram Jam Club on three further occasions - 3 November 1966, 28 January 1967 (two shows) and 3 June 1967.

ALL NIGHT RAVE AT THE FLAMINGO
27 AUGUST 1966, LONDON, UK

I WAS THERE: PETER BURKE

I WAS LUCKY enough to see Cream six times. The first time was at Windsor, their first official concert after they had played The Twisted Wheel a couple of nights earlier. My pal Bob Chappel and I hitched down to London from Scunthorpe and we went to the Marquee to see The Move and The Herd and then made our way to Windsor, but to be honest I don't remember much about the show. I also saw them at Spalding in a very full, hot and sweaty hall along with Hendrix, Floyd, The Move and Geno Washington. I saw them three times at

Peter Burke saw Cream six times

the Marquee. I would hitch down to The Smoke and queue up, pay my 7/6 to watch the show and then sleep in a Soho doorway and hitch back home the next day. I also did this three times for The Jeff Beck Group.

I also saw Cream at the Flamingo All-Nighter with support from Shotgun Express. Cream had played earlier that evening at The Ram Jam in Brixton. I was stood at the entrance to the Flamingo when they arrived. I was with Martin Stone (Savoy Brown, Mighty Baby, etc.) and a mutual friend. Eric knew Martin and stopped to say 'hi' to him.

When they played the Marquee they would go to The Ship for a drink. One time Eric was stood outside The Ship with his grandmother, Rose, who would come to see him play. I spoke to Eric, telling him that I would be going to see him at The King Mojo in Sheffield on the following Sunday. He said that he never knew where they would be playing one day to the next. I did go to The Mojo but they didn't show on that occasion.

I got to meet Eric a few times in later years. I did a spotlight on him on 39 solo shows at the Royal Albert Hall plus two ARMS concerts, four Hammersmith Odeon shows plus a few other shows here and there. His minder Alphie O'Leary (RIP) was a good friend, and I'm still good pals with Lee Dickson, who was Eric's guitar tech for over 30 years.

BEACHCOMBER CLUB
28 AUGUST 1966, NOTTINGHAM, UK

I WAS THERE: JOHN FLETCHER

John Fletcher was at the Beachcomber

I WAS 16 or 17 when I first became aware of Cream. I was a big fan of blues music as played by groups like John Mayall, who I saw live many time in Nottingham clubs such as the Beachcomber and Boat Club. I never did get to see him with Eric Clapton though. When Cream were formed I bought *Fresh Cream* and that was it - I loved the music. I went to see them at the Beachcomber Club in Nottingham more than once. I was underage for this club. However, a friend lent me his birth certificate and I blagged my membership. My card was duly signed as 'birth cert shown' accompanied by a comment of 'grow a moustache, son' from the manager!

The Beachcomber Club was situated in the Lace Market area of Nottingham on St Mary's Gate. The admission would have been less than £1. An old lace making factory, the club occupied three floors. The basement floor was where the small stage was situated, but when I say 'stage' it was more like a raised platform. The club had fairly low ceilings with mostly standing and dancing only. The acoustics were not great, and I recall that on one occasion Cream came on stage and after a few bars promptly left because the sound was so awful. But they returned several minutes later and it was okay. The atmosphere was brilliant and the close proximity to the stage and artists made these gigs so special.

CONCORDE CLUB, BASSETT HOTEL
1 SEPTEMBER 1966, SOUTHAMPTON, UK

I WAS THERE: JOHN STOREY
I WAS LUCKY enough to see Cream several times in the Sixties, after seeing many gigs by the Graham Bond Organisation featuring Ginger Baker. One show I remember better than most was Cream at the Concorde Club in Bassett, Southampton with Julie Driscoll. And I think members of Cream were at the Marquee Club in Wardour Street in London in the late Sixties one Sunday night for a tribute session to somebody who had died and who was well known to all the rock and jazz legends. People like Acker Bilk and Humphrey Lyttleton from jazz, but also rock greats like Long John Baldry were there, and it started with various groups performing but ended with a great jamming session.

I WASN'T THERE: RICHARD JONES
THE ORIGINAL CONCORDE Club at the back of the Bassett Hotel (now rebuilt as a care home) was just a stone's throw from where I lived as a kid. The club relocated to Eastleigh and in the 1980s I became a member. In the reception area were the original contracts with the early bands, all framed and on show for all to see. The Cream contract was most prominent and read along the lines of:
The Robert Stigwood Organisation agrees to provide the services of Jack Bruce, Ginger Baker and Eric Clapton collectively known as Cream to the Concorde Club on the given date for a fee of £££s.

BLUESVILLE 66, MANOR HOUSE
2 SEPTEMBER 1966, FINSBURY PARK, LONDON, UK

I WAS THERE: SUE RAINBOW, AGE 16

I WENT TO the Blues Room at Manor House on Fridays, mostly with my boyfriend Mick in his yellow bubble car! I had already seen John Mayall and Spencer Davis there. It was always crowded and always exciting, but it was earth shattering when Cream hit the stage and belted out 'NSU'. It was so fucking loud! That's the song I remember and remains my favourite even now. After the gig Ginger and Eric were sitting at a table having a drink in the downstairs bar and I asked them for their autographs. I'm kicking myself now as I had a purge on my possessions in the mid-Eighties and threw them out.

RICKY TICK CLUB, THAMES HOTEL
4 SEPTEMBER 1966, WINDSOR, UK

I WAS THERE: CHARLES BURY

I SAW CREAM a number of times at Windsor. I recall one time Ginger being carried to his drum kit either drunk or on drugs - or both. Then, when the band started, he was just fantastic as though he was a wind-up doll. Turn the key and - wow! They were a group with no equals. It all started with Eric really, with John Mayalls' Bluesbreakers and then the Yardbirds and Cream. I just followed him, like so many did, but seeing Ginger and Jack on the circuit too it was a natural progression. I was so lucky to see so many of the very best bands at the Ricky Tick in Windsor - Hendrix and Pink Floyd plus many others. But the eight mile walk home to Maidenhead nearly every Saturday night wasn't so much fun.

Ginger was fantastic, like a wind up doll

MARQUEE CLUB
10 SEPTEMBER 1966, BIRMINGHAM, UK

I WAS THERE: JOHN CHARLES
THE MARQUEE DANCE Club was on Navigation Street in Birmingham, behind New Street Station. It was a small club above what was Dora's Dancing School on the ground floor. Cream arrived in an old green Commer van. They only had a roadie with them. This was in the very early days after their formation, hence the low turnout of I'd say no more than 20 people in the audience. We could just walk right up to them as there wasn't much, if anything, of a stage in the corner. I remember them playing 'Spoonful' and 'Train Time' but nothing else.

SKYLINE BALLROOM
11 SEPTEMBER 1966, KINGSTON-UPON-HULL, UK

I WAS THERE: CHUCK MADSEN
MY WIFE AND I were at that fantastic gig. Prior to the Cream coming on stage - which was the dance floor - the warm-up band was The Move. Later in the evening, when they had finished their gig, we were in the bar when Ginger Baker came in next to us and ordered a drink that we in Hull were not familiar with, ie. a vodka and coke. A pint of bitter was my bevy! His dress sense was also strange. He was wearing a hat that looked like a leather RAF flying helmet. But it was a fantastic evening listening to Cream.

Some sources suggest that Cream played the Manor Lounge club in Stockport on this date.

RICKY TICK CLUB, CORN EXCHANGE
15 SEPTEMBER 1966, BEDFORD UK

I WAS THERE: BARRY THOMPSON
YES, I WAS there! Front row and my boot three feet from Jack Bruce. I was in a band at the time, and they were amazing. I'd never heard a sound like it. They opened the set with 'I Feel Free' and just blew me away. Terrific night.

HERMITAGE HALLS
16 SEPTEMBER 1966, HITCHIN, UK

I WAS THERE: GERAINT CATLING

I WAS THE entertainments secretary for the ICT Apprentice Association. I was pretty active in the area during the Sixties for promoting bands and had a number of friends in groups that weren't famous. I used to run monthly dances, mainly to try and boost the Apprentice Association's funds, and I also ran weekly dances at the local youth club. I ran the dance at Hermitage Ballroom. The ballroom was run by a profit-making organisation, which would let out the ballroom on a Friday for private functions for free but take all the bar profits. On that night they must have made a lot of money.

I booked the Cream for £70. I'd seen the forming of the group on the front page of the *Melody Maker* in late June or early July and I believe I was the first person to actually book them, hence the low price, although it wasn't the first time they played. Dave Baxter Entertainments was the guy that I used to book all the bands through, and he made the enquiries on my behalf. Their representation was via the Robert Stigwood Organisation, who were dithering at the time as to what the fee should be.

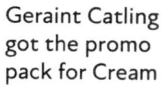

Geraint Catling got the promo pack for Cream

Originally, they were going to be booked for Hitchin Technical College but we had a bit of vandalism and people ripped the toilet washbasins out at a previous dance so we got stopped from booking the hall there and swapped the venue to the ballroom. I also booked the support band, then called the Farinas and which later became Family. They were a very popular support band around this area and the bass player, Rick Grech, eventually left Family and joined Blind Faith. I think it was the first time that the Cream had also met Family, and it's claimed that Eric made John Whitney an offer for his twin-necked Gibson guitar but he wouldn't sell.

I wasn't expecting the response that I got. I had some fellow apprentices on the little box office downstairs and we ran out of change. In fact, we ran out of everything so we gave up charging admission. Anyone that came late just got in for free and I have no idea how many came altogether. The capacity was normally about 300 and we were way over that - we stopped counting at 600.

The capacity was normally about 300 and we were way over that - we stopped counting at 600

I've got a couple of pictures of the ballroom and it is absolutely solid with people, just crammed in. There was no way you could dance there. Everyone was head-to-head, jammed solid. I did hear that the

Below left, Eric in action at the Herm. Right, Cream at the Herm

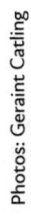
Photos: Geraint Catling

Jack at the Herm

ballroom had a visitation the following month from the health and safety but we never got any feedback from the ballroom management staff that there was any problem. Perhaps they just got a warning.

People were just mesmerised, looking at and listening to the Cream. I remember Ginger Baker's drum solo, which may have been longer than 10 minutes. He smashed his cymbal and cracked it and had to change it, but people were just staring at it. Ginger was the spokesman for all three and what I would call the driving force. Eric was a very quiet person. I hadn't got any stipulation on the contract I had as to the time that they were due to finish whereas the Cream's contract said that they would play no later than 11pm, so I had a 'polite discussion' with Ginger - because he was definitely the negotiator - and ended up paying for one of their sessions at time and a half because it was past eleven o'clock when they finished. This worked out at an extra £17.50 which, when you're trying to make a bit of money for the Apprentice Association, is a bit of a shock. But they were worth a damn sight more than the original £70 I paid.

It was a brilliant evening. It was talked about for months after. Everyone really enjoyed it, and because the Family were a group that always played in this area, that just enhanced the crowds. It still sticks in my mind, and those of a lot of my friends who were there as well. I think that was the biggest coup of my promoting career, because I got them so cheap. I remember taking a leather bag stuffed full of money to the Barclays Bank night safe afterwards, duly escorted by a couple of the taller apprentices.

I WAS THERE: RAY DONEY

I WAS AN engineering apprentice and we used to run a social group. I used to run the concerts for them and do bits and pieces for them, and then I started booking bands into the local youth club as well. I got offered two dates for Cream. I ummed and aaahed to be honest, because I usually booked bands in at two 45-minute sessions and Robert Stigwood said 'well, we'll only do an hour' and I thought 'that's no good'. Believe it or not, they cost me £75 each for each date. And because we thought we'd get quite a lot of people we actually hired the Hermitage Halls to put them on. We've got an hour. What do we fill the rest with? And so I got Family to come down and they supported them that night. I'd known Family for quite some time as they'd done a few gigs for me over the years.

We booked them in and the rest, as they say, is history. Cream did quite well. That gig got Rick Grech the gig with Blind Faith. I think they were very impressed with him. I didn't make any money personally because I was doing it for the apprentices. It was absolutely packed. We had to shut the doors because we just couldn't get any more in, it was so full. A friend of mine who was a pro drummer said to me recently 'that's emblazoned in my memory'. People who were there remember it.

I WAS THERE: ROGER COOPER

Roger Cooper had been a fanatical Yardbirds fan

THIS WAS AN especially memorable gig for me because I was a fanatical fan of the Yardbirds and John Mayall and wanted to see what Eric Clapton was getting up to in his new band. I'd seen The Beatles 1963 Christmas Show and other live bands, but always in the company of grown ups.

My obsession with live music had begun on my fifteenth birthday when my next door neighbour's daughter, a lovely 17 year old named Annette, took me to see the Yardbirds at the Marquee. She had a boyfriend living in London who often took her to London clubs. I've always looked young for my age, but had no trouble getting in with a buxom mini-skirted 17-year-old girl on my arm. I don't think the bouncer even looked at me! We met her boyfriend inside.

It was the first time I had ever seen Clapton live, and it was the night the band recorded Five Live Yardbirds. It was an amazing experience which I will never forget, and it's still one of my favourite records. I had also seen Jack Bruce and Ginger Baker before as members of the Graham Bond Organisation.

I saw Cream at the 'Herm'. It had a tiny stage and was on the first floor, so it must have been a nightmare for the roadies getting all the equipment up and down the stairs or the rear fire escape. The Hermitage was one of many good gigs in the area. We also had Bowes Lyon House and the Mecca in Stevenage and the California Ballroom in Dunstable, plus London was just 50 minutes train ride away. I lived in nearby Letchworth and at the time was a sixth former at school in Hitchin, so the Hermitage was an easy Saturday night option if there was nothing else special on.

I went with a schoolfriend named Richard Hyne. I can't remember why I didn't go with my girlfriend but I do remember Jack Bruce at one point cutting his finger on his guitar strings and Rick and I, being at the very front of the audience, getting splattered with blood. Not a lot, but enough to ruin my really nice shirt.

I remember Jack Bruce at one point cutting his finger on his guitar strings

The second memory is of Ginger Baker playing 'Toad'. Drum solos were de rigeur in those days, but this one was special. The first indication that it wasn't just a run-of-the-mill run around the drum kit was when Bruce and Clapton put down their guitars, lit up cigarettes and left the stage! The tempo sped up, slowed down, mesmerised and went on and on and on... until the guitarists had finished their cigarettes and saddled up their guitars again for the grand finale. In the bar after the performance, that drum solo was the talk of the evening.

I WAS THERE: PHIL NEWSTEAD
BEING A FAN of John Mayall I was at the Herm the night Cream played there and I can still recall the buzz. The event was barely advertised - it was more word of mouth - but the place was rammed and rocking. There were no tickets. As I recall it cost three and six (17.5p) to get in and you had to pay at the door. Slowhand, Bruce and Baker gave a great performance, probably one of their best as they were sober and up for it! It was a great night.

I WAS THERE: IAN SAGGERS

I LIVED IN north Hertfordshire where one of the main employers was International Computers and Tabulators (ICT). Every summer the company would throw an evening of entertainment for their apprentices, who numbered in the hundreds. I was invited along by one of my near neighbours who was just such an apprentice. Before that evening I had no idea who they were. From that evening on I became a fan. It was the one and only time I have seen Eric Clapton live, but what a player. It was truly a great night. One story that went around was that during their break Ginger Baker went up to the bar and ordered a half pint of vodka and lime. Some 30 minutes later his drum solo, which lasted something like 10 minutes, brought the house down - together with most of his drum kit.

DRILL HALL
17 SEPTEMBER 1966, GRANTHAM, UK

I WAS THERE: JOHN DICKENSON

I WAS INTO the Yardbirds with Eric Clapton. On the Saturday afternoon I discussed with my wife (she was then my girlfriend) who to see - Otis Redding at Boston Gliderdrome or Cream at Grantham Barracks? Needless to say - I won! The gig itself was brilliant with lots of blues plus a long (boring) drum solo by Ginger Baker. The audience was very sparse, about 50 or 60 people. I think everyone had gone to see Otis. I remember we were stood right in front of the group and Ginger kept winking at my girlfriend, which she found very becoming. It was a very enjoyable experience and to think a couple of months later they were playing in front of 10,000 people.

I WAS THERE: KEVIN EBBINS

OTIS REDDING WAS playing at the Gliderdrome in Boston, Lincolnshire and a bus load went to see him. I was with my friend Dave and we went to see Cream. There were only about 30 people there. Cream decided not to play on the stage but on the dance floor. They played a full set and really went for it. Ginger Baker nailed his drum kit to the floor. It was a time when they were at their best. I regret at times not seeing the great Otis Redding, but if l I'd gone to see him I wouldn't have been as close as I was to the three legends that were Cream.

TECHNICAL INSTITUTE
24 SEPTEMBER 1966, KINGSTON-UPON-THAMES, UK

I WAS THERE: ALLIE STEWART

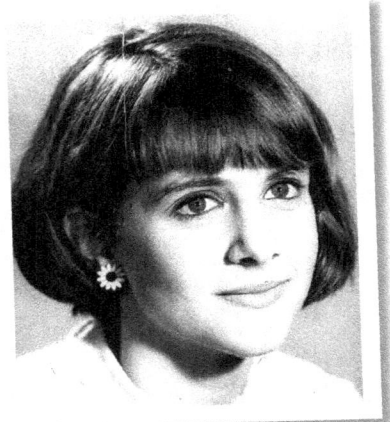

Allie Stewart saw Cream and wished she could smell some Lynx!

ALTHOUGH IT FEELS like yesterday, over 50 years have passed since I saw Cream. The Technical Institute was not a huge venue. To be honest I didn't know who they were, having just started to get interested in the vibrant music scene of Kingston and Richmond. The tickets were seven shillings and sixpence (37p), which was a lot for a young schoolgirl to find back then. The buzz in the assembly hall at the Institute was palpable, with everyone milling around and lots of body odour as we were quite tightly packed - there was no Lynx in those days! - and as it was standing only you got quite close up to the next person.

I recall being taking aback by the volume of the sound when Cream appeared, with Ginger Baker waving his drumsticks like a cross between a wizard and a banshee. What they played hasn't stuck in my memory, but what I did take away and have kept until today is knowing that I was at the forefront of an exciting change in music. Somehow, Cream had got into my blood and that thrill has never gone away. I also had my purse pinched from my bag, which I accidentally left in the cloakroom. I had to walk home and I remember it was dark and chilly.

RICKY TICK CLUB,
30 SEPTEMBER 1966, HOUNSLOW, UK

I WAS THERE: ROBERT SCOTT

I SAW CREAM at the Ricky Tick in Hounslow, although their show is in the 'I vaguely remember' category. I definitely remember going to Hammersmith with my mother to see The Beatles and the Yardbirds, as my cousin was the drummer, Jimmy McCarty. Seeing them backstage was more important than seeing The Beatles. I wore a suit and tie! Eel Pie Island in Twickenham was the best, from Muddy Waters for five shillings to the Stones and The Who for only two and six (12p).

REGENT STREET POLYTECHNIC
1 OCTOBER 1966, LONDON, UK

I WAS THERE: WENDY GREENE

I WENT TO a student gig. We paid about half a crown (13p) to get in - even though we weren't students - and with that got a free beer. Cream were just starting out. We'd previously seen them at one of the Wardour Street clubs when they hadn't even got lyrics to some things. This time they brought on stage a friend from America called Jimi Hendrix. Everyone was stunned by his playing, using his teeth and playing behind his head, which I'd only ever seen Joe Brown do four years before on the Billy Fury tour, with his teeth and with loads of feedback and volume. When he went off, Eric Clapton played his socks off, not wanting to be shown up. We also saw them at the Saville Theatre and the Royal Albert Hall. At their farewell concert we had a seat almost level with Clapton's side of the stage. This delighted my then husband who was a brilliant guitarist himself, later joining forces with Jim McCarty of The Yardbirds.

I WAS THERE: NEIL MAURER, AGE 20

I WAS AT boarding school in Mill Hill and on a Saturday night a friend used to bring his car up to the school dormitory and I'd sneak out through a window and go into London for a gig. Then he'd drop me back at boarding school in time for breakfast on Sunday morning. I used to go and see Georgie Fame at the Flamingo Club, and fairly regularly to the Marquee Club in Wardour Street. I saw Eric Clapton there with John Mayall's Bluesbreakers, and I was there when they announced one evening that Eric was leaving to join Cream and that Peter Green was taking over.

I was not long out of school when a friend who was studying at North London Poly called me and said, 'There's a group called Cream playing tonight. Do you want to come up and we'll go?' so off we went. It was at Titchfield Street, just off Oxford Circus. They played the first half and during the interval they said, 'We've got a brand new guitarist going to join us for the second half. None of you will have heard of him.' It was Jimi Hendrix. He came on and played the second half with them, which was quite amazing. He was playing the guitar with his teeth. We were all absolutely amazed at what we were watching. He was lucky he didn't electrocute himself.

I WAS THERE: JOHN SMAIL, AGE 21

AS A KEEN follower of British blues guitarists of the Sixties I attended many concerts, mainly in and around London, and saw live on stage such names as Eric Clapton (several times with the Yardbirds, John Mayall's Bluesbreakers and Cream), Jimmy Page, Peter Green, Pete Townsend, Jeff Beck, Keith Richards and many others. I was fortunate enough to be present at a Cream concert when Jimi Hendrix, having just flown over from the USA the previous weekend, was brought on stage as a guest guitarist. It is no understatement to say that this was a defining moment in musical history. Little was known of Jimi - he had been 'spotted' by Linda Keith in New York and brought over to the UK by Chas Chandler.

I still have my tickets, numbered 478 and 479 on the reverse. The ticket price was 2/6d - 12½p in decimal currency. As I remember it, the audience was not particularly large - hundreds rather than thousands.

Jimi's stage presence was immediate. I am no musician but it was clear that Jimi was more than capable of playing with the excellent and experienced band that was Cream. At one stage during the session, the electricity seemed to switch off and there is still speculation as to whether it was a power failure or whether the band (in particular, Eric) pulled the plug, being overwhelmed by Jimi's sensational guitar skills and

John Smail was at the Great Portland Street gig where Jimi got up and jammed with Cream

Photos: John Smail

struggling to compete. The music resumed but I cannot recall how long Jimi's session lasted. The evening was so memorable and special - a 'sixth sense' almost seemed to tell me that history was being made that night - so I retained the tickets as souvenirs.

I WASN'T THERE: DAVID RITMAN
MY MATE RAN a folk club in Richmond. He was there to see Cream and says the audience, him included, booed Hendrix loudly. Cries of 'get him off, we came to see you' apparently rang round for all of two minutes.

Jimi came on and stole the show… He played the guitar behind his head, between his legs, with his teeth, slapped it round on the ground a bit. I just went, 'Yeah - this is it! This guy is bound for glory!' **Eric Clapton**

Chas Chandler later found Clapton with his head in his hands. Clapton allegedly looked up and said to Chas, 'You didn't tell me he was that fucking good!'

FALMER HOUSE, UNIVERSITY OF SUSSEX
8 OCTOBER 1966, BRIGHTON, UK

I WAS THERE: KEITH HURLEY
I PLAYED SUPPORT to both Cream and John Mayall's Bluesbreakers when Clapton was with them! My band was called Russel's Clump. The Cream show was an all night gig. There was an all night restaurant and we had booked a time and a table. It turned out that sitting at the same table opposite to us were Cream. Clapton was uncontactable and obviously drugged up and Ginger Baker was so drunk he had to be helped to his drumstool. Jack Bruce was normal and I did exchange a few words. In the steamy windows of Sussex University, people wrote 'Clapton is God'

Ginger collapsed during his solo on 'Toad' and was diagnosed with acute exhaustion and influenza.

ORFORD CELLAR
12 OCTOBER 1966, NORWICH, UK

I WAS THERE: ANN CROUCHER

I HAD A terrible cold (so sorry to everyone I must have spread it to) and felt awful but I was determined to go. I was standing quite near the front and remember the drum solo because Ginger Baker had a halo of sweat flying off him.

I WAS THERE: TREVOR DYE

I SAW CREAM perform live in Norwich. As a fresh faced 16-year-old who had just joined a local band I, along with a couple of older lads, went to the Orford Cellar. The performance blew me away and things would never be the same again for me musically. I was hooked.

Trevor Dye was hooked by Cream

I WAS THERE: VAL KEATES, AGE 16

EVERYONE WAS HOT and sweaty and the music was very loud. I was very angry because Ginger Baker's hair was longer than mine! The rest of the evening is a blur. I wasn't supposed to be there as my dad had forbidden me to go. My only other memory is of a police raid upstairs in the bar. It must have been about capacity in the cellar. I remember slow hand clapping and people mumbling 'all coppers are barstewards'. There was also a large rush to the toilets to flush away incriminating substances. The police had a good look round and were making their way out but stopped at me. He asked me my name, age and address. Having said I was 16, he asked if I had been drinking. I said, 'No, I'm under age, I just told you I am 16!' He stared at me and I stared demurely back. Plod went and I turned round, grasped the vodka and orange that had been sat behind me while we were having our conversation - and downed it!

STUDENTS UNION, UNIVERSITY OF SHEFFIELD
15 OCTOBER 1966, SHEFFIELD, UK

I WAS THERE: JOHN LANE
I WAS OBVIOUSLY aware of Clapton's reputation from the Yardbirds and John Mayall's Bluesbreakers, and I'd also seen Baker and Bruce at a club in Sheffield when they were in the Graham Bond Organisation. I remember Cream appearing at the University of Sheffield Students Union in 1966. It was a Saturday. Surprisingly, they were the support act to The Four Pennies, a pop group who'd had a few hits in the mid-Sixties but were on the wane. This was still an era when most people went to gigs to dance rather than watch, and when Cream performed, the majority of the crowd remained in the bar while maybe 50 people, myself included, watched their set. I'm afraid I can't remember the set list, but they were very good and very loud.

The dancing ceased soon after this gig and crowds actually watched the acts. The Students Union was a great venue, but the problem was that tickets could only be sold to genuine students, who had to show their union card at a desk manned by university porters when the entered the building. However, if you arrived before the porters set up the desk, about 6.30pm to 7.00pm, you could get into the bar and buy a ticket. This we did on a regular basis, the only downside being that by the time the acts appeared we'd been drinking for quite a while. Happy days!

CARNIVAL DANCE, WILLENHALL BATHS ASSEMBLY HALL
20 OCTOBER 1966, WILLENHALL, UK

I WAS THERE: ROG WARD, AGE 19
I USED TO go to a youth club in Willenhall in the West Midlands. They played for the youth club annual dance at Willenhall Baths, where they covered the pool over for concerts. The audience limit was about 300 and it was free for the youth club members and their friends. The line up was Baker, Clapton and Bruce and I remember how Baker

looked very spaced out and creepy whilst Clapton was his brilliant self. The youth club also had the Spencer Davis Group and The Hollies for other dances. And The 'N Betweens, who became Slade, rehearsed at the club.

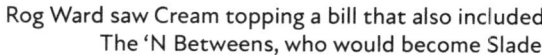
Rog Ward saw Cream topping a bill that also included The 'N Betweens, who would become Slade

HE WAS THERE: DON POWELL, SLADE DRUMMER
I REMEMBER CREAM were paid £125, we were paid £6 and Robert Plant got £4. We all shared the same dressing room, a store cupboard at the side of the stage. Ginger Baker had his double kit set up in there. No one could move. Planty went up and asked if he could move them. Ginger's reply started with 'F' and finished with 'off'.

UNIVERSITY OF LEEDS
22 OCTOBER 1966, LEEDS, UK

I WAS THERE: ALAN POYNER-LEVISON
IN THE LATE Sixties and early Seventies I was with a group called Iron Grape. We played all over the area of South Yorkshire, and we used to hang around Leeds University because they had a good recording studio. The leader of the students union at that time was a guy called John Biz-Brown. He used to allow us to use the facility at weekends when it was not in use. When Cream came, I was in the hall while the roadies were unloading the stuff and setting it up. They brought in Ginger's drums and set them up on a parquet floor which was very highly polished. Realising that they were bound to slide around once the maestro descended on them, they promptly went out to the truck returning with two six-inch stakes which they hammered into the floor on both sides of the bass drum, smashing the floor to pieces. An official from the university went crazy with the roadies, but the roadies won the day having come to some arrangement - probably by refusing to play!

By now the hall was getting filled up, but soon they were ready. I had heard their first single, 'Wrapping Paper', which I was not too fond of. But then came 'Tales of Brave Ulysses' which was more to my sort of thing. The speaker cabinets were stacked two high either side of Ginger, and boy they were loud. I was stood in the front by now and Jack's bass thundered through my body. I moved to the back to get a more even sound experience. The band was everything I had expected and more as they went through their repertoire, beginning with 'Spoonful' and 'Wrapping Paper' and then they played 'Stormy Monday' and then one I had never heard which sounded like the 'March of the Elephants' as Jack's bass pounded it out. I was later to find out it was one they had just tried out - 'Politician'. They continued with 'Strange Brew' and finally 'Sunshine of Your Love'. It was a thoroughly great evening.

'WRAPPING PAPER' RELEASED
25 OCTOBER 1966

Cream's first single, which didn't feature on their first album released a few weeks later, reached number 34 in the UK charts.

NEW YORKER DISCOTHEQUE
27 OCTOBER 1966, SWINDON, UK

I WAS THERE: ALEX WILKINSON
I'M PRETTY SURE I saw Cream at the New Yorker Disco in Milton Road back in the Sixties. John Mayall's Bluesbreakers also did a gig there but it is a bit of a blur, purely because we saw many, many great acts in Swindon back then, particularly at the Locarno which has been left now derelict.

I WAS THERE: JIM BIRD
AS THERE WAS no drinks licence we all used the Rolleston pub across the road and the members of the groups used to be in there for a drink. Other groups who played there were Pink Floyd, Zoot Money, Georgie Fame, Free and Geno Washington.

I WAS THERE: DAVE PARRY
I REMEMBER GOING to the New Yorker Discotheque in Swindon to watch them. The warm up act was the fabulous Geno Washington and the Ram Jam Band, who did a two hour set from 10pm to midnight followed by Cream from midnight to 2am. Wonderful times, wonderful music.

I WAS THERE: IAN TITCOMBE

THE NEW YORKER Discotheque was definitely the Mod place at the time and hosted many of the London-based R&B and soul groups of the mid-Sixties. I cannot recall anything that Cream actually played, but knew from the music press that Eric Clapton was being lauded as one of the top guitarists in the country following his stints with other groups. One of the problems with the New Yorker was that the local council would not grant it an alcohol licence, so at the break a whole bunch of loosely affiliated Mods got pass outs and headed over to the back bar of the local pub, The Rolleston. Obviously, someone had told the members of Cream where to get a drink as they duly turned up and stood at the bar, totally left alone by us to enjoy their beverages.

IL RONDO
28 OCTOBER 1966, LEICESTER, UK

I WAS THERE: BRYAN HEMMING

I SAW CREAM three times as far I can remember, but it may have been four. As you might imagine, I'm a bit hazy on some of the dates. The first time was at Leicester's Il Rondo. There was a long queue as the band already had a big reputation, despite the fact they'd only got together weeks before. Back in those days, bands like John Mayall's Bluesbreakers had a following mainly composed of Mods and students. When we heard Clapton, Baker and Bruce had teamed up, the atmosphere of expectancy was electric. The queue at the Il Rondo was massive, and mostly Mod. The size of the queue only served to increase the excitement, even though the band had hardly played any live gigs at that point. Their first single, 'Wrapping Paper', had only just been released. The crowd was almost too much for the ticket office to handle. A lot of people were disappointed.

Bryan Hemming saw Cream three times, or possibly four

If I remember rightly the set started late, which may have been due to the fact that, while we were queuing, Ginger Baker was in The Churchill pub opposite the Il Rondo in Silver Street, downing a few drinks. I only found that out later, because one of my art college friends, George Blynd - who couldn't get in - was having a drink and chatting with him. The Churchill was a favourite haunt of the Mod crowd at that time, and later the hippy crowd.

I WAS THERE: CELIA JONES

I REMEMBER GOING down the Rondo to see them one Friday night, full of expectation. They didn't disappoint! 'Spoonful' sticks in my mind. I was about six months pregnant with my eldest daughter and during the solos bit of the tune she started 'dancing' inside me. She's still a Cream and Clapton fan to this day!

MIDNIGHT CITY
29 OCTOBER 1966, BIRMINGHAM, UK

I WAS THERE: FRANCES LEWIS, AGE 17

I WILL NEVER forget the atmosphere that night. I sat on the fire escape at the back of the club and knew I had witnessed something special. According to my diary, earlier in the evening I went to see the Walker Brothers at the Odeon and later went on to the Midnight City. I was 17 at the time and am now 71 but I will never forget that night. I went out a week or two later and bought their LP *Fresh Cream*, and I still have it along with

Frances Lewis was at Midnight City to see Cream

Frances Lewis's diary records her seeing Cream in 1966

hundreds of others in the bottom of my wardrobe. Sadly the Midnight City didn't last long but that night will remain with me and I am proud to say when I saw Cream they were probably at the height of their fame! How lucky I was.

Frances Lewis's Midnight City membership card

THE PAVILION
2 NOVEMBER 1966, HEMEL HEMPSTEAD, UK

I WAS THERE: LINDA EVANS, AGE 14

I WAS A 14-year-old schoolgirl who had never heard of them before. I stayed on late at school with a couple of other girls that night, killing time and then dressing up for the gig. I was surprised my mum had let me go. I was very naive musically at 14, but I knew I was listening to something amazing! I was astounded by their music and have never forgotten that concert or how brilliant they were.

I WAS THERE: PHIL HOBBS

I WAS STILL at school and was 15 and 4 months old at the time. My friend, Keith Hall, a drummer who later had a number one record with Pickettywitch and then moved on to Gerry and the Pacemakers amongst others, told a few of us about this gig. As I recall, it had not been advertised locally and I had not even heard of Cream, but was aware of Eric Clapton because of his John Mayall involvement. As I had previously missed

Phil Hobbs was still at school when he saw Cream

out on a trip Keith had organised to see Jimi Hendrix at Aylesbury in a very early UK performance, I did not want to miss out again.

The gig was not particularly well attended with the Pavilion being perhaps half full at most, which would be 500 to 600 people. This supports my theory that it was not advertised much or, at least not very well. I enjoyed support act The Cortinas (who later became the excellent Octopus) who I knew from our local youth club dances in Berkhamsted. Most of their set was cover versions.

I distinctly remember Cream opened with 'NSU', which I've loved ever since. I remember them doing other numbers like 'Spoonful' and 'Sleepy Time Time'. I know they didn't do 'Wrapping Paper', which I could not believe was Cream when I heard it a short while later! Whilst I was already into music with blues influences and anything that was a bit different, this concert made me a Cream fan and was a major change in my musical life.

By coincidence, I saw Eric Clapton at the Pavilion again in a 'secret gig' in the mid-Seventies (I remember Yvonne Elliman being a backing singer) when he made a comeback from his problems. My mate came in my office the day before the gig and asked if I wanted a ticket (£2, I think) which were just being sold by word of mouth. The answer, of course, was yes!

I WAS THERE: STEVE RICHES

I WORKED FOR the *Hemel Hempstead Gazette*. One of the advantages of being on a local newspaper was getting free tickets to various places and events, which went some way to making up for appallingly low wages. We had press passes to the cinemas, the bowling alley, the swimming pool, the nightclub (there was only one), social clubs, all the sports grounds and to every function organised by the council and anyone else hoping for (and usually getting) a plug in the paper. But the jewel in the ticket crown was a pass to Hemel Hempstead Pavilion, which during the late Sixties and early Seventies hosted a whole string of touring bands from the brilliant to the truly terrible. I almost always went on a Friday or Saturday as the holder of our Executive Pass for Two, the Gazette being staffed by no

Steve Riches considered Cream the cream of all the acts he saw as a local journalist

other people who were remotely interested in the music of the day. That treasured pass enabled me to see a huge variety of live acts I would otherwise have been unable to afford. Not all of them were much cop. Indeed, I can still see and hear with complete horror the likes of The Foundations, The Barron Knights, The Walker Brothers, Crispian St Peters and Dave Dee, Dozy, Beaky, Mick and Titch. But I saw some great acts too.

Out of all that talent, I have to go for Cream at the Pavilion as my headliners. I had never seen anything like it and still haven't. They played with consummate skill and enthusiasm, yet without any fuss. They just got on with it, rattling through classics like 'White Room' and 'Spoonful' and raising the roof with 'Sunshine of Your Love'.

Ginger's eyes were staring like a madman, his drumsticks twirling between his bony fingers

They were musicians rather than a musical act, like so many. And yet I have never forgotten the climax of the show, although I'm still unsure whether this was rehearsed or completely unplanned. The romantic in me sides with the latter. Eric and Jack had already had their share of solos, when drummer Ginger was let loose as the crowd cramming the dance floor went wild. His eyes staring like a madman, his drumsticks mesmerisingly twirling between his bony fingers, he went musically bonkers. After a couple of minutes of bashing the daylights out of his drum kit, in a fashion he had personally invented, Eric and Jack plonked their instruments on the stage floor and walked off. But not exit left or right. They simply walked down the steps at the side, up the spiral staircase from the dance floor and straight up to the bar. There, they ordered a pint of beer each, downed it in fairly rapid time and walked casually back the way they came. They picked up their instruments, playing Ginger out of his trance, finished the song (I can't even remember what it was), bowed a couple of times and walked off. That was it. Class, pure class.

WARWICK ARTS CENTRE, UNIVERSITY OF WARWICK
4 NOVEMBER 1966, COVENTRY, UK

I WAS THERE: GRAHAM BELLAMY
I FIRST SAW Eric Clapton when he was playing with John Mayall's Bluesbreakers at the Leofric in Coventry and had seen them a few times. So I was very interested when they formed Cream and Cream was a very apt title as they were all individually brilliant. The first time was at Warwick University. The stage was about two inches high. There were maybe a hundred people in the room, if that. I stood about two feet from Eric and watched him play.

Ginger Baker was the first drummer that held my attention throughout his drum solos. One of the girls with us, Carol Jones, got back stage and shared a joint with them. At a later date, they played at Manchester Polytechnic. As was normal those days, there was always a party on a Saturday night and Ginger Baker and Jack Bruce came to it without Eric. They sat in a corner smoking a few joints.

I WAS THERE: JOHN TREFOR RICHARDS
I STOOD NEXT to Ginger Baker at the bar during the interval. It must have been a fairly small gig as they simply played on a foot high platform placed by the wall.

EAST HAM TOWN HALL
5 NOVEMBER 1966, LONDON, UK

I WAS THERE: CHRIS HOLLEBONE
THE FIRST GIG I went to was John Mayall's Bluesbreakers with Eric Clapton. In those days I was a bit more of a blues follower. I was becoming interested in what was happening to Eric after he left John Mayall, and I was there at the first performance by Cream at the Windsor Jazz Festival. That was also the birth of many other bands - Fleetwood Mac were also appearing there, and the Aynsley Dunbar Retaliation. The spin off groups from John Mayall were rife at the time.

I saw them a few times after that when they were still a club band. Although I didn't live in London my friend did and we used to go to the Manor House a lot because Cream and all the other blues bands of the time used to perform there, along with other clubs like Klooks Kleek and the Marquee.

The other memorable gig was when they did a gig at East Ham Town Hall. I used to have some pictures of that performance but I've mislaid them. The East Ham gig was a bigger venue, so obviously the crowds were beginning to build up. They then started getting hit records and getting going so they disappeared off the scene as far as I was concerned until we got to the 'Goodbye' concert at the Royal Albert Hall, which was the next time I saw them. So I saw them right at the beginning and right at the end.

It was an exponential growth in terms of the racket they made and an assault on the ears

They were pretty polished from the beginning. What we weren't used to at the time was a three-piece band making such a great job of it. Hendrix came along pretty soon afterwards but Cream were the ones that really kicked off that trio ensemble. And because they were all exceptional players, I think everyone was a bit gobsmacked, not just by the music but the technicality of it. Jack wasn't exactly a conventional bass player, Ginger certainly wasn't a conventional drummer and by any standards Eric Clapton was slightly better than most guitarists. It was a pretty strange bill really.

I used to see The Who which was the closest thing we got to that, because they were a three piece with a singer but had the same kind of approach, where the playing was a bit more adventurous amongst the three musicians. The style of music was slightly different but the approach to it was full on in every department. I would imagine that Cream took a bit of inspiration from bands like The Who in terms of how they presented themselves. The sheer volume was the other thing that was noticeably different between the John Mayall days and Cream. The decibel level went up substantially. Instead of just using a little Marshall amp that he used to stick on a chair, as Eric did with Mayall, Cream went to two Marshall stacks behind each player. It was an exponential growth in terms of the racket they made and an assault on the ears. The one thing they didn't pick up from The Who was smashing all the gear up, which I always thought was a little bit sad with The Who. It was part of the act but it was never one I particularly enjoyed.

Cream started to veer off a bit in directions I wasn't totally happy with at various times in their career. I particularly loathed the first album. I thought it was lacklustre production and not particularly great in the way it was presented and that it and the first couple of singles were really just manufactured crap. 'Wrapping Paper' was an abomination compared with what I was used to on the live sets. 'I Feel Free' was slightly better but I lost faith for a while after that. *Disraeli Gears* restored my faith a bit, and was a major step in the right direction in terms of going back to doing the sort of things I liked.

LIVERPOOL UNIVERSITY
12 NOVEMBER 1966, LIVERPOOL, UK

I WAS THERE: STEF BRAMMAR, AGE 20
I JUST CHANCED upon Cream. I was into the Beatles and the Stones and all that stuff. I was working as a secretary, but my boyfriend was at Liverpool University so our social life revolved around the student social life. Being in Liverpool was very exciting because there was a lot going on in terms of music. We went to the Union and saw the Small Faces, Julie Driscoll and Brian Auger, the Nice and Cream, really good big bands. The college circuit developed because bands needed bigger venues to play and the arenas hadn't yet been built. We got there an hour early so that we could be down at the front near the stage. The atmosphere was just amazing. I'll never forget that first time, and that opening riff. Cream have always been my favourite. I still listen to them.

REDCAR JAZZ CLUB
13 NOVEMBER 1966, REDCAR, UK

I WAS THERE: JOHN ROBERTS
CREAM PLAYED REDCAR Jazz Club on this date for a fee of £75. When they returned on 9th April 1967 their fee was £285.

VILLAGE HALL
18 NOVEMBER 1966, HOVETON, UK

I WAS THERE: RICHARD PILCH

HOVETON VILLAGE HALL is in a small village just outside of Norwich. This was in the very early days of Cream and to play such a small venue was wonderful for us star struck lads. There were no pre booking in those days, so you had to turn up at the door and pay, which I think cost me 7/6d (35p). We had a little band at the time called Three's Company and our drummer, Roger Cooper, was hitching a lift to the gig, a distance of about 15 miles. My friend Vincent and I got there quite early and (in pre-mobile phone days) said we would meet him at the door. About 7pm a Rover car came into the car park and in it was Roger in the passenger seat and Ginger Baker driving. Roger got out of the car and of course we were so jealous. Apparently Ginger had seen him hitching and, as Ginger was lost - again, pre satnav days, stopped to ask Roger the way to Hoveton. When Ginger was told that Roger was actually going to the gig, he thought his luck was in so gave him a lift, and to thank him invited Roger, myself and our lead guitarist Vincent into the band room for a drink. What a great bunch they were. Eric, Ginger and Jack couldn't have been more accommodating. None of us had to pay to get in and Cream performed a wonderful set and we all went home happy bunnies.

I WAS THERE: CHRIS GUDGIN

THEY WERE SUPPORTED by The Continentals. I can't remember much about it other than a fight occurred!

I WAS THERE: MIKE ROSE

I BELIEVE THIS was a warm up gig prior to them heading over to Paris. I was around 17 or 18 and had been listening to the likes of John Mayall and particularly the blues guitar playing of Eric and Peter Green. I started getting the *NME* and read about this new supergroup called Cream and found out they were coming to Hoveton Village Hall. On the evening the hall wasn't even particularly full but what stood out for me was the fact that you had three excellent musicians all playing an equal part. I couldn't believe a bass player could be so up front in a band, plus the drum solo of course. I live only three miles from Hoveton and still get nostalgic whenever I drive past.

BLUE MOON CLUB
19 NOVEMBER 1966, CHELTENHAM, UK

I WAS THERE: VICTOR FOSTER
I WENT TO the Blue Moon Club from '66 to '68, when I was 18 to 20. I'm a Gloucester lad. Me and a mate used to go to a club in Churchdown called Sandycroft. A couple of Cheltenham lads used to go there and they were all always on about this Blue Moon Club that had opened and said we should go. It was opened by a couple of chaps from London called Eddie Norman and Bill Reid. It was just something completely different.

It was dead easy in those days. You'd get on a train in Gloucester for sixpence, get to St James Station and walk the rest of it. You had the Cheltenham lot and the Gloucester lot who were Mods, so it was more of a Mod club than a rockers club because the greaser lads were down the road at a place called the Aztec Club, a good quarter of a mile from the Blue Moon. It was a great big room. They didn't sell drinks, so if you wanted a drink you went to the local bars and then you either fell up the stairs or down them.

Cream were there quite often. Ginger Baker was a little bit volatile. I remember a couple of Cheltenham lads asking me for a cigarette and I turned round and said 'get your own'. The next thing I remember is going flying across the drums and getting a smack in the head from the drumstick thanks to Mr Baker.

The club lasted for about two and a quarter years and that was it. I think it closed because of drugs, when the purple hearts started coming in from America when the Vietnam War was on. And then a Gloucester club started and the next thing the Moon was gone and it became the Spa Lounge. I don't remember going there again. We've got a plaque in the pavement outside where the club used to be.

I also saw John Mayall's Bluesbreakers at the Top Spot in Ross-on-Wye in a church hall. I was one of the scooter boys so I used to go by scooter. There were loads of rockers there and we'd be upstairs. They'd be looking for a fight but we'd manage to ecape without getting into too much trouble.

I WAS THERE: MARY BEARD, AGE 15
I WAS STILL at school and I think it was a school night so would have gone with schoolfriends. We could dance right by where the acts were playing. The Moon wasn't licensed and it cost about 2/6d to get in. That's 12 ½p to see Cream!

I WAS THERE: ROB WILKINSON
WE - THE LOCAL Cheltenham Mods - all used to go to the Blue Moon. It was a very fashionable dance club and 'the' place to be, attracting people from Gloucester, Swindon, Bristol, Stroud and Newport, South Wales. The music taste in the club was very dance orientated with soul, British R&B and English soul. It was always a strange night when Cream took to the stage and the DJ would finish his set, because most of the dancers would walk off the floor because it was not the kind of music the audience wanted to hear and try out their latest dance moves to. It wasn't only the Cream who were insulted in this way. Many of the louder R&B bands like Zoot Money got the same treatment - because they were undanceable to!

One thing I clearly remember about Cream's stage show was the wildest rendition of 'Toad' you could imagine, complete with mad eyes and flaring nostrils, which was always met with huge cheers and stamping of feet. And Jack and Eric always gave a beltingly good version of 'I Feel Free' at the end of the night to huge acclaim.

PAVILION
21 NOVEMBER 1966, BATH, UK

I WAS THERE: RICHARD BOND, AGE 19
I FOLLOWED CREAM later in life but although I was at the Pavilion in Bath, I can't say that I remember much detail from the evening - and certainly didn't realise that I was in the (very near) presence of future greatness! I do remember Ginger had a cracked cymbal. The primary memory of the night was our driver losing the keys to his E-type Jag and having to remove the rear window to gain access… and get home.

I WAS THERE: STUART THOMSETT, AGE 16/17
THEY'D JUST BROUGHT out the single 'I Feel Free'. I went with my twin sister. I don't remember Cream being that loud. When Led Zeppelin played Bath Pavilion, Robert Plant's voice was so loud in a confined space that my ears were really hurting. And The Who were really loud as well.

Stuart Thomsett doesn't remember Cream being louder than Zeo or The Who

BRISTOL CHINESE R&B & JAZZ CLUB CORN EXCHANGE
22 NOVEMBER 1966, BRISTOL, UK

I WAS THERE: RICHARD EVANS
CREAM WERE WITHOUT doubt a huge favourite of mine. I saw them quite a few times from their inception in Bristol and Brighton where I was a student. Their live performances with improvised and extended soloing were remarkable. I'm told that originally the reason for extending the songs was that they only had a very limited number of numbers to play. In the middle of one of those solos, Eric collapsed backwards over his loudspeakers and was carried off stage. I think he was very stoned. The performance finished there!

Cream performed at the Corn Exchange on two other occasions: 24 January 1967 and 9 December 1967.

CORN EXCHANGE
26 NOVEMBER 1966, CHELMSFORD, UK

I WAS THERE: FROG GODDARD
THE FIRST TIME I saw them was at the Corn Exchange in Chelmsford in Essex before the first album came out. I was aware of their pedigree but I was really knocked out by their performance.

Frog Goddard was 'knocked out' by Cream

BIRDCAGE CLUB
3 DECEMBER 1966, PORTSMOUTH, UK

I WAS THERE: DAVE ALLEN
THEIR PERFORMANCE WAS truncated when Ginger fell off his stool and was taken to hospital. I was there and still have a diary with notes about the night, set list, etc. There is also a poster 'out there' advertising them playing the Birdcage two months previously but it matches no other evidence from that time and I'm sure that earlier gig never happened. I don't remember anticipating it - and since I loved Cream, and went to the Birdcage that weekend - I reckon I'd have been very disappointed to miss it. In my diary I described Cream as 'great' and listed some of the songs they played, plus some earlier/original performers: 'From Four till Late' (Robert Johnson); 'Rollin' and Tumblin'' (Baby Face Leroy); '(Sitting) on Top of the World', 'Down in the Bottom' (Howlin' Wolf); 'Cat's Squirrel'; 'Sweet Wine'. I believe the police found out what had happened, suspected (reasonably) that drugs might be involved and raided this all-nighter at some point, but I wrote nothing in my diary about that!

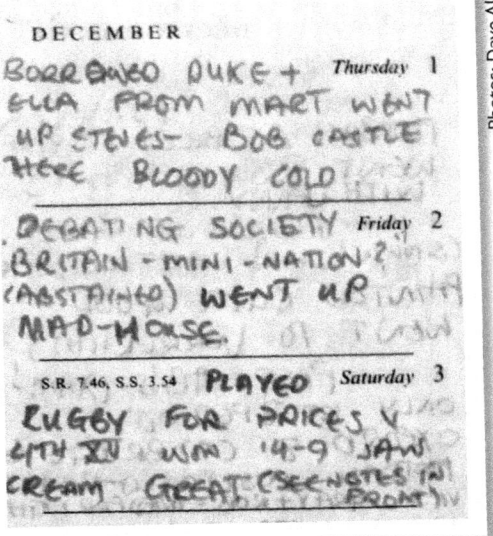

Dave Allen's diary records that he saw Cream and they were 'great'

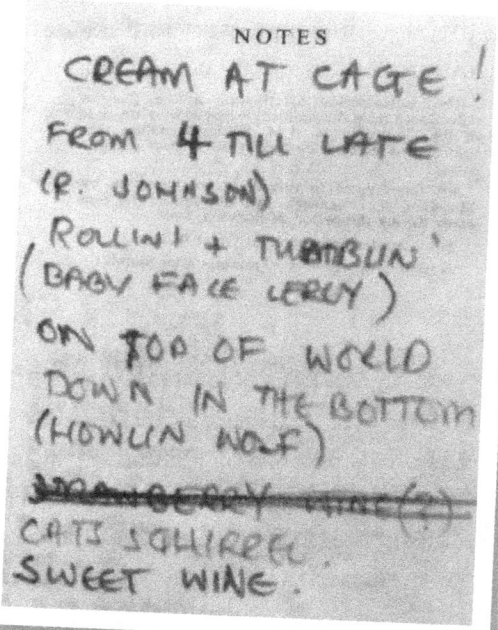

Dave Allen noted Cream's set list at the Birdcage

HORNSEY COLLEGE OF ART
8 DECEMBER 1966, LONDON, UK

I WAS THERE: DAVID RITMAN

IT WAS AN unpleasant winter's evening. 'Come on, we're going to see Cream tonight.' 'Who are Cream?' 'Clapton, Baker and Bruce.' 'Really! Where are they playing?' 'Hornsey Art College, just up the road.' 'We won't get in, you have to have a student union card.' 'We'll wing it. Tell them on the door we forgot our cards but we're in the ceramics department.' 'How much is it, I've only got a quid?' 'We'll give it a go.'

We blagged our way in for three shillings and while the backing band were on (I think it was Free) we tried to get the very snooty fine art girls to dance with us, but no joy. When Cream started all the blokes crowded the stage, leaving the girls on their own at the back of the hall. There were no more than 150 people there. The band was superb. It was in that six to seven month period when they played colleges to get their act together before launching themselves on the road.

'I FEEL FREE' RELEASED
9 DECEMBER 1966

Recorded in September and entering the charts at number 50 on 17 December 1966, Cream's second UK single 'I Feel Free' was omitted from the UK album release of Fresh Cream, climbing to number 11 at the end of January 1967.

FRESH CREAM RELEASED
9 DECEMBER 1966

Critics' views on Cream's debut album are mixed. New Musical Express says that the group 'really startle the ears with their changes of volume and tempo' but Crawdaddy concludes that 'there is too much unfulfilled experimentation to make this a really first rate album'. In the UK charts, the album reaches number 6. Released in January 1967 in America, it gets to number 4.

BROMEL CLUB, BROMLEY COURT HOTEL
14 DECEMBER 1966, BROMLEY, UK

I WAS THERE: KEITH SEARLE
I KNEW THE group from watching Mayall and Graham Bond Organisation and was very disappointed. They were okay at best. They were stoned and almost incoherent. They were at least an hour late arriving, perhaps more. By that time they hadn't built up much of a back catalogue and were experimenting, but seemed to be playing more for themselves than the audience. It got quite boring and quite a few people left after a while. I went to get a drink from the bar which was never a quick process at the BCH, probably 20 minutes, and when I returned they were still playing the same riff and it went on and on. I think it was 'Cat's Squirrel' but it might have been 'Wrapping Paper'. Ginger Baker fell of his stool a couple of times. By the time they finished half of the audience had left. The highlight of the evening was Ginger Baker breaking his drumsticks and throwing them into the audience. I never went to see them again. I stuck with Mayall and his ever-changing band.

WINTER GARDENS
20 DECEMBER 1966, MALVERN, UK

I WAS THERE: MARTIN WILLMOTT
ERIC FIRST CAME to my attention during his days with John Mayall (I still play 'Hideaway' from the *Beano* album today). I went to see John Mayall at Malvern Winter Gardens, expecting to see Eric, but was devastated to find that he had left. Instead, I was disappointed to see a replacement in the guitar spot - Peter Green. Halfway through the gig one of my pals said, 'Hey, he's as good as Eric....' At the time I was having none of it. John came to the bar at half time and we spoke to him. He was very cool about Eric and, in retrospect, I bet he was tired of hearing about him. Suffice it to say, I have come to love the playing of Peter Green, God rest him, and I've come to love his early work. But on that night I had wanted to see Eric....

John Mayall's live gigs were quality musical experiences. You could hear all of the instruments and the vocals. They were a reasonable representation of what you might have heard on their records. This was true of some bands I heard at Winter Gardens, including the Manfred Mann and The Animals. However, most bands were loud and not balanced. I saw The Who at the Winter Gardens, and lots of lesser-known bands, such as Simon Dupree and the Big Sound. These band were very visual and the volume was part of the excitement. It was awesome to a teenager like me. But vocals were almost always drowned out as poor sound was the norm in the late Sixties. Volumes went from 30 watt Vox guitar amps to 100 watt Marshalls, then to banks of Marshalls and so on.

I will never forget the first time I saw Cream

I will never forget the first time I saw Cream. They started with 'NSU'. Ginger Baker began the song with his crashing drum introduction - twin bass drums and flurries of hard-bashing drumming around his kit, accurate and powerful. I had never heard anything like it. You could feel the vibrations in your chest. In those days, drums were not miked up. He just played with sheer power. I think only John Bonham has ever matched this feeling from unamplified drums. I still 'feel' that feeling now when I listen to the *Fresh Cream* album. It's remarkable, timeless. He stunned everyone.

Then Eric came in with his arpeggiated, jangling guitar - but loud. At that time, he was still playing his Les Paul. Then a semi-subdued Jack Bruce on the vocal lead, having to shout more than he wanted over the din. The whole thing just shook you. On that night, they played most of their first album and this was the clearest I was ever to hear them, because on the next two outings that I attended they were even louder. We used to ignore that! We all knew the music anyway, so knew what we were supposed to be hearing, and the feeling and the spectacle were amazing.

ASSEMBLY HALL
22 DECEMBER 1966, WORTHING, UK

I WAS THERE: GEORGINA HAY
I'D SEEN CLAPTON a few times with the Yardbirds. I particularly remember Ginger Baker's drumming and his hair!

I WAS THERE: IAN LIDBETTER
MY WIFE TERRI and I first saw Eric Clapton with the Yardbirds, so when we saw he was with Cream and heard 'I Feel Free' and that they were playing in Worthing, West Sussex, we jumped at the chance. We stood at the front of the stage, only a few inches away from Eric. They were amazing and played with so much energy, especially when they played 'Toad'. Ginger's drum solo was breathtaking and one of his white-ended drum sticks broke and the brass washer landed near Terri. She still has it somewhere.

Ian and Terri Lidbetter were at Worthing's Assembly Hall

I WAS THERE: STEPHEN DAVY
I WAS THE bass guitarist for English group Steamhammer from 1968 to 1971. I am one of Cream's biggest fans and saw them twice in the Sixties. The place was Worthing, a seaside town in West Sussex. Fred Bannister, a local promoter, put on concert dances every Thursday for which entrance was only five or six shillings to see all the top groups of the time. They were held at either the Pier or the Assembly Hall. It was at the latter that I would watch Cream play twice.

The first time I saw them was soon after the release of their first single 'I Feel Free', which went to number 11 in the charts. I turned up with full expectancy as these chaps had each been voted the best on their instruments in the *Melody Maker* polls. They must have been the first supergroup of the time. I remember thinking, 'Do I stand in front of

Jack or Eric?' to watch them. In the end I opted for Eric. When they walked on stage, I knew it was going to be exciting.

They opened with 'NSU'. I recall Ginger, his eyes glinting, playing his double bass drum Ludwig kit with a lit cigarette in his mouth, his arms flailing around the drums. Jack was moving around the stage while playing bass and Eric was standing composed. They played most of the material from the first LP, *Fresh Cream*, and reeled off 'Sleepy Time Time', 'Spoonful', 'Rollin' and Tumblin'' and so on. Myself and the crowd were very impressed.

I WAS THERE: CEDRIC PAINE
I RECALL ERIC wearing a very elegant white suit and I think the ticket cost all of six shillings (30p)!

TOP OF THE POPS
29 DECEMBER 1966, LONDON, UK

I WAS WATCHING: MIKE MURTAGH
IN 1966, MY life changed irrevocably one Thursday evening with a performance of 'I Feel Free' by Cream on *Top of the Pops*. I had never seen or heard anything quite so thrilling! I was always a massive Cream fan from that point, being particularly interested in the huge contribution of Jack Bruce as opposed to Eric Clapton, about whom everyone was starting to rave. I didn't want to be part of the crowd as far as music was concerned, and swoon at the poppy stuff usually seen on *Top of the Pops* at that time. Cream and what was called 'progressive music' offered me a particular niche and I grabbed the opportunity to be a bit different.

Prog rock has become bastardised to represent the excesses of the big stadium rock bands with their light shows, stereo systems, stage sets and so on, which are nothing like the ideals of actual progressive music, as its adherents understood it. We valued lack of ostentation and high standards in our music - almost the opposite of a lot of what prog rock became.

Cream was a great example of this striving for higher musical standards. Two out-and-out jazzers - very capable musicians - teamed with an up-and-coming blues guitarist. Jack Bruce once said, 'Cream was a jazz band. We just never told Eric' - and he was absolutely right! Extended improvisations, tricky time signatures and so on represented just what we were looking for in our new music. Cream were admired by Leonard Bernstein and Igor Stravinsky - very heavy duty admirers with impeccable musical credentials.

Cream was a jazz band. We just never told Eric! **Jack Bruce**

TESCO'S
1966, NEASDEN, LONDON, UK

KEVIN MCKEEVER

I LEFT SCHOOL in 1966 aged 14 and three quarters to work in a local supermarket in Neasden, NW10. After a year I moved to a smaller Tesco shop in the same high street. There I met a colleague whose daughter I dated a couple of times and whilst chatting she said she babysat regularly for Ginger Baker, who lived in her road - Braemar Avenue in Neasden. I recall she said that as you entered the front door the whole downstairs hall and living areas were covered in white fur of some type of animals. I thought it odd at the time that he would be living there, although it was certainly an okay area. Twiggy was born and raised in Neasden too. And Spike Milligan did some sort of ditty to Neasden which put it on the map.

GUILDHALL
13 JANUARY 1967, SOUTHAMPTON, UK

DAVID FULFORD, AGE 14

I KNEW ABOUT the *Beano* album with John Mayall but I didn't see Eric until Cream as I was only 14 in early 1967 when the Bluesbreakers played the Guildhall and I couldn't travel far. I unfortunately missed Cream's Concorde performance in Southampton. At the Guildhall there were about 150 people in the audience so I could just walk up to be in front of Eric. They were pretty young but brilliant. The *Fresh Cream* album had been out a couple of months. Eric was a Mod and he still used his black Les Paul.

David Fulford (second right) with his band Phantasy

When they played 'Rollin' and Tumblin'', Eric was not required as the song comprised of drums, harmonica and vocals. He went behind the amps for a minute and came out with the longest cigarette I'd ever seen. It was a couple of years later that I realised what he was actually smoking!

Ginger was playing 'Toad' and because of the acoustics at the Guildhall, it literally sounded like a herd of elephants coming in, absolutely deafening and brilliant. The intro for 'Cat's Squirrel' went on and on and on for ages, with just Eric strumming the same E/Esus4 chords. Then, the next thing you know, he's leaning right back on the Marshall stack with his eyes closed and fires up at the top of the neck for the solo, unforgettable and unbeatable. The band were telepathic. They were one of the top bands ever and, like all of them, they were really only kids with very old souls.

Later in the year Hendrix played at the Winter Gardens in Bournemouth (which was unbelievable) and Led Zep played at Kimbells Ballroom in Southsea, but they were disappointing by comparison. Watching Eric and the boys inspired me to want to be a blues/rock lead guitar player. My first band was called Phantasy and our lead singer, Terry Scott Jr, went on to play in a band called Heaven in 1970 alongside Jimi Hendrix at the Isle of Wight. Apparently, he shared a joint with Jimi.

I WAS THERE: ROBERT GORMAN, AGE 15

I WAS AT the Jimi Hendrix gig at Southampton Guildhall. I was in a band and myself and my drummer and bassist intruded the dressing room long before he arrived. He was hungry and asked, 'Is there any place to eat around here?' We walked him down to the Windsor Fish Bar. He bought saveloy and chips and offered to buy us something but we were too awestruck! I asked him for a plectrum and he gave me one and asked for one of mine, which I only reluctantly parted with. I also went to see Cream there. Eric actually spoke to me. He said, 'Get out of the dressing room!'

Robert Gorham got into Cream's dressing room - but not for long!

LANCHESTER ARTS FESTIVAL, LANCHESTER COLLEGE
14 JANUARY 1967, COVENTRY, UK

I WAS THERE: TREVOR SUTHERS

ALL I REMEMBER is the venue being very non-descript but my being genuinely blown away by Jack Bruce's voice and charisma, with Eric Clapton and Ginger Baker seeming very much in the background. They easily seemed to replicate the singles I knew. I can't remember if there was an extended Ginger Baker drum solo - but there probably was!

Was there an extended Ginger Baker drum solo? Probably!

LEICESTER COLLEGE OF ART ARTS BALL, GRANBY HALLS
19 JANUARY 1967, LEICESTER, UK

I WAS THERE: NICK HAIRS

IN 1966 I was hitchhiking around Europe. Arriving back back in the UK I met a couple of lads at Victoria Station returning home from the Windsor Jazz and Blues Festival. They told me about Cream, how Eric was bending his strings and the powerhouse that was Jack and Ginger. I was hooked and knew I had to see them as soon as possible. I was a big Clapton fan through the Beano album and John Mayall's Bluesbreakers, but had never got to

Nick Hairs saw Cream five times

see them. I had seen Ginger and Jack with Graham Bond. I went on to see Cream five times. The first time was a student rag ball. After a false start of the opening song, 'NSU', due to sound problems, they went on to do about an hour or so long set. They were so dynamic and unique. I even managed to snaffle one of Ginger's drum sticks after he threw then into the crowd. I lost it over the years.

I WAS THERE: LIZ HENFREY

I DIDN'T GO to many shows but I went to this one!

Liz Henfrey was at Leicester's Granby Halls

I WAS THERE: PETER WICKHAM

I REMEMBER BEING at the Granby Halls that night. Also on the bill was the Geno Washington Band so after a few beers in the town centre myself and three friends decided to head there. We didn't have tickets but were hoping to be able to gate crash. When we arrived, there was quite a throng milling around the closed doors. The one that we chose must have already had about 50 hopefuls congregated and we all formed a human battering ram and managed to burst open the doors and gain entry, quickly rushing into the crowd to stop the stewards catching us. We had a great night and the temporary bar run by the students was very cheap so we carried on drinking and enjoying the show.

CLUB A'GOGO
20 JANUARY 1967, NEWCASTLE, UK

I WAS THERE: LAWRENCE CONNELLY, AGE 18

I WAS WORKING at Long Benton in the Ministry of Pensions and National Insurance. I had heard about the Club a'GoGo but had never been. One night I went there with Tommy Greggs from work and three other lads from Consett in my 1961 Ford Anglia, vehicle registration number 3889 UM. It was a bit of a squeeze with five lads. We went round Newcastle beforehand and had a few bottles of Newcastle Brown Ale to get in the mood. It was our first time at the club and Tommy said he'd heard a group called Cream were playing. I had never heard anything like it. I loved all the songs they played and Ginger Baker on the drums was amazing. I seem to remember Eric Clapton or Jack Bruce - or possibly both of them - wearing long leather overcoats as they went to the stage.

I just loved their music - the drums, Eric's guitar playing, the bass of Jack and their vocals - they really went for it. I became a fan that night and am still one today. Just before lockdown due to the Covid pandemic, I sang 'White Room' on a karaoke night at the British Legion in Thirsk. There were some guys in from Newcastle for Thirsk races and they said I was brilliant!

Lawrence Connelly had a few brown ales before heading into the Club A'GoGo

CORN EXCHANGE
27 JANUARY 1967, BRISTOL, UK

I WAS THERE: TONY PHILLIPS
I WAS INTRODUCED to Cream by my late brother-in-law Chris. The venue was the Corn Exchange, Bristol, the date was 22 November 1966 and the ticket price was six shillings (30p). I was all excited as it was my first gig, aged 16 years old, only to learn that Eric Clapton had broken his wrist so the gig was cancelled. I was very disappointed to say the least. Cream then returned to the Corn Exchange, Bristol on 27 January 1967 and the price of the ticket was seven shillings (35p). They more than made up for the previous disappointment with a night I shall never forget. Eric had to go off stage several times as he had broken a string on his guitar.

PUBLIC HALL
4 FEBRUARY 1967, WALLINGTON, UK

I WAS THERE: JOHN BLACKLEY
I SAW CREAM three times in the Sixties, including their last gig at the Royal Albert Hall in '68. Then I was lucky to see them again in 2005, once again at the Royal Albert Hall. As a teenager who was electrified by the whole music scene of the Sixties, they were something else as far as I was concerned. Apart from the pop explosion around The Beatles, Stones, etc., I remember being hooked by Ray Charles' 'What'd I Say', John Lee Hooker's 'Smokestack Lightning' and Chuck Berry's 'Roll Over Beethoven' and 'Johnny B Goode'. Then the blues really got me. So I was getting into going to gigs. The leader of the group that I was in was really into the Yardbirds. We saw them with Eric and I was blown away. Then we heard that this new group who we had never heard of called Cream were playing at Wallington Public Hall. We went to see them and - wow!

CITY HALL
9 FEBRUARY 1967, SALISBURY, UK

I WAS THERE: TOM THATCHER

THE BLUES OR the white version of it first grabbed me when I heard the album *Blues Breakers* by John Mayall - it was my Christmas present from reluctant parents. The Beano album featured Mayall on vocals, keyboards and harmonica, Hughie Flint on drums, John McVie (later of Fleetwood Mac) on bass and, of course, Eric Clapton on guitar and some vocals. Clapton's passionate solo on 'Have You Heard?' completely blew me away as I listened to it for the tenth time on Christmas Day, as did his brilliant and fluent playing on the instrumentals 'Stepping Out' and 'Hideaway', the latter by the fabulous Freddie King. Not long after, it was announced that Eric had left the Bluesbreakers.

Tom Thatcher with his band Heap

Before the show they were seen having fish and chips in the chippy opposite

He teamed up with two stunning musicians, Jack Bruce and Ginger Baker, and Cream came into being. In all honesty, most people had barely heard of Jack and Ginger but they soon would. *Fresh Cream* was a huge success and although many people bought it just to hear Eric, it was clear within a few seconds that the others were of the same extraordinary calibre. Although many have stated that this was a blues album, it wasn't entirely by a long way. The band's own songs - 'NSU', 'Sleepy Time Time', 'Dreaming' and 'Sweet Wine' - were true pop/rock songs which featured, amongst other things, perfect vocal harmonies, bass guitar played like lead guitar, jazz-type drumming in unusual tempos (often 5/4 and 7/8) and some fiery guitar work too. Unable to afford the album when it came out, I bought it from a girlfriend, Sheila, whose father had given it her as a birthday present. She hated it and I bought it from her for three shillings - 15p!

My excitement at seeing Eric and the band in February 1967 was almost unbearable. Before they took the stage, they were seen having fish and chips in the Yorkshire Fisheries, the most well-known chippy in Salisbury, just opposite the City Hall. I spotted Ginger walking up the side alley to the hall's back entrance and asked if I could accompany him. He said yes. I asked how the gigs were going so far. 'Alright.' Me: 'Do you enjoy these provincial gigs?' 'They're alright.' Me: 'How do they compare with the big London shows?' Ginger, clenching fist, 'Don't be so fucking nosy.' End of conversation!

The band played like gods and we guitar hawks at the front of a half full hall watched in amazement as Clapton broke a top E-string during a driving version of 'Rollin' and Tumblin'' but just changed strings and frets in mid-song without breaking stride or looking down. Others remember the gig as being ill-tempered: I just remember being absolutely astonished that three people could sound like ten, and that the quality of the vocals and harmonies was far beyond my wildest dreams. Jack's bass was like nothing ever seen - a complete rhythm section on its own, and Ginger brought power, unusual timings and new patterns to the show.

BATH PAVILION
11 FEBRUARY 1967, MATLOCK, UK

I WAS THERE: ANGELA WORTHY
WHAT A GREAT night it was. The room was filled with all the trendy people, including Mods in their mohair suits. The atmosphere was electric. The concert was reported in the Derby *Evening Telegraph* a week later when they said, 'Take Jack Bruce, Ginger Baker and Eric Clapton - shake well and you have the Cream, recognised as the top blues group in England.' We were photographed at the show - on the second row!

Angela Worthy and her friend Susan were at the Matlock Bath Pavilion

STARLITE BALLROOM
19 FEBRUARY 1967, GREENFORD, LONDON, UK

I WAS THERE: JOHN HOLMES

I SAW CREAM play three times. The first time was at the Starlite Ballroom in Greenford, near Wembley, which had a dubious reputation for fighting and general trouble but still put on a lot of top acts. I personally never saw any trouble. The support group that night was apparently The Gods, with Mick Taylor, but I don't remember them at all. I do recall curtains being across the stage when the opening drum pattern to 'NSU' started. The curtain on Eric's side went back when he came in and the same happened on the other side when Jack came in. Ginger was using his double kit (the painted one), and split a bass drum skin in the first number. The entire bass drum and tom tom was exchanged for an identical one!

I made some notes at the time and can confirm that, apart from 'NSU', they also did 'Tales of Brave Ulysses', 'SWLABR', 'Sweet Wine', 'Rollin' and Tumblin'' and 'Toad'. I also recall the songs being not much longer than the recorded versions, so they hadn't got into the really long improvisations at that time.

BROMEL CLUB, BROMLEY COURT HOTEL
22 FEBRUARY 1967, BROMLEY, UK

I WAS THERE: CELIA CRONIN

I HAD ALREADY seen the individual members of Cream at the Black Prince pub in Bexley through the mid-Sixties on Sunday nights when they played in different bands. Ginger Baker played with the Graham Bond Organisation, as did Jack Bruce sometimes. So each Cream member was familiar to Black Prince regulars. And I was in front row at Bromley Court Hotel for Cream with my friend Martin Wright. It was wonderful. My favourite bit was the guitar solo in 'Born Under a Bad Sign'. Ah, memories….

I WAS THERE: MARTIN WRIGHT

CREAM WERE WHAT lots of people had been waiting for. We all knew what we wanted, but no one knew how to put it all together - blues, rock and roll, jazz and a fusion/mix- before Cream. And they played it loud, the loudest I'd heard at small venues. That in itself made a difference, not just because they were loud for the sake of it but because it sounded better because of it. And because they were a three piece, and each one was on the top of theior game, the sound was clean. Each instrument was separate, and together, and they topped it off with vocals, voices that fitted and harmonised, and they could extemporise. So it was new and refreshing and fast moving. We were all in the mood. Good music, sexy girls - what was there not like?

There were lots of emerging bands, and lots of local music venues with lots of stuff going on in pubs. So if you liked the idea of loud music in a pub/club setting there was much to choose from and enjoy. People 'in the know' - that is, people like me (!) - got to see the best of each of these playing in other bands before Cream was formed. These guys with many others, were all going the same way, and at speed. Loads of names that could be seen close by were John Mayall and the Bluesbreakers, the Graham Bond Organisation, the Yardbirds, Chicken Shack, Pink Floyd, Peter Green and Fleetwood Mac, etc. Venues were places like The Black Prince, The Marquee, The Greyhound in Croydon and Bromley College, plus loads of others. For me, checking out who was doing what with who was much influenced by Jack Bruce, Eric Clapton and Ginger Baker. The bonus was when they formed Cream.

Whilst I had seen them all separately, the gig at the Bromley Court Hotel was the best ever. It was a small venue, able to hold maybe 200 to 250 people. All standing, and then muscle your way as close as possible, and with your beer. I went with my friend Celia, and we got to the front. There was no security - just the stage about six feet high, right in front, and then the band and all their gear. There was a double bass drum kit in the middle, with the two guitar players either side, plus a wall of speakers behind all of them.

There was no poncing around with extended sound checks

Then it started. There was no poncing around with extended sound checks. There were minimal introductions, and they were off! And very loud. The very best way they could start. Perhaps the only way.

It might have been too loud for the wiring, because a short way into their set there were technical problems with sparks and flames coming out of the amps. All was shut down. A roadie-type guy and others came out, and a short announcement of apology was made, and I thought 'what a fucking bummer!'. It had just got going. I genuinely thought we'd all be going back to the bar, and then back on home to play the record on Celia's Dansette. But it seems we got more than we first thought. They fixed the fuses or whatever the problem was, apologised, and announced that because of the interruption they would play all the way through with no interval. Then they started and tore the arse out it!

They seemed determined to do better had the problem not happened. There was loads of improvisation but keeping to the song, and I could tell they were in their element. And so was I and everyone else in the hall. I don't think Celia and I bothered too much about wrestling our way to the bar and back to get drinks. Where we were and what was going on was too good to miss.

Celia Cronin was at the Bromley Court Hotel with Martin Wright

I really think that at the time we saw them, and in the way and 'style' we saw them - in a small venue, not yet in the superstar league, only one album behind them, and so still really creative and pushing - was the very best time. Some might say they got better as time went on. But there and then, where we were, was the best ever.

I wouldn't bother with Wembley or the Albert Hall, sitting at the back of beyond and paying hundreds of pounds. But I'd do Bromley Court Hotel again!

ULSTER HALL
1 MARCH 1967, BELFAST, UK

I WAS THERE: RENE FULTON

I WAS AT the Ulster Hall gig with my boyfriend (now my husband of 48 years) and I remember it well, mainly because it overran and I missed my last bus and had to ring my dad to come into town from Dundonald to bring me home. Ginger Baker was the drummer and had decided to play a drum solo so we just couldn't leave until he finished now, could we? So it was well worth the telling off my dad gave me. It was a wonderful night! It's really my husband Tommy who was the fan. He reckons Cream were the best band ever. He took me that night but it was so long ago the only other thing we can remember is that it wasn't seated - at least, we weren't seated. We saw everyone who came to Belfast in the Sixties, including The Beatles and the Stones and Cilla!

I WAS THERE: GORDON HUNT
I ATTENDED THE Cream concert in the Ulster Hall and although that was some ago, I can still remember it - well, a bit, as things are a bit hazy from then!

I WAS THERE: SAMMY MCADAM
THE GROUP I played in, The Interns, were a support group to the Cream when they played at the Ulster Hall and at the Union Dining Hall at Queens University the following night. I was a full time professional drummer, and I was 21 or 22 at the time. We played rhythm and blues and Tamla Motown. We also supported The Who, The Herd, Spencer Davies, Alexis Korner and the Small Faces with Stevie Marriott. Ginger Baker had two Ludwig kits which were the same colour as Ringo Starr used when he started with The Beatles. At the Union Dining Hall at Queens University, Ginger dropped a couple of sticks while he was playing. I was standing beside him so I gave him a couple of sticks. There seemed to be a bit of arguing on the stage, and I don't know whether they went too long after that.

I WAS THERE: TONY N, AGE 15
I WAS A 15-year-old schoolboy at the time. It was six or seven shillings for the ticket. Eric wore a flowery shirt, and green trousers. They did 'Train Time', 'Rollin' and Tumblin'', 'I'm So Glad', 'Spoonful' and 'Toad'. It finished just before 11pm and I got the last bus home.

QUEENS UNIVERSITY STUDENTS HALL
2 MARCH 1967, BELFAST, UK

I WAS THERE: ANN SMILLIE

I WAS AT the Queens University Students Union and saw Cream in 1967. The thing I recall most about the gig, apart from the music, is that someone had stolen Eric Clapton's sunglasses that his current girlfriend had bought him and he refused to come on stage until he got them back. I guess they were returned as he came on stage to a rapturous welcome. Sunglasses on stage before Bono!

My friend Jeannie was at Queens with me and also remembers that Eric Clapton lay down on the stage. There was absolutely no security. We were right at the front of the stage along with many others. Our friends worked in the Students Union and we got in for free. My memory of the night is hazy as I guess we were on a half of Carlsberg Special each!

Ann Smillie (right) was at Queens with her friend Jeannie

Cream arrive in Denmark on 5 March for the start of a short Scandinavian tour but are initially refused entry as they have forgotten to bring any money with them.

FALKONERTEATRET
6 MARCH 1967, COPENHAGEN, DENMARK

I WAS THERE: MIK BREUNING, AGE 15

I WAS LIVING in a suburb of Copenhagen. I had been to concerts before with Danish bands but tonight there was going to be a big name from the UK. I hadn't heard about them and actually I didn't really care. I only went because my pals did, and I didn't want them to experience anything without me. How could I know that this night would change my life forever?

The concert began with many Danish bands playing support. That was possible because the theatre had a revolving stage, so when one band was playing another got ready behind the rear curtain. At one point Eric Clapton came on stage to receive a music award. The Danish musicians all had Beatles haircuts and suits but here came a man with an afro style hair (he had just met Jimi Hendrix - we didn't know who Jimi was at that time), blue jacket and screaming red trousers.

Then the support was over. For the first time the front curtain came down. When it went up the music began and... lo and behold! We had

Mik Breuning saw Cream all three times they were in Copenhagen

never seen a Marshall wall before, we had never seen such a huge drum setup. We had never felt such an energy. These guys were musicians, not boys having a little band for fun. At first you thought Ginger was a wild, crazy person with all that red hair and beard. He sat higher behind the drums than other drummers, like a raptor over its prey. And then you realized he actually played the drums, and wasn't just drumming the beat.

I thought, 'Welcome to this duck pond,' and I later learned that a fan had stood backstage and shouted 'jazz is dead, maaan!' This was shock, this was innovation, these were new times. Do I have to explain how the Danish bands began to appear on stage after this?

The second time Cream were in Copenhagen, they started the show with a monster version of 'Tales of Brave Ulysses'. Eric had now a more Captain Hook-style haircut and a rather thick moustache. Jack wore a white jacket with fringes, probably the same he wears on the cover of Songs for a Tailor. Again, we went home with music in our ears and excitement in our hearts.

The third time wasn't planned but as they were in Copenhagen to appear in Erik Balling's movie, *Det Var en Lørdag Aften (It Was a Saturday Evening)*, they gave an afternoon and evening gig in Tivoli's concert Hall. Here I was witness to the 'battle' between Eric and Jack. Every time Jack would turn the volume up, Eric would do the same. Poor Ginger in the middle. I was there in the afternoon and when I went out, I was jealous of the people on their way in. Why hadn't I bought a ticket for both shows?

I failed to get tickets to Cream's reunion which I will always regret. But as a friend said, 'Would you exchange my experience of the reunion for one of your experiences when they were young?' I think not!

LORENSBERGS CIRKUS
8 MARCH 1967, GOTHENBURG, SWEDEN

I WAS THERE: P O HESSELBOM

I SAW CREAM twice in 1967 in my home town of Gothenburg. There was a club in Gothenburg during the Sixties called the Cue Club whose owner was Styrbjörn Colliander, a very nice man who sadly was killed outside his club by some lunatic. But he arranged lots of concerts in the Sixties, including two by Cream at Lorensbergs Cirkus. This was, as the name suggests, a place where circuses performed but also where lots of bands like The Beatles and The Who appeared.

P O Hesselbom was at the Lorenbergs Cirkus show in Gothenburg; these posters were advertising the previous day's show in Stockholm

The first Cream gig was on March 8, 1967, and the second was November 15, 1967. Some books say the November show was at the Cue Club or at Liseberg, an amusement park in Gothenburg where many bands including Jimi Hendrix played, but Cream didn't.

The Cream also stayed at Styrbjörn's apartment the first time they were here. I remember the ticket price was five Swedish Crowns (today about 45 Crowns, one dollar is about ten Crowns) and for that price you also got four Swedish bands as well - Steampacket (not the English group), The Gonks, Annabee Nox and The Jackpots. When the opening acts had finished there was a long pause and you could hear some hammering. Later on, I

Eric in action in Sweden

understood that they were nailing Ginger's drums to the floor.

I'd seen the Hollies and they performed like The Beatles, eager to please, and there's nothing wrong with that. But Cream came in looking very serious, no smiling, and started to play with a skill I'd never heard before. It changed my whole view of music and opened up a whole new world for me. Every solo Eric Clapton did he turned his back on the audience, inspired by Robert Johnson. Ginger did a drum solo, something I never heard before. Clapton played on a Les Paul, Jack Bruce had a six string bass and Ginger had his double bass drums and lots of tom toms and cymbals. In a review in *Göteborgs Posten* (the *Gothenburg Post*) journalist Hans Sidén wrote about Clapton, 'He sounds like a lightning strike in a guitar factory.'

Ginger (left) and Jack in action in Sweden

Photos: Rudi Jelinek

WELLINGTON CLUB
12 MARCH 1967, EAST DEREHAM, UK

I WAS THERE: MARTIN BOOTH
I REMEMBER HAVING a chat with Ginger Baker in the bar, although I can't remember what it was about. When they were playing one of Ginger's pom pom drumstick heads came off and I caught it. I still have it somewhere. The other thing that happened at that gig was that a bloke came up to me and clocked me right between the eyes for no apparent reason. I think he was drunk as his mates led him away. I did not react as I am not a fighter and, more importantly, I did not want to get thrown out of the club before I had seen Cream!

Martin Booth (here with wife Sandra) was in the wars at Dereham 67

I WAS THERE: DEBORAH EVANS
I GOT THEIR autograph, along with Jimi Hendrix's as he also performed there.

KING'S HALL
14 MARCH 1967, ABERYSTWYTH, UK

I WAS THERE: DAVID DAVIES, AGE 17
I DID BAR work for Gerald Morris, landlord of either The Angel or the White Horse at the time. Gerald had the concession to provide the bar facilities for all the university functions at the King's Hall. I was asked to work at the gig and as always it was always very busy. But when the big acts such as Cream appeared on stage the bar went very quiet. I went down towards the stage during their performance and was especially mesmerised watching Ginger Baker perform his drum solo for what appeared to be for a long time. If Gerald felt the takings were good (which they usually were for any uni gig), a band would be given a 40oz bottle of vodka. I was asked to go backstage with this offering and met Eric Clapton, Jack Bruce and Ginger Baker.

STUDENT UNION, UNIVERSITY OF BRISTOL
18 MARCH 1967, BRISTOL, UK

I WAS THERE: JOHN FLETCHER
FROM THE SIXTIES through to the Noughties I've seen many of the best bands and artists, often in small halls and including the Stones, Zep, The Beatles, the Animals, Otis, Janis, Little Richard, Dylan, Elton and Floyd, and I can say that Cream was easily the best - in March and again in December 1967. I first saw Clapton with the Yardbirds in February 1965 in a town hall and then in November 1965 with John Mayall in a Red Cross Hall. I saw Cream in the best possible venue - a university union. I was right up front and I was blown away: Clapton (pre complete heroin addiction) with some unbelievable licks, Ginger drumming his heart out (where did he get the energy?) and Bruce very competently

making up the overall unique sound. Just writing about it is a thrill. They were superb!

LOCARNO BALLROOM
22 MARCH 1967, STEVENAGE, UK

I WAS THERE: TERRY MCNAMARA
A GOOD FRIEND of mine, who had a big influence on the type of music I listened to, asked me to go to the 'Herm' in my home town of Hitchin to see a band called Cream. I can't remember why I didn't go but have kicked myself ever since. We also used to go to the Mecca (Locarno Ballroom) in Stevenage every Wednesday where some great bands played, including The Who in their equipment smashing days. When I found out Cream were due to play there and made sure I didn't miss them this time. I was awestruck at what I was seeing and hearing. I think I just stared open mouthed as Ginger Baker played 'Toad'. These were three top class musicians producing something that was entirely different to what I had listened to before. That was it - I was hooked. When I hear their records now, I am transported back to those wonderful Sixties when I was a teenager, and especially to that night at the Mecca.

In March 1967, Cream visited the United States for the first time.

MUSIC IN THE FIFTH DIMENSION RKO 58TH STREET THEATER
28 MARCH 1967, NEW YORK, NEW YORK

I WAS THERE: RANDY DANNENFELSER
MURRAY KAUFMAN WAS a New York disc jockey known professionally as Murray the K. He greatly enhanced his reputation as New York's 'Boss Jock' by arranging somehow to worm his way into The Beatles' entourage when they came to New York on their first tour and obtaining exclusive interviews with them from their hotel rooms. He shamelessly promoted himself as 'The Fifth Beatle', although he was not the only radio personality in the States to do so. Since the late

fifties, Kaufman had been putting together live holiday rock and roll shows during Christmas and Easter breaks each year, combining American pop, soul and folk acts on the bill and lately, sprinkling a couple of 'British Invasion' bands into the mix. My three friends and I, then 19 and denizens of Long Island, went to see one of Murray's last-ever shows in Manhattan during Easter week of 1967.

The show's headliners were Mitch Ryder and the Detroit Wheels, Wilson Pickett, and Smokey Robinson and the Miracles. The next acts billed were The Who and 'The Cream', both bands making their first appearances stateside. The British bands were the reason we were making the trip. A major Who fan, I had played my *Fresh Cream* album until the grooves were worn down. There were no bad cuts on that album, no songs to be skipped. Cream's music struck me as close to rock and roll, but not really; close to jazz, but not really; and close to blues, but not really. Rather than combining these genres, each element tended to blur the identity of the others in Cream's style, so that what you had was not rock 'n' roll, jazz and blues but an original music form. I realise now that Cream were, for better or worse, the fathers of what we now call 'Progressive Rock'. And I couldn't wait to see these guys in full flight.

Randy Dannenfelser saw Murray the K's introduction of Cream to the USA

'I Feel Free' was the song that was receiving airplay on the radio

---

Including the lower carded bands and performers, there were nine or ten acts on each bill. Kaufman's shows were presented in old vaudeville format; each act would come onstage, do a couple of songs, and be hustled off so that the next band could get on. Each show lasted two hours, at which point the theatre was cleaned of rubbish and audience members hiding in the rest rooms, hoping to sneak into the next show, and then the next group of ticket holders were let in. The theatre opened mid-morning and Murray was able to squeeze in five separate shows a day before Ryder finished up for the final time at around midnight. This lasted for nine consecutive days during Easter break. Our tickets were for the last show on Tuesday. So since we knew we were going to get, at the most, three songs from Cream, we wondered which three would they be? 'I Feel Free' was the song that was receiving airplay on Murray's radio show, and so I was positive that would be one of them. My favourite Cream song was 'NSU' and so I was hoping that one would be in the set. And I made a bet with one of my friends that 'Sweet Wine' would surely be one we'd hear.

We took public transport into Manhattan - driving into the city was always a pain, as was finding a reasonable place to park on a college student's budget. I remember the theatre was a smallish one on the east side of midtown, several blocks beyond the theatre district. Our seats were located toward the back right side of the orchestra level. The opening acts were painful to sit through, bands with names like The Chicago Loop and Mandala. Jim and Jean were a nice folk duo, but out of place in this venue, as were a comedy troupe called The Hardly Worthit Players, whose leader was a Bobby Kennedy impressionist who 'sang' a parody of 'Wild Thing'. (Ugh!)

Then, the time had come. From offstage Murray announced in a solemn tone, 'Ladies and gentlemen, direct from England, please welcome... The Cream.'

Ladies and gentlemen, direct from England, please welcome... The Cream

---

The curtain went up and the lights went on. Ginger Baker began the controlled, syncopated attack on his floor tom. I realised, as Eric Clapton began to pick the opening notes, that I was going to get my wish. My heart was racing. Jack Bruce was now involved in the intro with his thunderous bass, although I don't remember if it was the four or six string Gibson he was playing. He stepped up to the mic and began: 'Driving in my car... smoking a cigar...' I was in ecstasy. I jumped up in my seat and began to shout along. I sang along with the 'ahs'. My buds were probably embarrassed because none of us was stoned.

'NSU' lasted for almost five minutes. As the boys did their grand finish, I think I was cheering loudest of anyone in the audience. Now, what song would be next? Totally unexpected, at least to me, they followed with the fourth cut on side two of my *Fresh Cream* album, 'I'm So Glad'. Good, I thought, because 'I'm So Glad' was under four minutes long, and they'd have time to do another song after it. Little did I realise that they would turn it into a live jam song, with Eric taking an extended lead solo and Ginger doing what, for him, was a relatively brief drum solo. The entire song clocked in at between eight and nine minutes. Then it was 'thank you and goodnight'. No 'I Feel Free'. No 'Sweet Wine'. They had played nearly 15 minutes, far longer than any other act that had appeared before them. I was left delighted and disappointed by their song choices. It was a mixed bag of afterglow from the greatest prog rock band ever.

I would see Cream play once more. It was the following year on a night when their sound system crapped out early. After Ginger had played a drum solo for almost a half hour while technicians frantically and fruitlessly tried to patch things up, the boys apologised and left the stage for good. As horrible as that night was, in the long term it made my memory of the Murray the K show a little more sweet. It made me appreciate that once upon a time on a weeknight in New York City, I was lucky enough to see a band for the ages perform a couple of songs as they were hitting their stride.

I WAS THERE: BILL C EVANS

AFTER THE BEATLES burst into our lives, a few of my friends and I were inspired to take up instruments. We started a band and played a couple of dances. We were in junior high school. Our drummer Scott's older brother, Neil, was in the band that played at all the high school dances. We looked up to Neil and he was more than happy to share his love of music coming out of the UK with us. One day after practicing a few songs, Neil came running in with a record album. 'You guys have to hear this drummer! I read about this band, The Who, in a magazine and ordered the album from England.' He put *My Generation* on the record player and played the song, 'My Generation'. It's safe to say, our lives changed that day. I doubt if our parents appreciated it very much.

Bill Evans was at the RKO Theatre for Murray the K's 'Music in the Fifth Dimension'

As our adolescent band got louder and more free-spirited, other British records that we were discovering at the time were the Yardbirds, John Mayall and the Bluesbreakers and, shortly thereafter, Cream. Eric Clapton hit our radars. It wasn't long before *My Generation* and *Fresh Cream* were released in America. So when Murray the K announced shows at the RKO Theatre in New York, New York that included The Who and Cream, we begged our parents relentlessly to let us go. They gave in, and one of our dads drove to the show and picked us up afterwards.

I WAS THERE: ANDY SZEGO

EACH GROUP HAD only like five minutes - there were about 15 acts - and it ran all day. I read later that both groups hated it but needed the US exposure. I recall Cream doing 'I'm So Glad' and being amazed at the psychedelic guitars and Bruce's six string bass. I had never seen one before. It was a great show and a musical education for a 13-year-old. The Who did 'Substitute' and 'My Generation'. Watching them destroy their equipment was both exciting and sad - we could barely afford any for our band!

Andy Szego saw the Murray the K show

I WAS THERE: THOM LUKAS, AGE 14

I SAW CREAM a few times. I saw two or three shows at the RKO 58th Street Theater and then a few months later at the Village Theater. I got backstage too. I was 14 the first time, at the Murray the K shows. I had heard a few songs on the radio and bought *Fresh Cream* about a month before seeing them. I could recognise and sing along with both songs they played at each of the shows that I saw.

At the Village Theater, I recognised all three or four songs they did, because I had also bought the John Mayall LP before seeing their set. I got kind of dragged backstage after the show by a 32-year-old member of the Group Image commune. We barged into a design room where Ginger Baker and Richie Haven were having a lively conversation. I recall being shocked by Havens having his front dentures out. No front teeth! I was also surprised at how tall, slim and friendly Ginger Baker was. He had a huge grin and he was amused by my friend and her request that Cream play a free concert to benefit the struggling Group Image and the work they were doing to clean up the East Village. All he said was, 'Good image, good group!'

I WAS THERE: JONATHAN GILBERT

I GOT TO see them twice. The first time was Cream's first performance in the USA. There was a DJ in New York - Murray the K - who would put on shows with six to eight bands each doing two or three songs. It was Easter weekend 1967, in my senior year at high school. It was at a movie theatre in Manhattan. I think there were three shows a day for three to four days. The show I was at had Simon & Garfunkel, a group of comics who ended up on *Saturday Night Live*, The Who (their first US performance), Cream, Wilson Pickett and the headliner - Mitch Ryder. Pete Townsend smashed his guitar and Keith Moon kicked his drum set over. We were all 'what the hell is going on?' If I remember, Cream did 'Spoonful', 'I'm So Glad' and 'Toad'. Instead of the 15 minutes they were allotted they played for half an hour or more. I then saw them the next year in Columbus, Ohio, near where I went to college. Unfortunately, I don't have much memory of that show, except Eric being mesmerising and Ginger going on and on.

Jonathan Gilbert remembers Cream exceeding their allotted 15 minutes

I WAS THERE: RICHARD CORNETTO, AGE 15

I SAW THEM twice, the first time at the Murray the K RKO show, where they only played 'Cat's Squirrel' and 'I Feel Free', and six months later at the Village Theater. In March of '67 they had no airplay at all. I knew Clapton didn't do too much with the Yardbirds ('For Your Love') and I hadn't heard of Mayall yet. They were good.

Richard Cornetto remembers Cream playing 'Cat's Squirrel' at the RKO 67

I WAS THERE: ALAN CHILDS

I HAD A friend who in early 1967 somehow got a flight to London from NYC. We grew up in a housing project in Brooklyn. All our friends couldn't figure out how he got the money for this trip. He was a keyboard player. I was the drummer. We were 15 years old. When he came back to Brooklyn, he came to my apartment with two LPs. He was very intense. He insisted that I listen to these LPs. It was John Mayall and the Bluesbreakers with Eric Clapton (the *Beano* album) and *Fresh Cream*. Not only did my life change musically, but it set my path to a very nice career.

Alan Childs was introduced to Clapton by the Beano album

Cream were and remain a major influence on me. In March 967, I saw them for the first time (and The Who as well) at the RKO 58th St Theatre in New York City. They were advertised as coming 'direct from England' on the Murray the K show. Murray was a New York DJ who was also known as the Fifth Beatle. It was both bands' first trip to the USA. About 15 other acts played as well. I can only remember that I was witnessing something groundbreaking. The sound was not very clear, but I could feel it. Each band did two or three songs. I'm sure I heard 'NSU' and possibly 'Sweet Wine'. I'm not sure I understood completely what I was hearing, but it moved me.

I asked Ginger, 'What do you think of America so far?' 'How the fuck should I know? I've only been here 35 fucking minutes' **Al Kooper**

The months that followed put me into an obsession mode musically. I was hooked. At this point I knew what I was listening to (I mean in a musical sense). In October 1967 I saw Cream at the small Cafe Au Go Go in Greenwich Village. Sitting at the next table from my friends and I were the Blues Project (Al Kooper's band). Cream were in NYC recording the *Disraeli Gears* LP and did a few gigs. Clapton turned his back to the audience only to turn around to sing. It was loud. It was amazing. I now understood the high calibre of musicianship.

Cream arrive back in the UK on Friday 7 June after a 10 hour delay at Kennedy Airport due to bad weather.

IMPERIAL BALLROOM
8 APRIL 1967, NELSON, UK

I WAS THERE: BRIAN DOBNEY
I ONLY SAW them once, at the Imp. I think there had been a bust up between Jack and Eric before they came on as, when they arrived on stage, Jack shouted something at Eric and threw his harmonica on stage. It didn't affect the performance. I don't remember any individual songs, just being super impressed by them and especially by Ginger's drumming!

REDCAR JAZZ CLUB
9 APRIL 1967, REDCAR, UK

I WAS THERE: CHRISTINE SWIFT, AGE 18
I WENT WITH my future husband because he was a massive fan. I really enjoyed them. What I remember is that towards end of the concert Jack Bruce fell flat on his face. Rumour was that this was because he was so drunk!

RHODES CENTRE
15 APRIL 1967, BISHOP'S STORTFORD, UK

I WAS THERE: AUSTIN REEVE
AFTER SEEING THEM at the Windsor Festival in 1966, when they'd been billed as 'Eric Clapton - Jack Bruce - Ginger Baker', the next time I saw the band they had a name. Cream came to our

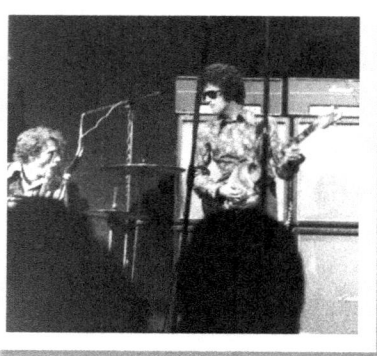

Photos: Austin Reeve

local venue, the Rhodes Centre, in April 1967 and it was to be another memorable night. I knew that the band had arranged with The Fool, a couple of Dutch artists, to decorate a set of instruments, so I took my camera (no restrictions in those days) hoping to get some interesting shots. When the band came on stage, Eric's Gibson SG Standard had been decorated with multi-coloured psychedelic images, as had Ginger's drum kit. But Jack was playing an unadorned Danelectro Longhorn bass. I heard later that he didn't like the decorated Fender Bass VI and only used it for TV appearances.

Both Lawrie and Jeff, who were with me, were disappointed that Eric wasn't playing his Les Paul Gibson but the SG had a great rock tone. Eric was dressed to kill - Afghan coat, permed hair, floral shirt and ski pants - while the other two were much less flamboyant. The music was brilliant - they kicked off with 'NSU' and the full house audience loved it.

I got pretty close to the stage and took a roll of film with my old Russian rangefinder camera. It was not easy to focus or keep steady in a crowd but I got several pictures which sum up the atmosphere that night. Cream played two sets and, in the interval, Jeff followed the band down South Street to the Jolly Brewers pub where they refreshed themselves. Jeff longed to go in and chat but he was too young for pubs at that time! After the interval,

Photos: Austin Reeve

Cream at the Rhodes Centre

the band waded in with 'Cat's Squirrel' and were met throughout the rest of the evening with rapturous applause. Unfortunately, with all the extended solos, they overran the allowed time slot and the Centre caretaker cut the power to the amps, leaving them to shout to the audience that they couldn't play any longer. All in all, a great evening.

In 1968, I went to Sunbury to the Jazz Festival which had moved there from Windsor after the complaints about noise. There was no Cream performance as such as they had announced that they were going to break up shortly. A drum battle between Ginger Baker and Phil Seaman was on the menu and, although they can get a bit boring after a while, I settled down in the middle of the audience to watch. After five or 10 minutes of hard work by the two drummers, a guitarist came on stage unannounced, plugged in and proceeded to give an amazing extended adlib solo which both drummers joined in. It didn't take the audience long to work out that it was EC, so it was two thirds of Cream - better than we could have hoped for!

I didn't see Cream again - I couldn't get tickets for the farewell concerts and anyway I was starting at university in October 1968 which meant finances were tight, so I had to make do with an early American copy of *Wheels of Fire* which came from a local USAF airbase. Live gigs were sorely missed but I did manage to see Eric and Ginger in Cream's evolution band, Blind Faith, at their huge free concert in Hyde Park in June 1969. With 120,000 in the audience, it didn't seem much like the old days at Rhodes.

Photos: Austin Reeve

DAILY EXPRESS RECORD STAR SHOW EMPIRE POOL, WEMBLEY
16 APRIL 1967, LONDON, UK

I WAS THERE: PETER CHARLESWORTH

I REMEMBER THEIR rendition of 'Toad'. All started normal enough then after a few minutes Clapton and Bruce just walked off the stage. Nothing was said to a bemused crowd. However, a certain Mr Baker was left at his quite considerable drum kit doing what only he could do. It seemed to last forever. I'm guessing this drum solo was not the classic that everyone knows now. Then with as little fuss as when they left Jack and Eric came back and finished the set.

Peter Charlesworth remembers Ginger's drum solo lasting 'forever'

Cream had to walk off after two numbers when their bass amp blew up. **Dave Berry, talking to Record Mirror**

CORN EXCHANGE
18 APRIL 1967, BRISTOL, UK

I WAS THERE: JOHN HARRIS

BRISTOL IN THE Sixties was bursting with live music. Word was that there were 500 local bands. Folk fans went to the Troubadour, acoustic blues purists to the Old Duke, but for the latest bands the place to be was the Corn Exchange. Here Uncle Bonnie ran the exotically named Bristol Chinese R&B Jazz Club every Tuesday evening, attracting big names to a venue small enough for fans to get very close to the action. Advertising was sketchy - cheap duplicated hand-drawn flyers; the odd poster; an announcement from the stage about next week's band - but word got round quickly and gigs were usually full. There were no tickets in advance: you queued up on the night and hoped you'd get in. The secret was for someone you knew to join the queue early, then join them once you'd

John Harris supported Cream at the fabled Bristol Chinese R&B Jazz Club

changed out of your school uniform and caught the bus into town. But for us this time there was no queueing: we were to be the local support band.

Clapton was God; all three members of Cream had at some stage served time with our hero, John Mayall; this was the first supergroup. Our teenage blues band had played with The Troggs and Zoot Money, but for us this was the big one. We were desperate to support Cream. We had pushed and pleaded and, amazingly, found ourselves arriving early that evening at the Corn Exchange with our kit, ready to play. We tried to smuggle some friends in with us, to be met with a firm no: 'Sorry, boys. The band tonight are on a percentage of the gate, and I want them to have as much as possible.'

Setting up was a serious challenge. Cream's road crew were already in action, driving huge nails into the front of the stage floor to prevent Ginger Baker's double drum kit from sliding off, and hauling double Marshall stacks to either side - all of it well forward and filling the tiny stage. We asked for room for our modest kit, to be roundly told to 'fuck off'. The best we could do was for two of us to perch with our amps on the thin strip between Jack Bruce's stacks and his microphone, and for the bassist and drummer to cram in on the thin strip on Eric Clapton's side.

We asked for room for our modest kit, to be roundly told to 'fuck off'

Of course, we wanted their autographs on our Ilex Blues Band cards, so we filed into the space behind the stage which served as their changing room. Our bassist saw Ginger relieve himself unceremoniously into a pint glass. The contrast between the three Cream members was striking: Jack Bruce warm, friendly and open; Eric unassuming and shy; Ginger glazed and silent.

What should we play? As blues fans we'd taped an early radio broadcast of Cream playing 'Crossroads' live. What we didn't realise was that the BBC sound engineer had failed to turn on the vocals for the third verse - all we heard at that point was the pounding rhythm, no words, so that's what we learned. This had become our signature piece, opening and closing our sets. With the arrogance of youth we decided to play as normal - 'Crossroads' bookending blues classics and a couple of our own pieces. After all, Cream hadn't released 'Crossroads' yet; and couldn't it be seen as a tribute? At the end of our set, we stacked our gear as best we could to give Clapton and Bruce space to stand, and squeezed into the three rows of chairs which were always directly in front of the stage, to watch every movement of Clapton's hands.

Cream were at their peak, and experiencing them for the first time, from just a few feet away, was overpowering. All three commanded the Corn Exchange - Bruce through his stage presence, Clapton with his technical brilliance, Baker through his sheer energy. Together, as a power trio, they were electrifying. They were mesmerisingly skilful. They were exciting. And they were loud. We had seen the first supergroup, the band of the moment - and, more than that, we had met them and opened the bill for them.

Afterwards it was back to everyday life: we collected our amps and guitars and, as we so often did after a local gig, took them back home on the bus. Next day would be school again.

BRIGHTON ARTS FESTIVAL, THE DOME
21 APRIL 1967, BRIGHTON, UK

I WAS THERE: IAN GRANT
IT WAS MY 16th birthday. I bought two tickets to see Cream and The Who at Brighton Dome. The second ticket was for a girl I fancied but alas she wasn't allowed to go, or didn't want to. It was to be my first concert experience. I gave or sold the second ticket to a classmate and we both got the train, very much excited about the evening ahead of us. I had the *Fresh Cream* album so was looking forward to hearing Eric, Jack and Ginger playing most tracks from it. Crispian St Peters ('The Pied Piper') was on first, then The Merseys ('Sorrow') and then… there they were. - Cream!

It's 54 years ago so I can't remember too much (Pete Townshend said to me recently, 'I'm surprised you can remember anything about it') but I do remember being transfixed and in total awe of the occasion. It was loud and the musicianship was astounding. It was great to hear 'I Feel Free' and 'NSU' but 'Crossroads' and 'Toad' were the scene stealers because of their length and the improvisation. I was spell bound.

And then The Who. What an initiation. I had seen the light and was never to be the same again. What I didn't know was that, in two years' time, I would be doing lights for the Pink Floyd in this very venue and have several bands I managed headline there. And that in three years' time I would be promoting Deep Purple in my home town of Worthing and that I would have a 50 year career in music. Just to think, it all started with this gig. If I hadn't wanted to date the girl I fancied, I might not have been so inspired to see more bands and have the motivation to get involved in the business of music.

I WAS THERE: ROGER ADAMS, AGE 15

I SAW CREAM twice, both times in Brighton. The first time was at the Dome on a package tour where they were second on the bill to The Who. My dad was a jazz trombone player who was into, amongst others, Chris Barber - the true father of the blues in Britain. I was a blues fan from the age of 14 and had old records by Howlin' Wolf and Muddy Waters. I liked the Bluesbreakers, had seen the Yardbirds a few times on TV, read in the *Melody Maker* about Cream forming, bought their first album and bought tickets to see them at the Dome in 1967. I was already playing a bit of electric blues guitar. The Dome show was part of the very first Brighton Festival. Ginger's solo got a standing ovation and when The Who came on, they obviously couldn't follow it. They gave up after a few short songs, smashed the gear and walked off.

I came away a Cream convert, and went to see them again when they played the Top Rank Suite, where they were supported by a local band called The Span (previously the Mike Stuart Span). By this time, we were doing Cream songs in a little band I had formed with some school mates. Cream were undoubtedly the best band I ever saw - by a country mile.

I took my family to the Thursday night reunion gig at the Albert Hall in 2005. It was a very different, more measured musical approach from all three of them in their later years, but I still enjoyed it a lot. I was also lucky enough to see 'Sons of Cream' when they somehow ended up playing at our local pub. It was a bit weird because we had already bought tickets to see Kofi, Malcolm and Will at the 100 Club in London (I'd booked a hotel room and all!) and then my daughter who worked behind the bar in the Duke of Wellington, Shoreham phoned me up to say 'you're going to kick yourself - guess who's playing here this afternoon?' So I saw the 'Sons' twice too.

PAVILION BALLROOM
25 APRIL 1967, BOURNEMOUTH, UK

I WAS THERE: RICHARD ANSTEY

I WAS A grammar school student and very much aligned with the Sixties rebellion against the establishment. Cream presented a genre of music that was vogue in our group and when they performed at the Pavilion in Bournemouth there were four of us that booked tickets. I can picture the performance even now - the audience was standing in a semi-circle around the stage and I would guess there would have been no more than 150 people. Initially we were up front near the speakers but then moved to the sides to relieve our ears.

One outstanding memory is of Jack Bruce and his cherry red Cuban-heeled boots. I don't know why but I have never forgotten them. They had everyone in awe. Ginger Baker certainly performed as we had come to expect - an absolute maniac on the drums and completely off his head. Eric Clapton went on to be the most famous but from their performance they were a tight team and no one was better than the others. All three were brilliant. I certainly remember 'White Room', and 'Sunshine of Your Love' was another stand out performance I will remember forever.

Richard Anstey saw Cream at Bournemouth's Pavilion Ballroom

'Sunshine of Your Love' was another stand out performance I will remember forever

---

Between 1966 and 1971 I was a student and we were able to see many bands that had their day in the sun, but none stand out to me like Cream. That may be because they broke up shortly after and the others became more commercial. We all loved The Beatles and the Stones and even now marvel at their innovation and talent, but I always felt Clapton Bruce and Baker were spiritual blues musicians which may not have appealed to the commercial public as much but they were nonetheless deeply talented musicians. Fleetwood Mac moved far away from the early roots of their formative days, while Savoy Brown was another band that did the college circuit and we went to the Ritz Ballrooms on the cliff at Bournemouth beach to see them. Our school band was called the Electrons and featured sixth former Bob Fripp, who later formed King Crimson. Cream introduced us naive teenagers to the emerging and proudly UK variant of the blues - rhythm and blues - and in my opinion established a genre that has never been equalled.

BIRDCAGE
26 APRIL 1967, PORTSMOUTH, UK

I WAS THERE: HELEN SHERWOOD
I SAW THE Cream in a nightclub in Portsmouth in the Sixties, called The Birdcage, in the Eastney area of Portsmouth. I only went along with my then boyfriend (who became my husband) because he was a great fan of Ginger Baker. This club never gets much of a mention in Portsmouth memories but they certainly hosted some good names there. It was opened by Mike and Bernie Winters!

MUNICIPAL HALL
5 MAY 1967, PONTYPRIDD, UK

I WAS THERE: JUDITH JONES
LITTLE DID I know when I went to work in Cardiff University that later that day I would get to meet one of my favourite bands - Cream. Knowing that I was a fan, the son of one of my workmates had left a message to say that Cream were playing that night in the Rhondda Valley town of Pontypridd, some 12 miles from my home town of Cardiff. My best friend Jaci, another fan, had the use of her father's minivan and, all togged up in our trendiest hippie gear, we set off for Pontypridd and its Municipal Hall. Pontypridd being a valleys town, it was a little backward when it came to music, preferring the likes of Shakin' Stevens and of course their own Tom Jones. So that night the audience consisted of Jaci, myself and a handful of diehard fans. We didn't care. It just meant we could get right up to the stage and sing and dance and show our appreciation of the band.

After the show the audience dispersed quickly mainly due to the 'jobsworth' on the door, and we soon found ourselves outside on the pavement. We decided to hang around in the hopes of seeing our heroes and, sure enough, after a few minutes a small door next to the main entrance opened and out stepped Jack Bruce and GInger Baker. We called out to them and they crossed over the road towards us.

Jack Bruce was carrying armfuls of Mr Kipling's Cakes, which he handed over to me saying, 'If you want our autographs you'll have to hold these but don't drop them as we haven't eaten all day and we're starving.'

Jack Bruce was carrying armfuls of Mr Kipling's Cakes

We stood around chatting and Ginger Baker said to hang around as 'Eric would be along in a minute.' Sure enough, a few minutes later a big black car with smoked windows drew up, the window on the passenger side slid down and there sat Eric Clapton. Jack introduced us to a very monosyllabic Eric who just nodded and thrust his hand out to give us his autograph. Seconds later, after a handshake from Ginger, a nod from Eric and a quick peck on the cheek and a cheery 'see ya girls' from Jack, they were speeding up the deserted street and we were left staring at the rapidly disappearing tail lights of their car.

MARQUEE CLUB
23 MAY 1967, LONDON, UK

I WAS THERE: ALAN ALPHONSO HARDING, AGE 15

1967 WAS MY first year of gigging. Inspired by John Peel and his radio sessions and the sessions on *Saturday Club* with Brian MatThews I bought *Fresh Cream*. Already digging the Stones, the Yardbirds and Mayall, I first saw Cream in May '67 during the Summer of Love. The gig was at the Marquee and full of sweaty, spotty, hair-growing herberts like me. Cream played a number of new songs destined for the yet-to-be-released masterpiece *Disraeli Gears*. So it really was the shock of the new. It started with 'Tales of Brave Ulysses' and most of us had never heard wah-wah before live on stage. It was a revelation and so in tune with psychedelia in 1967. It was a magnificent evening. I went home deaf on the Tube. And I was deaf for the next week back at school. Those were the days!

'STRANGE BREW' RELEASED
26 MAY 1967

Cream's third UK single reaches number 17 in charts. In Disc magazine, guest reviewer Lulu says 'the opening sounds just like Jimi Hendrix. Very much like Hendrix, in fact. Naughty.'

GOLDSMITHS COLLEGE
26 MAY 1967, NEW CROSS, LONDON, UK

I WAS THERE: JOHN STARKEY

I STILL HAVE my ticket for the Goldsmiths Summer Ball in May 1967. I attended this event with my then partner, now my wife of 51 years. They were billed as 'The Cream' but it was definitely them. As there were a number of different venues and performers were performing at various times I don't recall 'being there' when Cream were performing.

John Starkey was at Goldsmiths when Cream played

BARBECUE 67, TULIP BULB AUCTION HOUSE
29 MAY 1967, SPALDING, UK

I WAS THERE: BRYAN HEMMING

1967 WAS MY second year at Loughborough Art College. Posters announcing the gig had been slapped up all over the town. The Jimi Hendrix Experience, Cream, The Move, Pink Floyd, Zoot Money and Geno Washington and the Ram Jam Band, all on the same bill. All playing at the small Lincolnshire market town of Spalding. All on the same day. None of us could actually pinpoint Spalding on the map, despite the fact it was little more than 50 miles from where we lived. No matter, we knew it was somewhere not far away, so George sent off for tickets. That's the sort of thing George did.

The sleepy, little county market town of Spalding lies in the aptly-named South Holland district of Lincolnshire. Aptly-named because much of Lincolnshire is very flat, has dykes, windmills and is renowned for its own flowers, tulips. Officially designated as part of the East Midlands, it would be more appropriate for it to fall under the rule of East Anglia, as both geographically and historically, that's where it is and always has been.

The morning of May 29th, 1967 dawned in typical English fashion in the little town of Syston, north of Leicester. Misty, damp and chill, only one thing was different. A fixed Spring Bank Holiday had been introduced to Britain for the very first time. To be celebrated on the last Monday of May, it would replace Whit Monday. Up until then the annual public holiday had always been dictated by the moveable feast of Pentecost, which marks the end of Easter.

Thousands of people from all over the UK had flocked to the venue

I hardly had time to splash my face before George Blynd picked me up in his 1950s Morris Minor. George's little Mog headed down Barkby Road to Leicester Road, where we picked up Mick Kouzaris. Mick lived above the family fish 'n' chip shop. From there we went into Leicester to meet Terry Bryan. Our gang of four pootled merrily along the country roads to Spalding. But it wasn't all fun and joy, as the four of us insisted on enriching the oil rag and petrol fumes clinging to the old Morris' interior with clouds of nicotine-enhanced fumes. A 50 mile drive at 40 miles an hour in a smoke-choked, rusty old can on wheels, stinking of petrol, begins to seem endless after the first 10 minutes.

Smoked and choked we finally arrived. Though early, we weren't the first by any means. The town was already packed with knots of ticketless youths wandering about in the hope of scoring tickets. The event had been advertised over the entire country. Though there were no official figures, thousands of people from all over the UK had flocked to the venue. So many without tickets, there might have been a riot, were it not for the fact there were so many forged ones available. The police presence was virtually nil.

An unlikely place for Britain's Summer of Love and a musical revolution to kick off, the inhabitants of Spalding had no idea what had hit them. A small group of bemused locals stood leaning against a wall, trying to appear nonchalant. It was blatantly obvious they were getting nervous at the numbers of strangers gathering on their patch. Giving the distinct impression not much had happened over the seven-and-a-half centuries since King John lost his jewels, it became evident they were looking for the right opportunity to slink off unnoticed without losing face. As they melted into the mass, we new arrivals surveyed our freshly-won territory, like the invading army we had become.

Soul and R&B had been all the rage among Mods and students, before the Summer of Love came along, so there was no surprise Geno Washington and the Ram Jam Band were topping the bill. However, it was the rest of the line up that led to Spalding going down in history. Within a couple of years, three of them would number among the best-known rock bands in the world. Despite being virtually unknown beyond the blossoming UK underground scene in early 1967, by the year's close Hendrix and Clapton were well on their way to becoming the world's most famous lead guitarists.

Hendrix and Clapton were on their way to becoming the world's most famous guitarists

To see Jimi Hendrix play a Fender Stratocaster with his teeth really was mind-blowing. It was clear right from the start he wasn't happy with the instrument. Unable to tune it quite the way he wanted, he seemed unsettled by the large number of fans who had come just to see Geno Washington. Their impatience overflowing, not far into his set, they began chanting 'Geno, Geno, Geno!' at the top of their voices, which was quite usual at Ram Jam concerts. They had done the same through Cream's performance. So frustrated did Hendrix appear to become he began tearing at his guitar strings towards the end of the set. But it was only when he started slamming the Strat against the amplifiers that he caught the Geno fans' attention. Getting one of his roadies to squirt lighter fluid over the Strat he pulled a box of matches from a trouser pocket to set it aflame. The crowd erupted into an ear-splitting roar of approval.

I WAS THERE: JOHN FLETCHER

MY NEXT EXPERIENCE of seeing Cream was at the famous Barbeque 67. This gig was allegedly the first rock festival ever held, although it's been disputed since. The venue was 50 to 60 miles from where I lived and I drove myself and a couple of friends to the venue. We didn't have tickets, and when we got to the large bulb auction house building all tickets (£1 each) had been sold, but we managed to buy three 'pass outs' from a guy in the crowd outside the venue and got into the gig.

Looking at the artist line up today it seems amazing - Jimi Hendrix, Cream, Pink Floyd, Move, Geno Washington, Zoot Money plus local bands and a disco. The venue was not ideal for the quality of the sound, but as a live performance for me it was fantastic. The atmosphere was really good, very friendly. The only downside was that at the end of the night my car had been stolen and we had to scrounge a lift back to Nottingham with a party of fans who had hired a bus. Thankfully, I got the car back a few days later.

I WAS THERE: RICHARD PILCH

BY NOW CREAM were becoming very big indeed. It went on from three in the afternoon till midnight. Cream were the main attraction with Jimi Hendrix going on before them. After Hendrix had done his guitar routine, we thought there was no way Cream could follow that but with everything turned up to 11 they played their full set and won the night over. It took forever to get out of the car park and I had to call in sick in the morning as I only had about two hours' sleep.

I WAS THERE: FROG GODDARD

THEN I SAW them at a festival at the Tulip Bulb Warehouse in Lincolnshire. I'm a drummer and I drove my band van full of my mates from Braintree, Essex up for the gig. On the way we stopped and removed a very large poster advertising John Mayall at the same gig and strung it across the front of the van, just for fun. On arrival at the gig, we were waved straight into the band car park and embarrassingly parked right next to John Mayall's van where Hughie Flint was sitting there, fixing up his drums. He just gave us a weird look as we all piled out of the van.

I WAS THERE: ALAN MASON

THE GIG WAS in a World War Two aircraft hangar in the middle of nowhere. We all went to see Clapton, Bruce and Baker but there was also Hendrix. We slept the few hours left in the public restrooms as it was winter and frozen rain was falling on the fields outside.

I WAS THERE: STEVE COBHAM, AGE 16

I JOINED THE fan club, Cream Addicts Anonymous, and went to Moscow Road in Bayswater and surprised the secretary - who I think was Dutch - by arriving on the doorstep and saying 'I'm in the fan club'. I was probably 16 at the time.

I've always been into music. I was playing guitar by the time I went to see Cream, and I was already gigging. I suppose Clapton was the person I leant most from. The record to have at school was the *Beano* album, with Clapton and Mayall. And when Clapton left Mayall and joined Cream, it was Cream from then on. Before Cream I was listening to the Paul Butterfield Blues Band album, the Stones and Dylan.

The Tulip Bulb Auction House was a horrible, horrible, horrible venue

I was very disappointed with their first album. The first track I heard was 'Wrapping Paper' and I thought 'good grief, it's got to be better than this'. Fortunately, the flip side had 'Cat's Squirrel' on and that had the guitar on so that made me a bit happier.

I was living in Bletchley, which is the home of Marshall amps. It was quite good transport-wise, because we used to go down to London and see various bands. A kid in school had connections to a local coach firm and had organised a trip to see The Who at Bedford Corn Exchange the previous year. He organised a trip to the Spalding Festival. We never saw the Floyd. We got there and they were playing but we couldn't actually get into this awful corrugated iron building that was obviously what it was named as - a tulip bulb auction hall. But then the doors opened. I read afterwards that the organisers of the gig made off with the money and just left everybody to

Steve Cobham was at Barbecue 67

it. We managed to get in. It was a horrible, horrible, horrible venue. It was dark. The lighting wasn't very good. It stank of the smell of onions which was probably bits of tulip bulb lying around all over the place. You could cut the air with a knife it was so thick from this dust. Any lights that were there shone through the dust as shafts of light. There was a lot of dope being smoked as well, and that didn't help.

I can remember being extremely excited at seeing Cream. I actually remember very little about it but I vividly remember Clapton getting really irritated with his stack. He grasped the upper speaker cabinet in both hands and proceeded to kick in the bottom speaker cabinet. I can't remember whether Hendrix had been on before him or after him, but Hendrix smashed a guitar that night and I can remember thinking 'well, Hendrix smashed his guitar and all Eric did was seem to lose his rag with his stack'. I thought it looked a bit silly compared to what Hendrix had done to his Strat.

I can remember it being horrendously loud. In a building that's built of corrugated iron it wasn't a very good sound acoustically. We were quite close to the stage, about 10 or 12 feet away from the edge of the stage.

I was as hippy as I could be. I was 16 when I first saw them, 17 when I saw them the second and last time. I was living at home. I was going to grammar school. My parents were on my back about length of hair and that sort of thing. But I was as hippy. I went a bit more hippyish when I left home and went to college.

On the way down, they played 'Strange Brew' on the coach radio and we thought, 'Ooh, we're going to hear this,' and I don't think they ever played it live!

I WAS THERE: BRIAN THURLEY

DETAILS ARE SKETCHY. I don't even remember who I was with. Spalding is famous for tulips and the gig was in the Tulip Shed. I believe it was the first music festival, but because it was technically indoors, it was not considered so. Thousands turned up. Back then I was lucky enough to see many top acts, and being aware of these acts I remember finding my way close enough to appreciate them. On this occasion I was watching Clapton, Baker and Bruce along with Pink Floyd and Jimi Hendrix. It is documented that Jimi Hendrix was not on form and that Pink Floyd were psychedelic at the early stages of their development.

But I do know that I was so lucky to be in the presence of Cream. I knew of Eric with John Mayall and from the Yardbirds. I was only 17 and was leaning towards The Who, but some mates were huge Yardbirds fans and to them Eric was God. That day in 1967 turned me on to Eric and of course Jack and Ginger. I'm still a huge Eric Clapton fan and bigger venues and perfect mixing decks are great, but the thrill of watching these greats, close up and raw, will live forever in my probably rose-coloured memory. I just wish I'd realised at the time that I was witnessing musical history in the making.

I WAS THERE: MARTIN WILLMOTT

I SAW THEM again at the Tulip Festival in Spalding in May 1967 and it was all change. Eric had an Afro haircut and very tight velvet jeans with hippie-like scarf and shirt. They played some songs from the forthcoming *Disraeli Gears* album, including 'Sunshine of Your Love'. I have sometimes wondered if that was its first outing. Eric played his 'The Fool' SG. The vocals and the sound balance were dreadful. Of special significance to me was the pairing of Cream that day with the Jimi Hendrix Experience. Sound balance was terrible for both bands. Eric was being compared very unfavourably with Jimi. I adore the playing of both but there is no doubt in my mind that, on the night, Eric eclipsed Jimi Hendrix.

I WAS THERE: NICK HAIRS

MY SECOND CREAM gig was at the now legendary Spalding Tulip Bulb Hall festival. There was a massive crowd and it was a very hot day. Cream were good but beset with poor sound. Jimi Hendrix also had sound problems and was heckled with comments like 'give it to Eric to tune'.

These kids stating pelting us with pennies, which wasn't very nice
Eric Clapton to Disc, about the Bristol Locarno show, 8 June

WELLINGTON CLUB
10 JUNE 1967, EAST DEREHAM, UK

I WAS THERE: LEWIS BETTS, AGE 17

I DIDN'T KNOW much about their music. It was more the reputation of Ginger Baker being a bit of a wild thing that we wanted to see. There were not many mental drummers about at that time, or that's what my memory tells me. I was too young to drive so my father in his beloved Morris 1000 Traveller took me and my mates to the club. The venue was known as the Tavern Club situated in the Market Place. But it closed sometime in that June and reopened shortly after as the Wellington Club. The place was absolutely heaving. The quiet small town of Dereham had seen nothing like it.

Cream were about two hours late but when they came on, boy did they give a show. I remember Eric and Jack walking off the stage to leave Ginger playing the most amazing drum solo I have ever heard. He seemed to go on forever - a mess of ginger hair, teeth and sweat. The crowd went mental at the end. For sleepy little Dereham this was huge and was talked about for many weeks after.

We had strict instructions to be outside the club at 10pm when the gig was supposed to finish. However, as Cream were two hours late it was past midnight before we came out. My dad was not best pleased.

THE ASSEMBLY HALL
15 JUNE 1967, WORTHING, UK

I WAS THERE: TREVOR GRAY

I REMEMBER SEEING Cream play Worthing more than once, and possibly as many as three times, as The Who did. The Pier Pavilion put on shows but in the Sixties most bands played the slightly larger capacity Assembly Hall. All were standing concerts of course. On one occasion that Cream played, I and my mates from a local band which I played drums with met Ginger Baker before the gig in a nearby pub and had a brief chat with him.

I WAS THERE: STEPHEN DAVY
AT THE SECOND Cream show I saw, promoter Fred Bannister came on stage and announced they would be arriving late due to recording *Top of the Pops* at the BBC in London. The large audience were hanging around for a good hour after the start time when Fred again came to the microphone. This time he said, 'Sorry, the group won't be coming at all.' Then, just as everyone was leaving and had reached the back of the hall, we heard him shouting into the mic: 'Cream are here!' There was a massive rush to get to the front of the stage by overjoyed people.

Since their time in the USA, they had become truly great and were more psychedelic. They had permed hairstyles and wore hippy clothes. The guitars had been painted in bright colours. The numbers had got longer with improvisations reaching peaks not heard before. 'I'm So Glad', 'Strange Brew', 'Tales of Brave Ulysses' and 'We're Going Wrong' all took my breath away. It was one of the best concerts that I have ever been to.

Cream had appeared earlier that evening at the BBC's Lime Grove Studios in London, miming to 'Strange Brew' for a live broadcast of Top of the Pops.

UNIVERSITY OF SUSSEX
16 JUNE 1967, BRIGHTON, UK

I WAS THERE: MO MARSH
I SAW CREAM at the University of Sussex Summer Ball. I remember queuing for our 4am supper slot!

CARLTON BALLROOM (LATER MOTHERS)
24 JUNE 1967, ERDINGTON, BIRMINGHAM, UK

I WAS THERE: MALCOLM PARKES
I SAW CREAM at Mothers Club on the High Street in Erdington, Birmingham in the smallest room you could ever imagine. They were absolutely brilliant and even today no one can touch their music.

I WAS THERE: ALAN RUTHERFORD

I ONLY SAW them once, at Mothers in Erdington. My memory, such as it is, tells me that it was a great show and it sparked a lifelong interest in the band that had not existed previously. The gig stands amongst my all time favourite shows, along with Captain Beefheart, the Stones et al.

Alan Rutherford was at the Carlton

TUESDAY BEAT SESSION, WINTER GARDENS
27 JUNE 1967, MALVERN, UK

I WAS THERE: MARTIN WILLMOTT

I SAW CREAM again at Malvern, when Ginger Baker and Jack Bruce had the most vicious and - frankly - frightening shouting match on stage. They came on stage almost an hour late and played with visibly reduced enthusiasm. Hardened fans ignored that. They were still our heroes. It was the night before one of my Latin 'A' level papers. I was not in good odour with my old man, who took a dim view of Cream anyway...

I WAS THERE: KEITH GOULDING

I WAS AN apprentice in the Army and home on leave. I wasn't even sure who Jack Bruce and Ginger Baker were. I had obviously heard of Clapton from his John Mayall days. I also saw quite a few other bands around that time including The Who, John Mayall, Ten Years After, The Troggs, Manfred Mann and a few others. When I saw Manfred Mann, Jack Bruce was standing in for their bass player. On the night I saw The Troggs, me and a couple of mates had a lift back to Worcester with their roadie, who bought us all fish and chips at Honky Fletcher's.

Ginger and Jack had the most vicious shouting match on stage

FLORAL HALL
28 JUNE 1967, GORLESTON, UK

I WAS THERE: TREVOR DYE

AFTER THEIR APPEARANCE at the Orford Cellar, Cream came to Norfolk a further three times - at the Wellington Club in East Dereham in June 1967, the Floral Hall in Gorleston and the Industrial Club in Oak Street in Norwich. I was present at all of these venues. I was there too when Eric appeared a few years later with Derek and the Dominos at the Lads Club on King Street in Norwich.

The Gorleston appearance was particularly memorable as they turned up two hours late with no equipment as the vehicle containing it broke down on the way. They borrowed the local support band's equipment. Eric played a Watkins Rapier guitar with a Vox AC30 amp and still made it sing (no gimmicks) but Ginger's fingers were bloody by the end of the performance from hitting the drums harder than usual as there was no miking up.

I WAS THERE: MICHAEL LADBROOKE

AFTER A LATE arrival they got there but without their equipment. I'm fairly sure that there were enough local band members in the audience to get enough equipment together for them to perform. Unfortunately for me it was a school night so after all that I didn't get to see them. And pocket money constraints at the time didn't stretch to the second show. (Cream returned to the Floral Hall to fulfil the engagement on 12 August 1967). When I started my apprenticeship at Birdseye, the claim to fame of one of the guys I worked with was that he had lent an amplifier and guitar that night.

I WAS THERE: MIKE ROSE

AS WELL AS Hoveton Village Hall in 1966, I was also at a Cream gig at Gorleston Floral Hall. Unfortunately, the band's equipment did not turn up. They used the support band's equipment instead but had to cut short their set a bit as Ginger had blood all over his hands because of using an unfamiliar kit. It was still a memorable night. They were a great band!

I WAS THERE: MARTIN BOOTH

THE FIRST BAND I saw was the Graham Bond Organisation at the Orford Cellar, with Alexis Korner on vocals and Jack Bruce on bass. I saw Cream at the Sunshine Rooms in East Dereham and twice at the Floral Hall in Gorleston, and later at the Industrial Club in Norwich. The first time they appeared at the Floral Hall their equipment did not arrive so they played with the support band's stuff but only did three numbers. We all got free tickets for their return. Again, their stuff did not turn up but this time they did a full gig using the support band's stuff. In the end they had to stop because Ginger Baker's hand were running with blood, I assume from using the wrong drumsticks.

BLUESVILLE 67
30 JUNE 1967, MANOR HOUSE, LONDON, UK

I WAS THERE: VERNON NORTHOVER

I LIVED IN north London. I spent a lot of time in London seeing bands, and I've also been a musician for a long, long time. I was in my first band in London in Tottenham in 1965. Like any other band we played a lot of Who and Beatles and Yardbirds and Stones stuff. But every time we had a rehearsal, the songs I came up with were blues songs. Although I loved them, I was never so much into playing The Who's stuff. I followed Eric Clapton with the Yardbirds and I saw Jack Bruce with Manfred Mann and Ginger with Graham Bond. And when they formed a band, I read about it in the *Melody Maker*. I just couldn't believe that these three guys were going to be treading the same boards. So as soon as they came to the Manor House - they called it Bluesville 66 in those days - I went down to see them.

It was a pub - it wasn't a big arena - and I just couldn't believe what I was seeing. I've played

Vernon Northover was at the Manor House pub in London to see Cream

with Les Paul, I've played with Dave Mason, but I've never had an experience like that night. I'd never heard a drummer like Ginger Baker, and I didn't realise how good he was because I'd never seen him live before. And Jack Bruce was playing bass with the harmonica around his neck doing things like 'Train Time', and then there was Eric. You didn't know who to watch.

Most of their act was songs from *Fresh Cream*, which had just come out. They probably played the whole album and I don't remember them playing anything that wasn't from that. They were so good they didn't really even need to rehearse too much. They just got up there and did it. I'd only been playing guitar for two years at that point and when I walked out of the pub I was thinking, 'Do I really want to keep playing guitar or should I just grow peas for a living? Because I'm never going to sound like Eric.' It wasn't until about a day later that I came to my senses.

You didn't know who to watch

During that time I saw Hendrix and used to go to every Rory Gallagher concert.

I was a regular at the Marquee, and saw the real Fleetwood Mac and John Mayall and all those blues guys like Freddie King. But I've never enjoyed a concert more than when I first saw those guys. They toured the States for most of their life as a band, which kind of pissed everybody off, but when they did the farewell thing at the Albert Hall, obviously I was there.

I had a band called Slowhand Graffiti which celebrated the whole history of Eric Clapton, so my appreciation of Mr Clapton is not lightweight. I've been to just about every concert he's played over here in the US. But I couldn't get tickets for the reunion. I was pretty pissed off about that. I was willing to fly over to London just for that. And I couldn't get tickets for Madison Square Garden, although apparently that wasn't quite so good.

SAVILLE THEATRE
2 JULY 1967, LONDON, UK

I WAS THERE: RICHARD LUETCHFORD
THE NEXT TIME I saw Cream was at the Saville Theatre in Shaftesbury Avenue which had been taken over by Brian Epstein and in which he staged some fantastic concerts over a couple of years. The bill included Clapton's old boss John Mayall with his band's new young guitarist Mick Taylor, and the Jeff Beck Group with Rod Stewart and Ron Wood. A year since the Windsor Jazz and Blues Festival appearance in 1966, the band were now heavily into psychedelia and much more confident, improvising freely over their original songs as well as the old blues standards. Clapton had guitars suspended from the ceiling, feeding back from his Marshall amplification, while he soloed over the top. Again they were very loud but really stretching the limits of a three piece band. This was a great concert all round, but Cream deserved their top billing despite some very strong competition from the support bands!

BEACH BALLROOM
8 JULY 1967, ABERDEEN, UK

I WAS THERE: DAVID MIDDLETON
IN THE MID to late Sixties many big groups came to Aberdeen, and in particular either the Beach or the Capitol cinema. I saw the Stones in 1965 (four rows from the front for 15 shillings or 75p), the Small Faces, The Who and many more. All I really remember about the Cream concert was how together they were with their music, and dancing to 'Sunshine of Your Love' while watching Clapton (with his purple hair in an afro) playing so brilliantly.

KINEMA BALLROOM
9 JULY 1967, DUNFERMLINE, UK

I WAS THERE: JOHN FOSTER, AGE 19
IT'S ONE OF the greatest experiences I've ever had and I've been to

many a gig since. Like most kids in the Sixties, my musical interests started at school. I had a great interest in the guitar, and listening to the Shadows triggered it. After that it was Chuck Berry and my interest moved towards the blues. And then of course the Beatles arrived and I had the great honour of actually seeing them live in Kirkcaldy in 1963. That was an experience. It was roughly ten days before Beatlemania, which didn't really take off until their appearance at the Royal Variety Performance in London and John Lennon's 'rattle your jewellery' joke. Triggered by all that I just moved on. The Rolling Stones came along but my tendency was towards the more progressive type of music thereafter. It was all new and exciting.

John Foster saw Cream at Dunfermline's Kinema Ballroom

I had the *John Mayall's Bluesbreakers* album with Eric on it (the Beano album) prior to him joining Cream so he wasn't new to me as a guitarist. By the time I started working, my six shillings and seven pence was spent every Friday night on a single at the local record shop. The first single I bought was 'Wrapping Paper' by Cream. It wasn't typical of what Cream was to become but there was some great guitar work there and the bass and vocals sounded good so I bought that and the follow up, 'I Feel Free', and even the follow up to that, 'Anyone for Tennis'. When the *Fresh Cream* album came out, I played it to death. Then I got the word that they were coming to Dunfermline so I immediately snapped up a ticket and my brother and I went to the gig. I remember feeling quite excited at the prospect.

It's one of the greatest experiences I've ever had

The Kinema Ballroom in Dunfermline had a capacity of 500 at most, although it was a very popular venue in the mid to late Sixties. The Small Faces played there and The Who played there three times. The tickets only cost four and six (23p). The venue itself had two stages. The ballroom had a large stage at one end of the dance floor for the bigger bands and a small stage at the other end. Cream appeared on the small stage so it was a very intimate and close up performance. People were right up against the edge of the stage.

We got a decent position near the front. There was no alcohol there - there was a separate bar - but just next to the stage was a cafeteria area where the kids used to go for a coke and a burger. I glanced to the left and there was the three of them - Jack and Ginger and Eric - sitting round the table with a coke each and enjoying a smoke. This was literally five or 10 minutes before they were on stage. They must then have got the signal as I saw them quite nonchalantly and casually finished their cokes - Ginger still had a cigarette hanging out of his mouth - and it was like, 'Well, let's go up and do our thing,' and they went up on stage.

They went through this psychedelic phase and were each wearing multi-coloured kaftan tops with coloured drainpipe jeans. Eric was wearing purple. Eric and Ginger both had afro hairstyles. I don't remember Jack having one. The three numbers that I am absolutely 100 per cent certain they performed were all pretty lengthy. Jack Bruce did his 'Train Time', Ginger Baker did a lengthy version of 'Toad' (they were all lengthy but this one seemed to last forever) and 'Spoonful'. They maybe did 'Crossroads' as well, which would kind of figure as those are the four live ones that appear on the *Wheels of Fire* album from the Fillmore. Most of the stuff they played was from *Fresh Cream* like 'Rollin' and Tumblin'' and 'NSU'. They might even have done a couple off *Disraeli Gears* which was just coming out at that point. And they might have done 'Tales of Brave Ulysses' because I remember the wah-wah guitar.

You've got to put yourself in the place of a youngster at that time to appreciate how revolutionary it was. I saw The Beatles and one or two other bands, all of which were good, but seeing Cream was the seminal moment for me. I thought, 'This is more than pop music. It's taking it to a whole new level.' They opened the door to many bands and artists that came after. It was mesmerising to just stand there with your mouth open listening to this. The chemistry between the three members just beggared belief.

They did part of the set and I thought, 'Oh, it's going to be one of these short efforts. Where you get real value for your money!' But Jack Bruce came up to the mic and said, 'We're just having a wee break now but we'll be back.' And away they went. But they came back after 10 or 15 minutes and did the other half of their performance.

At the very end, which might have been 'Spoonful', Jack and Eric took off their guitars and hung them up on the front of their respective amps and walked off. Leaving their guitars hanging on the amps created a feedback on the bass and on Eric's lead guitar which built up in terms of volume. My memory is of the sound resonating, coming up through the wooden ballroom floor and the soles of your feet and right through your body. It was a very strange experience. You were blown away by the fact that you'd just witnessed a great gig, and then there was this energy from the two guitars hanging on the amps resonating up through the floor and up through the audience's bodies. Everybody just stood there, applauding and surrounded by this sound.

When I heard that they were splitting up, I was sad but I thought there was an inevitability about it. I couldn't see them going on much longer because there were tensions in the band. I hesitate to say that Clapton was destined for greater things but he must have thought that himself. I always think Clapton is at his best when he's playing the blues or anything blues-related, which has been proved to be the point over the years. By his own admission he's a bluesman.

I WAS THERE: TOM PORTER

I SAW CREAM play at the Kinema Ballroom in Dunfermline and it was the best gig ever until I saw Jimi Hendrix live at Woburn Abbey! It's rumoured that the Ballroom attracted bands like Cream because of the amazing lead guitarist, Manny Charlton, in the house band, Nazareth. All of the star bands played there. The only two major bands that didn't were the Beatles and the Stones. The Stones still might! I became aware of Cream when we heard that Eric Clapton had formed this new band after leaving John Mayall's Bluesbreakers. Prior to that I knew little of Jack Bruce or Ginger Baker. The gig was absolutely jaw-dropping. All three band members exuded musicality of the highest standard. An unforgettable moment was when Eric and Jack left the stage part way through a number, leaving Ginger to play this amazing drum solo on 'Toad'. He was breathtaking and totally unique. I also remember Eric's beautiful playing but also how Jack was almost competing with his own solo style on bass - what a man! The vocals were brilliant too, Jack's being the stronger but Eric had and still has a lovely timbre and tonality.

I WAS THERE: NORMAN TAYLOR
SUNDAY NIGHTS WERE usually quiet compared with Friday and Saturday, so high profile bands and artists were always on a weekday or a Sunday. The Cream gig was not that well attended. They performed on the smaller stage at the far end of the hall after coming up the stairs. The main stage at the top of the stairs was for the resident showband, the Red Hawks, who also performed that night. Most people stood in front of the small stage and others were dancing next to the main stage. When I got into work on the Monday, one of my work mates asked what I'd done at the weekend. I told him about the Cream concert. He replied, 'Oh, that's who those guys were.' He and his mates had been talking to three guys in a café in Glenrothes, where he lived, and they'd said they were playing in Dunfermline in the evening. I asked him to describe them and sure enough he'd met Cream. They had stopped off for a coffee and something to eat.

BALLERINA BALLROOM
11 JULY 1967, NAIRN, UK

I WAS THERE: ROB MILNE
THE BALLERINA BALLROOM in Nairn was a small but legendary venue for live music in the late Sixties. Cream were on a short Scottish tour just after their very successful first tour of the USA and ahead of the release of *Disraeli Gears*. The gig was to take place on a Friday evening but I was skint and couldn't afford a ticket for the gig. However, by a quirk of fate, while Cream turned up their equipment and roadies didn't - a van breakdown, I think.

Clapton played his psychedelically painted Gibson SG

Cream were to be supported by a local band from Elgin called The T Set, a cover band. They kindly offered Cream their equipment so they could play. This offer was declined but all three band members appeared on stage to explain the situation. They promised to return to play the gig on the following Tuesday after they played the final Scottish gig in Fife and all tickets would be valid. Then I got lucky! My friend Jimmy Groat was in attendance on the Friday night but due to work commitments could not make the rescheduled gig and kindly gave his ticket to me. As promised, Cream returned to play a storming gig. Clapton had the permed hairdo at that time and played his psychedelically painted Gibson SG. It was a memorable performance in that most intimate of venues.

At that time, it was par for the course for the support band to open with a short set before the headliners and then return for a second set after the headliners finished. This is what happened with Cream. After they finished their set, I went to the box office when the support band returned. This was normal for me as there was a free bus from Inverness to Nairn for the gig but you were expected to purchase a ticket in order to board the bus for the return journey. This cost was the princely sum of two shillings or 10p! This was also the time of unscrupulous promoters, some of whom were known to abscond with the cash when the star act was performing. Just as I was approaching the box office window, I was brushed aside by a drumstick-thin Ginger Baker, by this time wearing a buckskin-fringed suede jacket. He pushed past me and entered the tiny box office right in front of me. All I heard him say to the startled employee was, 'OK, we are done so where's the fucking money?' I could not believe how skinny he was but he was certainly scary and aggressive. Cream were duly paid and all was well on the night.

Jack Bruce quoted in his biography how galling it was to have to play these small venues after such a successful tour of the USA. He actually mentions this gig in his book but gets the venue wrong. He thought Cream had played a venue in the nearby town of Elgin but it was definitely the Ballerina Ballroom in Nairn. I know - because I was there!

I WAS THERE: WILLIAM CRAN

WE CAME ACROSS on the Friday night to see them, when they were originally scheduled to perform, but the van carrying their equipment had a breakdown. They were sat in the refreshment area (there was no alcohol in those days) in deep conversation. I got their autographs on the inside of a cigarette packet. I wish I still had it!

The concert was rescheduled for Tuesday and we all got tickets. A rather dreary support band was playing 'Sgt Pepper' until it was time for the main event. I made sure that I and my then girlfriend (she dumped me at the end of the concert) were about five rows away from the elevated stage. This was my first real rock concert, and I was absolutely mesmerised, especially with Jack Bruce's 'Traintime' and me being an aspiring harp player. The time flowed like water, and my ears were ringing for four days after hearing 'Toad' and all the classics. I decided to walk back to Inverness - a 15 miler - thinking my mates were ahead but they were actually behind me. I managed to get a lift from the Inverness cops, who checked me out as they drove past at 1am and finally picked me up at 5am. When I got to Singapore in 1968, all my RAF mates were green with envy that I'd seen Cream!

There are more Clapton connections. My niece was in the same dance class as his daughter and they are still good friends. When I was at Guildford in 1997, who should I find myself standing next to watching the first appearance of the Big Town Playboys but Eric? He screwed up his face when I spotted him but I shook my head and turned away. Everybody deserves a bit of privacy!

Eric screwed up his face when I spotted him but I shook my head and turned away

---

FLORAL HALL
12 JULY 1967, SOUTHPORT, UK

I WAS THERE: TERRY PYE, AGE 18

I FIRST HEARD Cream in 1966 on Radio Caroline. They had just released their single, 'I Feel Free.' My two brothers and I were staying at our grandparents' house in Southport in July 1967 when we saw in the local paper that Cream were appearing at the Floral Hall that Saturday night. I went along with Michael, my brother. He wasn't a Cream fan, he just went along for something to do. They were brilliant, and played all the best numbers like 'I'm So Glad', 'White Room', 'Rollin' and Tumblin'', etc. Then Ginger went solo on the drums with a piece called 'Toad'. Even after a couple days our ears were still ringing. I think I converted Michael to a Cream fan that night. I didn't get the chance to see them at their reunion concerts at the Albert Hall in 2005. But thanks to technology I can watch the concert on YouTube. Jack's solo with the harmonica during 'Cat's Squirrel' is something to behold. I don't think there will be another band to match Cream. They were and always will be rock icons.

CITY HALL
4 AUGUST 1967, PERTH, UK

I WAS THERE: JOHN (JOCK) SALTER, AGE 16

I WAS ALREADY a seasoned concert goer, having seen The Who, Small Faces, John Mayall's Bluesbreakers (with Eric Clapton) and the Yardbirds. The Cream concert, was, and indeed still is, the best concert I ever attended. It was a packed hall, even on the balcony. As a support band, the Bonzo Dog Doodah Band largely eclipsed the main act with 'Urban Spaceman', etc. - perhaps a tribute, perhaps a parody - ecstatically received by the sell out crowd. They were a hard act for Cream to follow.

Clapton was, as always, Clapton, supremely competent. Jack Bruce was, and is, the greatest bassist Scotland has ever produced and an underrated singer/songwriter. Drum solos are not really my cup of tea. Ginger Baker is overrated and conceited - the weak link. I bought the DVD of the reunion and watch it when my wife and neighbour are out. More usually I listen to Bach's Mass in B Minor.

MCGOOS
6 AUGUST 1967, EDINBURGH, UK

I WAS THERE: GRAEME SELKIRK, AGE 16

MY PRETTY HIP older sister turned me on to John Mayall's Bluesbreakers. She had just bought the *Beano* album and I noticed a track on it called 'Hideaway' which I listened to thinking it was going to be the Dave Dee, Dozy, etc. version. It certainly wasn't - it was ten times better and was my introduction to 'God'. Not long after she told me about the formation of this fantastic new group featuring the best musicians on the London scene. They were called Cream (or, modestly, The Cream at the time) and as soon as I heard the first album I was hooked. I'd only

Graeme Selkirk's 'pretty hip' older sister turned him on to Clapton

heard of Eric Clapton but as an aspiring drummer it didn't take me long to become familiar with Ginger Baker. I was also impressed that, like me, Jack Bruce was a Scotsman.

Perusing the *Some months later, as an end of term*, I spotted a tiny advert at the bottom of one page stating that Cream were playing at McGoos club on the High Street. I couldn't believe my eyes and had to read it a few times. I mentioned it to my sister and she thought I was winding her up. Her loss! Anyway, off I went (it was a Sunday evening) with a few of my mates, still not really believing I was about to see my heroes in person. The first sign something exciting was happening, apart from the long queue to get in, was a large van (a Commer walkthrough, no less) parked outside the club with a sign in the back window saying 'Free the Rolling Stones', two of whom were imprisoned at the time for some minor drugs offence. On entering the club, I looked up at the stage and there glittering under the lights was the biggest drum kit I'd ever seen. One bass drum had a psychedelic design on it and the other a painting of a dish full of cream. So - it really was happening!

I couldn't take my eyes off Ginger

Once the local support band finished their set Cream came on stage. The excitement was palpable and seeing these guys who were already legends so close up was surreal. Eric was playing his psychedelic painted Gibson SG, which only added to the atmosphere. The band had a pretty relaxed and informal attitude (I now know why) and didn't seem to come prepared with any set list. After the obligatory tuning up (which in their case took around five seconds) they opened with 'NSU'. Ginger Baker's precise and powerful tom tom rhythms, combined with his flaming red hair and baleful demeanour, immediately set the tone. The crowd started shouting out requests and I recall Eric turning to Jack and saying, "I'm So Glad' - let's do that one then.'

I couldn't take my eyes off Ginger - he just looked so spectacular, not to mention his skill as a drummer. It's easy to forget, with so many great musicians around nowadays, just how jaw-dropping their musicianship was for a band of that era. I realise now how lucky I was to see the band at their height, before things gradually turned sour. Some months later, as an end of term treat, my music teacher allowed us to give a lecture on our favourite music. I of course chose Cream and turned up with a copy of *Disraeli Gears* tucked lovingly under my arm. As I remember, I played 'Sunshine of your Love' and/or 'We're Going Wrong' and talked about Jack Bruce's classical training and love of Bach. This still wasn't enough to impress the music teacher who, to my chagrin, stood by looking like he'd just got wind of a fart in a lift. However, a good few of my classmates came up to me afterwards and said how knocked out they were to discover a band like Cream existed which made the whole exercise worthwhile. Around a year or so later I was sitting in the pub with some buddies, trying to look old enough be in there, when one of them said Cream were splitting up. It felt like a punch in the solar plexus but little did I know Led Zep were just around the corner. The king is dead, long live the king. Funny that I can remember so much of that night over 50 years ago but can't remember what I was doing last Tuesday!

I WAS THERE: DAVE JOHNSTONE, AGE 18

MCGOOS WAS A small club in Edinburgh High Street. The band had already broken nationally. Perhaps they were insisting on honouring their commitment to the small gigs. The club was full, and I'm guessing it held around 400. I just have a general picture in my head of the band on stage. I know I enjoyed it. I remember asking Willie Finlayson, lead vocals and lead guitar with the backing band, Writing on the Wall, what he thought of them. He summoned up a barely complimentary 'they were alright'.

I WAS THERE: ANDREW MCCRACKEN

I HAD FINISHED first year at Edinburgh University and was doing a summer job as barman at the Forth Bridges Motel, sharing the lounge bar with a barman about my age called Jake from Bo'ness. An English customer told us he had tickets to see Cream and invited us to join him. It was a great concert, and we stood about 30 feet from the three of them with their afro hair, psychedelic clothes and a couple of girlfriends hanging around beside the stage. My clearest memories are of them playing 'Sunshine of your Love' from their

Andrew McCracken saw Cream and Hendrix in 1967

'new' album, *Disraeli Gears*, but most memorably of 'Toad', when Clapton and Bruce left the stage and had a smoke in the wings during Baker's amazing drum solo which I knew well from *Fresh Cream*. Jake didn't know their music, and spent the journey back to South Queensferry trying to convince us they'd been miming!

Later that year a few of us fellow students travelled through to Green's Playhouse in Glasgow for a Jimi Hendrix concert. I had become a massive fan after a fellow student along the corridor from my room used to play 'Hey Joe' on a loop at top volume every evening for at least half an hour, and I would open my door for a better listen. *Are You Experienced*, *Axis: Bold as Love* and *Disraeli Gears* were my albums of choice that year. Hendrix and Cream, 1967; amazing.

Many years later my wife and I went to a Clapton concert in Glasgow, and happened to sit next to Tommy Gemmell, another hero, whom I had seen a few days earlier give a farewell speech at the leaving do of the Head at St Joseph's School in Tranent. I had not seen or thought of him since watching him score that famous goal in 1967. We chatted for a bit before the music started. Memories.

I WAS THERE: KEN BROGAN

I WAS AT Edinburgh University, and decided to stay in town for the summer rather than go home to Liverpool, getting a job at a timber yard in Granton and then at the Scottish & Newcastle brewery at the bottom of the High Street, where the Parliament is now. Tickets for Cream were about five shillings in old money (25p) and I could only afford one, so did a quick exit from my girlfriend of the time without revealing where I was going to, promising to see her later.

Ken Brogan remembers the post-gig feedback from the guitars

As a big fan of Cream at the time (I still am today, if I think about it), I really wanted to see them and wasn't disappointed. My memory is fuzzy but says it was a small club where you could stand pretty much in front of the low stage - there was no separation from the audience. They played their usual stuff and were totally brilliant. I specifically remember Ginger doing 'Toad' while the other two wandered off for a smoke. If my memory isn't playing tricks, they also propped the guitars against the amps at the end and walked off, leaving a load of feedback until some roadie came in and switched them off.

HE WAS THERE: PAT KEOGH

MY HUSBAND JOHN Keogh and his friend Freddy Dignan, both 16 years old, were at one of the gigs in 1967. John said McGoos was jumping and the concert was fantastic. At the end of the gig, Freddy jumped onto the stage and managed to get one of Ginger Baker's drumsticks which he subsequently gave to his sister Margaret. He said it was a brilliant night and that he will never forget that gig.

I WAS THERE: JIMMY HAY

I REMEMBER ENJOYING it so much that it almost seemed like an honour to be there. When Clapton wanted to change guitars the roadies passed them from the back of the hall over the heads of the crowd. It took place in the basement, which was surprisingly small for such a famous band. I had recently seen The Who at the same venue, and they played in the much bigger converted cinema upstairs. Apparently, when Ginger played his drum solo in 'Toad', Clapton and Bruce nipped out to the nearby World's End bar for a quick pint, secure in the knowledge that Ginger would play till they came back. The icing on the cake was meeting the band on the pavement outside the stage door afterwards having a fag. I was overawed at being able to shake Eric Clapton's hand, but had the presence of mind to shake Ginger and Jack's hands too.

I WASN'T THERE: TOM HAMILTON

CALVIN MUNROE, WHO owned the World's End pub, told me that when Ginger Baker did his drum solo, Eric Clapton and Jack Bruce came into the pub and had a pint. He asked them if they were worried about leaving him alone and they said it didn't matter how long they were away - he would just keep playing!

I WAS THERE: PETER FERGUSON

I SAW THEM three times - their first performance at the Windsor Blues Festival, then McGoos and finally in the Ballroom at Kirkcaldy. I was right down at the front and so lucky to get within touching distance of your heroes. I got one of Ginger's drumsticks

Peter Ferguson saw Cream three times

that flew into the crowd. I can't find it now! I'm not the most reliable witness (it was the Sixties, man) but I don't remember McGoos having two performance spaces. I saw The Who and think it was on the same stage as Cream.

My first gig was Chuck Berry supported by Graham Bond Organisation with Ginger and Jack. At the tender age of 15 my naive parents allowed me to hitch down to London with a friend. We were really crap at hitching and took a long time! Festivals in those days were small affairs - perhaps 5,000 strong - but the line up for the Windsor Blues Festival was stellar! It was £1 for a weekend ticket. They allowed you to bunk down in the marquee after the bands had finished. It was about a thousand folk in the dark - a symphony of snoring and farting. Cream were of course fantastic but the whole festival was plagued by a poor sound system and we got used to a lot of feedback!

When I found out they were coming to McGoos I must have been first in the queue as I was right down at the front, within touching distance of my heroes. They were in their psychedelic pomp, and when Eric took off his waistcoat I made some remark. He replied that it was good to have an audience with a bit of life in them. I'm gutted that I can't find Ginger's drumstick and I've lost the Windsor poster I had too.

When I saw them in Kircaldy, we were near the back and had a poor view of the stage. The music was still great but it wasn't such a memorable experience. It's only now, having seen a number of documentaries, that you realise they were off their faces on every possible drug and that violence was a regular feature of their off-stage lives.

I WAS THERE: VERONICA ANDERON
I CAN'T RECALL if it was August or October, because they played there twice. But you could not get near the front as it was packed with guys standing, listening and staring in awe at the band and their amazing music.

PALACE BALLROOM
8 AUGUST 1967, DOUGLAS, ISLE OF MAN

I WAS THERE: DAVID HALSALL
WE WERE VERY lucky in the Isle of Man to get most groups over in the late Sixties. A friend had an LP of Cream so when they came

over we went to see them at the Palace Lido. The problem was that it was a bank holiday weekend when we had boat trips over from Scotland and they liked was more Mod-type stuff. These lads clad in black coats and cropped hair started to boo the band and someone threw a bottle at Ginger Baker, who stood up and threatened to take the guy outside. Overall, the evening was a washout but the music was good.

David Halsall (left) remembers a less than appreciative crowd

I WAS THERE: FRANK HARDING

I GUESS EVERYONE has different (wrong) memories of events from a long time ago, but the long demolished Palace Ballroom was certainly a large space that had been used in World War I as a factory for making military balloons. At one time the dance floor area was said to be one of the largest in Europe. It had just a few seats scattered round the dance floor itself with some seating upstairs. Hence the dance floor that night was heaving with standing people, and myself and friends were standing near the front of the stage.

The support band that summer was Sounds Incorporated, 'The Kentish Wall of Sound', who might have played that night, though I have no recollection of them doing so. They were unusual, in an era of guitar bands, to have a brass line up.

Ginger said, 'Whoever is throwing fucking peanuts on the fucking stage, will they fucking well stop it?'

At one point during the Cream set, Ginger Baker suddenly stopped playing and strode towards the front of the stage. A big man with a shock of red hair, he was an intimidating presence from a few metres distance. Both Eric Clapton and Jack Bruce stopped playing and stood still, looking down at the stage

Frank Harding was at the Palace Ballroom

floor, clearly anticipating an outburst. Ginger said, 'Whoever is throwing fucking peanuts on the fucking stage, will they fucking well stop it?'

With that Baker turned on his heel and went back to his drum kit to complete the remainder of the set, which I think finished with 'I'm So Glad'. Shortly before he died, my old schoolfriend Tom, who was present that night, said that he remembered Clapton or Bruce saying that we had been an unappreciative audience. It was Tom who loaned me his first Cream record - it might have been an EP with 'NSU' on it - and then his copy of *Disraeli Gears* until I could buy my own. We thought the record sleeve artwork and the name epitomised Sixties cool, and when we discovered that the name was inspired by a malapropism in a coffee break chat during its recording, we thought this very funny. Someone had intended to ask if another person's new bicycle had derailleur gears.

I WAS THERE: IVAN BRATTY

I WAS A big Eric Clapton and John Mayall fan, and bought *Fresh Cream* and loved it. When I found out that Cream were on at the Lido I couldn't wait. They played a few of the tracks from the as yet unreleased *Disraeli Gears*. I seem to remember they played 'Strange Brew' and 'Sunshine of Your Love'. Ginger Baker's drum solo seemed to go on for 25 minutes or more. The crowd started throwing pennies at him but he drummed on.

I WAS THERE: PAUL KERNAN, AGE 19

THE ISLE OF Man in those days was booming. In the holidays lots of people came over because it was a big touristy place. A lot of groups would come over on the boats for a one night stand and play the Palace Ballroom. The Palace Ballroom was very grand, with one of the old sprung floor ballrooms, similar to Blackpool's ballroom. In the summertime you'd get people coming over here for the season to work. There was a Scottish gang that came over from Glasgow, working as waiters over the summer, and they were a bit nasty. They used to deliberately start fights in the ballroom. When Cream came on, they played three songs. There were coke bottles and everything flying around and Ginger Baker was hit with coins and all sorts while he was doing his drum solo. So the three of them walked off the stage and that was it. They'd had enough.

I saw the Rolling Stones twice there. The atmosphere was unbelievable. Loads of girls fainted before they came on. The second time they appeared, they'd built a barrier in front of the stage with a gap for the bouncers and a police dog handler had his dog in the gap between the stage and the audience to stop people getting on stage. I saw the early Who, with Keith Moon kicking his drums over and Pete Townshend smashing his guitar. Pete changed his guitar for the last song and smashed up an old one, not the one he had been playing. I saw Pink Floyd before they became famous. They had a transit van with 'Pink Floyd' written on the side in lipstick. And The Animals were at the top of the charts with 'We Gotta Get Out of This Place' when they were over here. They were heady days, but if I could go back and see just one of those concerts again it would be Cream, because I had really been looking forward to it. But I'd like to see them perform more than three songs!

I WAS THERE: ROBIN SMITH

THE GIG OCCURRED during the Glasgow Wakes Weeks, where all the factories in Glasgow shut down and people went on holiday, many to the Isle of Man. There were many there from the Glasgow housing projects of Fleet and Easterhouse, who did not like each other much, so there were quite a few fights during the concert. During the band's performance many in the crowd were throwing pennies at the band - the pre-decimal big penny. I'm not sure why. Ginger Baker went into his 'Toad' drum solo; Eric and Jack left the stage. Just before they returned Ginger stopped his solo, stood up and said to the crowd, very aggressively, something like, 'If any of you fuckers throw any more pennies at us, I will be down there myself to sort you out.' My recollection is that no more pennies were thrown.

Ginger said, 'If any of you fuckers throw any more pennies at us, I will be down there myself to sort you out'

Although I liked Cream, I was not a big fan. My focus was more American bands and singers. The Byrds were booked to play the Palace Ballroom in early August 1965. They had a gig the previous evening in Morecambe. Then they were summoned to appear on *Top of the Pops*, so the Isle of Man gig was cancelled at the last minute. That did not make them any new fans in the Isle of Man.

FLORAL HALL
12 AUGUST 1967, GORLESTON, UK

I WAS THERE: SHEA FIDDES

JACK BRUCE AND Ginger Baker had quite a following in Great Yarmouth, where I spent my teenage years. The Graham Bond Organisation was a hard working band that appeared at Great Yarmouth College of Art and Design and at places like West Runton on the North Norfolk coast. I still have my copies of *The Sound of '65* and *There's a Bond Between Us*. But I hadn't seen Eric Clapton as by the time The Yardbirds visited Great Yarmouth it was with Jimmy Page and, I think, Jeff Beck.

I bought a ticket to see Cream at Gorleston's Floral Hall, a circular 1950s dance hall, now known as The Ocean Rooms. There was not a big crowd such as for Manfred Mann or The Hollies. It would have been during the summer holiday season. My copy of *Fresh Cream* was a treasured possession. I was a 19-year-old student and wanted to watch groups closely, often standing in front of the band while the regular teenage clientele danced behind me using the dance floor!

I stood waiting at the raised walkway around the dance floor and opposite the small stage. Eventually the announcement was made that Cream were there but the van carrying their equipment was not. Disappointment and refunds all round. I did bag a horrid day-glo pink poster from a wall and produced by the town hall entertainments department.

To my delight a few weeks later it was announced that Cream would return to the Floral Hall. Same drill, only this time the announcer said that while Cream were there, the van was not (again). But Cream would play their set with the support band's equipment. It was the regulation local band set up, a couple of tinny amplifiers and a basic drum kit. And so our heroes strained every sinew to make a noise worthy of their act. They hammered and crashed the instruments for all they were worth, and bellowed into the house microphone. It was recognisably Cream, but not as we know it. I don't know what happened afterwards because as soon as

Shea Fiddes saw Cream in Gorleston

they had completed the set they vanished. No encore or goodnights. You cannot blame them.

It seems odd now that a group like Cream would play at a seaside dance hall but practically all the pop acts did then and I imagine that the booking was done before they became the supergroup. That same summer I sat in a sparsely attended afternoon Great Yarmouth theatre to see the very popular Move close the first act. Top of the bill was Billy Fury!

7TH NATIONAL JAZZ & BLUES FESTIVAL, BALLOON MEADOW
13 AUGUST 1967, WINDSOR, UK

I WAS THERE: ALEX FRIEDMAN, AGE 15

I SAW CREAM at the 1967 Windsor Jazz and Blues Festival and also at the Marquee. My schoolfriend and I hitched to Windsor and camped there. It was the first big gig I had been to. Jeff Beck, Zoot Money, Al Cohn and Zoot Sims, Fleetwood Mac - it was an amazing line up. Cream were very tight by then. But competition was fierce - Arthur Brown and his band, for example. For some reason Jeff Beck played the entire set with his back to the audience. Amen Corner were (very unfairly, I thought) booed off stage. I'd never seen that before or since.

At the Marquee gig I was in the musicians' enclosure when I overheard a journalist asking Eric if he had taught Bob Dylan anything when he was in the States. Eric looked at the guy and said, 'No! Who the hell do you think I am?' I think it showed humility and respect often missing in rock musicians. Well, I was impressed! I used to go to the Marquee a lot as I had a friend who worked there and would sign me in - I even saw Jimi Hendrix's first gig there.

Alex Friedman was at the Windsor Festival in 1967

I WAS THERE: LAURENS VAN HOUTEN

AGED 17 AND 18, I went with my schoolmate Jan from Sweden to England for the Windsor Festival, with Cream as the headliners. As a photographer who was just starting out, I was able to take a picture of Eric with his lady and photograph the band on stage. Ginger was throwing sticks, used and new, into the audience. Backstage later, I asked them to autograph one of the damaged sticks. We were there a year later at the Sunbury Festival, when Ginger performed with Phil Seaman and Eric appeared as a 'ghost' guest.

Laurens van Houten photographed Cream at the 1967 Windsor Festival, and Ginger and Eric at Sunbury in 1968

Photos: Lauren van Houten

I WAS THERE: NICK HAIRS

AFTER HEARING ABOUT their debut at the festival the year before, I just had to go to this gig, my third time of seeing Cream. It was my first festival proper. The highlight was Peter Green's Fleetwood Mac. They just blew me away and I followed them for a long time after. Cream did another great set and received rapturous applause from the crowd. I then saw the Saville Theatre gig, but to be honest I can't recall much about that one, although I'm not sure why. It wasn't due to drugs, I might add!

I WAS THERE: MIKE GODWIN

I WAS AN asthmatic suburban teenager listening to Buddy Holly and Eddie Cochran when I discovered the blues, thanks to a school friend who took me to the American Folk Blues Festival at the Albert Hall in 1966. I heard Otis Rush, Junior Wells and Big Joe Turner before I was even aware of Peter Green and Eric Clapton. I certainly saw The Animals and The Yardbirds on *Ready Steady Go* but it wasn't until early 1967 that I saw John Mayall's Bluesbreakers. By then the lead guitarist was Peter Green. The first time I saw the Cream was the Windsor Jazz and Blues Festival, when they topped the bill.

I think it is only in retrospect that I recognised what an amazing line-up there was on that day: Fleetwood Mac (making their debut); Chicken Shack featuring Christine Perfect; the Jeff Beck Group with Rod Stewart; Donovan; and Denny Laine's Electric String Band. I had also seen The Pink Floyd several times by then, who were emphatically not playing blues. Unlike many of my later blues purist friends, I was relaxed about the Cream venturing into non-blues experimentation. The story from that day is that Eric Clapton, in scarlet psychedelic poncho and afro perm, said to Peter Green in his white t-shirt and jeans, 'You're going to have to brighten up your image if you want people to take notice of you.'

I WAS THERE: ROGER HILLIARD

I WAS AT Windsor Blues and Jazz Festival in August 1967, where I watched Cream plus the first ever appearance of Peter Green's Fleetwood Mac. Cream were playing in a small marquee powered by their Orange amps, and I was watching wearing a kaftan made out of a blanket we were using for camping. I was bemused as a 17-year-old why festival goers were continually asking me for gear? Looking back, I realise it was probably because I was wearing a homemade kaftan and a necktie round my head! But watching Cream that balmy night, it was obvious even to a green 17-year-old like me that they were going to go far. With limited equipment by today's standards Ginger, Jack and Eric looked the complete outfit as they rocked the marquee they were performing in. If there was a time that encapsulated the Sixties for me, it would be that balmy night in August when Cream came on and shook the night skies of Windsor.

Roger Hilliard was a 'green' 17-year-old when he saw Cream

I WAS THERE: STEVE MEW

THE SUMMER OF 1967 saw me back at the Windsor Jazz and Blues festival. Eric was now sporting his Hendrix-style perm. What can I say? They were again superb. This weekend had been somewhat spoilt by council restrictions on sound levels. However Cream were having none of that, having graduated to two double Marshall stacks each. So ended the last time (regrettably) that I saw Cream live. I still love their music to this day and regret that they split. I don't think that any of them have been as good since (apart) as they were in their heyday together.

Ticket for the 7th National Jazz & Blues Festival

I WAS THERE: AUSTIN REEVE

I WENT TO the Windsor Jazz and Blues Festival again in 1967 and Cream played one of the headlining sets. I can't remember any detail of the performance (maybe I was drunk?). All that I recall is that the weekend was plagued with PA problems, stemming from WEM's 1000 watt amplifiers which kept breaking down. The volume of the music was often so low that it could barely be heard by those unfortunates at the back of the audience and any attempts to turn it up met with complaints from local residents and the council, which didn't go down well with the bands.

I WAS THERE: CHRIS RINGSHAW, AGE 16

I WENT WITH my friend Tom Houlihan, who is now sadly gone. We saw some billboards mentioning the festival being held at Windsor Race Course so being into music we decided to go. It was £5 for three days.

Chris Ringshaw was at the Windsor Festival

Although I had a TV175 Lambretta, we got a tent from somewhere and went there by bus. We were both wearing parkas. Windsor was packed with hippy types, Mods and Rockers but it was all very peaceful. We entered the course, were given a tent spot and then went looking for food and beer. I was a Mod at the time and wore a smoking cap retrieved from a shed in Sunninghill at my sister's flat. A hippy type bloke liked the hat so I sold it to him for five bob. We spent the first day milling about drinking and smoking - not weed.

Tom was into Dylan and Joni Mitchell and that genre, whereas I was more The Who, Small Faces, Animals and Beatles. We saw Donovan from the first two rows back and he was good. This must have been early, about 10-ish in the morning. Then Cream came on. They were a sort of unknown (to us, anyway). Clapton had the biggest afro I'd ever seen, Ginger Baker looked mad with his long ginger hair and Jack Bruce seemed normal. They played after much tuning. Clapton seemed as though he was not there. They were pretty good but very loud, and some people were walking around not listening although many were.

And we met some girls from London, but best not dwell on that.

EXPLOSION '67, TOWN HALL,
15 AUGUST 1967, TORQUAY, UK

I WAS THERE: DAVID MORTIMER, AGE 16

CREAM HAD FIRST appeared in Torquay in 1966. Myself and my twin brother Paul saw their return visit to Torquay Town Hall a year later. We were on a family holiday and it was the day after the offshore pirate radio station Radio London ('Big L') was closed down. My diary for the day says 'Only Radio Caroline left now'. We sat around that day, being so pissed off about the pirate radio shut down.

As Yardbirds fans, we knew all about Eric

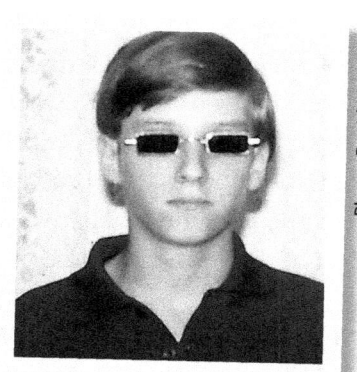

David Mortimer and his brother Paul were in Torquay for the return of Cream

Clapton and Cream, and I'd bought the *Fresh Cream* LP and their singles when released in 1966. The band had toured the USA in the spring of 1967 and recorded their *Disraeli Gears* album in New York. A massive buzz surrounded the band in the Summer of Love. Cream

were at the peak of their immense powers. It was an incredible year to be aged 16. We got tickets and hung around outside the Town Hall hours before, in the hope of seeing the band arrive.

We only encountered Ginger Baker, who drove up outside alongside the steps to the main doors, parking very clumsily in his new Rover 2000. I think he'd backed it into a concrete bollard! We recognised him as he got out of the car, looked at the rear bumper and scowled, and grunted as he strode in past us. We didn't see Eric or Jack arrive - they were probably inside already, waiting for Ginger to join in the soundcheck.

It was a fantastic gig, the band resplendent in psychedelic garb, Clapton with a brightly painted multi-coloured guitar. The stage was about four feet high and we were first in as part of an all-standing crowd. As little twins - at 16 we looked about 12 - we were so small up against the stage and had to gaze up in wonder throughout. The songs I noted included 'I Feel Free', 'NSU'. 'Steppin' Out', 'Sleepy Time Time', 'Sweet Wine', 'Spoonful' and Ginger's solo, 'Toad'. The guy next to us was losing it a bit in pure ecstasy during the incredible performance of 'Spoonful', banging the beat on the edge of the stage and singing along as Jack howled out those Howlin' Wolf words!

It was packed in there, but I don't remember anything about audience reaction. Their music was just so mesmerising, we got completely lost in it - without drugs or alcohol at our age! They may have done 'Sunshine of Your Love' and other classics from *Disraeli Gears*, but the LP didn't come out until November so we wouldn't have recognised the tracks. The band didn't engage the audience much with banter, or introduce those new songs. There were support bands on too - The In-Sect and Phaze (both of which I noted in my diary as 'good'). It's one of my all-time top 10 gigs in a lifetime of hundreds.

I WAS THERE: PAUL MORTIMER

WE'D ARRIVED IN Torquay for a holiday on the previous Saturday; as we arrived in Torquay after our long car journey, we spotted a poster advertising Cream at the Town Hall! We hadn't even arrived at the holiday flats, but made our dad stop his shiny new Cortina estate car to drop us off. We skipped off to find the Town Hall, got the precious Cream tickets and then found our way on foot to the holiday accommodation. I'd just treated myself to a new Kodak Instamatic 25 camera and flash cubes.

Ginger arrives at Torquay Town Hall

We went to the Town Hall for the gig in the early afternoon, wanting to be sure to get stage-front when doors opened; we were tiny lads! (That modus operandi still applies at most gigs today). We had only been to a few gigs by then - but good ones for starters - The Who, Spencer Davis Group, The Move and The Yardbirds with Beck and Page, so we were already on our way to becoming rock veterans! As we waited, Ginger Baker arrived in his new white Rover 2000. He parked it haphazardly, moaning about other vehicles or obstacles, barely acknowledging our chirpy 'Hello, Ginger!' as he went into the venue.

Eric at Torquay Town Hall

Ginger at Torquay Town Hall

As Cream came on stage and tuned up, I took photos of Eric, Jack and Ginger. They were amazing, tight,

Photos: Paul Mortimer

loud, bluesy; our idols - close up! It was a very heady gig with the legendary trio in their psychedelic blues-rock prime. I remember being temporarily disappointed when they played 'I Feel Free', as Clapton went straight into the guitar chords and riff. They'd skipped the 'ba ba ba ba-bob-bob' and the hand claps that open the single. I had so wanted to clap along! They also played 'NSU', 'Crossroads', 'Steppin' Out', 'I'm So Glad', 'Sleepy Time Time', 'Sweet Wine', 'Spoonful', 'Toad' and more. A gig forever etched in the memory.

Jack at Torquay Town Hall

I PROMOTED THEM: LIONEL DIGBY

ALMOST EXACTLY A year later they came back to Torquay and did a second appearance. I paid £75 for them first time round. Second time I paid £300. I usually put a bluesy band called Package Deal on as the support band. The lead guitarist, Martin Pugh, wanted to go pro. The second time Cream came to Torquay I said to Eric, 'What do you think of the support band?' He said, 'They're good. Whenever we do a job for you, they seem to support us.' And I said, 'What do you think of the lead guitarist?' He said, 'Yeah, he's good.' I said, 'The thing is, he wants to go pro but

Package Deal supported Cream at Torquay in 1967

Lionel Digby promoted both of Cream's performances in Torquay

the band doesn't. Is there anything you could do for him?' He said, 'Send him in.' So I went outside and said to Martin, 'Eric wants to have a word with you.' Martin went into the dressing room and came out and said, 'I've got to go and pack my stuff - I'm going back to London with Eric.' Eric took him back to London and put him with Steamhammer, who Eric knew were looking for a lead guitarist.

After their May 1967 visit, Cream returned to North America in August of that year.

FILLMORE
22 - 27, 29 - 31 AUGUST, 1 - 3 SEPTEMBER 1967, SAN FRANCISCO, CALIFORNIA

I WAS THERE: BRUCE WOODWARD

I WAS FORTUNATE to see Cream in their heyday. I saw them twice in August of 1967 and also in March of 1968. The first two times were a week apart at the Fillmore Ballroom. The first time they were playing with Charlie Musselwhite's South Side Sound System and the Paul Butterfield Blues Band. The second time, also at the Fillmore, they were with the Electric Flag and also Gary Burton. I happened to be having a bad acid trip at the first concert and Cream brought me out of it. After they began to play my bad trip disappeared. I went to the very front of the ballroom and sat on the floor half way between Jack and Eric. I kind of have both of those first concerts melded together in my memory. At any rate, they were the best band I had ever heard, hands down. I had followed Eric Clapton since his days with the Bluesbreakers and purchased *Fresh Cream* right when it came out so I was familiar with the songs on that album.

Cream opened with 'Cat's Squirrel' and proceeded quickly to 'NSU'. They played 'I Feel Free', 'Rollin and Tumblin', 'Sleepy Time' (my favourite - listen to *Live Cream* to hear Clapton's superb playing) and 'Sweet Wine' - I literally saw sparks come off Clapton's guitar during that one - acid induced, no doubt! They played 'Traintime' and ended with 'Toad'. When the song was over, they all walked off the stage with the guitars feeding back and making a huge sound. The roadies then came on and turned off the amps. I don't really recall what Jack and Ginger were wearing but I think Eric had on a Western-style long sleeved shirt and reddish pants. He had his hair done in a natural perm. They were larger than life to me that night.

The second week's concert included 'Spoonful', 'Tales of Brave Ulysses', 'Sunshine of Your Love' and several of the songs from the first album. I also remember 'Strange Brew'. What struck me about them was their sophistication and how each member was so perfect for the band. I was definitely awestruck by their prowess on the instruments they played. Jack Bruce's voice was so strong and clear, Baker's playing was perfect and Eric was… well, the best I have heard before or since.

The next spring they came to Fresno and played at the Selland Arena and it was a good concert but they didn't seem to be as into it as they were those nights in SF.

I did hear 'Crossroads' on that occasion, though. Thinking back, it was probably the Fillmore that made it such a good place to see them. It wasn't a huge venue and you really couldn't be far away from them. I always loved seeing bands there. I have seen The Beatles, the Stones, The Who, Led Zeppelin, Jimi and many other bands from the Sixties and Seventies, and Cream is still my favourite for a live band.

I WAS THERE: JULIO STABEN, AGE 18

I WAS AT the front of the stage watching Eric and Jack singing and rocking, playing all of the *Fresh Cream* album in their British clothing. Eric's hair in an afro and watching Ginger Baker on the 'Toad' drum solo with only a strobe light dazzling everyone is something I will never forget. Their wild hair and musicianship were excellent. Because I played in bands during that time, they were a huge influence on me. We would lie on the floor a bit high and play the album until it wore out. Our band, Wakefield Loop, played 'Spoonful'.

I WAS THERE: DENNIS LEVERENZ

MY BUDDIES AND I went to this one record shop in San Fran that had UK editions of records by new groups. I always followed the Yardbirds, Eric and Jeff Beck. I was aged 17 or 18 when I saw two great Cream shows at the original Fillmore. There were only 250 or 300 people there. What stood out was Eric, whose hair was permed and stood about 12 inches from the top of his skull. It made him look eight feet tall. The music was like I never heard before. To this day I love *Disraeli Gears*. Sometimes being old is a good thing.

I WAS THERE: MICHAEL E ROMERO, AGE 14

MY VERY HIP older brother would take me and some of my friends to Fillmore West and Winterland. My first concert was the Jimi Hendrix Experience. Cream was probably the third show I went to, at Fillmore West. I smoked so much pot I fell asleep and was only woken up by Ginger Baker playing 'Toad'!

I WAS THERE: RENEE WELCH

I WAS 16 or 17, in a pot induced state, when I saw them at the Fillmore - or it could've been Winterland! I would sneak out of the house and hitchhike up to San Francisco four to five nights a week. I hadn't really heard much about them but I knew I was in the presence of something special.

I WAS THERE: TONY WRIGHT

Tony Wright was in SF for the Summer of Love

IN OCTOBER 1965 at Sheffield University Students' Union I see my first gig in the Lower Refectory. All the dining furniture has been pushed into a back room and there's a low stage at what would be the front. There are no seats, just the floor. It's the Saturday night dance and John Mayall's Bluesbreakers are playing. I've never seen a name band before - I am from Barnstaple, North Devon - and I ignore all the lovely young women and stand right next to the band, who are just feet away and only a foot off the floor. The volume is ear splitting. I watch Eric Clapton from no more than five feet away. He's reeling out solos and fills. It's an astonishing sound. He doesn't smile - he's so into his playing that he's almost in a trance. I have listened to Bluesbreakers albums before, but this is far, far better. In the interval I am in the toilets. As I finish my wee, I zip up and look up to find my way out. Clapton has been standing next to me (really!). God's wee! It was like that in those days, when bands came to the Union - they drank in the students' bar and used the student toilets. No superstars then. During the second set, there is a small group of students shouting 'Eric is God!' Eric waves shyly.

Later in 1965 at the same venue, we have the Graham Bond Organisation. A sensational sound, like nothing I'd ever heard. Amazing music and individual virtuosity. The drummer is utterly wild and dominant: Ginger Baker is spectacular. There's a bass player who's all over the fretboard, and with an amazing voice: Jack Bruce. I'd heard about Clapton, but didn't know anything about Baker and Bruce until then. Graham Bond came back again in 1966, but Bruce was already doing other stuff. Baker even more amazing this time, doing a 10 minute solo while the rest of the band went for a pint. When they formed Cream, I rushed off to buy *Fresh Cream* and hoped and prayed they'd do Sheffield Union. They didn't... but I got to see them eventually.

Clapton was standing next to me at the urinal

In August 1967 I was in San Francisco to experience the hippy scene as part of a trip around the US on Greyhound buses. My first day was at a huge free gig in Golden Gate Park - Grateful Dead, Big Brother and the Holding Company and Jefferson Airplane. Quite a start to my week there. Next up, ambition fulfilled. Cream live, at the Fillmore in Haight-Ashbury, a rundown baroque theatre with a parquet dance floor.

I got a ticket for the opening night of their run there. It was packed and I have no idea how many people were there. Everybody was sitting on the floor in front of the low stage - I only ever saw these guys on low stages. I managed to get near the front. The warm up act was the Gary Burton Quartet and it was weird to hear jazz in a rock concert, I thought. But they were very good, although I didn't like jazz at that time. I wanted to hear and see the best rock group in the world at the time: Cream.

They looked more than a little stoned when they appeared from the bowels of the theatre, but just tore into it from the off. The instrumental breaks seemed to last forever. Baker and Bruce straining every muscle; Clapton standing like a statue, stretching his guitar sound to the limits. Every song fantastic, many of the crowd on their feet doing whirling dervish dances. I joined them for some numbers. Baker played 'Toad' for what seemed like a week. Jack and Eric disappeared and left him to it. Ginger's bass drums were nailed to the platform, but he was playing so hard one broke free and rolled off the side of the stage. He didn't seem to notice. Roadies repaired the kit when he was done. The psychedelic light show on the ornate décor was very trippy. It was perhaps the wildest, most mind-stretching gig I ever went to. It was so good I went back the next evening. Electric Flag were the support act then and they were exceptional. But Cream were peerless, as good - if not better - on the second night. My ears were ringing two days later. Those Marshall stacks!

I never saw Cream at home in Britain, but those two nights at the Fillmore were more than compensation.

The standard of musicianship, the improvisation and interplay between Clapton, Baker and Bruce was pure jazz; I am now a big modern jazz fan, and Cream were my gateway to this music. There's no doubt in my mind that they were one of the most innovative and influential of all Sixties bands. They set the tone and direction of complex instrumental music and high individual standards. I followed Ginger and Jack's solo careers, but lost Eric when he started to become a pop-rock singer.

I WAS THERE: GREG LIMA
I HAD SEEN *Fresh Cream* in the record store and knew Clapton's name because I was a huge Yardbirds fan but I hadn't heard a song off the album when I went to see them at the Fillmore. Butterfield was the headliner and Charlie Musselwhite (billed as the South Side Sound System) was the opener. When we walked in Charlie was playing and Harvey Mandel was cookin' on guitar. I was buzzing enjoyably and I told my friend a couple of times 'that little sumbitch can play his ass off'.

Greg Lima (right) was at the Fillmore in '67 and back at Winterland in '68

That was the last song of their set and as they left a woman who was standing in front of me, who I can probably get away with calling a bull dyke for clarity's sake, turned around to me and said, 'He's heavy but he's not as heavy as Clapton.' I'd never heard the word used that way before, though it was about to start being used commonly, but I understood exactly what she meant.

After the 10 to 15 minute setup Bill Graham announced Cream and they were off and running with 'NSU'. Everyone was standing and I'm only five feet eight so I was struggling to see them all through the taller people. Finally, I turned to my taller friend and said, 'I can only see three of them.'

He looked at me and said, 'That's because there ARE only three of them.'

By the time they finished their first set they had become my favourite band. Later that night, they finished their second set with 'Toad', which was Ginger Baker's showcase. After Ginger's drum solo Bruce and Clapton came in hard and lifted the song to a blistering crescendo and then they both slipped off their guitars, leaned them against their amps, still blaring, waved and walked off. The crowd was going nuts while the guitars kept roaring. After a minute or two, a stagehand walked over to Jack's Marshalls and shut them off, then did the same to Eric's, and we all stood mesmerised as both guitars slowly faded away. I felt really bad for poor Elvin Bishop having to come out and follow that up. He and Butter and the band gave it their best, but the concert was pretty much over after Cream's exit.

I turned to my taller friend and said, 'I can only see three of them'

Cream played the following weekend also. This time the Electric Flag was the headliner (a term much less significant in the days of the Fillmore than it was going to become in the stadium rock days). I don't remember who opened but after they were done Bill Graham announced that the Flag was not going to be able to play because Bloomfield was sick (code for too high on heroin, we were sure), that the Flaming Groovies would play next and that Cream would close, and that anyone who wanted their money back could be reimbursed upon leaving. There was a group of six or seven people near me and the arrogant alpha male was all pissed off and said they should just leave. I leaned over to the guy closest to me and told him he might want to consider sticking around to see Cream. I don't know what they did but I stuck around. Nothing matched that first appearance - how could it? - but I did not leave disappointed.

I WAS THERE: RICHARD URBINO, AGE 17

CHARLIE MUSSELWHITE WAS the opening group and Butterfield was the headliner. Cream had Indian-style outfits and Eric and Jack had Hendrix-style hair. They did the first album. Eric and Jack had two Marshall stacks each and they both played Gibson SGs. I was very close. There was limited seating and the show cost three dollars.

I WAS THERE: TOM BRODY
I SAW CREAM during their first American tour at the Fillmore. I went with Drew Johnese and his brother Randy, who co-led my rock 'n' roll band, Fellowship of the Ring. The opening act that night was the Gary Burton Quartet. And I saw them again at Oakland Coliseum in Oakland, California when the opening act was It's a Beautiful Day. On entering the concert hall, I noticed that one of the concert-goers was a man wearing a tuxedo - clearly an anomaly. This tuxedo-wearing man was not shocking to me and, in fact, I was under the impression that this was his way of showing respect to the performers. The Fillmore concert began with several plodding thunderous notes from Jack Bruce's electric bass, which introduced 'Spoonful'. I'd never experience such bone-jarring bass notes. Immediately before that, Bill Graham played an excerpt from the *Sgt Pepper's Lonely Hearts Club Band* album, which had just been issued. (Rock concerts were never generally initiated by playing a record album for the audience.) The second act was Gary Burton Quartet. At that time, Bill Graham usually included a jazz act during his rock 'n' roll concerts. I remember Gary Burton introducing his composition, 'General Mojo's Well Laid Plan'. I thought that he was saying 'General Motors Well Laid Plan'. 50 years later Gary Burton's Duster album is still one of my top-ten favourite jazz albums. The opening notes took the form of Jack Bruce's bass line for 'Spoonful'. The bass line was thunderous and like an earthquake, providing the sensation of being vibrated, as though I was on a jittery roller coaster ride.

Tom Brody (right) and Drew Johnese (left) with Drew's garage band

I WAS THERE: ELLEN ATKINS
IT WAS THE year I graduated from high school, the Summer of Love. The Fillmore was the perfect place to see them. It was packed to the rafters and everyone was buzzing. The acoustics were great and the stage was low and it wasn't huge but big and close enough so it felt intimate and you could see everything. You walked in the door and up

the stairs past all of psychedelic posters, signs and amazing artwork. It was dark and cool and everyone was jamming in anticipation of seeing Cream live for the first time. It was like being in a club. It was a great show. Lots of blues which everyone was into. We hadn't seen Cream live before and everyone was grooving in anticipation. When Cream came on, it was like an epiphany. Ginger Baker on drums was indescribably awesome. Eric Clapton's vocals blew everyone away. Most of us knew him from the Yardbirds so we already loved his voice. Jack Bruce made 'Sunshine' as a contrast. His bass made Clapton's lead soar. I'm getting goosebumps now. They put out so much music it was hard to believe there were only three of them... like a wall of music coming at you. It was thrilling - a great session and a great summer to see amazing music everywhere and anywhere.

I WAS THERE: GEORGE B FIEST

I WAS A DJ at the time at college and I was able to go backstage and interview Eric Clapton. I sat with him for about an hour. I didn't record it but I was able to take pictures and I still haven't found the pictures to this day. I asked him how much they made for their performance and he told me that they didn't get any money for the performance but they were flown out

George B Fiest interviewed Eric

here and put up in a small hotel and Bill Graham paid for that at the end of the show. I was excited so I jumped on the stage and shook Eric Clapton's hand and told him what a great show it was and just at that moment Bill Graham grabbed me by the collar and told me 'get off my fucking stage.'

Bill Graham grabbed me by the collar and told me 'get off my fucking stage'

Paul Butterfield was on the bill and he and Ginger Baker went off and got drunk but Ginger still did a phenomenally long 'Toad'.

I WAS THERE: JUDI HISCOX

I WAS 20 or 21 and living in SF. We went to the Fillmore and the Avalon Ballroom all the time. We also saw The Who there. Mostly it was the Grateful Dead, Quicksilver Messanger Service, Jefferson Airplane, Big Brother, etc. but we loved whenever the British bands came. They were very, very pale that is what I mostly remember and thin. They did not talk much but they did mingle then. Back then bands would walk through the crowd and come and talk with us. They were not guarded or rushed in and out of venues. They were interested in the hippie lifestyle we were living but maybe they were shy. Later we heard they used heroin so maybe this was part of it too. Compared to us, they were very thin and very pale. The music was fantastic though. I wish I could go back for one day, or even an hour.

Judi Hiscox was at the Fillmore

I WAS THERE: MICHAEL BUCHANAN CLARK, AGE 17

Michael Buchanan Clark remembers a packed out Fillmore show

SAN FRANCISCO WAS a wonderful place to grow up, not that I did. I was part of the scene in a big way. My friends and I went to concerts two or three nights a week from 1967 until 1977. I was a junior at a Catholic College Preparatory High School and had a young, black and very hip brother (in a cassock) physics professor who turned me on to Cream. When they came to SF, I didn't miss it. The Fillmore was a really small place. There must have been five or six thousand people in a venue that probably was licensed for about 1,200. It was incredibly sweaty and hot. I recall being amazed by Jack Bruce's vocals and Ginger Baker's incredible energy. Also of note was the understated Eric Clapton. I was playing guitar in bands at the time and Clapton was a god! Because of guitar players like him, I gave up guitar and became a keyboard player. The piano introduction to Janis Joplin's 'Turtle Blues' sealed the deal. Shortly after, the *Disraeli Gears* album came out. My physics professor loaned it to me and I recorded it on a reel-to-reel that my father used to take depositions.

WHISKY A GO-GO
4 - 6 SEPTEMBER 1967,
LOS ANGELES, CALIFORNIA

I WAS THERE: DENNIS AIDEN LOCKHART, AGE 23

I FOLLOWED THE British music scene as closely as I could in those pre-internet days. *Billboard* was a main source of information as was the *Los Angeles Free Press* and there were some hip FM deejays. I knew about Cream from the start. I saw them twice in 1967, at the Fillmore in San Francisco (a friend and I had driven up from LA to check out Haight-Ashbury) and a couple of days later at the Whisky a Go-Go. I lived about a block away from the Whisky, off the Sunset Strip. They were loud at the Fillmore (a hall) but they were much louder at the Whisky (a club). I used to hang outside

Dennis Lockhart heard Eric hit a bum note... and saw him smile to himself

the Whisky, always barefoot, because the scene on the sidewalk was usually more interesting plus Mario, the manager (who recently died at the age of 93) would open the doors at 1.30am so you could see the last 20 minutes of the main act for free. I remember standing right in front of the stage at the Whisky and looking right up at Eric - the stage at the Whisky is up high. He was playing a solo and he hit a note that didn't sound right. I looked up and he was smiling to himself.

I loved *Fresh Cream* and *Disraeli Gears*... *Wheels of Fire* not so much. 'Tales of Brave Ulysses' is probably my favourite song, over the much inferior 'White Room'. I was watching a show on Cream and they said at one concert Eric turned off the volume on his guitar - and Jack and Ginger never even noticed!

Back on the East Coast, a two week residency at Boston's Cross Town Bus Club falls through and Cream are instead booked into a makeshift club.

PSYCHEDELIC SUPERMARKET
7 & 10 - 16 SEPTEMBER 1967, BOSTON, MASSACHUSETTS

I WAS THERE: ANDREW KASTNER, AGE 17

I WAS WORKING at a rock club in Boston and the Cream was the first band to play the club when it opened. They played seven nights in a row, two shows a night, so I saw them 14 times in one week and I was their gopher.

In 1967 I was fully entrenched in the Boston music scene. I fondly remember hanging out at Unicorn Coffee House, a tiny venue at 825 Boylston Street that held maybe 75 people, and seeing The J Geils Band, Ultimate Spinach with Skunk Baxter, Jefferson Airplane and Spirit. It was there that I also met Unicorn owner George Papadopoulos, an encounter that led me on one of the most memorable adventures of my young life.

Papadopoulos was building a new rock music club outside of Kenmore Square, and my brother Stanley and I asked him if we could work there. He agreed, but our 'payment' would be free access to shows. It sounded like a good deal to me. After school and on weekends, I, my brother Stanley, and some friends from Newton South High school would jump on the MTA (Trolley) and head from Newton to an underground parking garage at 590 Commonwealth Avenue, just west of Kenmore Square, to help the carpenter Papadopoulos had hired build what would become The Psychedelic Supermarket. Complete with backlight rooms, a head shop, and all the typical hippy clothing stores, the Supermarket probably held 300 to 400 people and there were no seats.

One day in early September 1967, Papadopoulos grabbed me and said, 'I want you to go to the top of the driveway and meet the band that is playing here this week.' A few minutes later, two yellow cabs pulled up and out came three weird guys dressed in fringed suede jackets and moccasins. They had curly unkempt hairdos and

Andrew Kastner was at the Psychedelic Supermarket for the whole 14 shows Cream played there

were almost literally straight off the plane from the hip London scene. From my conservative Boston perspective, they looked like aliens. It turned out that these three were the soon-to-be supergroup, Cream: Eric Clapton, Jack Bruce and Ginger Baker. (Their classic second album, *Disraeli Gears*, wouldn't be released until November that year.)

I walked the trio to their dressing room and hung out with them for an entire week. For some reason I can't remember, Cream hated Papadopoulos, so to get back at him they turned their double Marshall stacks to 11 and played as loud as they could in a venue not known for its acoustics. They were very uncomfortable in Boston, sticking out of the crowd; rather than explore the city, they just stayed in their hotel rooms when they weren't at the club for their seven-night, two-shows-a-night engagement. The three band members were going stir crazy and on one occasion took spray paint and sprayed the dressing room walls with crazy graffiti: things like 'Black Jews' for Jack Bruce and 'Berry Craptown' for Eric Clapton.

I remember for some reason the stage wasn't built quite right so it wobbled and on many occasions that week during their performances my job was to stand on stage and hold up Jack Bruce's amplifier from behind because his thundering bass and Ginger Baker's drumming would cause it to almost fall over. One night Clapton asked me if I could get him some uppers and I had no idea what he was talking about. On another memorable night, he handed me his painted SG and showed me how to play 'Sunshine of Your Love'.

That week was something I would never forget. For 14 shows, I was backstage or on stage listening and hanging out with Eric Clapton, Jack Bruce and Ginger Baker. This was the start of an amazing music scene experience in Boston and I was there to witness all of it.

I WAS THERE: MIKE ANNESE

I KNEW ABOUT Clapton of course. The word 'supergroup' was heavily used for the first time for the formation of Cream. A music-mad friend was home from a trip and wanted to go to the Boston gig so we called for directions to get to this place. I remember the operator couldn't find it in her directory and my friend saying, 'The dumb bitch probably thinks 'psychedelic' starts with an S.'

The show wasn't heavily promoted at all. If my friend hadn't told me about it I would've missed it. The promoter, I learned later, was a fast-buck artist who didn't know what he was doing. The gig was literally held in a former underground garage; all dark and all concrete. There was no eye-candy lighting, etc., just maybe one light on the band. I think Clapton got mugged in Boston - these were his beehive hair days. My memory may be playing tricks but I seem to have a picture of him playing most of the gig with his back to the crowd of about 50 people. Thinking back, it was like a Fellini movie, watching Cream in a dark cement garage with less than 70 people; there were no chairs and people were mostly sitting on the floor with the rest standing. I can't remember the songs they played that night. I, like most Clapton fans, went to see him burn the place down with his Strat. There was zero interaction with the audience. They probably hated being talked into this gig, playing in a dungeon.

The reunion shows at Albert Hall have become my faves now. They lack the fire of the early days but it was still great to see them together after so many years and with so much history under their belts. Those shows are my go to on YouTube - full blast with nice headphones. I followed Clapton closely, buying almost everything he did after. Jack Bruce is one of the most underrated rock voices ever. I felt his passing with sadness. I related heavily to his personal life - Ginger, who I greatly admire, not so much. But I enjoyed the documentary *Beware of Mr Baker*. He should win a Nobel Prize in science to have reached 80. I used to go haul on a spliff on any drum solo. Drum solos were not my thing.

I WAS THERE: JOHNNY PRESS, AGE 16 OR 17

I WAS IN high school. Five of us drove to the club. It was an underground garage. The stage was loaded with gigantic amps called Marshall. These were new to us and I had never seen one before. Cream came out and blasted right into 'Crossroads'. The power coming off that stage was something I had never experienced before. Being a guitarist, I focused on Clapton. He played a red Gibson SG all night through two cranked Marshalls. No pedals. He had curly permed hair. When the band went into 'Toad', Clapton walked to the side of the stage and lit a cigarette. Women flocked to him. I immediately thought, 'This is what I want to do for the rest of my life!' Jack Bruce

Johnny Press got an afro after seeing Eric with one

did almost all the singing. He also played through two Marshall stacks, using a red Gibson EBO bass. I don't believe anything was miked and they only had a couple of lights on them. The sound was roaring and we were in shock. Seeing that show changed everything for me musically. On the way home all we talked about was those Marshall amps.

I WAS THERE: ANN GOLDMAN

THE PSYCHEDELIC SUPERMARKET was a dark and dingy converted underground parking garage in Kenmore Square. It was damp and cold. I don't remember there being any stage and I don't remember an opening act. I do remember there weren't very many people there and we were standing, unless one wanted to sit on a concrete floor. Eric Clapton was on the right side about 15 to 20 feet in front of me. I couldn't get over how good they sounded and I really enjoyed Clapton's guitar playing. I don't remember any specific songs that they played, only remember what a great concert it was in spite of the venue. Several months later I saw them again at the Back Bay Theater which was a regular theatre. By then they had tripled the amount of amps set up. It was a disappointing concert because the super loud amps just muddled everything and I couldn't hear the individual notes Clapton was playing.

I WAS THERE: BRIAN MAGOON

ON THEIR FIRST American tour Cream were booked for five nights at a club in Brighton, Massachusetts called the Crosstown Bus. The Club closed before their tour and a brand new club, The Psychedelic Supermarket on Commonwealth Avenue in Boston, was created specifically to have Cream there. I went the second night, was blown away and so went back two nights later. At the first night I saw at the Psychedelic Supermarket, Clapton had on snakeskin boots, white sailor-style bib front pants and a brightly-coloured flowery shirt with a big collar. His hair was in an afro style. I saw them again the following year in Boston, and Derek and the Dominos in 1970 at the Fillmore East and Clapton four or five times after that.

I WAS THERE: DAVID SOKOL

I WAS STILL in high school. I was right at the beginning of the line, hours before showtime, and was interviewed by legendary Boston deejay Dick Summer who approached me, microphone in hand. I don't remember too much other than the excitement I felt that night at being able to see this wildly exciting trio and be so close to the stage inside this odd and uncomfortable concrete basement club. There was certainly the feeling that we all were in the presence of something very new and special, and for me, just starting my junior year of high school, it all felt quite magical. I had to leave early into the second 'solos' set, during Jack Bruce's 'Traintime', so I wouldn't miss the last train out of the city.

I WAS THERE: ANDY PRATT
I WAS IN a band called Butter and our assignment to join the band had been to learn and play *Fresh Cream*. At one point Clapton went to the mic and said 'it's Saturday night and I just got paid, gonna go out and... get laid'. It was hippy heaven.

I WAS THERE: STEVE HORWITZ, AGE 16
I HAD ALREADY seen Clapton when he played with Mayall so I was excited to see the band. The evening was one of frustration boarding on anger. The band played on Commonwealth Avenue directly across from Boston University. The club was in the basement so everything was concrete. Cream came out and I was close to the stage. I can't quite explain how unpleasant it was. The band was so loud. Volume was normally not a problem because I was seeing live music frequently and was accustomed to load music. This was beyond loud. It became so unbearable that I had to leave. Because it was a sold out show the crowd on Commonwealth Avenue was huge, full of frustrated fans who just wanted to be close.

I WAS THERE: BILL SULLIVAN, AGE 17
I SAW THEM twice. The first Cream show I saw was one of the greatest ever. There were only about 20 or 30 people in attendance. It was in a dank garage called the Psychedelic Supermarket - a piss hole in the snow! Admission was $1.25. It was a cellar with concrete walls, floor and ceilings. Horrible acoustics but we were standing directly in front of the three foot high stage! The music

Bill Sullivan saw Cream twice

was over the top. During intermission, Eric and Jack sat on the edge of the stage, smoking cigarettes and asked how we had heard of them.

I WAS THERE: WAYNE ULAKY
I SAW THEM at a short-lived rock club called the Psychedelic Supermarket near Boston University and again at a stadium concert in Rhode Island. I was in a rock band of my own, and played frequently at the Boston Tea Party in the early days. Then we heard of a 'new' place that had opened called the Psychedelic Supermarket, and I took a girlfriend there to see Cream. Unfortunately, the venue was a converted concrete parking garage and the acoustics were horrible. The Cream, of course, were quite loud with a wall of Marshalls. The concrete floors and walls reverberated the sound in so many directions it sounded like mush. It was so loud that we had to leave after only one song.

The only place that wasn't outstanding was in Boston, where we played the opening of a brand new club. **Ginger Baker**

VILLAGE THEATER
23 SEPTEMBER 1967, NEW YORK, NEW YORK

I WAS THERE: RICHARD CORNETTO
AFTER THE RKO performance I saw them again at the Village Theater, where they played all blues and not many of their hits. Canned Heat opened for them because Moby Grape didn't show up. Henry Vestine was my favourite blues guitar player for a whole half hour. When Cream came on, Clapton came out in his Davy Crockett fringed suede jacket and blew my 15-year-old self away. They played blues songs that were 15 to 20 minutes long without getting boring. Clapton could bend strings and play real fast at the same time. He would start a solo a half key lower and then bend it right. It was stuff I had never heard anyone do before. I wasn't crazy about Bruce's fuzzy tone on the bass but it was probably necessary to fill in holes in a trio, and I had no idea what Baker was doing on the drums. It wasn't as full sounding as I expected with all those drums.

I WAS THERE: RONNIE RUSSO
I WAS VERY young but went anyway. My mother was about to kill me when I got home but it was worth it. They had recorded *Disraeli Gears* in New York and I went to listen by the trailer that was recording them.

To say that was unreal would be putting it lightly. They did 'Sunshine of Your Love', 'Politician', 'I'm So Glad' and more. At 11.30pm I was in my seat. I could not control myself. I loved Ginger. He was something I never saw before and I bought another set of drums so I could play double bass like him. Eric was top notch and Jack was very heavy. I will never forget that night.

I WAS THERE: JOSEPH VINDIGNI, AGE 18

I SAW THEM when they played at the Village Theater, later to be called the Fillmore East. I'd stopped hanging around Bensonhurst Heights in Brooklyn and was hanging around in Greenwich Village. I was a beatnik then - hey, I'm still a beatnik! I went into a record store on 8th Street and saw three albums - *The Doors*, *The Grateful Dead* and *Fresh Cream*. I had no idea who these bands were. I bought them for maybe 10 bucks altogether and took them home and listened to them.

The Village Theater was like a movie theatre. You'd go there and somebody would open up the door on the side and you'd get in for free, because everybody would just run in. There was no conformity. There were a lot of people just doing what they wanted. When they opened the Fillmore East, you had to sit in your seat. When it was the Village Theater you could go up on the stage. I remember sitting up on the stage with the Vanilla Fudge with the amp to my back. It was so loud I thought I was going to die.

Cream were very loud too. I think I was stoned. They were wearing Indian-type moccasins but boots. And very flashy costumes. One of them could have been wearing snakeskin-type boots. I remember a lot of hair, a lot of people smoking pot and nobody saying anything. A lot of people were smoking pot in the aisles and people were dancing if the music was danceable. Each of them took solos for half an hour or more. At that time we weren't really used to listening to music that took an hour. They could be on stage for an hour just playing 'Spoonful'. I remember Ginger Baker playing drums and Jack Bruce and Clapton walked off the stage and they came back about 45 minutes later. I remember they played 'Spoonful' and 'Rollin' and Tumblin'' too.

In 1968 I went to photography school for about a year. When I came out they were ready to draft me so I went into the Navy. I was in boot camp when we found out about Woodstock. We wanted to be in upstate

New York, listening to Jimi Hendrix. But there I was, doing drill in bootcamp with an M16 in my hand.

We wanted to be listening to Hendrix at Woodstock, but I was in bootcamp with an M16 in my hand

I WAS THERE: PATRICIA CESTARE

I WAS 17 when I was introduced to the Cream. My drummer friend told me to come over and listen to this new album. I had been jamming with people and been in bands. As a rhythm guitarist, I had played guitar for four years. I went over and listened to what was Cream's first album and I was mesmerised. I had no idea what the guitarist was doing. When I saw them live, they were very loud - but Eric shone!

Patricia Cestare remembers Cream being very loud

I'd better shit or get off the pot. **Leslie West, on seeing Clapton**

CAFÉ AU GO GO
26 - 30 SEPTEMBER 1967, NEW YORK, NEW YORK

I WAS THERE: PAUL SIMEONE

WHEN I WAS younger, I was a drummer and the boys in the band I was in, Jim Zaleski and Teddy Tedesco, started following different types of music. We got hooked into the Yardbirds. Hence following Eric Clapton after he left the Yardbirds and went into John Mayall and then Cream. We heard that Cream was going to make their United States club debut in New York City so the three of us took a train and went up to New York City and a place called the Café au Go Go. I was maybe 15 or 16 years old at the time. We were there very early, walked around the outside and then went into the club early to try and get a seat.

We walked backstage and found the dressing room door, pushed the door open and much to our surprise - and I'm sure to theirs too - we found Eric, Ginger and Jack sitting in the dressing room. With our mouths open, we stood and stared at each other for a few seconds. Nobody said anything. And then Jack Bruce said, 'Hello boys, can we help you?' We said, 'We came here from Philadelphia to see you guys,' and Jack asked, 'Well, where's Philadelphia?' We said, 'It's about 100 miles south of here,' and he jumped up off his seat and started shaking our hands and going 'you guys travelled 100 miles to see us?'

Ginger Baker was sitting on the floor with bare feet. He was painting his feet with dayglo paint. And if you see early pictures of Eric Clapton with Cream, you can see that his hair was very curly. In the dressing room we noticed that Clapton was setting his hair in a product called Spoolies, curlers that a woman would use to give her hair curls. He had them all over his head, giving his hair this curl effect. It was very bizarre to see him do that.

GRANDE BALLROOM
13 - 15 OCTOBER 1967, DETROIT, MICHIGAN

I WAS THERE: CANDYCE RAMON, AGE 18

THE GRANDE BALLROOM was the place I went every weekend. I saw so many groups with friends there. Time was free and music was the best. I took these pictures while sitting on the right side of the stage. What a beautiful time in my life. I will never forget it!

I WAS THERE: JIM OEHL

Candyce Ramon got a few snaps of Jack in action at the Grande

I SAW CREAM live at least three times at Detroit's Grande Ballroom. I also saw Eric come on stage while John Mayall and the Bluesbreakers played there with Mick Taylor. Mick handed Eric his guitar, announced 'Eric Clapton!' and walked offstage.

I WAS THERE: KATHLEEN CRAWFORD, AGE 17

I SAW CREAM a couple times at the Grande. I thought they were great. Eric Clapton had a perm the first time, and between strobe lights and popular but illegal substances that pretty well wraps it up.

I WAS THERE: KEVIN KELLY, AGE 16

I WAS JUST getting started in sex, drugs and rock 'n' roll. Being a novice young guitarist led me to hanging with older 'bad influences'. I saw Cream the first time they came to in Detroit in 1967. I worshipped Cream and Clapton. The place was packed. The house band the MC5 opened and Cream were next. It was an awesome show. I saw Rob Tyner, the singer/front man from the 5 and asked Rob if he would get me back stage to meet Cream. He said, 'Come with me!' Tyner was a big dude, like six foot three and a solid 225 pounds. We walked down the hall to the dressing rooms. There was Jack Bruce. Tyner, much to my surprise, leaned over Jack and started telling him that Detroit was MC5 turf and 'you little English fucks weren't shit'. A couple of roadies ran to Jack's defence. Rob turned to me and let out a sly laugh! Well, so much for meeting Cream!

Being a guitarist led to Kevin Kelly hanging with 'bad influences'

Rob was really a man of peace and great talent but typical of the bravado that Detroiters' became notorious for. RIP, Rob.

I WAS THERE: CATHERINE PLEAK

I WAS YOUNG and went with some friends. We went to concerts every weekend back in those days. We could easily afford it. It was different times, and all about the music. They were amazing. The only vivid memory I have is of Ginger Baker beating his drums for so long that he stood up and fell to the ground. He lay there a few minutes and was taken backstage.

I WAS THERE: MARC FALCONBERRY, AGE 18

I HAD BEEN playing guitar only three years professionally. At our ballroom in Detroit, which I'd played, the Cream were scheduled to appear for three straight nights. Being a big Yardbirds fan and trying to get better on the guitar, I went to see every guitarist who played with the Yardbirds. A buddy of mine went to the very first gig Cream played in Detroit on Friday. The crowd was pretty small, maybe 300 people in a place that held 1,500. Almost everybody there knew nothing about the band. But a friend of mine had seen them at the Fillmore in San Francisco and said they were very good, which was an understatement!

The first thing that struck me was the equipment set up. I had never heard of Marshall amps and never seen two stacks on each side of the stage plus double bass drum set with cymbals stacked on top of one another on single stands. All for just three guys? They came out and Eric had cowboy chaps on and I thought, 'What is this?' Their first song was 'Tales of Brave Ulysses' and I was immediately impressed with the finesse and power of the equipment plus Jack's voice which soared over the so-so sound system. It was also one of the first times I heard a wah-wah pedal live. Then it was 'NSU', which was totally original sounding with a long jam in the middle. I was so happy to see this because all live pop bands back then (including us) weren't allowed to have songs more than three minutes long with a single guitar solo or they wouldn't play it on the radio.

It went from people standing with arms folded at the start to mouths hanging open

I was afraid for their success since they seemed to have a devil-may-care attitude about it. Jazz guys I had seen were like this but not rock bands. I remember they did two sets and everyone there was amazed at the virtuosity. I knew from experience Detroit audiences were hard to please, but it went from people standing with arms folded at the start to mouths hanging open, even from other musicians I knew there. I was totally captivated too and Eric had great tone and felt like a kindred spirit, but they were older with a lot of experience, especially Jack and Ginger with their melting pot of blues jazz rock and psychedelic sounds.

There was no stopping me from telling everybody to go see them and buy their records

Each guy would take the lead at different times which I had never seen before in that form of music. Still, there were detractors, eg. some of my musician friends who were jealous and critical, but there was no stopping me from telling everybody to go see them and buy their records. I also left there that night totally upset and thought I should quit playing because I could never be as good as that. And the British wave of bands was too powerful in people's minds. The bar was raised so high that us locals were expected to play like and have equipment like the English guys or you wouldn't get work.

I went back the next night. The word had got out and I got to see them again with a full house. Again I was witness to incredible harmonica, vocals, drum solos and - of course - Eric. A few months later in December 1967 they came back with a new song - 'Sunshine of your Love' - which I thought was great but I was not sure it would be a hit because I thought the band needed, and deserved, better promotion. Their work ethic was one thing I learned from them and really admired. Again, I attended both the Friday and Saturday shows.

The next trip in was in June 1968. I went on Sunday and there were a few problems. It was in the summer about 300 degrees and the band seemed out of gas. 'White Room' was not out yet and it seemed they were burned out from touring, etc. Their last performance was later moved to Olympia the hockey stadium. I didn't go, and after that they broke up. In my opinion the best stuff I saw Cream do was not recorded. They were trailblazing. I'll always love them.

I WAS THERE: LINDA ASCIONE NIMAN, AGE 17

YOU HAD TO prove your age to get into the Grande, and I didn't have a driver's license yet. I would bring my actual birth certificate. One night the cop at the door would not accept it as proof and wouldn't let me in. I had come with my two girlfriends who were already in. I had no way to get home from downtown Detroit, so when the cop wasn't looking, I made a mad dash up the stairs and disappeared into the crowd.

Linda Niman (far right) with her hippy friends from the Grande

I always went with my two girlfriends. We couldn't always get the money from our parents to go out every week, so we chose the weekends when our favourites were playing. We saw all the big musicians before they were famous for about $1.50. Coffee houses were cheaper. No cover and all you had to buy was a coke. It was the best era ever to be young.

I saw Cream a couple of times. I remember Clapton's furry white chaps and his very long leads in every song. It seemed every song turned into a Clapton guitar-playing marathon, but the crowd loved it.

I WAS THERE: MARK SMALL

THE GRANDE BALLROOM was wide open and filled to overflowing with a couple of hundred kids, all head bobbing when the music started. People always say the drummer attracts more attention, especially amongst the young ladies. But Ginger Baker was larger than life - I'm not the only one to have noticed - with wild frenzied red hair and a back beat that slapped you silly. The thing about hearing them at the Grande was the amplified sound in those close quarters. I think the big Orange speakers with Custom Reverb Twin MKII were on each end of the stage, probably 100 watt versions, saturating my body with sound until it vibrated. Detroit was famous for its loud sound and we were all delighted with the body rush Cream gave us. I can still feel the guitar reverb and the explosions of Baker's drum heads. During breaks we wandered in and out of the Green Room with abandon. I'll never forget it.

Mark Small was at the Grande

I WAS THERE: RICHARD SHACK

AS A FORMER James Gang member, I was focused in on the great guitarists - Hendrix, Clapton, Beck, Page, Peter Green, etc. With the release of the first Cream album, we were pumped. 'I Feel Free' was a unique debut tune and they were doing things no one else had even considered. They jammed like a jazz group except they were rocking hard. Jack Bruce and Ginger Baker made

Richard Shack travelled from Cleveland to see Cream

for an incredible rhythm section and Clapton was Clapton. They came to Detroit early and played at the Grande Ballroom. I had a popular band in Cleveland called The Case of ET Hooley and we travelled to Motor City to see them. They left us speechless. We had to re-examine our musical goals and aspirations. Their energy and power were unprecedented. Jack Bruce was a brilliant player with a great voice who could compose.

Cream return to the UK on 17 October 1967 via New York. A planned Irish tour is postponed. Robert Stigwood describes the US tour as 'extremely uneconomical'.

SAVILLE THEATRE
29 OCTOBER 1967, LONDON, UK

I WAS THERE: TOM THATCHER
AFTER SALISBURY, I determined to see the band as many times as I could and saw in *Melody Maker* (the gig bible of the day) that the band was playing at the famous Saville Theatre on Shaftesbury Avenue in central London. But - disaster - the Melody Maker announced the next week that all tickets for Cream at the Saville had sold out. Undeterred, I walked from home to the nearest main road, having finished all farm work for the day, and hitchhiked to Hammersmith and then caught the Tube to Piccadilly. It had been pouring with rain, so I was soaking wet but really excited about the possibility of seeing the band. It was heaving with people outside the Saville Theatre and touts were asking £10 to £20 a ticket: it might as well have been £20,000! After two hours of milling about and asking if anyone had a spare ticket, I overhead a group of three people saying, 'Well, if he doesn't bloody well turn up in the next five minutes, I'm selling his ticket.' I immediately asked them if I could hang about with them and buy the ticket if their mate didn't arrive, and 10 minutes later the chap said, 'Right, it's yours - face value.' So I paid the face value, which was I

Tom Thatcher got a ticket at face value for the sold out Saville Theatre show think seven shillings and sixpence, and in we went!

The line-up was the most unlikely pairing of Cream and The Bonzo Dog Doo Dah Band, of whom Eric was a huge fan. The other act was The Action, who did not turn up. The Bonzos were quite exceptional - beneath the chaos and lunacy, a mixture of The Temperance Seven and the Goons, there were some real musicianship and fine songs - and they went down a storm.

Cream played out of their skins. Despite the sedate all-seated audience, they ran through a lot of their by now popular songs and also produced an excellent extended workout on both 'Toad' and 'Spoonful'. The sound was good, the band looked happy - Jack and Ginger were not actually snarling at each other - and the audience was delighted. Alvin Lee of Ten Years After was in the audience, sitting just a few seats away from me. I hitched home again, arriving around 4am and still soaking wet after more rain, but it was worth it.

I WAS THERE: RICHARD LUETCHFORD

MY FINAL CREAM gig was again at the Saville Theatre. This was a different band to the one I had seen only a few months earlier. Recently returned from a US tour, they seemed tired and somewhat self indulgent and overly loud with long improvised solos and a lack of communication with their audience. The earlier 'warm up' acts were, in contrast, brilliant - the Mod band The Action and then the superb Bonzos and the hilarious Viv Stanshall.

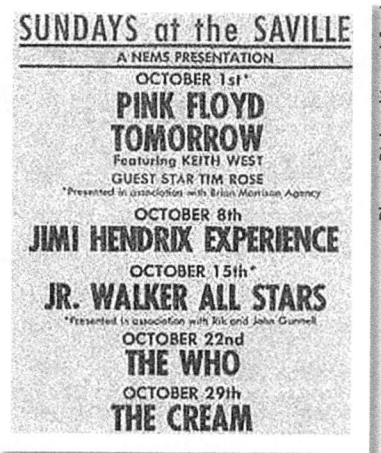

Cream played Brian Epstein's Saville Theatre twice

I WAS THERE: MIKE R GODWIN

AFTER THE WINDSOR Festival, I saw Cream at the Saville Theatre supported by the excellent Bonzo Dog Doo-Dah Band. I have to confess that the Saville concert made an unforgettable impression. They opened with 'Ulysses' and played 'Spoonful', 'We're Going Wrong', 'Traintime', 'Toad', 'I'm So Glad' and some others which I forget. That Saville Theatre impression wasn't confirmed at later gigs. By the time of *Goodbye Cream* the tensions between Jack Bruce and Ginger Baker meant they were still capable of improvising well on stage but between songs the atmosphere was distant. On the other hand, they did play 'White Room' which presumably replaced 'Ulysses', which has a similar riff. I saw both houses of the Farewell concert at the Albert Hall. I saw a photo where Eric was playing a Firebird, which must have been either in the first house or at a different concert altogether, as at the second house, filmed by Tony Palmer, he plays a 335 (or is it a 345 - I can't remember!) throughout.

Mike Godwin was at the Saville Theatre show

A rich friend also bought a gang of us tickets for the 2005 reunion where Eric played a Strat ('Blackie'). The 2005 show was the only one I saw where Ginger Baker recited 'Pressed Rat and Warthog'. They also did a nice 'Deserted Cities of the Heart' which I don't remember seeing them play before.

ROMANO'S BALLROOM
2 NOVEMBER 1967, BELFAST, NORTHERN IRELAND

BOB ADCOCK, CREAM'S TOUR MANAGER
WHEN THE CREAM formed, they didn't have a professional tour manager working with them. They had a friend of Eric's, who was no more than a driver and who drove them from gig to gig when they started out. But he couldn't cope with it and Stigwood asked me to do it. I stepped in and that was it basically. I was 22 years old.

I started out when the Merseybeat thing was happening back in the mid-Sixties. I worked with a couple of bands and ended up working with the Merseybeats who were very big at the time. Their manager was Kit Lambert, who also managed The Who, and the agent for the Merseys was Robert Stigwood who later managed Cream and the Bee Gees. That's how I knew Stigwood. I was very much aware that I was at the centre of what was happening musically in Liverpool through working with the Merseybeats. It was so different being involved with a professional band compared to being in a nine to five job. I'd never had a nine to five job. The first band I worked with in Liverpool, I was one of the few people who wanted to do the job because of what it was.

At the start Cream didn't have a professional tour manager working with them

The person who did it was usually a friend of whoever was the most important guy in the band, a frustrated musician who really wanted to be in the band but couldn't play a musical instrument or sing and wasn't good looking enough. All you had to do to be good at the job in those days was get to the right gig on time, set the gear up and drive everybody home to where they lived at the end of the night. But you'd be amazed how few people could do it. They couldn't find the right town. They got there late. The gear didn't work. They crashed the van. They did this. They did that. All you had to do to stand out was not do any of that. You didn't have to be particularly smart to be a good roadie in those days. I don't think the term even existed then but I wanted to be the road manager. I wanted to be the guy who drove the van, put the gear and the band in the back of the van and drove the van to gigs.

I went down to the Cavern one night to watch The Who. Richard Cole, who went on to be Zeppelin's tour manager, was working with The Who then, and Neville Chesters, who had previously been the equipment manager with the Merseys, was working with Richard. And they said, 'Well, come down to London with us at the end of the night.' And that's what I did. I hopped in the van, drove down to London and stayed at Roger Daltrey's for a couple of days. And the Merseys phoned me up when I was staying at Roger's so a couple of days after moving down to London I started working with the Merseys. I never moved back to Liverpool after that.

Stigwood invited me to come down to London. While I was a professional road manager the guy before was a hippy. Stigwood didn't want to be surrounded by hippies. He wasn't into that kind of culture. And that's why he asked me to do the job. I went round to Ginger's maisonette in Neasden. We had fish and chips and a few pints of Guinness and talked for about four hours, and at the end of it he said, 'You'll do.' Jack and Eric weren't involved. It was just Ginger. Ginger was the prime mover with getting Cream together. I was very reluctant to start. Stigwood called me three times before I finally said I'd do it. I was put off was by this aura surrounding Cream which I didn't think I would enjoy. I was never a hippy, and they had this hippy image and Ginger was supposed to be manic and the others were always fighting and I said, 'I don't want to get involved in that. I've just spent two years on the road with a pop band.' On the third call, Stigwood said, 'Look, I'm desperate for someone to start right now. They're doing a tour of Ireland. Do the tour for two weeks and then leave. Just do the tour. Give me two weeks to find someone else.' So I said, 'Yeah, okay. Let's do that.' I did that two week tour and my eyes were opened. It was a different world. None of the publicity that I'd heard before I'd met the band was true. They were three fantastic guys to work with. I really liked them as people.

The audiences were nothing like I'd been used to. They weren't a pop-drawing audience. They were intellectuals, they were into music. It was a totally different world for me. And I jumped at the chance of working with them instead of going on trial for two weeks and me auditioning them to see if I wanted to stick it out. I was just really grateful to be given a chance to do the job, because I thought they were fantastic. I loved the music, but that's not important. When you're looking at it from the point of view of working with a band the music they play is totally irrelevant. You certainly don't get to hear it because there's so many other things to be done during the show that you never get to hear them anyway. The music they play is not the reason you decide whether you want to work with someone. It's how they are on the road. You spend 24 hours a day with them for months at a time. You've got to be able to get on, and to like them. And I did. I got on with them, very well and liked them very much.

I WASN'T THERE: TONY N

THIS SHOW WAS scheduled for 19th October but had to be postponed as they were just back from the US and their equipment was still in transit. Rory Gallagher and Taste, the support band, played the gig and those who wanted got their money back. I wasn't there but a mate gave me a photo taken backstage at Romano's.

Tony R wasn't at the November 1967 Romano's show but got this photo of Cream backstage at the Queen's Hall from his mate

SILVER BLADES ICE RINK
6 NOVEMBER 1967, STREATHAM, LONDON, UK

I WAS THERE: NIGEL ENEVER

I SAW CREAM twice in London. The most odd - and memorable - of these gigs was at Streatham Ice Rink. My friend and I were standing one side of the ice rink and Cream were playing on the other. People stopped skating momentarily, but then started up again, ignoring the group. Cream were almost a side show.

DISRAELI GEARS RELEASED
10 NOVEMBER 1967

Cream's second album is released, having been recorded in five days between 11th and 15th May 1967 in New York. Melody Maker's review says 'this is the creation of pure energy - from the top, centre, the bottom, all the way through - Cream.'

We didn't know you were meant to take months and years to make an album. A lot of the tracks were first and second takes. **Jack Bruce**

11 NOVEMBER 1967
SCANDINAVIAN TOUR

I WAS THERE: BOB ADCOCK, CREAM'S TOUR MANAGER

SHORTLY AFTER THAT we did a Scandinavian tour which ran off fine and then we went to America for the first time and that was like moving from a black and white world to a world of colour. It just changed everything I'd grown up with and believed in. I had an insatiable appetite for touring because I wanted to see the world. And I thought, 'If you want to see the world it's better if someone pays you to do it rather than you putting a sack on your back.' And it was travelling on an extent that I never would have believed possible. I spent my whole life on the road and loved every part of it.

KONSERTHUSET
14 NOVEMBER 1967, STOCKHOLM, SWEDEN

I WAS THERE: ANDERS RÅDLING

I SAW CREAM at Stockholm's Concert House. It was the best band I have ever seen. I had been listening to The Beatles and the Rolling Stones for a couple of years but was keen to hear something rougher. That was the beginning of my interest in Jimi Hendrix and in Cream and their bluesy sound. The audience were ecstatic and I was so impressed by Jack Bruce's voice. I have a live CD from this concert.

Anders Rådling has a boot of the show by the best band he ever saw

LORENSBERGS CIRKUS
15 NOVEMBER 1967, GOTHENBURG, SWEDEN

I WAS THERE: P O HESSELBOM

THE SECOND GOTHENBURG gig had three opening acts - Young Flowers (a Danish group), The Red Squares (an English group living in Denmark) and the Fabulous Four (a Swedish band). Eric, with an enormous bow tie and with hair like a judge from the 18th Century, played on a painted SG and Jack had a four string EB3. During the last song, 'Spoonful', there was some problem with the PA system and the microphone was cutting out. But when Jack Bruce sang without a microphone he could still be heard. Talk about a loud voice! In the end he became so angry that he slammed his bass right into the floor so that it broke into pieces and the gig was over. As a teenager I was deeply impressed! In a review in Göteborgstidningen, a Gothenburg newspaper, journalist Gösta Hansson wrote, 'Despite the enormous volume level, we got to hear some good pop music served by perhaps the best pop group there is.'

Cream returned to the UK after their Scandinavian tour.

CLUB A'GOGO
23 NOVEMBER 1967, NEWCASTLE, UK

I WAS THERE: COLIN BRANTHWAITE

Colin Branthwaite (right) remembers the queues to get into Newcastle's Club A'GoGo

I'D SEEN JACK Bruce and Ginger Baker in the Graham Bond Organisation a couple of times and Clapton in Bluesbreakers several times before they formed Cream. Needless to say, I was knocked out by them, particularly John Mayall's band with Clapton. When Clapton left Mayall I was devastated, but thankfully he recruited one or two other guitarists afterwards who were decent players! When Cream were formed, my spirits were lifted as I was familiar with the work the band members had done previously. And the term 'supergroup' entered our language.

I remember Cream at the GoGo well, although not how I got tickets. We queued along Percy Street outside the club and managed to get in without difficulty. I was in the Young Set as I wasn't old enough for the Jazz Lounge. It was heaving and we had to stand around for ages waiting for them to appear. They did everything I wanted them to, but I was disappointed that they did a long drawn out set of nearly all instrumentals and a drum solo covering only about three songs. It lasted less than an hour and wasn't what I wanted really. I did attempt to see them in The Jazz Lounge but couldn't get in. But the experience of seeing them was fantastic and when I saw them play a full set it was just amazing. The atmosphere was always unbelievable and people were just incredulous that these three musicians of such calibre were playing in front of us.

After Cream disbanded Clapton and Baker formed Blind Faith and I was lucky enough to see the band play their first gig in Hyde Park on a hot summer's day. It wasn't Cream but with Steve Winwood and Rick Grech in the line up, another super group was formed. Happy, happy days.

I WAS THERE: CHARLIE REAVLEY, AGE 17

AS A SCHOOLBOY in the mid-Sixties I was exposed to the surge of beat groups as well as an American folk singer (Bob Dylan). This interest developed into blues via the Marble Arch UK budget issues of LPs - American Folk Blues, Howlin' Wolf, Muddy Waters, John Lee Hooker, Sonny Boy Williamson, etc., but had yet to really experience the emergence of homegrown interpretation of Chicago and Delta Blues.

Charlie Reavley was hooked by 'I Feel Free'

Picking up latest sounds courtesy of the pirate radio station, Radio 270, and Radio Luxembourg became the evening pastime. It was possibly these stations or the BBC Light Programme that drew me to this three piece called Cream. Their release of 'Wrapping Paper' set them apart from the norm, and I was unaware of any other trios of this ilk. I didn't buy the single but when 'I Feel Free' was released late in 1966 as a single I knew this was a group I'd want to follow. I bought *Fresh Cream* on its release and was immediately swept up with 'I'm So Glad', 'NSU', 'Cat's Squirrel', 'Spoonful' and the epic Ginger Baker drum solo of 'Toad'. My exposure to drum solos had been limited to Sandy Nelson and 'Let There Be Drums'!

Fresh Cream was subsequently shared with school friends, and I remember loaning the LP to another couple of mates so they could learn tracks for their group - namely 'Rollin' and Tumblin'', 'NSU' and 'Sweet Wine'.

At that point a solitary concert featuring Tommy Steele, The Viscounts and The Vernon Girls was my only exposure to live music. This changed in 1967; having left school with a clutch of O levels I entered the world of work. When the opportunity to attend a Hallowe'en dance at my old school arose, I was definitely going to be there. The Junco Partners - a star North East attraction - were playing. Here, whilst discussing the merits of different groups, I learnt Cream were coming to Newcastle.

I remember the anticipation and excitement of me and my two pals, Colin Ellar and John Miller. The train journey to Newcastle, the walk from the central station to the GoGo on Percy Street - and the queue. The Club a'GoGo was situated on the first floor so access was via a flight of stairs, and the queue stretched onto the street. We were not going to be put off though and joined the throng.

But what to do in terms of entrance price? It was 7/6 for the Young Set and 12/6 for the late night in the Jazz Lounge. Do we go the whole hog? A decision was made and the Jazz Lounge it would be, without any thought of the consequences for getting home. I was just gone 17 with a youthful face and was nervous about the possible embarrassment of being refused entry, with some pretty mean-looking guys on the door casting their eyes over the queue. But I needn't have worried and, 12/6 each handed over, our wrists were stamped for Jazz Lounge entry and we were in! We made our way into the Young Set room, which was not large by any standards and absolutely packed and waited for what seemed forever.

Ginger looked like the wild man with his double bass drum

Eventually, on they came. Clapton with his long hair in a permed hairstyle, moustache and the fabulous Fool-decorated Gibson SG, Ginger Baker looking like the wild man with his double bass drum arrangement, and Bruce with his fretless bass. Their set contained only five numbers as they gave themselves extended work outs. In no particular order we heard 'Cat's Squirrel' and 'Sweet Wine' and particularly long workouts on 'Train Time', 'Spoonful' and 'Toad'. 'Train Time' and 'Toad' gave Bruce and Baker plenty of freedom with Clapton superb throughout. All were rapturously received but after 45 minutes it was all over. For us, however, the thrill of a second set awaited, so we trooped into the adjacent Jazz Lounge discussing what we had witnessed - the sound, their appearance and what they may play in the second set.

The Jazz Lounge set seemed to fly by with another 45 minutes of sustained brilliance and again only five or six numbers. I remember 'Rollin' and Tumblin'', 'I Feel Free' and 'Tales of Brave Ulysses'. Before we knew it, it was over.

Then came the realisation the last train home to Sunderland was long gone. A taxi journey was way beyond our combined resources, and back then taxis only seemed to be transport for the better off. After trudging the streets of Newcastle for a good hour and huddling in shop doorways, we ended up back at the train station. Securing a bench in the waiting room we dozed until 5am before making our way onto the platform to buy tickets for the milk train back to Sunderland. Back home in time for breakfast, dear knows what my parents thought but what a night and something that has always stayed with me - seeing Cream up close in a smoky club!

MARQUEE CLUB
28 NOVEMBER 1967, LONDON, UK

I WAS THERE: JOHN HOLMES

THE SECOND TIME I saw them was at the Marquee. I have a book about Cream, *Strange Brew*, which notes that this gig was cancelled, but I know it wasn't! The Marquee was a very small, sweaty club which probably wasn't supposed to hold more than 200 people but I'm sure it regularly had far more than that. Non-members queuing one side of the door and members the other side. Those queues used to extend a very long way for bands like Cream.

They had a few rows of seats at the front but everyone else stood. If you had to go to the toilet (which I didn't need to very often in those days) you had little chance of getting back to where you were. The support band was Remo Four, who once backed Billy J Kramer. The guitar player was hammering on notes on his guitar whilst using the other hand in a sort of abracadabra motion over the fretboard. It would have been okay if he had been Jimi Hendrix but for someone who was nothing special at all it was rather embarrassing. If Clapton was watching, he would have had a good laugh. I don't recall much else, apart from waiting in the queue when Clapton walked past. My (very short-term) girlfriend said 'hi Eric' and he said 'hello Pam'. I was aghast - she'd never told me they were acquainted!

I WAS THERE: PETER B TIDBALL

WE WENT IN a coach trip to see them when I was at Trent Park College of Education. I thought that it would be bigger, but the atmosphere was electric. As we walked in Cream were just starting 'Tales of Brave Ulysses'. We were so close to the low stage.

Peter B Tidball was at the Marquee

Nowadays we would be watching on a large screen, miles away. It all seemed so much more real in those times. It was a feeling that I have never forgotten, as the vibration from Jack Bruce's bass filled my whole body, with my stomach vibrating in unison. What music! I couldn't believe the musicianship of all three, each one supreme in their field. Jack playing bass so tunefully, Ginger awesome, and Eric's lead guitar like nothing I have ever heard before. The gig ended with the encore of 'I'm So Glad'. I've been replaying the songs in my mind.

I also saw them when they played Ramsgate's Supreme Ballroom in July 1967. I was with my dad, fishing, at the same time as all three members of the greatest group in the world were walking on the opposite side of the road, having a breather. I left them in peace. I didn't hear them that time, but just seeing them was an awesome experience.

GRANDE BALLROOM
8 DECEMBER 1967, DETROIT, MICHIGAN

I WAS THERE: BOB BURWELL

MY GROUP WILSON Mower Pursuit played for the first time at the Grande Ballroom in Detroit, opening for Moby Grape. We opened our set with the Cream song, 'Tales of Brave Ulysses'. Our lead guitar Paul Frank Koschtial is a born-perfect pitch, and along with his wah-wah pedal, nailed Clapton's guitar part. Hearing this from their office, Grande founder Russ Gibb and manager Tom Wright jumped up and ran out to see what was happening, as they were sure that Cream had shown up two weeks early by mistake.

Cream return to the United States on 11 December 1967 to record more material at Atlantic Studios in New York.

The band Bob Burwell (far right) was in, fooled the Grande's management into thinking Cream had arrived two weeks early!

GRANDE BALLROOM
22 – 24 DECEMBER 1967, DETROIT, MICHIGAN

I WAS THERE: BOB ADCOCK, CREAM'S TOUR MANAGER

THE VERY FIRST time we ever played the Grande in Detroit, Mick Turner and I went to see it. Mick Turner was the stage manager who also Ginger's drum tech and he'd been with hm from the days of the Graham Bond Organisation. And he used to be a professional wrestler at one point in his life. We drove down to check out the gig and parked opposite in a really rough part of town. Although it was a white kids' rock club it was right in the middle of the ghetto. And as we got out of the car a carload of black guys got out, about four or five of them with a knife, and we got mugged by the guy with the knife. Not that we gave up anything. We had a bit of a battle with them. That was our introduction to Detroit.

Cream returned home to the UK on Christmas Day 1967.

INDUSTRIAL CLUB
5 JANUARY 1968, NORWICH, UK

I WAS THERE: PETE GOODRUM

THE PLACE WOULD change its name to the Melody Rooms but it was still The Industrial Club when Cream played there. It wasn't unusual for the club to book big names, but as I recall the Cream gig was put on on a Friday night, at short notice, as opposed to being a Saturday night big attraction. So many of us spent so much time in that club, on week nights and at weekends.

Pete Goodrum saw Cream at Norwich's Industrial Club

The band were in their stride by then and 'Strange Brew' had been out as a single in the previous summer. I remember that they had only just returned from the USA before coming to Norwich. I definitely remember the place feeling even more crowded than usual. What they played was more complex than most other bands at the time. Clapton in particular was hugely admired. They still had that aura, that concept, of being a 'supergroup'. Seeing three men, on the same stage, and knowing that their joint histories covered The Graham Bond Organisation and John Mayall's Bluesbreakers - that's without the Yardbirds - was exciting. It was about credibility, even if Bruce had 'gone commercial' by being in Manfred Mann for a while.

My overriding memory of the gig has to be Ginger Baker. I'd never heard drumming like that before. There were times when he seemed to be producing more sounds, more beats and more rhythm from his feet than any other drummer could produce from both feet and both hands. He was mesmerising. What he played was complicated, bordering on jazz in its freedom and improvisation, and yet it still keyed the band in to the beat. The timing. We'd heard him on Cream records but on stage he was breathtaking.

I WAS THERE: PETER WATT
THEY HAD JUST come off their first US tour, and sounded great in the intimate setting of the Industrial Club. Clapton had permed his hair and it was tied back with a sailor's bow, plus he had a droopy moustache. Ginger's cymbals had rivets in them and several stands had more than one cymbal on them. I've never seen a drum kit like it.

I WAS THERE: MARTIN BOOTH
I USED TO go to gigs on my trusty Honda 50. I was definitely at the Cream gig at the Industrial Club in 1968. They were brilliant but I can only remember that they were on the stage on the left, which had the go-go girl cages.

Martin Booth remembers going to the gig on his Honda 50 - and the cages for the go-go girls

I WAS THERE: TREVOR ANDERSON
GINGER LOOKED LIKE a wild man but boy could he smack the drums. Clapton had a Russian fur hat on. We'd seen Cream and Hendrix in Spalding the year before and got the full deal, with Jimi setting fire to the guitar and playing it with his teeth.

I WAS THERE: ANN CROUCHER

I HAD A terrible cold, so apologies to everyone I must have spread it to, and felt awful but I was determined to go. I was standing quite near the front and remember that drum solo because Ginger Baker had a halo of sweat flying off him. I didn't realise at the time how lucky we were to see so many terrific acts in Norwich.

I WAS THERE: JOHN FIELDER

GINGER'S DRUM SOLO was probably the most memorable part of the evening for me too. We were mesmerised.

I WAS THERE: TIM CLAREY

GINGER'S DRUM SOLO seemed to go on for over five minutes! He looked shattered at the end but then again he always looked that way. I seem to remember a pretty full Industrial Club that night, with the dance floor packed!

I WAS THERE: JOHN WALLER

THEY WERE AMAZING. I'd never heard or felt such sounds before. Ginger Baker's drumming was thunderous, Jack Bruce's bass and voice dynamic - and Clapton? Truly incredible. It was fantastic. Only The Nice were comparable in my experience.

I WAS THERE: SUSIE GREAVES, AGE 15

I REMEMBER BEING right in front of them. I was with my first boyfriend who was really into them. I'd not heard of them until then. As an impressionable 15-year-old I went on to be a big fan.

I WAS THERE: DAVID PASK

IT WAS THE only time I saw Cream but I have seen Eric about 30 times live since, including the annual pilgrimage to the Albert Hall where he used to play every year. I saw many bands of the time at the Industrial Club and the Orford Cellar in Norwich, which was famous for bringing big names like Hendrix, Clapton and The Who to name but three - and the venue was pretty small!

COATHAM HOTEL
14 JANUARY 1968, REDCAR, UK

I WAS THERE: TONY REAY

I WENT TO the Coatham Hotel in Redcar, a seaside town on the bitterly cold North East coast, to see Cream play again, having already been to every concert I could manage by this, by far my favourite band. Redcar was close to home (my parent's house) and the venue was a small club in the mini ballroom of the hotel. The fire limit was probably 200 people, although I'm sure there were half as many again that night.

My mate Chris and I hitched from our respective parents' homes and got there early, which is why and how we were at the load-in entrance when the band's equipment arrived. We asked if they needed a hand with the gear which they gratefully accepted, and we lugged the amps and speakers and Ginger's drum cases along the dark and narrow hallway into the main room and heaved them all onto the low stage.

We stayed until the last echo of the last note

The gig itself was wonderful, maybe one of their best in the early UK days, and we stayed until the last echo of the last note. And then a little while longer. We spotted the man who had 'allowed' us to load in the gear and asked him if we could help him take it all back out again, and while talking to him Eric walked over and offered us each a guitar pick and shook our hands as we assured him how fabulous the band had been. In retrospect, it was probably one of their finest gigs ever. Before the endless full volume noodling and soulless jamming took precedent over tight and tasteful solos, they were an unbelievably advanced band, a unique and innovative blend of blues and jazz, and in this small hall they had every opportunity to expand and expound on their own living experiment.

TOP RANK
19 JANUARY 1968, BRIGHTON, UK

I WAS THERE: RICHARD BATES

I STILL HAVE memories of this gig, maybe because of the very attractive girl I was with and who claims to be in the picture on the cover of *Disraeli Gears*. I remember the large stage with massive amps, Jack Bruce wailing the night away and us hanging over the balcony watching the gig. I also did one of the original farewell shows at the Royal Albert Hall and I was always amused that so many people said 'I was at the first farewell' when there were twice as many shows for the 2005 reunion and half the first timers probably didn't go in 2005, including me!

ST. MARYS COLLEGE
27 JANUARY 1968, TWICKENHAM, LONDON, UK

I WAS THERE: CHRISTOPHER BAGGOTT, AGE 18

WE WERE RIGHT on the edge of the stage and we were so close we could have touched them. Ginger Baker did his drum solo on 'Crossroads', which lasted around 15 minutes. It was just out of this world. It was amazing because they were so famous but it was like a club gig. And we were drinking Newcastle Pale Ale out of the bottle then, which you cannot get nowadays. They were good days.

I WAS THERE: ANNE REYERSBACH

I SAW CREAM at the Saville Theatre in July 1967 and again at St Mary's College, Twickenham. I also went to the first of the two farewell concerts, which Tony Palmer filmed. Between The Beatles and Cream, you had the Rolling Stones, John Mayall and The Who. They were all edgier and rougher than The Beatles, who were pretty sanitised by comparison. The Swinging Sixties didn't start off edgy, but became so very quickly and by '67 it was. I was 16 or 17 and of course it was just sex really. When Robert Plant said 'squeeze my lemon, babe' there was no doubt what he was talking about. It wasn't subtle. It was extraordinarily loud music, brilliantly played, that went through you. My mother must have spent the entire time in a state of complete worry about what was going to happen to me. I lived in Pinner in north west London and somehow I had to get home from Twickenham. I had a friend with me and I can't remember how we did it.

They were quite spectacularly talented. Those basslines that Jack Bruce pumped out, and those drum solos and the guitar solos. They were just amazing. They must have been hugely influenced by jazz to do all that improvisation. They looked fabulous too. Eric had that very, very curly hair and extremely tight velvet bell-bottomed trousers. And they wore interesting waistcoats. They were each idiosyncratically turned out and conscious of their image.

The lyrics were really interesting too. I was also into poetry - Brian Patten, Michael Horovitz, Roger McGough, Adrian Henri and Pete Brown. Pete came to my 'nice' girls school to do a reading and after that he started seeing one of my friends. So I vaguely knew the guy who wrote the lyrics. I was deeply impressed by this. And I knew the woman that Pete Brown wrote 'White Room' for, Elyse Dodgson, because I later worked with her.

The music was loud, the lyrics inaudible, but it was stunning

Going to the Albert Hall for the farewell concert was a much more mainstream thing to do. I was going to the Albert Hall anyway for the Proms. I remember going to Way In, which was a very trendy boutique in Harrods, before a prom to buy a copy of *Wheels of Fire*. I arrived at the Albert Hall and met some of the promenaders, who I knew, and they did not understand that you could listen to Eric Clapton and Johann Sebastian Bach. I remember thinking then how that was really small-minded. If you liked it, you liked it.

I wondered why I liked them so much. I think that even at the age of 16 I knew they were consummate musicians. I had been brought up on classical music - Kathleen Ferrier, Bach and Handel. At the same time as I was going to gigs, I was going to the Proms and to musicals - *My Fair Lady*, *Fiddler on the Roof!* I have always loved talent, even then. I had no idea that Eric, Jack and Ginger were coked up or whatever - and if I had known, I wouldn't have cared. The music was loud and the lyrics pretty inaudible and incomprehensible but it was stunning. I bought the albums and listened as much as I could - I had won a record player on *Take Your Pick!* I still have the albums. One of my *Desert Island Discs* is 'Layla'. Like so much of Cream's output it is immediately recognisable from the opening chords.

I was in floods of tears when Cream split up

I was in floods of tears when Cream split up but headed off the day before my English 'A' level to see Blind Faith in Hyde Park. I used to have one of Ginger Baker's drum sticks. I don't remember how I got it. He might have thrown it out into the audience. It was a treasured possession for quite a long time, but my mother had a clear out and threw it out, along with all my original copies of Time Out and Spare Rib - all the things I would really have like her to keep

TECHNICAL COLLEGE
2 FEBRUARY 1968, NOTTINGHAM, UK

I WAS THERE: MARTIN DYER, AGE 20
I WAS AT university. I was already a fan of Clapton who I had discovered when he was in John Mayall's band. But I hadn't heard of the other two until that night. I'm afraid all I remember is how exciting they were, particularly Baker's drumming. I remember thinking I was witnessing something really important. I'm not sure I can remember much else. But I've never forgotten it. I would never have thought then that the songs they played that night would still be played regularly 50 years later.

CARNIVAL '68, UNIVERSITY COLLEGE
3 FEBRUARY 1968, LONDON, UK

I WAS THERE: LINDA JAY
WHEN I ATTENDED the sixth form of Hornsey School for Girls in north London, a friend obtained tickets to see the Cream. As far as I remember they performed at the UCL in London. It was a small venue - a college hall - and all that separated us from them was a small rope barrier.

Linda Jay remembers just a small rope barrier between her and the stage

I was close enough to have touched them, particularly Eric Clapton. My stand out memory is the very long drum solo by Ginger Baker.

I WAS THERE: PHIL WILLS

I WAS A student at the time. As it was the biggest college, the union could afford to book the best groups and it cost 2/6d each Saturday. We had a lot of big acts, including Quo, the Bonzos, Move, Julie Driscoll, Pentangle, The Tremeloes, Alan Price and Geno Washington. Cream were 15 shillings. They played under the dome of UCL. People were hanging from the rafters so to speak and so it was difficult to see much. I remember they played 'I Feel Free' and 'Crossroads'.

I WAS THERE: DAVE POPLE

I ATTENDED WITH my Scottish fellow student who was totally addicted to them. It took place in a basement room which was completely inappropriate for the huge crowd that turned up on the night.

I thought my hearing had been affected

The organisers were taken by surprise and it looked as if the concert would be cancelled at the behaviour of all the students, standing on tables. The room was overcrowded and noisy. Somehow it started. I was right at the front, a foot away from Eric Clapton and one of the huge amps. The volume in that room with a low ceiling was unbelievable. My fellow student reckoned it was the best night of his life and was on a high for days afterwards. As for myself, I remember Ginger Baker sweating profusely and looking really ill and I thought my hearing had been affected.

I WAS THERE: TOM THATCHER

WE WERE NOT starved of bands in those years. My diary from 1968 reads like a who's who of musicians of the day, under the heading 'Bands Seen':
Sat 20th January - Aynsley Dunbar Retaliation
Friday 2nd February - Savoy Brown and Jethro Tull
Saturday 3rd February - Cream
Tuesday 20th February - Jeff Beck Group

Sun 25th February - Peter Green's Fleetwood Mac
Friday 1st March - Savoy Brown and Chicken Shack
Saturday 2nd March - Peter Green's Fleetwood Mac
Friday 25th March - Savoy Brown
Saturday 16th March - Aynsley Dunbar Retaliation
… and so on!

Gwyneth, a close friend from Salisbury, was doing a medical degree at University College London, called me to say that Cream were playing at the Union but that it was not publicised at all as it was the University Annual Ball and would I like a ticket? The support bands were The Millionaires, The Soundtrekkers and Two of Each. Until recently, I had the only surviving ticket from this gig, which was barely even known about, and I still have the university paper write up, which barely mentions the band.

Here's what I wrote in my diary: 'Strangely enough, I did not get too knocked out by Cream's performance. They seemed like three very tired people running out of inspiration.' Sadly, I can still remember how lifeless the performance seemed. They were in completely the wrong place - I guess that the organisers had wanted a 'popular' band - and the long jams were tired and wearing. But, while saying that, they were still about five times better than most other bands could dream of by a light year! I slept on someone's floor that night and hitched home early for work on a sheep farm on Monday.

OWENS UNION BUILDING, UNIVERSITY OF MANCHESTER
10 FEBRUARY 1968, MANCHESTER, UK

I WAS THERE: KEITH MULLARD
I SAW THEM at Manchester University with Jethro Tull in support. I had seen Hendrix at Sheffield City Hall a couple of weeks earlier so it was a good comparison. Admission was six shillings (30p). When I came into the hall Tull were already playing. But then I turned around and saw everyone was looking at the other end of the hall where the main stage was. They had Triumph PA speakers that were never that good. But Cream came on and it was good. Great bass playing, great vocals and the

guitar playing was perhaps not Jimi but it was tight and worked well with the band. Ginger was Ginger and played a great solo. All in all, it was a great show and well worth the six shillings!

I WAS THERE: MICHAEL KINGSLAND

IT WAS JUST an amazing night. I remember asking one of the roadies which mic Clapton would be standing at. All this went on as other road crew nailed Ginger's drum kit to the stage to stop it moving forward. They opened with 'Tales of Brave Ulysses' from *Disraeli Gears*. It was a fabulous gig. Clapton's cherry SG tone is burned into my memory.

Keith Mullard (second right) saw Cream supported by Jethro Tull for 30p

I WAS THERE: BILLY LYDIATE

I SAW ERIC with John Mayall at the Oasis Club in Manchester and with Blind Faith at Hyde Park. And I loved Cream. That night at the students' union was excellent, with us being right at the front to watch them - and all for six bob (30p)!

Cream arrive in New York on 12 February 1968 for a week of recording before embarking upon their second full North American tour.

I WAS THERE: BOB ADCOCK, CREAM'S TOUR MANAGER

THE DIFFERENCE FOR me was the way Cream toured with so few people. Before 1973 and the oil crisis, the airlines operated totally differently. Every time you got on a plane it was never more than half full wherever you were going. That meant that you never had a problem taking amps and drums with you on the plane. I didn't handle that. Mick Turner and Bruce McCaskill did. The two roadies handled all the gear. So they would turn up at the airport. They'd take all that equipment on the plane as excess baggage and in most instances weren't even charged for it. This meant there were no limits to where you could tour. We often did New York on Monday and then be in LA on Friday, Miami Saturday, Vancouver Sunday. If the airplanes went there you could go.

Cream were the last band to tour the States without their own sound and light. This made a huge difference. The sound system and the lighting system were always provided by the promoter. When Cream split up, that all changed. Bands like Led Zeppelin started taking their own equipment on the road, their own sound and their own lights, which had a big benefit to them because they had the same systems every night. But it meant you couldn't schedule two gigs that were more than a couple of hundred miles apart because the trucks couldn't get there. So all that long touring that we did with Cream from coast to coast suddenly ended overnight.

Cream were the last band to tour the States without their own sound and light

And you couldn't tour with three crew. You started getting 20 crew. And instead of doing it with a panel truck then you'd need three or four artics. It's developed and nowadays people tour with their own stages. Taylor Swift has just (2019) done an American tour using over 100 trucks because they take their own stage with them. It's like trying to organise an army. But we were still doing the same sized gigs as Taylor Swift, just with a lot fewer people.

'SUNSHINE OF YOUR LOVE' RELEASED
FEBRUARY 1968

An edited version of the track on Disraeli Gears is released as a single in the US. It reaches number 5 in the charts. 'Sunshine of Your Love' is not released until September 1968 in Britain, where it charts at number 25.

CIVIC AUDITORIUM
23 FEBRUARY 1968, SANTA MONICA, CALIFORNIA

I WAS THERE: SCOTT WHITE, AGE 17
WE WERE GOING to see a called The Hook (formerly known as The Leaves, they did 'Hey Joe' before Jimi). We drove by all the clubs on the Strip in Hollywood - the Hullabaloo, the Palladium, Pandora's Box and the Whisky A Go-Go - and on the Whisky's marquee my buddy saw 'Cream' in big letters. We all looked at each other and pretty much said, 'Who the hell

is Cream?' At that time, we had no idea. A few months later we caught them at the Santa Monica Civic, a fairly small venue with a seating capacity of about 3,000. The opening acts were the Electric Prunes and Steppenwolf. It was a killer show. They came back later in '68 and played the Anaheim Convention Center. Spirit opened for them then, and we could only get seats behind the stage. We didn't give a shit as long as we were there. They were - and are - the best trio ever and are responsible for some of Clapton's best work, next to the *Beano* album.

Scott White saw the Civic Auditorium show

I WAS THERE: IRA KNOPF

THE CREAM GIGS I got to see were all in 1968, and I still have the ticket stubs and programmes. I saw two shows in one night at Santa Monica. The first show set list was 'Tales of Brave Ulysses', 'Sunshine of Your Love', 'Steppin' Out', 'Traintime' and 'Toad' while the second show set list was 'NSU', 'Sunshine of Your Love', 'We're Going Wrong', 'Steppin' Out', 'Traintime', 'Toad' and 'I'm So Glad'. Clapton used The Fool SG and Jack his EB-O bass. Both shows sold out. The opening acts were Penny Nichols (first show only) and Steppenwolf. They were loud and clear and each show went off without any tech problems.

Ira Knopf with Ginger

EARL WARREN SHOWGROUNDS
24 FEBRUARY 1968, SANTA BARBARA, CALIFORNIA

I WAS THERE: BRUCE REED

IN MOVING TO a new town in the summer of 1966 I made friends with a musician and rabid collector of English rock music albums. This was a new world to me and I was immediately attracted to the music of the Yardbirds and Cream. In the US, *Fresh Cream* was released before John Mayall and the Bluesbreakers and I was stunned by their powerful sound and the guitar playing of Eric Clapton.

I was already a huge fan and well acquainted with the music of Cream by the time I first saw them at the Earl Warren Showgrounds Exhibit Hall, a small venue in Santa Barbara, California. The small hall had

Bruce Reed was already a fan before he saw Cream

a flat concrete floor (there was no seating) and constructed temporary plywood stages for the concerts that were periodically held there, usually by a local promoter named Jim Salzer. Taking advantage of being approximately an hour and a half away from Los Angeles, Salzer wisely tapped into the availability of major rock acts appearing in Los Angeles during national tours.

Eric lit up the longest cigarette I had ever seen

Upon entering the hall, I quickly worked my way to a place in front of where I knew Eric Clapton would be situated, to Ginger's left. I patiently listened to the fantastic opening acts, James Cotton Blues Band and Taj Mahal and his band, but wiggled (standing only!) even closer to the stage when they finished. Since photographs of the bands were few and far between in those days, I was mesmerised when seeing Eric, sporting long hair and a thick moustache, take the stage holding his brightly painted (later named) 'Fool' SG.

They plugged into their twin Marshall stacks, tuned up and quickly launched into music so powerful that I was stunned. I was 20 feet away from my idol and soaked it all in. As Ginger launched into his solo in 'Toad' I recall seeing Eric light up what was the longest cigarette I had ever seen - a dark, thin, 100mm 'European' one - and crouch down beside his amp to patiently watch. When the solo was finished, he slowly stood up and ended the song as the crowd went nuts.

Cream had not yet achieved the enormous popularity they would soon have, so the relatively small crowd that night appeared to know each song and appreciated every note. Jack's amazing voice cut through the wall of sound and Ginger's powerful playing was met with yells and shouts all through the show. Eric's guitar playing was other worldly and surpassed my already high expectations of what I hoped I would hear. I went away that night with a huge smile on my face and, after vowing to never play my guitar again, will always clearly remember what I saw, felt, and heard.

I WAS THERE: ROB JORGENSEN
THE STAGE WAS about one foot high and we were close enough to touch them - but didn't. The light show was very rudimentary with an overhead projector. It was an amazing experience!

Between 29 February and 10 March 1968, Cream played a clutch of shows at the Winterland Ballroom and Fillmore Auditorium in San Francisco.

WINTERLAND
29 FEBRUARY - 2 MARCH & 8 - 10 MARCH 1968

FILLMORE AUDITORIUM
3 & 7 MARCH 1978, SAN FRANCISCO, CALIFORNIA

I WAS THERE: BRIAN STEARNS
I HAD ONLY been out of the Navy six months. I went to the first Winterland concert. We were so stoned that night everything seems completely surreal. When Ginger Baker broke out into a solo it went on for almost an hour. Eric Clapton and Jack Bruce went off stage. They

also did this in the second concert that I saw. Ginger Baker was on fire that night, and then when Eric Clapton and Jack Bruce came back out on stage, they were high as a kite and the concert just exploded. There were so many people in the Winterland and everybody seem to be moving completely in sync to the rhythm!

I WAS THERE: SAMUEL PASSO
I WAS VISITING my cousin's wedding. It was surreal for us Indiana Hoosier teenagers. We heard Ginger Baker on drums, in front of a large stage, with lots of psychedelic lights. Most of the other guests were too stoned to talk to us. So we left!

I WAS THERE: PETER POHLE
THE VENUE WAS in the shape of a rectangle. Two sides were screened off. When setting up for Cream to play next the screens were blue and green, resembling the earth. When they started playing the screens erupted with an assortment of colours. It was like a volcano eruption, but with the earth exploding. Their performance surpassed their recordings. When Ginger Baker did his drum solo he played a portion with his hands and at the end, he threw up his hands and they appeared bloody.

I WAS THERE: ELLEN ATKINS
I KNEW I had to be there when they came back. Bill Graham set it up at Winterland. You didn't have the intimacy of the Fillmore, but Cream blew the roof off the place even better because Winterland was so huge and their music filled it up. As incredibly cool as Winterland was, I liked the acoustics, the darkness and the intimacy of the Fillmore better, maybe it was because it was the first time I saw them, and because we felt like we were jamming with them. Winterland was more brightly lit and felt more commercial, but their performance there was still outstanding, with a lot of people still jamming. I still love Cream's music - play it loud!

I WAS THERE: KENNETH LISS
I SAW CREAM at Winterland and then at the larger Oakland Coliseum. At the Winterland show they were a well-oiled blues machine. Jack Bruce's vocals were amazing as was Ginger Baker's drumming and Clapton's guitar playing was perfect. The Oakland Coliseum show wasn't as good,

mainly because Bruce's vocals were shrill all night long. He must have been whacked out of his mind on something. Even though it paled by comparison to the first time I saw them - hey, it was still Cream!

I WAS THERE: REBECCA ANNE, AGE 15/16

I REMEMBER THEIR first song starting and then the LSD kicked in (hey - it was the Sixties!) I remember snatches of stuff like how smooth Clapton's playing was and how bone-thin Ginger Baker was but not much else. But I do remember how awed I was by their sound. And I can still hear it in my head. I was definitely out without permission. I felt the music wash over me, it felt transcendent. I went to another place - me, the music, and heaven. For a while, Ginger looked like he was on fire, drumming his heart out. I've been a fan ever since, and I'm now almost 70!

I WAS THERE: GARY WASSERMAN, AGE 19

THEY WERE AMAZING - Ginger becoming one with two drum kits, Jack Bruce making his bass sing and Eric, with knee high boots and a ruffled shirt, looking like he was channelling a swashbuckling pirate. The visual was electric and the music was crazy powerful. I loved Fillmore. I think we saw everyone of the guitar heroes of the day. When Ginger commenced his drum solos it felt like time stood still. The band was a perfect blend of musicality, energy, talent and visual presence that owned the venue. The Sixties were magical and Nor Cal from Sacramento to Big Basin were magical for this young man.

Gary Wasserman was at the Fillmore

Eric looked like he was channelling a swashbuckling pirate

I WAS THERE: KATHLEEN VAN VELSOR

AN OLD FRIEND, Janet Perez, and I caught a Cream performance at either Fillmore West or Winterland in 1968. She usually drove us in her Karmann Ghia up from the peninsula. There were times when we hadn't heard any recordings prior to a performance and this was one. I recall that we were both surprised at the hard edge and hard driving quality of the band. We were literally and figuratively blown away. The sound was so huge that I think we counted the racks of amps and at one point thought about asking the sound managers to dial it back a bit. Although they didn't connect well with the audience, Cream certainly left an impression.

I WAS THERE: PHIL MONTALVO

I WAS A junior in high school and this was the first *Bill Graham Presents* concert I attended. *Fresh Cream* had a lot of airplay on the underground radio station, KMPX FM. All my friends were buzzing about the blues guitar of Eric Clapton and the drumming of Ginger Baker. Upon entering Winterland, my senses were overwhelmed in this cathedral of music. Sweet smells of incense and the pungent smells of marijuana permeated the air. Visually, the light show pulsed with swirling patterns in rhythm with the music. My memory was that Jeremy and Satyrs were the first band to play and a jazz band also opened the concert. Bill Graham was prescient to often include jazz and authentic blues musicians along with the rock bands of the day. All I remember is the soaring flute solos by Jeremy Steig and being anxious to see Cream. James Cotton was up next and he startled the crowd by forcefully hitting the mic to start off his set, as if to say, 'Pay attention, y'all.'

Cream finally entered the stage. I cannot remember which songs were played but I wanted to hear 'Spoonful', 'I'm So Glad', 'I Feel Free' and 'Rollin' and Tumblin'.' I remember 'Toad' as being this drumming tour de force, and never having seen a double bass drum set as pioneered by jazz drummer Louie Bellson. I was awe struck by this band and my only regret was not staying to see Blood, Sweat & Tears.

I WAS THERE: TOM HENNEBERRY

I WAS IN London for much of 1966. I missed Jimi Hendrix and Cream but saw the Spencer Davis Group, Manfred Mann and the Yardbirds at the Marquee in Soho and also, thanks to my girlfriend, the Stones, Animals and Yardbirds (again) live on the jaw-dropping *Ready Steady Go*. I loved reading *Melody Maker*, *New Musical Express*, *Disc* and *Music Echo* to keep up with the beat groups. I caught Cream the second go round on March 8, 1968 with James Cotton and Blood, Sweat & Tears. The band was loud and powerful, and I became a disciple immediately. Winterland was a fairly small arena so the sound was thundering, and the band was firing on all cylinders.

The band was firing on all cylinders

They focused on tracks such as 'I Feel Free', 'I'm So Glad' and a stupendous 'Spoonful', a highlight for me. The Jack Bruce - Eric Clapton tandem was earthshaking, along with Ginger Baker keeping perfect time on the skins. I had never seen a power trio before (they were the first), and I was blown away. Three months later, I witnessed the Jimi Hendrix Experience at the Monterey Pop Festival and my year was made....

I WAS THERE: JOHN ELDRIDGE

WHAT YEAR WAS it? '67? '68? Damn those drugs. They were loud. At the time I was more interested in hanging out and milling about. What I remember most was riding on the back of my friend's Lambretta, right in front of the concert, and him pulling out in front of a big Cadillac with a big bullet chrome bumper. That memory will always be with me!

I WAS THERE: GREG LIMA

WHEN CREAM CAME back through for the second time, they were huge and so were Bill Graham's shows. He began holding his Friday and Saturday shows at Winterland because of its much greater capacity. They were again there for two weeks in a row. I know I went twice but one was much more memorable. This time Cream was clearly the headliner, which meant they would play third and sixth. After the second band the crowd was getting ramped up (we had all come to see Cream) when Bill Graham came out and announced that Ginger Baker was caught up in the Haight and he was going to bring out the first two bands again and that Cream would do a super long session at the end. So the first two bands played again and then they set up for Cream. They came out and played in their usual dynamite way and then after what would amount to one normal length session they waved and walked off. The crowd, which had been applauding the last song, fell silent. We all just stood there slowly taking in the fact that they were done and we'd been 'brutally' misled. By this time in concert evolution, encores for the headliner were standard fare but on that night there was no encore. We all just stood. I don't even remember anyone bitching or yelling, just stunned silence. After a few minutes we turned and headed towards the exits. There was little talking going on but one could just feel everyone in the crowd muttering a silent 'fuck you' as they were leaving.

I WAS THERE: STEPHEN P LEAR

I GREW UP listening to rock and roll and then to surf music in Southern California, specifically Dick Dale and the Deltones and the Centurions, who my brother played rhythm guitar for. During my time in the service, I started listening to bands like the Temptations, Smokey Robinson and the Miracles and even James Brown. My brother-in-law lived in San Francisco and he was that one who got us into that Cream concert. It was definitely a different experience, and my first introduction to the psychedelic era. It still took me a year or two after that before I bought my first pair of bellbottoms, but my wife and I decorated the stairway in our apartment with concert posters and we definitely had one from Cream.

I WAS THERE: CRAIG BRADSHAW

I WAS AT both the Fillmore and at Winterland. I mostly remember the lovely redheaded woman that accompanied me. Their stage versions were different from the studio versions as Eric used little of the wah-wah on songs like 'Sweet Wine' that he employed in the studio.

I WAS THERE: DAVE RAMPTON, AGE 24

I WAS AT the Winterland performance 1968. We, four 'flower sailors' unfortunately still in the Navy, had to make a decision - Cream, which we had only heard of via a single speaker FM radio, or Blue Cheer at the Avalon Ballroom. We went with Cream and were blown away.

I WAS THERE: JOHN KORNIS, AGE 19

I WAS IN Radar School in the US Navy, stationed on Treasure Island in 1968. A shipmate, Tony Sutton, and I went to Winterland. I'm sure it was less than $5 to get in - remember, we were on Navy pay. Cream were just hitting their stride. We'd never seen a group like this. It was totally eye opening. Lots of grass was being smoked and I'll assume other drugs but it was a friendly atmosphere. There was a light show going on behind the bands as they played. The whole concert was late into the night. 'Toad' was like nothing I'd seen and the blues played like this set a standard still unmatched. Later that year I saw them in San Diego with my girlfriend, now my wife. It was more of a set concert, and not as free flowing as Winterland with all the hippies and love children.

John Kornis was in the Navy when he saw Cream

I WAS THERE: BOB ADCOCK, CREAM'S TOUR MANAGER

BILL GRAHAM WAS absolutely fantastic, the best promoter I've ever worked with. He made the changes. He was a tough guy to deal with but if you'd done deal with him, he always stuck by it. He cared so much about the artists and the public. He wanted to put on the best show possible. He wanted it to run smoothly. His standards of professionalism changed the business. He brought in running orders and specific time slots for bands, the hospitality in the dressing room, towels - all this kind of thing that nobody else was doing. Every other promoter was there to make money and nothing else. If you made money for them, they liked you and you got on well with them. If you didn't make money for them, they ignored you. There was no comparison between Bill Graham and all the others. There were a few exceptions on the east coast - Barry Fey and a handful of others, but you could live without the rest. I remember standing on the steps of the Fillmore East in New York when he took his belt off to about 12 hardened Hell's Angels and drove them out of the foyer of the Fillmore East on his own. That takes balls, that does. He was a very tough guy but very fair.

Bill Graham was the best promoter I ever worked with

The nearest we ever got to security was Bill Graham's gigs where he had t-shirted security as opposed to, in those days, usually somebody from a Mafia movie or someone in suits and ties. Bill introduced t-shirted security but it wasn't to protect the band. It was because right in front of the stage was a wide alley where people couldn't stand. And if they did, he risked losing his licence. So he had t-shirts for security which said 'don't stand in the aisle' and these guys would patrol that aisle to keep people out. Nowadays you have big meetings with the head of security and you spend an hour discussing the gig with them beforehand and there's 50 or 60 of them at the average gig. But then? There was none. But nothing ever went on inside the gig which needed security. We were always able to cope with whatever went on.

I WASN'T THERE: PAUL BURKE, AGE 13

I WAS JUST a bit too young when the Cream played the Fillmore. There were people I knew that saw them and described to me those early shows on that first tour. I was a major Cream freak though. If you've never been to the original Fillmore Auditorium, it's a really small room with an 800 person capacity. Bill Graham packed 2,000 people in there for Cream. I only wish I could go back in time and witness the recording of *Wheels of Fire* at the Fillmore, and at Winterland two blocks away.

The double album Wheels of Fire was released with four tracks recorded live - 'Toad' was taken from the 3 March 1968 show at the Fillmore and the remaining three tracks from the 10 March performance at Winterland.

SELLAND ARENA
13 MARCH 1968, FRESNO, CALIFORNIA

I WAS THERE: BOB GRANFLATEN

1968 WAS FILLED with turmoil in America. Early in that year the war in Vietnam raged on with no apparent end in sight, social unrest and student protests in response to the war dominated the evening news, and racial strife continued unabated. Against this backdrop for me was the refuge of music and an explosion of groundbreaking American and British rock-and-roll bands touring the states. One of the many bands I saw live in concert that year, while I was in my junior year of college, was Cream. I loved both their albums to that point, *Fresh Cream* and *Disraeli Gears*, and when word began to spread that the band would perform in concert in my college town, Fresno, California, I jumped at the chance to see the show.

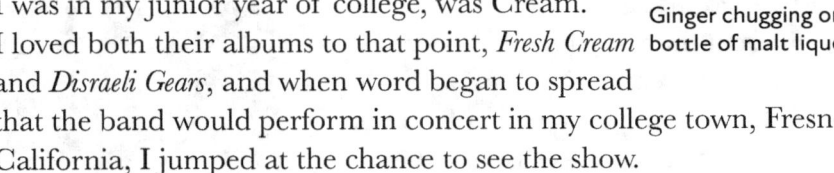
Bob Granflaten recalls Ginger chugging on a bottle of malt liquor

The band would perform in a show billed as 'England's No. 1 Concert Group' at Fresno's Selland Arena. A San Francisco band, Blue Cheer (likely named for a variety of LSD popular at the time), opened for the headliners. A light show by Ben Van Meter's North American Ibis Alchemical Co of San Francisco illuminated the stage as the bands played. Tickets were $3.50 a head.

My college buds and I were fortunate to snag seats very close to the front row, and we could see the performers' every move and facial expression as they pounded out their tunes. That long ago, I can't say for certain every song that Eric Clapton, Jack Bruce and Ginger Baker performed that night, but I'm pretty sure that they included 'Sunshine of Your Love' and 'Tales of Brave Ulysses'. One clear recollection is that Ginger had a can of Olde English 800 malt liquor squirreled away in his drum set that he would chug on between songs.

Cream were outstanding that night, one of the best live shows I was ever lucky enough to attend. Blue Cheer put on a great show too, that included their biggest single, a cover of Eddie Cochran's 'Summertime Blues'. To this day, I count among my blessings that I had the good fortune to see those legendary power trios live on stage and with such a great vantage point. It's sad that now Ginger Baker and Jack Bruce have passed into rock history and only Eric Clapton remains a living legend. Their show that evening in 1968 is and always will be an enduring memory.

I WAS THERE: CHRIS PEREZ

AT NINE YEARS old, I became a woman when I saw The Beatles on the *Ed Sullivan Show* - seriously! I loved their music. Then I heard John Mayall's Bluesbreakers on the radio and learned to love the blues. Then I heard Cream playing 'Sunshine of Your Love'. This became my new favourite song. I didn't know anything about the band members but I heard they were coming to my town so a friend and I bought a ticket. I realised that much of their music was way different than anything I had ever heard, and not different in the same way, but different in different ways. I couldn't figure out

Chris Perez saw Cream at the Selland Arena

what to call it, but I was mesmerised. It was loud, and I felt as though I was in another world. The standout for me was the guitarist. That sound was amazing! I can't remember whether it was before or after the concert when I first heard that the guy's name was Eric Clapton. I do remember how stoked I was when I found out he was the guitarist from the Bluesbreakers. Cream's unique sound can never be duplicated. Bands can take bits and pieces, they can experiment with Eric's woman tone, they can fuse jazz with sounds from 18th Century Britain, play Ginger's licks or sing like Jack - but no one will ever fully get it.

SHRINE AUDITORIUM
15 MARCH 1968, LOS ANGELES, CALIFORNIA

I WAS THERE: IRA KNOPF

I SAW CREAM play two sets in one night at the Shrine. There was a second night on the 16th but I didn't get to that. The first set was 'NSU', 'Sunshine of Your Love', 'Tales of Brave Ulysses' and 'Sweet Wine' and lasted about an hour. The opening acts were James Cotton and Buffalo Springfield. The second set was 'Spoonful', 'We're Going Wrong', 'Steppin' Out', 'Traintime', 'Toad' and 'I'm So Glad'. They were again loud and clear with no technical problems and they used the same gear as when I'd seen them at Santa Monica Civic. It was a packed house, with very little room to move.

I WAS THERE: DICK SAAR

I SAW CREAM four times, first in San Bernardino, twice at the old Shrine Auditorium in LA and at the farewell concert at the Forum. At the Shrine the James Cotton Blues Band opened for them. During Cream's set I was sitting on the floor with a friend and another guy next to me handed me a joint. I handed it to my friend, back to me, and back to the

Dick Saar doesn't just remember the music from one Cream show he saw

guy who gave it to me, a stranger. That joint went back and forth a few times. There was a person standing between us and I looked up. It was a woman. I realised she was very heavily pregnant, and we were passing the joint back and forth under her fat belly. I thought nothing of that until maybe an hour passed, and someone announced on the house PA, 'Is there a doctor in the house? There's a woman in the bathroom giving birth and needs help!'

There's a woman in the bathroom giving birth and needs help!

Holy shit! It had to be that same woman, had to be. And how cool did that kid turn out, being born at a Cream concert? Years later, I delivered my three kids at home, so I know how that goes. It would be very cool to find that kid....

ANAHEIM CONVENTION CENTER
18 MARCH 1968, ANAHEIM, CALIFORNIA

I WAS THERE: PHIL MONTANO
IT WAS MY summer between sophomore and junior years of high school. In the Sixties, Anaheim Convention Center was the ideal venue for acoustics and viewing the bands on stage. I had previously seen Eric Burdon and the Animals, Jimi Hendrix, Three Dog Night, Spirit and Donovan there. It was 'love ins', peace, love, beach parties and such - a real gas. When the flyer hit Orange County that Cream was playing the Convention Center it sold out quickly. The opening band was a Californian act, Spirit, who had a drummer in Ed Cassidy who was very close to Ginger's drumming skills. 'Sunshine of your Love', 'Tales of Brave Ulysses' - fantastic. But the real highlight was when Ginger Baker and Ed Cassidy, both with double sets, drummed 'Toad' for at least 20 minutes. I'm not sure if it a competition or friendly rivalry but it was intense! The next concert they did was The Who, at which disaster ensued. A riot and fights ended the Convention Center's use as a concert venue.

BELOIT COLLEGE
21 MARCH 1968, BELOIT, WISCONSIN

I WAS THERE: DON DARNUTZER

THE THING I remember the most about Cream's performance at Beloit College was that the band was at least 45 minutes late. I don't think there was an opening act. We had gotten front row seats at the foot of Eric's side of the stage, except there were no seats, only floor to sit on. While waiting for the band to arrive we must have gotten up to walk around and went out to the lobby of the basketball arena where many people were hanging out. All of the sudden the band came walking in the front door of the lobby and was met with stunned silence as they walked through the crowd. Nobody expected to be so close to famous musicians. Ginger Baker had his long red hair pulled to the top of his head and tied into the knot. I got an autograph off Eric but it's been lost to the sands of time. They did a great show of course.

CLOWES MEMORIAL HALL, BUTLER UNIVERSITY
22 MARCH 1968, INDIANAPOLIS, INDIANA

I WAS THERE: GREG GRIFFIN

I HAD DISCOVERED Cream listening to their music on vinyl 33rpm records at IRC Music Store in Indy, where I worked. I went with my girlfriend at the time. Cream put up a wall of sound and people were dancing in the aisles and everyone was blown away by their performance. Clowes Hall stopped allowing rock groups to perform there after that because the audience went crazy and some added to the experience by smoking marijuana. It's the best performance I ever saw and the sound quality was awesome. I also saw them in Chicago, with Frank Zappa and the Mothers of Invention. That was a great concert too.

Greg Griffin saw Cream twice

SHAPIRO ATHLETIC CENTER, BRANDEIS UNIVERSITY
23 MARCH 1968, BOSTON, MASSACHUSETTS

I WAS THERE: HARRY SANDLER

Harry Sandler played in the band that supported Cream at Brandeis University

I PLAYED IN the band Orpheus and opened for them at this show. I became friendly with Cream's road manager, Bob Adcock, and through him Eric, and went with them to many of their North East US concerts at the end of their run as a band. Whenever they were in the north east, they would reach out to me and we'd hang, get high and go to all their shows together. Jack would join us at times - smoking being a strong unifier - and Ginger would be along, but he was less than friendly like the others. We smoked a lot of weed together!

I WAS THERE: DENNIS ROACH

ERIC CLAPTON ALWAYS just hit the right nerve for me. I used to pick up a British magazine that we got over here called Rave and they had an article about the Yardbirds and that introduced me to Eric. About a month later they ran a story about this new band featuring Eric Clapton being formed with Jack Bruce and Ginger Baker. When their material was released here in the United States, I snapped it up right away. I had one of the first copies of *Fresh Cream* in my neighbourhood.

Dennis Roach saw Cream play a very late night show

The first show I saw was at Brandeis University, about ten miles outside Boston. The concert was held in the gymnasium and it was rather a big one. The crowd was really pumped to see the guys. We were enjoying balmy comfortable weather. It was almost hot. But they were delayed in some place like Minnesota or Missouri in a blizzard. Their plane could not take off to come to Boston.

The warm up act did their set and we waited. The people who were running the concert said Cream would be on their way. The warm up act did their set again, and did exactly the same show twice. Cream still hadn't arrived. The light show had two or three silent cartoons - Betty Boop-type stuff - so we watched those and finally we got the word that the plane had been able to take off.

It was a Saturday and as of midnight on Saturday night it was not legal to have the concert in the gymnasium at the school. I don't know if it was the law or the school's rules, but at that point the promoters declared it to be a party and because they weren't charging us admission anymore as a party it was okay to have the show. And we all waited. The entire crowd stayed.

When the announcement went out that there was a crowd waiting for Cream to show up, a local band that was practising at Brandeis University put all their equipment into their truck and brought it over to the gym and played after the warm up act while we were waiting for Cream. Their lead guitar player was really quite good and I was worried that he was so good that I wasn't going to be impressed with Eric! I was dead wrong. As wonderful as this kid was, Eric just blew me away.

At about 3am they started rolling some Marshall amps onto the stage

---

At about 3am they started rolling some Marshall amplifiers onto the stage and we were just elated. When the band hit the stage, they didn't look particularly tired or anything like that. They put on a fantastic show. My girlfriend and I had good seats, and seeing somebody of Eric's calibre so close up was like having ten years' worth of guitar lessons. It's just fabulous to see somebody like that playing and actually see how they do it.

Cream were wonderful that night. I think they played until about 4.35am. It was a wonderful show and they were in fine form. Jack Bruce did 'Train Time' and Baker of course played 'Toad' and they did 'Sunshine of your Love' and 'Tales of Brave Ulysses'.

I WAS THERE: RICHARD STEWART

Richard Stewart had to drop his date back at her college and come back for the show

A FRIEND AND I were in college and we had dates with women from nearby Regis College in Weston, outside of Boston. The opening act was Orpheus, a fairly popular Boston-based band, and they played for what must have been an hour and a half. People were getting a little restless.

Finally, the promoter of the concert went to the mic and said there was a problem. Cream were in Cincinnati. He didn't say what had happened but it sounded like somebody was in poor condition. We got the impression they didn't want to come, and it was already late. But this guy doubled the fee for their appearance and kind of bribed them to leave Cincinnati, even though one or more people were sick or out of it, and during the evening he chronicled the stages they went through to get the band with their equipment and their handlers and technicians to the show.

The promoter told us when they got onto the plane and when they were in the air. That flight would take maybe an hour and a half. They didn't tell us an estimated time of arrival and we wanted to see them, but people had to get back home. The two women we'd brought to the show were living at a Catholic women's college. They had a midnight curfew so my friend and I drove them back to campus. And I stopped by my parents' house to tell them that I wasn't coming home just yet.

Cream turned it up to number 11 on their dials

We went back to Brandeis. A lot of the people who'd been in the audience at eight o'clock had left because they had work or school the next day, so kids went around the campus dorms, waking the students up and saying, 'Hey, there's a free concert in the gym.' All of a sudden a whole bunch of Brandeis kids came pouring in who hadn't paid for a ticket.

Cream did get to Boston, they did come out to the university and they did play. They came on about two o'clock in the morning, or after. They turned it up to number 11 on their dials. It was ear splittingly loud, so loud it was uncomfortable. Do that in a natural amphitheatre and it could be okay, especially if you weren't too close, but this was an arena with exposed steel beams that was built for basketball, not concerts. The acoustics weren't that good.

I always thought Jack Bruce was great on the bass and Ginger Baker a force of nature on the drums. The drum solo in 'Toad' was fun. Seeing them together was exciting. Once they got into it, they seemed to enjoy themselves. But I was a kid using my parents' car. My parents wanted me home at some reasonable time so I stayed at the concert for an hour and a half or so and then had to leave. I think I got home about four in the morning.

I WAS THERE: CARYL WOODFORD

I WAS A student there. Their flight was late and they didn't get to the venue until around 3am, needed food, and didn't start playing until around 4am. A local Boston band opened the show and kept playing as long as they could. But for those of us who waited it out, sitting in the gym, it was worth the wait.

I WAS THERE: BOB ADCOCK, CREAM'S TOUR MANAGER

MOVING CREAM AROUND America was such a different world to today. It wasn't different in as much as three guys would get up on stage and sell out a 20,000 seat arena. But now a 20,000 arena sell out band would have 100 road crew. The whole time the Cream existed, right up to the last day at the Albert Hall, we never had more than three - two equipment guys and me. I was the tour manager and I didn't have a credit card because there weren't any. So simple things like renting cars all had to be paid for in cash. I used to collect the cash from the gigs. Consequently, I'd regularly be running around the States with hundreds of thousands of dollars in my briefcase. You paid for the hotels in cash. You paid car rental in cash. Any expenses went in cash.

Cream never had more than three road crew - two equipment guys and me

UNION CATHOLIC HIGH SCHOOL
26 MARCH 1968, SCOTCH PLAINS, NEW JERSEY

I WAS THERE: KEVIN MCDONOUGH, AGE 15

MY BEST FRIEND, Bobby Allen, turned me on to *Fresh Cream*. We were both sophomore high school students at Union Catholic. The Who and Cream were my two favourite groups, so when I was given a chance to see Cream, I jumped on it! It was general admission - first come, first served - so I intended to get there early to get a good seat. The first few rows of seating were for friends of the band, roadies, wives, girlfriends, groupies, whatever. Most of the concert was from the debut album. They may have introduced some material from their second album. They played in our gym, which was not ideal for acoustics or a light show, but it was a night I'll never forget. The music was incredible and it all seemed over too soon.

Kevin McDonough caught the Scotch Plains show at the Catholic School

I recall being impressed with Eric Clapton's guitar work, but as a drummer myself, I was hypnotically watching and listening to Ginger Baker's unusual style of playing. I had seen Keith Moon play a double bass set a year earlier. I know why they nicknamed him 'Moon the Loon', because he was entertaining to watch. Ginger Baker was polished, playing in an amazing mixture of both jazz and African-style drumming. I never heard anyone like him, not then and not since. When he played 'Toad' it was amazing. I later learned that he taught Keith Moon how to play double bass drums. Everyone pretty much agrees that 'Clapton's God' on guitar. I feel the same about Baker when he plays the drums with Bruce and Clapton!

When Ginger played 'Toad' it was amazing

HUNTER COLLEGE AUDITORIUM
29 MARCH 1968, NEW YORK, NEW YORK

I WAS THERE: ALAN CHILDS

THE THIRD AND last time I saw them was possibly the best Cream concert I attended, at Hunter College. They were way more polished as a band. This is the tour on which the live sides were recorded - on the West coast - for the *Wheels of Fire* LP. I even waited outside the stage door after the show to get a glimpse of them because I was such a fan. My drumming was very influenced by Ginger. I tried to dress like them. I definitely put in over 10,000 hours listening to them and their contemporaries. I eventually played drums for many recording sessions as well as touring with John Waite, Julian Lennon and a guy called David Bowie just to name a few. Cream changed rock music and the way we listen to music - it was excellent songwriting with high quality musicianship. RIP Jack and Ginger.

Alan Childs was influenced by Ginger and ended up drumming for Bowie

I WAS THERE: MIKE COHEN, AGE 18

I WAS IN college at the time. I have memories of their wild clothing and loud audio. They were my favourites along with Jimi Hendrix. My love for playing bass was because of Jack Bruce's improvisational riffs. I was blown away by Ginger Baker's style and double kick drums. Needless to say, Clapton's guitar was mesmerising. The real cool thing was that the auditorium was small, with maybe 500 seats.

Mike Cohen remembers an auditorium that held 500 tops

I WAS THERE: MARC SCHAEFFER

I SAW CREAM at Hunter College and at Madison Square Garden. I remember the volume of Clapton's Marshall stacks and the whirling dervish of Baker's drums, including the double kick drum, which I'd never seen before. 'Toad' was the first extended drum solo part of a rock show I'd ever seen. I remember enjoying how they improvised the jam sections of each song. At the time, Clapton and Hendrix were the guitar gods so hearing Clapton play live was a treat.

Marc Schaeffer remembers the volume of Eric's Marshalls

STATE FAIR MUSIC HALL
30 MARCH 1968, DALLAS, TEXAS

I WAS THERE: MIKE HICKS

Mike Hicks saw Cream just a month after seeing Hendrix

I WAS DRAFTED into the US Army in July. I saw Cream and Vanilla Fudge in the early part of 1968, just after seeing Hendrix in February. The regional band who opened were announced as being from the college town of Denton, Texas. They were called The Chessmen and featured a very young Jimmie Vaughan - Stevie Ray Vaughan's brother - and Doyle Bramhall, who co-wrote several of Stevie's greatest songs. The Chessmen did something I thought odd at the time, as they played 'Sunshine of Your Love'. I mean, Cream would be on the stage playing it probably within an hour. Weird, but back then groups did play a lot of covers.

Cream came out and I'd never quite seen anything like it. The amps - walls of amps, very tall walls of amps. Jack and Eric had a wall and Eric had a wall. I can't even estimate how many. And they were loud. I think they had more amplification than Hendrix. But they played an inspired, flawless set. This was the tour that would eventually end up on the *Wheels of Fire* LP set. They sounded exactly like they sound on that live portion of that record. It was great.

I WAS THERE: JEAN RICHARDSON
I WENT WITH a bunch of other hippies. I don't have a lot of clear memories, just that Ginger Baker was always switching drumsticks without missing a beat.

MORRIS CIVIC AUDITORIUM
3 APRIL 1968, SOUTH BEND, INDIANA

I WAS THERE: JIM ALEXANDER
TICKETS WERE $3.50 and I almost passed, but decided to go and take a girl. It was a Wednesday night and Cream were on their 'no sleep' tour. Clapton seemed exhausted. During 'Traintime' and 'Toad', he lay on the floor behind his amps with his head and shoulders propped up against the back of the speaker. He smoked a cig and just laid there. Ginger was all business. When he hit the drums they were loud - louder than the PA system. Jack was all fired up, bouncing in time with the music and extremely energetic. His voice was spectacular. Jack and Eric had 400 watts amps apiece and a 50 watt PA. Priorities. But I couldn't help feeling that they were largely just going through the motions.

Jim Alexander thought Eric looked 'exhausted'

BACK BAY THEATRE
5 APRIL 1968, BOSTON, MASSACHUSETTS

I WAS THERE: DENNIS ROACH
THE SECOND TIME I saw them was at the Back Bay Theatre. It was a formal theatre rather than a gymnasium and a well organised show. The warm up act was a bunch of guys with horns - definitely not a rock band! Cream came out and they were fantastic again. I don't remember as much about that show as I do the Brandeis show but I do remember

they wouldn't play 'Tales of Brave Ulysses' because some asshole had stolen Eric's wah-wah pedal.

During both shows, Eric played his Fool painted SG guitar. At this show, he broke a string and handed the SG off to the roadies and they handed him back a Les Paul - the same guitar he'd played in the Bluesbreakers - and they did 'Sleepy Time Time'. It was just amazing how this guitar sounded in the master's hands. It may have been the same Les Paul he later gave to George Harrison.

Clapton and Bruce left the stage when Baker soloed. Baker and Clapton left the stage when Jack Bruce did 'Train Time' as well, so it was just him soloing on the harmonica. I remember bouncing up and down in the seats while I listened to it. Both shows were really, really wonderful. As well as my girlfriend, another girl came along with us. She was a little younger and didn't understand it at all. She said, 'Are these people on drugs or something?'

There was a time when I was absolutely fanatical and wanted every recording that Eric was on. From YouTube videos I've seen of things he's done in the last five years, I think his guitar playing has become even more astounding than when he was younger. There's a video of Eric and Jeff Beck doing 'Moon River'. They complement each other incredibly well. I have nothing but admiration for Eric.

I WAS THERE: JADAH CARROLL

THERE WERE THREE music events we wanted to see. Cream were at the Back Bay Theatre, James Brown at the Garden and Taj Majal at Club 47. It was the night after the assassination of MLK, and James Brown was credited as saving Boston that night. I so remember Ginger Baker's 20 minute drum solo and of course the music was thrilling. But mostly I remember thinking 'where are Clapton and Bruce? They must be out in the alley smoking pot and getting high!' When Cream were done, we went to Club 47 to see Taj Majal, who stayed on that little stage just an arms-length from us and didn't take a break until 4am.

I WAS THERE: BILL SULLIVAN, AGE 17

AFTER THE PSYCHEDELIC Supermarket, the second show I saw was in the Back Bay Theatre and it cost $3.50 to get in. By then they weren't mingling with the audience but were protected like politicians. They were touring to support *Disraeli Gears* and it was a far more polished performance at a much better venue, more refined - if you can pair Cream and refinement in the same sentence! I think they were the original jam band. Some of their songs went on 10 or 15 minutes or more. It felt like Jack hit as many notes as Eric. His fingers were a blur and his voice like the voice of God, full of power.

I WAS THERE: BOB ADCOCK, CREAM'S TOUR MANAGER
THE NIGHT MARTIN Luther King got shot, we played in Boston and very close to a venue where James Brown was playing. They were both 10,000 seater venues. Cream were actually on stage when one of the high-ranking police officers from Boston turned up at the show. He came over to me at the side of the stage and said, 'We've got a problem. James Brown is across the road. Martin Luther King's just been shot. If word gets out, we're gonna have 10,000 black guys and 10,000 white guys meeting up on the streets. We can't have that happen. He's gonna play longer. You're gonna play shorter.' He wasn't asking. He was telling. Get off of the stage as soon as you can, basically.

The changeovers weren't exactly smooth. The band used to spend a fair amount of time wiping themselves down, having a drink. One guy would be talking into the mic while the other two were pissing around behind the amps. So at the end of the next song, I went over to Eric and said, 'Look, we've got to leave early. We've got to finish the show.' And he understood straight away. The rest of the band understood straight away. They finished the show and we got out of there.

WOOLSEY HALL
10 APRIL 1968, YALE UNIVERSITY NEW HAVEN, CONNECTICUT

I WAS THERE: BRIAN WOLFE, AGE 16
WHEN MY FATHER got his first stereo component system, instead of tossing the console unit to the kerb, he and I dragged it into my bedroom, down the end of the hall. It was on this unit late one night on the Yale FM station WYBC that I first heard The Cream's first LP, played in its entirety. It was one of those life-changing nocturnal emissions that changed the way I viewed playing electric guitar forever. My best friend Peter Mitchell and I promptly went to Merle's Record Rack in New Haven and bought the LP.

I had a trio at the time with Peter on bass and his brother John on drums. We started learning the *Fresh Cream* LP song by song. When we found out that Cream was going to appear a short drive down I-95 at Yale's Woolsey Hall, Peter and I knew we had to attend. I had been 16 years old for only three days, so my father drove Peter and me there.

Brian Wolfe (left) went to Yale - to see Cream

Our seats were front row balcony, almost in a direct line with Jack Bruce. The strongest recollection I have of the set was the first song, 'Spoonful'. It wasn't included on the US release of *Fresh Cream*, so the song was a complete surprise. I was transported to a state of ecstasy. Centred on just two notes, it went on for what seemed like forever, most likely about 20 minutes. A friend helped me figure out those two notes the next day! The other song from that show that sticks in my mind is the last song, 'Toad'. Ginger Baker's extended drum solo was equally as long as the extended guitar solo in 'Spoonful'. Eric Clapton and Jack Bruce left Ginger alone on stage. When they came back, both had a beer in their hand.

After the show, we went down to the stage to check out their amps. When we met up with my father, it was well after the concert. He asked, 'What took so long? Eric wanted to meet you. I told him you had a Les Paul and had spent hours learning his songs.' I was pretty sceptical. My father was known for being a joker. But when he showed me the beer he had from backstage I knew he was telling me the truth. My dad was in law enforcement and knew the police doing security backstage. They'd let him in, and he got to hang with Eric and Jack during the drum solo in 'Toad'.

THEE IMAGE
11 APRIL 1968, SUNNY ISLES BEACH, MIAMI, FLORIDA

I WAS THERE: BUD BRADBURY
I WAS HOME on vacation from Southern Methodist University in Dallas, and doing FM radio on KNUS-FM. It was an odd venue, a former bowling alley had been gutted except for the stage that rose to

maybe three feet below the existing bowling alley ceiling. There were no seats in the hall. Everyone sat cross legged on the cement floor. I arrived early enough to sit about 15 feet from left centre, on Jack Bruce's side. Eric was in excellent form. There were a few hundred in attendance making it a delightful hassle-free Miami evening. Except that the light show was mediocre and Ginger had a problem with the strobe operator. He would hold up crossed drumsticks at the operator and finally threw a pair at him. No more strobe....

Ginger had a problem with the strobe operator... No more strobe!

I WAS THERE: DOUGLAS NOECKER
I WAS JUST back from my tour of duty in the USAF, and friends of mine introduced me to Thee Image venue, a converted bowling alley on Miami Beach. It was only $3 to get in. There were lots of hippy types there enjoying the music and each other. There were lots of drugs there as well - pot, mescaline, LSD, etc. It was a very cool place to spend an evening at, with at least three different rock bands playing. It wasn't much for great lighting or speakers but it was small enough, holding about 500 at the most, to hear what Cream had to bring. They put on a great show that lasted about three hours or so, although I wasn't really watching the clock. Eric later bought a home on Golden Beach not far from that venue, and made an album named after the address of the house - *461 Ocean Boulevard*.

ELECTRIC FACTORY
12 - 14 APRIL 1968, PHILADELPHIA, PENNSYLVANIA

I WAS THERE: PAUL SIMEONE, AGE 17
I HAD A lot of interest in British bands and music in general and would take my camera to concerts that played in the Philadelphia area. Back then they didn't take any kind of interest in anybody carrying a camera. The Electric Factory was a venue in downtown Philadelphia that anybody who was anybody played back in the late Sixties. After the Café a Go Go show I saw in New York, Cream came down to Philadelphia and played Good Friday, Holy Saturday and Easter Sunday and I was there all three nights.

On the Friday night I was sitting outside the club. I was first in line. Finally, they opened up the door and let everybody in. The Cream were late getting there. I didn't know why until a few years ago, but it's because Eric Clapton's guitar was stolen and he had to go down to downtown Philadelphia to buy another. The guitar that he bought was the Gibson Firebird and I believe that night was the first time he ever used it. On my website there's a couple of photographs of Clapton playing that guitar and I think he used it a couple of times thereafter. I even got Ginger Baker's drumstick that night. Unfortunately, I can't find it today, but it had 'Ginger Baker model made in England' stamped on the drumstick.

Eric's guitar was stolen so he went downtown and bought a Firebird

A few years ago, my daughter was working in a gift store in Cape May, a summer resort town in New Jersey. The store would stay open until 10pm. One Wednesday night she called me right around 10 o'clock. I looked at my phone and thought 'this can't be good'. She said that, close to closing, a gentleman had come in the store with a woman and a couple of small kids. He had sunglasses and a hat on and was picking up all kinds of gifts and putting them on the counter. She was wondering why this guy was wearing sunglasses at 10 o'clock at night. Then he took his glasses off and my daughter just freaked out. She went, 'Oh my god. My dad. My dad. I've got to call my dad.' It was Eric with his wife and kids. He grabbed her hand and said, 'It's okay, just calm down.' His yacht, Blue Guitar, was moored in Cape May, New Jersey for a few days. I said, 'You didn't take a picture?' She said, 'I was shaking so much, I couldn't believe what was happening.'

I WAS THERE: JACK ECK

MY FRIENDS AND I saw them at the Electric Factory in Philly. They did a lot of *Fresh Cream* stuff and, of course, *Disraeli Gears*. Clapton wore a fringe jacket that I fell in love with and I went out and bought one. They wasted no time once they walked on stage but immediately launched into their set. They each had their own particular favourites, on which they would launch into a looonnnngggg solo. Ginger spent 42 minutes on a drum solo in the middle of 'Toad'. Bruce and Clapton simply left the stage for a while. Then Clapton took his turn on 'Crossroads' for about the same amount of time.

We went to see them again that summer at St John Terrel's Music Fair under a big tent in Trenton, New Jersey and then at the Spectrum in Philly that November, where they played lots of *Goodbye Cream* stuff. I took a camera and the guards let me go over the wall to get closer to them to take some pictures, but none of them came out. It was a Friday night as I recall. The following night, Saturday, they played Madison Square Garden for their last US concert and I went to that one also.

Jack Eck and his pals saw Cream in Philly

I WAS THERE: DIANE HICE, AGE 18

DURING SOPHOMORE SPRING break, my friend Susan (who lived in Jersey) and myself went to the Electric Factory in Philadelphia and heard a concert by Cream. The venue was not large so we ended either sitting on the floor or standing. It turns out those 'seats' were great, as we seemed to have a great, close up view of the band. Quite frankly, I don't think either of us really dug the music they played. We were mostly into Motown like the Temptations or Sam and Dave. I seemed to focus on the drummer's not too pleasant looking mouth and teeth, probably because I was a nursing student and would notice something like that. Ironically, I became a real fan of Eric Clapton as he moved onto other groups like Derek and the Dominos.

I focused on the drummer's not too pleasant looking mouth and teeth

THE CELLAR
26 APRIL 1968, ARLINGTON HEIGHTS, ILLINOIS

I WAS THERE: JACK FRYSCHMANN

THE CELLAR WAS a bowling alley converted into a place for kids to see local rock and roll groups perform. When the Cream played there it wasn't too crowded. I was able to stand a few feet from the stage to see them play and sing 'Sunshine of Your Love', which I already loved, and other songs from *Fresh Cream* and *Disraeli Gears*. I miss Jack Bruce. But he left us with his everlasting songs and tales.

COLISEUM
27 APRIL 1968, CHICAGO, ILLINOIS

I WAS THERE: VINCE BLACK

MY FIRST BASS guitar was a Beatle/Hofner style one and the first song I learned was 'Sunshine of Your Love'. When Cream came to the Coliseum in Chicago, I went to the show. As a local face, I was allowed backstage and took in most of the show from there. What can I say? They were brilliant! Ginger Baker did a really fantastic drum solo and, after the show, we could see how exhausted he was. Clapton was great and Jack Bruce, who was a big influence on me and inspired me to get a Gibson EBO bass, was brilliant. I went home happy!

Vince Black went backstage at the Coliseum

I WAS THERE: GARY A LUCAS

THE OLD CHICAGO Coliseum had been converted into a concert venue for a time - The Syndrome. I seem to recall a capacity crowd. Being the summer of 1968, they had the two albums to draw from. I certainly remember 'Toad', which was obligatory, and also Eric Clapton playing a Gibson Firebird. It looked like wood finish with a white pick guard. And I remember being quite thrilled to at last see them. The support act was another thrill for me - The Mothers of Invention. They too had several albums to play songs from. Clapton was mentioned in the liner notes for *We're Only in It for the Money*, and a sample of a riff that sounds like him and a British-accented voice saying something about seeing God.

I WAS THERE: BONNIE BENEFIELD

I SAW FRANK Zappa and the Mothers of Invention open for Cream in Chicago. My husband was the horn player with the original Mothers.

I WAS THERE: LOUIS DIAMOND

I WAS 14 when I first heard them. Growing up in a suburb close to Chicago, I had neighbours across the alley who were artists and musicians, the older one in a local band called The Dirty Wurds. They had the *Beano* record and then the import version of the Cream LP. I really liked the Bluesbreakers record. I was stoked to see

Cream at the Coliseum

Cream, but especially with the Mothers opening. Seeing Cream was just part of a wild day. There was also a big anti-war rally in Chicago which ended up with tear gas and cops chasing and beating people. Then - off to the show! I had been to many teen night club rock shows and a few big auditorium shows before this one. I remember dancing and dancing to 'Toad'. What fun. Alas, when I finally bought *Live Cream* it was not the shiny foil copy.

I WAS THERE: BRENDAN HOLLORAN, AGE 12

I WAS BLESSED with older cousins who took me to the show - and parents who allowed it! I had listened to their music on vinyl and was aware of their sound but was really taken by their ability to transform it live. All three members were very polished and very loud and energising. Their ability to sing a few bars and then just play endlessly without missing a beat was very impressive. It was really different from, say, The Beatles, who controlled pop music. Cream, to me, were delivering a message on music by playing extensive, creative jams. They were a real eye opener.

I WAS THERE: PAUL PETRAITIS

I SAW THEM three times, twice in big stadiums and once at a smallish hall on the University of Chicago's campus. They were absolutely underwhelming, failing to sound anything like their remarkable first album. I'm a guitarist, been playing since 1964 and I was hoping to be blown away by Clapton's 'loud blues'. I saw a couple of guys play in their instruments and I thought it was roadies doing the soundcheck. Then Ginger came out with no fanfare or introduction and they started playing... rather listlessly. Were they too high? I don't know.

Paul Petraitis thought the live Cream sound was too clean

Clapton's tone was dry, with little distortion, none of the trademark 'woman tone', and no feedback. Bruce was interesting but seemed to rarely pay attention to Mr Baker, whose drumming was never one of my favourites. It sounded like biscuit tins. The double bass drum was exciting but the overall sound was less than thrilling. I still get shivers upon hearing Eric's lovely Les Paul work on the first album. I was hoping Eric would be on a Les Paul and Jack would be on his Fender VI, but not in Chicago. I heard their first tour never got further west (from NYC) than Detroit. Their Chicago appearances were later when Jack played his 'burpy' Gibson EB3 bass. He was a stunning vocalist live.

I thought it was roadies doing the soundcheck. Then Ginger came out…

I found out about Cream from being an Anglophile and reading *Rave* magazine whenever I could get a copy. Friends got me the English version (purchased in Auckland, New Zealand) of their first album which oddly cut off the final chord in 'Spoonful'! Whatever happened to the amps Eric and Jack used on that album? I heard that they had the old original Celestion speakers removed from their 4x12 cabinets, replacing them with cleaner Altec speakers reasoning that 'Americans didn't like distortion'. What a strange thing to say! That distortion sound for me *was* Cream. Was it the new 'clean" speakers that made the live Cream performances sound so lifeless? They were still brilliant in the studio in my opinion - 'Badge', etc. - but I did not like the live Cream LPs.

Tom Dowd may have got that fat SG tone on *Disraeli Gears* by using the old 1950s trick of recording the guitar amp off the speaker leads, in the same way as Ron Malo at Chess recorded Hubert Sumlin (with Howlin' Wolf) and Jeff Beck (with the Yardbirds on 'Shapes Of Things'). You miss the articulate overly bright signal off the speaker leads (they used to use alligator clips) and step it down with a capacitor so it doesn't blast the input of the recording deck. The combination of distorting speaker and direct off the amp is a unique sound. I think that's what you hear on solos like 'Sunshine'. The occasional 'pop' you hear just has to be possible only with this method.

I WAS THERE: JIM STAHL

I SAW CREAM play live two different times in Chicago in the late Sixties. They would come out and play songs as a group, and then each one would do a solo number that would last as long as each wanted. Most people have seen and heard Ginger Baker do his 'Toad' solo act. However, Clapton and Bruce did incredible solo riffs on their own. All three of them would end their solos and merge their music back into the group to finish. They're still my favourite group of all time.

I WAS THERE: TERRY STARBUCK, AGE 14

I WENT WITH three friends. I have some vivid and some very fuzzy memories. We were probably the only four people in the audience who were not high!

I WAS THERE: BOB TIGER, AGE 20

IT WAS THE heyday of the hippy days in Chicago, and Old Town was jumpin' every night. Clapton was God. *Disraeli Gears* was a staple on the 8-track. There was a crew of four of us that hung out together, and when Cream came to Chicago, not being there was not an option. They were playing at the Chicago Coliseum. At the last stop before heading to the show, we dropped acid - standard procedure in those days before what promised to be an epic show.

For Bob Tiger and his crew, not seeing Cream was not an option

The Coliseum was an enormous barn. We found seats about halfway back from the stage, but as we got higher and higher, and I'm sure there were many others there in similar state of mind, sitting in a seat was not a thing. Everyone was walking around, and we ended up standing near the front, to the right as we faced the stage. The Mothers of Invention were the opening act. This was the full Mothers, including Flo and Eddy, Jimmy Carl Black - the Indian of the group - and what looked like about 10 percussionists. Those Mothers played frequently in Chicago, often on Mother's Day. They were great, as always. It was always a mindblower that they could play the crazy complex stuff on their albums exactly the same live. At one point, Frank told the crowd, 'Well, you're all stuck in this big barn-like place and you all have no choice but to sit here and listen to me play my 20-minute-long boring guitar solo from 'Lumpy Gravy'.' He proceeded to play it, but it was anything but boring; he was a much better guitar player than many people gave - or give - him credit for.

After the Mothers finished, the stage crew did their magic and suddenly (it seemed) there were two walls of Marshalls bracketing a huge drum kit with double bass drums and a wall of cymbals going two-thirds of the way around. The three legends in their own time took the stage, and it was on. They played the songs that were deeply ingrained in the brains of everyone in the real world. Perfectly. Loudly. To this day, it lives in my memory as one of the best concerts I've ever been at. Surreal. As I was at the height of the acid wave, Ginger played 'Toad'. He looked like he was made of pipe cleaners and holding four flying sticks in each hand, and he built up until he was hitting everything at once. I was standing in the face of a one-man hurricane of sound. I remember laughing out loud in astonishment. I've seen videos of him doing this, and I've listened to it cranked up and tried to re-envision what I saw that night, but nothing comes close to standing in front of the stage and feeling it. We all knew they were the best, and we saw it first hand that night.

Ginger looked like he was made of pipe cleaners and holding four flying sticks in each hand

Two weeks later, on May 13th, they returned to Chicago to play at Mandel Hall at the University of Chicago. It was a much smaller venue - what felt like a large high-school auditorium, especially compared to the Coliseum. Again, they played great, but it somehow seemed lower key, as if they were a bit tired. After the concert, we ran into a girl that we knew who said she knew where they were staying. We took her with us, followed her directions and ended up knocking on a door that Jack Bruce opened. There were a few other people there, so we hung out. It was the eve of Jack's birthday, so he was sort of celebrating, but he was stuck in a hotel room in Chicago on his birthday, so maybe not so much. He was walking back and forth across the room on his hands. Ginger was sitting cross-legged in the middle of the bed, rolling and smoking joints. Someone tried to put a Cream album on the stereo in the room, and both Jack and Ginger nixed that immediately. They were listening to jazz. Clapton wasn't there - he had gone up to the North Side to sit in with Paul Butterfield. Honestly, while hanging out in a hotel room with Jack Bruce and Ginger Baker is a pretty cool story, hearing Clapton sit in with Butterfield would have been much more fun.

Bob's memory of the Mandel Hall show on 13 May 1968 is not documented elsewhere.

I WAS THERE: BOB ADCOCK

THERE WAS NEVER any food provided at gigs. The necessity to do it was not there either, inasmuch as we didn't notice it wasn't important to have food there because the time spent at the gig was so much less. The crew didn't turn up until three o'clock in the afternoon. It's not like they were there from eight in the morning like they are today. The reason food is provided at gigs for crews is to stop them all going off and leaving the site to find somewhere to eat. That's the main reason that catering came in. But in those days there was no catering. The very first promoter that I ever saw anything close to catering was Bill Graham at the Fillmore. He would put a dustbin in the dressing room filled with ice and beers and that was the first time I'd ever had food or drink provided by a promoter. You just went over to the bin and took a beer out. It wasn't general. Otherwise, there were no drinks.

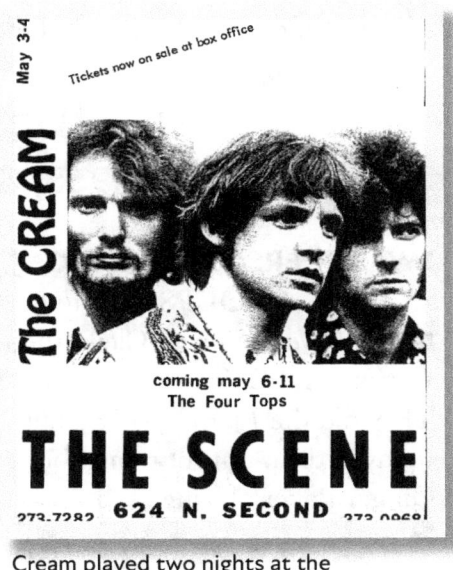

Cream played two nights at the Scene in Milwaukee, Wisconsin

I used to stop off and buy a couple of six packs for the band and that was it. That was catering. I've written riders since with bands I've worked with and they can run to ten pages with the band's requirements. But then? Absolutely nothing. But we never went hungry. There was always somewhere to eat. We never ate together anyway. It wasn't like everybody would meet up to go to the same place. I can't remember too many times when all four of us ate together at a table. Cream weren't like that.

CIVIC CENTRE
11 MAY 1968, AKRON, OHIO

MY BROTHER WAS THERE: TEDDY KARAM
WHEN MY BROTHER Joe was 16, he saw Cream at the Civic Theater in Akron, Ohio. He hung out afterwards and met Clapton, who let him hold the Fool SG and signed his t-shirt. My brother learned Clapton's vibrato to a T from seeing him that night. As a little kid I recall friends commenting to my brother, 'Man, you sound just like Clapton.'

MUSIC HALL
12 MAY 1968, CLEVELAND, OHIO

I WAS THERE: GARY LORIG
ALL THE GROUPS went to the big mid-West cities of Cleveland, Detroit, and Chicago - and still do. They did the *Wheels of Fire* album. I played drums and I remember Ginger Baker playing 'Toad'.

Gary Lorig (right) saw Cream and met James Brown (centre)

I WAS THERE: GARY JONES, AGE 16
MY FRIEND'S FATHER pulled some strings and got us second row, a contrast to two months before when we got nosebleed tickets to see the Jimi Hendrix Experience. Luckily, I had brought my binoculars.

Back to Cream: The curtain opened, Jack was standing right in front of me up on stage, Ginger and his huge drum were set in the middle with his name on it (instead of 'Cream') and Eric Clapton was off to the right. They opened with those power chords of 'Tales of Brave Ulysses'. Very moving. When Jack sang, he would rear his head back and unleash some of the most powerful vocals in rock history.

Until they played 'Sunshine of Your Love' I hadn't realised Eric began the vocals and that Jack came in with the second verse and his 'I'll stay with you 'til my seeds are dried up' line. After a few more songs, they went into their long, improvisational tunes. They did a long version of 'Steppin' Out', and the way Jack played bass was kind of battling with Eric on lead guitar, which was very powerful.

Towards the end of the show, Jack pulled out his harp and sang 'Traintime' with Ginger playing like a train rolling. Eric went backstage. They ended with 'Toad'. After setting up the theme, both Jack and Eric went backstage and let Ginger play for a very long time. Ginger built up to a climax when he had every cymbal, high hat, double bass drum going at once. What a show.

VETERANS MEMORIAL AUDITORIUM
14 MAY 1968, COLUMBUS, OHIO

I WAS THERE: TIM UMINA

I SAW THE Cream perform on stage from the middle front, third row. My most vivid memory, other than it was a great concert, was seeing Ginger Baker lose a drumstick and have another in his hand without losing a beat. His double bass action and drumming showed he was as formidable in his drumming as Eric was with his guitar and Jack as a bass player. To me they were hands down a 'supergroup'.

Tim Umina saw Ginger's flawless technique in Columbus, Ohio

I WAS THERE: JUDY GALLAGHER, AGE 24

THE ONLY CONCERT I had attended up to then was Doc Watson. Vets Memorial was an odd venue for a Cream concert. It was more suited to plays and such like, as there was only seating and no standing room. So everyone was seated obediently during the concert. Only on the last number or so did a few brave souls stand up and dance in the aisles - myself included! I do remember that Ginger Baker had a drum solo that seemed to go on forever.

I went with a woman friend who had scored free tickets. That day we went shopping for outfits, since part of going to a concert was the clothes. I found a pair of bell bottom pyjamas that looked like the *Disraeli Gears* album cover. I hadn't been a follower but the concert changed that. I immediately bought the album and played 'Strange Brew' over and over again. It wasn't just their lyrics but Clapton's guitar playing that made Cream stand out from other groups like the squeaky clean Beatles or the delinquent Rolling Stones. Cream sounded psychedelic. They were a holy trinity. Each one the best: Bruce the best voice, Baker the best drummer, Clapton the best guitar in rock. I didn't realise until later that I was pregnant in May '68, so I always remind my son that the Cream was his first concert.

Judy Gallagher was pregnant with her son when she saw Cream

I WAS THERE: PHROGGE KOEHLER

THEY PLAYED FOR an hour and a half and only played six songs. I sat right in front of the PA cabinets and couldn't hear for four hours after the show. A friend of mine is a friend of Clapton's and they chatted side stage while Ginger played his drum solo for 'Toad'. I also saw Blind Faith. An idiot rushed Ginger during the drum solo on 'Do What You Like'. Without missing a beat, Ginger jammed his drumstick into the guy's ear canal and you saw blood all over as the guy collapsed on stage and screaming in pain before security could drag him away.

Ginger jammed his drumstick into the guy's ear canal

ANAHEIM CONVENTION CENTER
17 MAY 1968, ANAHEIM, CALIFORNIA

I WAS THERE: KURT DRUMHELLER, AGE 16

I WAS A drummer in a garage band called The Nervous System. We played Beatles, Stones, Monkees and some originals. I still live about 10 miles west of the venue. Cream were very popular at that time. The show was highly energised and I vaguely remember a slight smoky haze of cannabis hanging in the air that night. My most vivid memory is Ginger Baker's 22 minute drum solo. I purposely timed it! He maintained the audience's attention throughout the entire solo with several stanzas or movements building momentum and reaching resolution and then starting a new portion. I remember the furious, accurate staccato high speed pounding of his double bass drum foot pedals anchoring the whole affair. His stamina was just jaw dropping. The audience erupted in spontaneous applause several times during the solo. As we all know, subsequently 'drum solos' have become the butt of many a joke, with most drummers now compelled to limit their solos to a few minutes at best. It wasn't like that with Cream in 1968.

Kurt Drumheller (left, with his band The Nervous System) was at the Convention Center

I WAS THERE: RUSSELL MOKER

I WENT WITH my best friend Steve and my cousin Tony. Spirit opened for them and after they finished, we went up to the mezzanine to grab a snack and soft drink. Spirit were there, in a roped off area for some press photos. When Cream finally took the stage, we were all blown away by their sound. We were seated high up and far away from the stage so it was difficult to see much. When they returned to So Cal, I saw them at the Forum in LA, where Deep Purple opened for them. I sat much closer to the stage and could actually see their faces while they were performing. I don't have any clear memories of the songs or the set list, but I do remember they sounded more refined and rehearsed that second time.

I WAS THERE: IRA KNOPF

THEY PLAYED MAY 17 and 18 in Anaheim and I attended the first night. The set list this time started with 'Spoonful' and 'Sunshine of Your Love'. On 'We're Going Wrong' Jack had mic problems and he had to grab Eric's mic to finish his vocal, but the problem was quickly corrected. After 'Rollin' and Tumblin'' and 'Steppin' Out', they played 'As You Said', the debut of a new song from the forthcoming *Wheels of Fire* LP with Jack solo on acoustic guitar. There wasn't a good response from the audience - in fact, there were moans and groans! They finished with 'Toad' and 'I'm So Glad'. Both shows were sold out. Spirit was the opening act. Other than Jack's mic problem, there were no technical issues and they used the same gear as on previous shows.

I WAS THERE: DARRYL GENIS

IN 1966 MY older sister went to Europe and Israel with a friend. She brought me back an album. I was hoping for *Revolver* by The Beatles but she brought me *Fresh Cream*. I had never heard of it and I'm not ashamed to say I was really disappointed. But I threw it on the turntable and just fell in love with it. It spoke to me and it became - and has remained - my favourite music. The comedian Chris Rock once said, 'The music you are listening to the first time you get laid is the music you listen to for the rest of your life.' All joking aside, I think he's right!

I was playing guitar and wanted a Gretsch guitar. My grandfather bought me a Gibson Firebird, one of the guitars that Eric played. The drummer in the band I was in was called Billy. His father, Roy Gerber, was the Beatles' representative in North America. I used to spend the night over at Billy's house. He had a drum set that Ringo had given to him, and a piano that Paul had given to him. And because of his dad's business, Billy always had front row seats and backstage passes, and because Billy was my best friend at the time I was always going to concerts. The first concert I went to was the Anaheim Convention Center where we saw Cream. We had front row seats and backstage passes and met all three of them. I also saw them at the Whisky and then for the farewell concert I saw them at the LA Forum and then drove down and saw them at the San Diego Stadium as well.

I don't have many regrets. But in 1969 Billy called me up at the last minute and asked me if I wanted to go to a concert to see Blind Faith.

I said, 'Without Jack Bruce, what's the point?' I was a 13-year-old musical snob who was broken hearted about Cream having disbanded and who saw Blind Faith as a second-rate substitute. I really regret that.

I WAS THERE: LAWRENCE STRID
THE FIRST ROCK concert I saw was Cream, with Spirit opening. Both were very impressive. Jack did 'As You Said' by himself on acoustic guitar. I saw them later at the Forum in LA for their farewell concert. Deep Purple opened, and again both were very impressive.

ICE PALACE
18 MAY 1968, LAS VEGAS, NEVADA

I WAS THERE: BOYCE VALENTINE
IT WAS AT the indoor ice rink. They covered the floor with plywood but with all the people there the ice kept melting. Cream rocked the house. Weed and white crosses fuelled the crowd. Many attendees rode the Super Chief train up to Vegas from LA, bringing large quantities of Owsley's White Lightning acid on sugar cubes. The jams were unbelievable. Everybody was wet from the melting ice and cold but just didn't care. After the concert, everybody went to the Teenbeat Club and Ginger and Eric dropped by and jammed with Sly. What a night. A close friend's father was VP of Capitol Records and we partied on all night with the crew!

Boyce Valentine remembers the ice, the weed and the acid

PHOTO SHOOT
19 MAY 1968, MONUMENT VALLEY, UTAH

I WAS THERE: STEVE ROSSMOORE, AGE 19
I SPENT A day with them when I worked as a roadie for a celebrity photographer. The photo shoot was supposedly for an album cover. I was handling the photography equipment. We met them when their

chartered twin-engined six passenger plane landed in the Grand Canyon Airport. After the shoot I flew back with them to Las Vegas, where they'd been playing. I sat next to Eric Clapton. Ginger Baker had forgotten his 'bag' in the VW bus I'd arrived in, the bag that had his heroin. I arrived with them in Las Vegas and continued on to San Francisco. I made $25, got to meet the Cream and got a free plane ride back!

Steve Rossmoore was in Monument Valley with Cream

COMMUNITY CONCOURSE, EXHIBIT HALL
19 MAY 1968, SAN DIEGO, CALIFORNIA

Sean O'Neil McCauley's PA was used by Cream

I WAS THERE: SEAN O'NEIL MCCAULEY

I SAW THEM four or five times. I did sound systems in San Diego during the Sixties, and one way or another saw just about everyone that came through town. I was a non-musician member of a college band and did all their setup. Our promoter used our huge PA system (and myself) on numerous occasions for bands coming through town. Cream used our PA twice. We had a lot of fun, and met a lot of interesting people. San Diego was a fabulous town back then.

Our band - Genetic Dryft - was supposed to open for Cream at the Community Concourse. At the very last minute (literally), we were replaced by a group called Framework. I can't relate just how upset we were. I had spent the morning setting up for our guys, and just about as soon as I was done, I had to tear it down again. Except the PA. The promoter wanted it up because it was the best system in town. At least I got to sit on stage left running the system while they played. They added an evening show at the last minute, so I got to do it twice. Afterwards, we came up missing a 500w DuKane PA amp from one side of the stage. Their roadies were so stoned, I doubt they realised.

They used Marshall stacks, usually three each for Jack and Eric. The Community Concourse was a closed off floor of the San Diego Civic Center, which included Symphony Hall and other buildings. I don't believe it was ever used for parking, as there were zero oil stains. The floor was tilted, as in most parking structures, so it made a good hall. The walls, floor and ceiling were solid concrete, so with all that amp power the sound just ate you. I left a nice set of ears at that concert.

I left a nice set of ears at that concert

I also found out later that our drummer had shoved a full-sized tape recorder under the stage, and plugged it into the PA system. We had a beautiful bootleg tape of them for a few years. Unfortunately, the drummer died in the Seventies and the tape is somewhere in the wind.

I saw Cream twice more during their farewell tour. All three of them were fantastic musicians, but I always thought that Cream was holding them back from bigger things and I believe history has proven me correct. The outstanding solos were a treat to watch, but they were basically doing the same thing at every show. Just how many times could Ginger Baker do 'Toad' without getting bored?

They were transformative. Their musicianship is legendary for a reason. Almost all of their live albums were highly accurate. On a fairly monster stereo, with a nice analogue turntable, you can do a pretty good job of reproducing the experience. If you can still recognise human language afterwards, you didn't have it turned up loud enough.

I WAS THERE: BOB ADCOCK, CREAM'S TOUR MANAGER

THEY BUILT UP a touring network where word of mouth spread. It was the college circuit in Europe that really got them moving. I don't know how to define Cream. Loud heavy blues music. Because at the end of the day it was blues. It wasn't rock and it wasn't pop. They were big in the industry - lots of other musicians liked them - but it took some breaking to get them off the ground with regards to the public. When we went to America and did the Fillmore gigs, that's where it absolutely took off. Word spread very fast. And Cream were one of the few bands that were big all over America. Most bands in those days were big in parts - the Midwest or the West Coast or the East or whatever - but Cream were big universally, right through. They were capable of going on for quite some time afterwards had they not broken up.

Gigs in America were so different to what we experienced in the UK

The gigs in America were so different to anything we'd experienced in the UK. The audiences were drugged out, there were light shows everywhere. It was Haight Ashbury at its prime. And you were in the middle of that lot. We weren't the first touring rock band. There were loads of them. We were competing in a big market with people like Buffalo Springfield, Grateful Dead and The Doors. There were loads of bands doing the circuit. When people came to see Cream on those big American tours it was usually for the first time and they were always happy with what they saw. I don't remember them ever doing a bad gig. In those days you could do a 20 minute drum solo and everyone thought it was fantastic. You'd never get away with that today. It was different to what people might have witnessed before. It was much louder than people had been used to. Cream didn't originate loud music. But there were other loud bands - Steppenwolf, The Doors.

CIVIC AUDITORIUM
25 MAY 1968, SAN JOSE, CALIFORNIA

I WAS THERE: TOM WENDT, AGE 15
LIVING IN THE South Bay would require a 45 mile trip to the Fillmore West so it was great to see a band like Cream in our backyard. A comedian opened. Eric Clapton had a wall of Marshall amps. Even then I found it unusual that Clapton did an instrumental from the Mayall *Beano* album with The Powerhouse on the *What's Shakin'* compilation, 'Steppin' Out'. Did Clapton see the 1963 American Folk Blues Festival tour as a young Yardbird? An overlooked and underappreciated aspect of Cream is Clapton's second guitar playing on the studio recordings.

His rhythm guitar indicates some real knowledge of counterpoint and harmony, as if Cream had two guitarists not just one. Being a multi-instrumentalist Jack Bruce was a good harmonica player. On *Fresh Cream*, he did some blues in his own right but I've wondered why he sang lead on 'I'm So Glad'. I didn't like the recorded live version of 'I'm So Glad'. The San Jose version is on YouTube and is better.

I WAS THERE: PAM MAZZUCHELLI, AGE 18

AGED 14 IN Campbell, California, I was not a fan of popular American acts like the Beach Boys or Elvis. My musical tastes were different than most girls my age. Perhaps I had been influenced by my parents. Sinatra, Streisand and classical music were always playing on the living room hi-fi. When I was 10, my favourite song was 'Slaughter on Tenth Avenue'. My mother, an Anglophile, spotted The Beatles in the newspaper, was taken with their hair and clothing, and suggested we watch them on *Ed Sullivan*. I was a goner... for a few years, anyway.

Pam Mazzuchelli was at the Civic Auditorium

The two years between discovering The Beatles and Cream now seems centuries ago, but also a long time between. The world and music had, and was still, greatly changing in those few short years, but I was a teenager with other teenage interests. On the music scene was Gerry and the Pacemakers, the Dave Clark Five, and others - to me, though, they were just Beatle knock-offs. I remember becoming frustrated because The Beatles were changing all the time and eventually just stopping keeping up with them. In 1965, a friend's older brother gave her some albums and 45s - 'British' music-bands like the Byrds and Yardbirds. To my teenage brain, the music these band members produced was different and more appealing than most I had heard before.

When 'Sunshine of Your Love' was released I immediately liked what I heard, especially the heavy bass intro. I've always loved the bass in any band. When my parents were out, I'd blast it on the hi-fi and dance around the living room. I had seen enough films to know exactly what Jack Bruce was singing about - 'It's getting near dawn, the light shining through on you.' I'm not a musician, but I realised too that the instrumentation supported the lyrics, as is the case with most of their songs. These musicians/writers had a special knack of getting the right notes with the right words. I completely appreciated their frequent incorporation of visually poetic lyrics, too; 'crouching tigers run down moonbeams in her dark eyes'. The moonbeams are lyrical and inviting while the crouching tigers are ready to attack, foreshadowing the breakup about to take place. The 'goodbye windows' also serve to show that the breakup is/was public and cruel.

As I got older, I also appreciated that their lyrics weren't obscenely suggestive. To me, they often suggested real love - 'I'll be with you when the stars start falling' - and what heartache really meant. I'm still intrigued by those poetic lyrics - and more appreciated their fancy word-work as an English major in college. And to top it all off, I never knew what any of them looked like, and I didn't care.

I was a senior at Campbell High School when I went to see them. My good friend Lorraine got the tickets, four or five dollars. The concert was general admission. When we walked through the doors, a lot of people were milling around and talking - the lights were dim. The auditorium wasn't that large. It was an older venue with arched balconies and the chairs had been removed. I had seen the Beach Boys here when I was 12 and, aged five, my parents took me to see Frank Sinatra. I fell asleep.

The aroma of marijuana was thick enough to get a contact high

That night, however, I was wide awake and the aroma of marijuana was thick enough to get a contact high. Security people walked the perimeter of the hall but most fans weren't phased. We waited and walked around wondering what they would play. Of course, I hoped to hear 'Sunshine' and it was the second of the few songs they played. They riffed on it for quite a while. When they began playing the first few chords, the crowd yelled and the bass reverberated through me. I realised after listening back to a live tape of the show that Bruce's voice onstage was not as strong as on the recording. The crowd moved up near the stage, but not rushing, and others stood back - some listening, others dancing and smoking, pot as well as cigarettes. Luckily, no one rushed the stage during any part of the performance or tried to jump up as was the habit at many concerts.

As was common then, black lights were everywhere and a lot of people had painted faces that reflected the black lights. Guys and girls approached us asking if we wanted to paint our faces. I declined - if I ever went home with paint on my face, I'd be questioned for hours. There was a projector behind the band with visuals that vibrated and moved with the beat of the music.

Listening to the live version of this concert on YouTube, I realise they sounded better than I had remembered, probably because of poor acoustics in the hall. Gladly, no one undressed or freaked out as we now see in footage of many of those outdoor live concerts. Most of this crowd was enjoying the excellence of these guitar and drum masters. My friend and I didn't get too near the stage as we were more interested in hearing the music. Baker did a solo at one point to rounds of applause. The electronics weren't as good as they are now, and though we didn't know that then, all I cared about was hearing live some of my favourite sounds. I honestly didn't know or care what Clapton, Bruce, or Baker looked like. After hearing the tape of that performance, I didn't remember how much the crowd yelled and clapped when they began the cheerily melodic 'I'm So Glad'. I heard some great guitar work in that live rendition.

EAGLES AUDITORIUM
29 & 30 MAY 1968, SEATTLE, WASHINGTON

I WAS THERE: RUSTY WILLIAMS
I SAW CREAM two nights in a row at the Eagles Auditorium. I sat on the stage both nights, right in front of Jack Bruce. Nobody stopped me. I dropped acid both nights.

PACIFIC COLISEUM
2 JUNE 1968, VANCOUVER, CANADA

I WAS THERE: MARK ALLAN
RAISED IN VANCOUVER, my first real live music concert featured my favourite band - Cream at the Pacific Coliseum hockey arena. Ginger Baker played literally a half-hour drum solo, which I thought was great

(it was all great). I had worn out my *Disraeli Gears* vinyl, but I had somehow overlooked the debut album *Fresh Cream* and the double *LP Wheels of Fire* had just been released, so I wasn't aware that 'Toad' featured a long drum solo. Imagine my surprise when Eric Clapton and Jack Bruce walked off stage and left Ginger out there for such a long time. 'Man,' I thought, 'they must be really angry at him.' As I discovered much later, Jack and Eric were often upset with their brilliant but antagonistic drummer They also played a scorching 'Sunshine of Your Love'. I've forgotten many details, but the power, volume and shimmering brilliance of the playing will be with me until the end.

Mark Allan was at the Pacific Coliseum show

I WAS THERE: PHIL NIELSEN

EPIC SHOW. GINGER did a wicked solo during 'Toad'. I remember the two axe patches were dayglo orange and were the only things you could see on stage except for the follow spot on Ginger. Jack and Eric had left the stage. I also met Eric the next year when he was with The Plastic Ono Band in Toronto. John called it *The Toronto Peace Festival*, but its actual name was *The Rock 'n' Roll Revival* at Varsity Stadium.

GRANDE BALLROOM
7 - 9 JUNE 1968, DETROIT, MICHIGAN

I WAS THERE: BURT KELLOGG

I WAS A great fan of the group, having cut my teeth as a bassist by trying to do as much as my meagre talent would allow to imitate Jack Bruce. I even bought a Gibson EB-3. *Fresh Cream* got the nod over *Disraeli Gears* in my world. *Wheels* was on the verge of being released. Up to that point, my concert activity consisted of two shows: The Blues Magoos, The Who and Herman's Hermits, and then Soft Machine and The Jimi Hendrix Experience, both in large venues in Flint, Michigan. The Who visit was the one where Moon infamously drove a car into the pool at the local Holiday Inn.

The Grande Ballroom was an old dance hall built in the Twenties, with an orchestra stage built into one end. It held around 1,800 people and had great acoustics. It became my portal into the world of English rock 'n' roll bands. As well as Cream I saw Jeff Beck, Jethro Tull, Procol Harum, John Mayall, Savoy Brown, Joe Cocker, The Who, Pink Floyd, Led Zep, Arthur Brown, Spooky Tooth and more, plus numerous American bands. The Grande was where The Who first played *Tommy*; they dropped a couple of the milder tunes from the album that weekend, so Detroit didn't get cred for being its premiere.

The Cream show was excellent. The temperature had to be around 100 degrees and a lot of clothing had been removed. The band had been pushed very hard by the opening act, the MC5, and they didn't take any prisoners. Most of the music was from *Fresh* and *Wheels*, with a few tunes from *Disraeli*. Just about every song featured extended interplay between Jack and Eric. Jack's tone was what I lived for; he really ran his Marshall 100s up to 11, distorting the daylights out of the 12 inch speakers that he liked to use. We were used to listening to the Motown bassists who, God bless 'em, played like wildfire, but with a tone that can best be described as thudding. Jack, and John Entwistle, changed that for bassists, much to our delight.

Eric had the first Gibson Firebird I'd ever seen outside of a music store. It's an overused word, but his sound can best be described as searing. He played like no one I'd ever seen before, leaving a lasting impression that ruined life for every other guitarist I worked with after that show. They really cooked. I was so attuned to Jack and Eric that I didn't pay a lot of attention to Mr Baker until 'Toad'. He held down the fort while his mates soared. I believe they encored twice, but I can't remember what the tunes were.

Eric had the first Gibson Firebird I'd seen outside of a music store

---

Four months later in October, they'd announced their breakup and embarked on the *Goodbye* tour. They played at Detroit's Olympia Stadium, a 15,000 seat hockey arena with the acoustics of a mud bog. With memories of the Grande show still fresh, it was a real disappointment. The stage was in the round and the sound was absolutely atrocious from our nosebleed seats, a garbled mashup. It would be several years before technology caught up to provide quality sound in large venues, and that sure wasn't even close to the beginning. 'Spoonful' seemed to go on forever. It was not a good night.

So I'm left with the memory of that one night in June of '68. Which is fine by me, because it was magical. I recall that show more than I do the girl I was with. In my mind, the essence of rock 'n' roll has always been the trio. Cream took that formation to heights that none of us dreamed possible, with grace and power that left us emotionally and physically drained. Their talent as musicians was beyond anything we'd yet seen, and it took quite some time for the rest of the music world to catch up. When I hear the word 'tenor', I see Jack Bruce; he may not have been an angel, but at times he certainly sang like one.

I WAS THERE: JIM BIELECKI
MY BROTHER WAS three years older than me and introduced me to Cream. He liked what we called at the time 'underground music'. He was into English blues rock which really started to take off in the mid-Sixties, and introduced me to the Yardbirds, Cream, Fleetwood Mac (when they were a blues band) and a bunch of other artists whose names now escape me. I remember when he brought home *Fresh Cream* from Dearborn Music, our local record shop. We listened to it together and I remember being blown away by 'Spoonful'. There's one riff where Eric plays blazingly fast and which knocked me on my butt. I had never heard a band play music like this before.

Jim Bielecki remembers it being very hot on that June '68 night in Detroit

The Grande Ballroom in Detroit was patterned after the Fillmore in San Francisco. It was the place to go in Detroit to hear good music. All British bands who were travelling America stopped by the Grande on their way to the West Coast. You had to be 17 years old to get into the Grande, so I had to wait until 1968 before I could go. The first band I saw was Cream, in June 1968. It was a hot day and when we walked into the Grande, it must have been 90 degrees. The place was packed.

I suffered through listening through the MC5, a local Detroit band, before Cream hit the stage. Memories are of Ginger playing 'Toad' and them playing 'Spoonful'. And I remember the interplay between Eric, Ginger and Jack. These guys were connected! I read someplace that once the band decided to break up, they played their best music, all pressure being off. That may have been the case in Detroit.

I saw Cream again on their farewell tour. They had outgrown the Grande and played their farewell concert at The Olympia, where the Detroit Red Wings hockey team played. The place was absolutely packed. What I remember most is Eric and Jack taking off their guitars and sitting behind the speakers talking while Ginger wailed away on the drums on 'Toad'. It was a good concert, but a sad one, because Cream was soon to be no more.

I saw many, many big bands play at the Grande - The Who, Led Zeppelin, Joe Cocker, Savoy Brown - and countless local ones. The best, by far, was Cream. To see and hear that much talent on stage, making music, still gives me shivers today. I count myself as very fortunate to have seen them twice.

I WAS THERE: RICK LANDERS

DURING THE 1960s, my brother and some high school friends were heavily into rock music. Many of us were musicians and we'd head to Detroit area clubs at weekends to see local area rockers like Bob Seeger, the Psychedelic Stooges, The Frost, Savage Grace, the MC5, the Unrelated Segments, Scott Richard Case, Mitch Ryder and the Detroit Wheels, Terry Knight and the Pack and more. Our centrepoint was a venue we called the 'old' Grande Ballroom, where kids would pack the place and line up along its short small stage. Big name groups would show up as featured acts. One I recall with no little awe and admiration was Cream.

Rick Landers with his Silvertone guitar

They played hard and played loud with abandon

Ginger Baker sat behind his double bass doubled tom drum kit, Jack Bruce held his ground with a cherry red EB-3 Gibson bass and a Marshall SuperBass amp, and Eric Clapton was harnessed to the Gibson Firebird he'd purchased two months before in Philadelphia. Cream launched their set with one of my favourite songs, 'Tales of Grand Ulysses', and were deafeningly loud, a full force gale of sound with Baker pummelling his kit.

Next up was 'Sunshine of Your Love' and I was surprised to watch Eric and Jack sharing the song's lyrics in a near call and response fashion. Their finale was Ginger Baker's 'Toad' drum solo, which I found a bit boring. As they were leaving, a roadie tossed me one of Ginger's drumsticks that is now sadly lost to the ages. Cream were a fashionable group decked out in clothes straight out of Carnaby Street; they played hard and played loud with abandon with some of the best songs I've ever heard.

Nearly 40 years later, my brother gave me two bricks from the now abandoned Grande. I had to smile to see that they had raised lettering on them by the brick maker that read 'J.A.M.'

I WAS THERE: JOHN TINTERA, AGE 14

IT WAS THE first concert I ever attended. There was a great deal of parental concern about this as it was the psychedelic era, and that meant more than just bell bottoms and fluorescent black light posters. An older friend was entrusted at 18 to drive to the concert. Strict warnings were given about drugs and alcohol. The concert was in downtown Detroit, home of Motown of which everyone was a fan, but no one except Hendrix and maybe Santana could touch the enthrallment of 'god' Clapton. And yes, the graffiti saying 'Clapton is God' was scrawled on the walls of the men's room, our generation's 'Kilroy was here'.

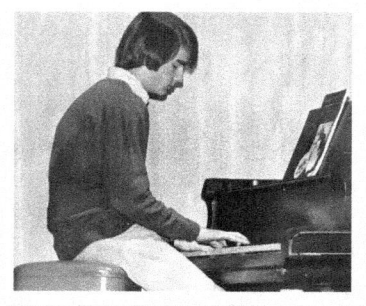

John Tintera was inspired to become a musician by seeing Cream in Detroit

A heavy cloud of dope smoke hovered over the large amphitheatre. Every few minutes another doobie passed by. The crowd was young and motley in dress but somewhat uniform in appearance, with beads and bright colours everywhere. The girls were long haired, lean and mini-skirted or blue-jeaned babes. All of us were full-throated rock fans, as only the very young and coming of age can be. Many of the female fans danced in place, swaying in time with the wild Baker's beat, a sight entrancing by itself. He was a madman on drums during 'Toad' and brought the house to its feet. Clapton and Bruce blew the roof off on 'White Room'. I knew walking out of the concert that I wanted to be a rock star for a lot of reasons, some noble, some just early teenage fantasies. It inspired my lifetime interest in amateur musicianship.

I WAS THERE: BOB ADCOCK, CREAM'S ROAD MANAGER

THERE WERE MAD dashes to airports sometimes. Catching the plane wasn't difficult if you excluded the major cities like New York, Chicago and LA. In other places you could turn up 15 minutes before the flight left and get on the plane with no problem. We rarely used limos. We used to use rental cars. Renting a car could be done very, very quickly because the rental car lot was usually directly across the road from the terminal exit. Nowadays they're miles away. You couldn't do it today. But back then you'd get there, you'd get your bags off the plane, rush over to the Hertz desk, rent the car - which never took more than a couple of minutes - and get across the road into the rental car. The band would get in, the suitcases would be loaded in and we'd drive off to the hotel. That happened every day. And the next day we'd turn up at the airport and do the thing in reverse. Leave the car outside the terminal. Go to the Hertz desk, give them the contract and they'd say 'thank you very much' and then you'd go straight to the check in desk, get on the plane and go. We never missed planes. We always got there on time.

We never missed planes. We always got there on time

Because I used to plan it well enough and because the three of them were quite reliable. They might have been branded as hippies but they'd turn up on time when they needed to. They were quite professional on the road. I don't remember ever missing a single flight with Cream because anyone was late.

ISLAND GARDENS
14 JUNE 1968, WEST HEMPSTEAD, LONG ISLAND, NEW YORK

I WAS THERE: KEVIN JOHN CLARKE, AGE 17

I REMEMBER BOTH my first ever concert - Cream - and the beautiful long-legged blonde with hot pants that attended the concert with me. What a combination. Who gets to see Eric Clapton, Ginger Baker and Jack Bruce? 50 plus years later I still listen to Cream and still values that music.

I WAS THERE: STEPHEN J GRILLI, AGE 16

I SAW THEM twice - in West Hempstead, Long Island and at their farewell concert at MSG that fall. At the first show the sound system broke down before they took the stage and, after an interminable delay, they came on and opened with 'NSU'. Bruce's vocals cut out almost immediately. Someone announced they were only going to do instrumentals, and if I remember, they only did 'Steppin' Out' and then 'Toad'. It was a short show and people were very disappointed.

Stephen J Grilli saw Cream twice

The farewell show at MSG in November was marred by a rotating stage that must have been hell for them and certainly was for us in the audience. They soldiered on gamely. By that time, I was positively enamoured with *Wheels of Fire* and listened to 'Crossroads' and 'Spoonful' endlessly. Frankly, I don't remember anything as dynamic as those two performances. I was a jock back then, and brought a few members from my high school football team to the show with me (we rode the LIRR in from our homes in Hicksville, where my first high school dance featured a local classmate named Bill Joel!). For the most part, they were pretty baffled by the whole experience. But I was thrilled hearing my idols.

WHEELS OF FIRE RELEASED
14 JUNE 1968

Cream's third album is a double, released in June in the United States and eight weeks later (on 9 August 1968) in the UK. One half of the album was recorded in the studio and the other half live. It goes on to top the Billboard chart and reach number 3 in Britain.

I WAS THERE: GORDON PHINN

I SMOKED SO much hash that I hallucinated on the cover of *Wheels of Fire* as if I were on acid. And I thought 'they designed it that way!'

The final show of the North American tour is in New Jersey.

CAMDEN COUNTY MUSIC FAIR
16 JUNE 1968, CHERRY HILL, NEW JERSEY

I WAS THERE: ROBERT BEECHER
THEY PLAYED AT a small venue called the Camden County Music Fair. There was a rumour that Ginger Baker had died. And when the show started you could only see Eric and Jack. But when the music started, I knew it was Ginger. I saw several other groups at the same venue, but that is one show I will definitely never forget.

I WAS THERE: JASON MCLEAN
CAMDEN COUNTY MUSIC Fair was a big tent with a rotating stage. A friend and I snuck under the tent flaps and saw an amazing show. The thing that sticks in my mind is Ginger's epic drum solo, after which somebody threw a bucket of water on him to cool him down. The band blew my young mind, and their music still sounds great today.

The band fly back to Britain that week separately, Eric appearing at Steve Paul's Scene in New York to jam with Jimi Hendrix and Jeff Beck.

I WAS THERE: ANNELIES HES
I SAW CREAM often. I was one of Eric's many lady friends for a short while.

Annelies Hes went out with Eric

'WHITE ROOM' RELEASED
21 SEPTEMBER 1968

'White Room' is released from Wheels of Fire to promote the American tour. It reaches number 6 on the Billboard chart, faring less well in the UK where it only gets to number 28.

After a long summer break, the band reassemble in Los Angeles in October 1968.

ALAMEDA COUNTY COLISEUM ARENA
4 OCTOBER 1968, OAKLAND, CALIFORNIA

I WAS THERE: TOM BRODY

AFTER SEEING THEM at the Fillmore, I attended another Cream concert at Oakland Coliseum. I attended this concert with my buddy, Jim Craft. We both played guitar and we both admired Moby Grape. The audience cried out 'Toad! Toad! Toad' because they wanted to hear this composition, and Ginger Baker replied in his microphone, exclaiming, 'I am not a toad!' The second act was It's a Beautiful Day. Their first song was 'Wasted Union Blues'. 30 seconds into this song, there was a vocal glissando, which I thought was ridiculous, so I imitated it out loud in an attempt to make fun of it. A girl sitting next to me in the upper balcony turned and scowled. I have no idea who she was.

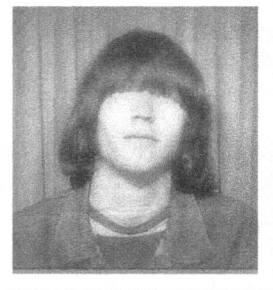

Dan Garvey was at the Coliseum

I WAS THERE: DAN GARVEY

I WAS SOMETHING of a regular at the Fillmore, the Carousel and Winterland so saw all the big bands - well, a hell of a lot anyway! I saw Cream at the old Fillmore in the late summer of 1967 and again early in 1968 at Winterland. I then saw them at Oakland Coliseum in the fall of 1968.

I WAS THERE: JERRY MILEY

I SAW THEM live three or four times in the San Francisco Bay Area in the late Sixties, and also Eric and Ginger with Blind Faith, and Eric and Dave Mason with Delaney and Bonnie and Friends. Being a blues guitar player, I became a huge fan of Eric when he was with John Mayall's Bluesbreakers so naturally became a huge fan of Cream. Eric and I are the same age and were similarly influenced by the same blues artists, so I was drawn to him immediately. With Cream though, I began to identify also with the talents of Jack and Ginger, and was totally sold on them. We saw them at the Oakland Arena. We were outside after the show and saw them get into a limo. Eric was sitting by the door with the window down and we spoke to each other and I asked for a pick. He seemed to be reaching for one but someone else rolled up the window, so I got to say hello but no souvenir. The show was just magnificent. Eric was hot that night!

I WAS THERE: ROBERT S CALICA, AGE 18
I SAW THE Cream in 1967 in San Francisco at the Fillmore West or Winterland and then the farewell concert tour at the Oakland Coliseum Arena. I found out about them from my friend, whose older brother had bought *Fresh Cream*. I then bought it, followed by *Disraeli Gears* and *Wheels of Fire*! It was an experience I'll never forget. I went with high school friends. I got really excited just watching them tune up, and it was loud. They had stacks of Marshall amps behind them and the sound was so powerful. My ears were ringing the day after the show.

I WAS THERE: STEVEN EGSTAD
I WAS IN my senior year of high school when I saw them in Oakland, California. Elton John warmed up for them. Having grown up during the San Francisco scene during the Sixties I got to enjoy a lot of great music but Cream really won me over. It just so happens I busted three of my teachers smoking pot at the show - and, yes, I was also! Eric is in my top three guitar players I've seen along with Jimi Hendrix and Stevie Ray Vaughan. I have always kept up with Eric's music through the decades. And I believe Cream had the best rock drummer in Ginger Baker. His drum solo on *Wheels of Fire* was unbelievable. I took *Wheels of Fire* with me when I went off to college.

UNIVERSITY ARENA, UNIVERSITY OF NEW MEXICO
5 OCTOBER 1968, ALBUQUERQUE, NEW MEXICO

I WAS THERE: SCOTT MACNICHOLL, AGE 14
I WAS A very naive 14-year-old steadily seeking out new rock and roll as I happened upon it. I was already a die-hard fan of the Rolling Stones and had discovered the Yardbirds, and then *Are You Experienced* turned everyone's heads sideways. Jimi Hendrix was a force of nature, while The Doors were also a big new discovery for me. My musical ears were often informed by friends' discoveries, often passed down by older

siblings, and finally the radio when it finally decided to expand past the tiring bombast of the Top 40 AM nicotine and caffeine-driven DJs playing the new hit single of the week four times an hour.

Scott MacNicholl discovered Cream whilst in Cape Cod

Born and raised in Albuquerque, I spent the summer of 1968 in Cape Cod, Massachusetts where radio, close to Boston, was a little more advanced. It was here I first heard 'Sunshine of Your Love'. I sought out *Disraeli Gears*, still one of the coolest album covers of the psychedelic age, and discovered *Fresh Cream*. I soaked up these sounds daily. Just before returning to New Mexico, I found *Wheels of Fire* in a Hyannis record store. I listened to Side 3 over and over - Clapton's blistering solo on 'Crossroads', followed by the long jam of Willie Dixon's 'Spoonful', which I listened to so much I could anticipate every moment of the track, followed by my mom from somewhere in the house saying 'please turn that down!'

From somewhere in the house I could hear my mother saying 'please turn that down!'

We got word that Cream were coming to Albuquerque. Many great bands of the Sixties didn't, and so my anticipation was over the top. Still seven weeks shy of turning 15, I dressed as hip as I could wearing jeans and an old army shirt with epaulettes my brother-in-law (a Vietnam vet) had given me. My hair was not long, unfortunately.

I went to the concert with a neighbourhood friend. The venue was where the University of New Mexico Lobos played basketball, nicknamed 'The Pit' as most of the structure is below ground level, and a very intimidating place for opponents to play as cloud and raucous crowds would rain down hell from the steeply stacked bleachers. My ticket was looked at but not torn in half. (Sadly my first piece of rock and roll memorabilia would be stolen from me some years later). I seated myself at a vantage looking down at my stage left. One of the openers was local band The Bounty Hunters, who mostly played covers of popular rock songs like 'In-A-Gadda-Da-Vida'. Finally, the lights were brought down for the main attraction.

The three members of Cream came down a ramp that would normally see a basketball team running down to man the court. They were on my side of the stage. Jack Bruce and Eric Clapton carried their guitars like soldiers with rifles, cradling the body of the instrument with the necks running up their chests and shoulders. They made their way to the stage, began plugging in, final tuning, etc. There was no introduction as the band launched into 'White Room'.

There was no introduction as the band launched into 'White Room'

Eric Clapton looked exactly as he would in the Royal Albert Hall final concert, with red shirt and jeans, while Ginger Baker was in a flowery loose-fitting East Indian-type affair. Closest to me was Jack Bruce, who drew most of my attention. He wore green velvet-looking pants and his stage moves seemed intense at times, his head cocking to one side as he belted out the chorus to 'I'm So Glad'. He would often back pedal into the instrumental sections of songs, hitting his Marshall stacks and making them rock back and forth. Eric was mostly focusing his concentration on playing his guitar.

Many late Sixties and early Seventies rock shows with long drum solos gave way to boredom. To fully appreciate Ginger Baker's mastey of his instrument, he had to be seen live. When he hit the crescendos of his solo, it seemed every drum and cymbal was being hit at once - faster, faster, faster! His head seemed buried in his snare drum, his arms and legs working their rhythmic magic! As he began the drum beat back into the full instrumental mode of 'Toad', the crowd simply exploded. For a 14-year-old, the show ended far too soon.

AUDITORIUM ARENA
6 OCTOBER 1968, DENVER, COLORADO

I WAS THERE: BOB COONTZ
THE CONCERT WAS in the round. Our seats were directly in front of the stage and about 10 rows back so the sound wasn't too bad. The

music was fantastic all the same. They played all the tunes I wanted to hear - 'Sunshine of Your Love', 'Spoonful', 'White Room', 'Train Time', 'Toad' and on and on. This concert is one of my favourite memories of my youth.

I had been getting into the blues without knowing it, first with the Rolling Stones, the Animals and the Yardbirds and then through Mayall and Butterfield. In the summer of 1968 I was working for the Denver Public Schools. We had a radio going all the time and were listening to KLZ- FM or KFML. Both were playing *Wheels of Fire*. The jam in 'Spoonful' really grabbed me. I was hooked.

Bob Coontz saw Cream in the round

Cream announced a concert for October 6 to be held at the Auditorium Arena and I bought two tickets as my (still to this day) very good friend Mike wanted to go. We got to the venue and smoked a little weed to set the tone for the evening. There was no opening act. Cream came on and launched into their programme. It was an hour to an hour and a half of bliss but the tension between Jack Bruce and Ginger Baker was evident. In the midst of a jam Jack would turn his amplifier up. Ginger would give him a nasty look and play faster and louder. You have to admire jazz drummers! Over all that Eric Clapton soared through a solo and brought the tune all together. It was a signature of Cream. I don't believe anyone has ever done it better.

I WAS THERE: GORDON REYNOLDS

I WAS IN school and several of us decided to get tickets and go. We just enjoyed their music and had the opportunity. We had to sit in the nose bleed section. As soon as the lights went down, the marijuana rose to the top. That was back in the day you could smoke inside. Happy times.

Gordon Reynolds had nosebleed seats

I WAS THERE: BOB ADCOCK, CREAM'S TOUR MANAGER

NOWADAYS THE BANDS have so much control over the shows, they can determine who plays support and how long they play for. You can say, 'I'm not having that band as a support act because they're trouble' or whatever. You couldn't do that then. Promoters chose the bill. The promoter said, 'This is the bill. I'm buying Cream. I'm also buying two or three other bands and this is the running order.'

In the Sixties there was no limit to how long you played, which is how these long, long sets started to develop. The Grateful Dead would play for something like three weeks at the one venue for the one gig. You had time to go home and have your dinner, or go on holiday and come back and they'd still be playing. Before the three hour thing came in, there was no limit and bands would play late. And nobody gave a care because times were different. Nobody in America cared about getting home at the end of the night. Everybody had cars and people didn't rely on public transport to get home. There were no restrictions on playing late. But having said that I don't remember many Cream gigs lasting more than a couple of hours.

When the unions started getting involved, they made show times three hours. The show could start whenever you wanted it to but it had to finish three hours later - to the second. And if it didn't the promoter had to pay huge sums in overtime money to the union. When the headline act started to realise that they had to finish by a certain time and the rest of the show determined when they went onstage, they said, 'If we've got to finish by a certain time then we'll tell you when we're going on stage.'

If the show didn't finish three hours later to the second, the promoter had to pay huge sums in overtime

It later developed to where record companies would say, 'If you're going to support Cream and you're playing to a sell-out audience, we're not going to pay you to play. Your record company can start paying us for you to play as support to Cream.' The band invariably played for a flat fee and that flat fee changed depending on how much the agent could screw out of the promoter and how wise the promoter was, and there were huge variations. You'd play one night for five thousand dollars and the next night for 25 thousand dollars. That all changed when bands started claiming percentages instead of fees. So they'd play for 90 per cent and the promoter got 10 per cent and he paid all of his expenses out of his 10 per cent.

CIVIC OPERA HOUSE
7 OCTOBER 1968, CHICAGO, ILLINOIS

I WAS THERE: JIM STAHL

I SAW CREAM play live two different times in Chicago in the late Sixties. They would come out and play songs as a group, and then each would do a solo number that would last as long as each wanted. Most people have seen and heard Ginger Baker do his 'Toad' solo act but Clapton and Bruce did incredible solo riffs on their own. All three of them would end their solos and merge their music back into the group to finish. Each of them wrote a lot of their stuff, too, which was very original and interesting. They are still my favourite group of all time.

NEW HAVEN ARENA
11 OCTOBER 1968, NEW HAVEN, CONNECTICUT

I WAS THERE: MICHAEL BLOOMFIELD

AS AN 18-YEAR-OLD flower child, I found myself in the middle of an incredible music explosion. Granted, listening to 'Cathy's Clown' and 'Hound Dog' on my 45 turntable as a Fifties child set the stage, but as I began college, I had already seen live performances of Simon and Garfunkel, Richie Havens, The Incredible String Band, James Taylor, CSNY, Jefferson Airplane, Fairport Convention, The Band, Traffic, Janis Joplin, BB King, Grateful Dead, Allman Brothers, Muddy Waters, Joni Mitchell, The Who, Arlo Guthrie, Frank Zappa, Judy Collins, and others, now a bit lost in a purple haze....

While I was aware of the Yardbirds and the

Michael Bloomfield is still learning 'Crossroads' 50 years on

Bluesbreakers, Clapton was not on my radar. But when *Fresh Cream* and *Disraeli Gears* came out? Bam! This was the music that said, 'I have arrived.' *Are You Experienced* blew me away and cemented my psychedelic identity, but Cream created a bridge from gritty earth to music heaven. When I discovered that they were to play the New Haven Arena, I found myself with a ticket and an itchy hitchhiker's thumb. The concert was near the end of their existence, and the band was - not surprisingly - late getting on and noticeably tired of it all, yet brilliant in their mastery. 50 plus years later, memory is less than crystal clear, and more of what is recalled are the larger circumstances around the band's tour - marching on Washington regarding the Vietnam War, civil rights, assassinations, student strikes, the draft. Nevertheless, Cream and Clapton are still the benchmarks for me as a guitarist and as the tap root of a lifetime of rock and roll enthusiasm. To this day, I am still learning Cream's version of 'Crossroads' from *Wheels of Fire*, one of life's ecstatic challenges. They appeared in my life at the perfect time and place, and their music still resonates.

NEW HAVEN ARENA
11 OCTOBER 1968, NEW HAVEN, CONNECTICUT

I WAS THERE: DOUG DESHONG, AGE 15
I STILL HAVE my ticket stub. Seats were $6 and $7.50. The stage was centre floor. I went with Robert, a school friend. We were in row 4 but behind the stage. A local band was on first, playing cover songs. Their last song was 'Hey Jude'. Our parents had given us $1 each for sodas and snacks which was about right for the time. *Farewell Cream* posters were on sale before the show for $1.50 but neither of us would give the other their $1 for them to get the poster. Bob wanted it more than I did. I didn't care for it. Jack had that leather hat on that looked like a poor attempt at a cowboy hat. I just never liked that photo.

Ginger was to my right, sat up on a corner. I could see Jack's back, and occasionally Eric, but mostly saw a lot of

Doug's ticket from the October '68 New Haven show

Marshalls. They opened with 'White Room'. Jack did 'Traintime' and I liked his harmonica playing. He also made a point to come to the back of the stage and play to all us folks on that side. Most everything they played was off *Wheels of Fire* - 'Politician', 'Deserted Cities of the Heart', 'Crossroads', 'Traintime', 'Those Were the Days'. Of course, with Cream a full show could three songs. The crowd wanted 'Spoonful' but they were running on and had a second show to do, so closed with 'Toad'. I couldn't have been more than 20 feet from Ginger and had a great view of his left side. His feet were amazing, the way they never stopped.

I mostly saw a lot of Marshalls

I spent my life wishing they would reform. Those three together put out an energy - an aura - I never felt from any other band. I saw Blind Faith in Bridgeport, Connecticut on their one tour. It wasn't the same with Rick Grech and Steve Winwood but without Jack Bruce. The magic was just not there. And I saw Jack and Ginger in the short lived BBM with Gary Moore. Again, there wasn't the special chemistry that the three Cream generated together. It's why Jack and Ginger had less than A list careers. Eric got along well, but his slowish folk blues style did nothing for me. I often wondered if heroin had put the fire out permanently.

His playing at the 2005 reunion showed me it was there, dusty but still there. I tried to get tickets to the London shows and was up at 3am for ticket sales but my Visa credit card would not allow a charge in pounds. By the time I got hold of Visa and explained it was not credit card fraud tickets were sold out. It would have been a huge to go to London from Missouri but my wife knew how much it would have meant to me.

Had Cream stayed together they were going to team up with Steve Winwood. I don't know if they would still have the same aura and mystique if that had happened. Maybe they could have played together a while, as Eric could have gone off with Steve when Jack and Ginger wanted to kill each other.

I have always wondered why a trio that was so damn successful and special would break up. It sounds like Ginger was a quiet guy with a very short fuse, and his heroin addiction probably did nothing for his stability, while Jack was a bit of a bully who would get him riled. Jack would sometimes get on Ginger, and while Ginger would not start a fight he would never run from one either.

I WAS THERE: BILL POUTRAY

IT WAS A short but incredibly high energy show, basically the live stuff from *Wheels of Fire*. They ripped ass, Clapton and Baker chasing each other full out. The rumour was that Baker, being a speed freak, would die on stage during his big 'Toad' drum solo. Not to disappoint, he appeared to pass out and was dragged offstage to the astonishment of all. Obviously, he survived. One of the greatest rock shows I ever saw.

I WAS THERE: TONY DESILVIS, AGE 17

I SAW *FRESH Cream* at a friend's house in 1967. I wasn't familiar with it and forgot about it. But music was starting to change. You had the San Francisco thing going on and seven or eight months later 'Sunshine of your Love' and *Disraeli Gears* came out and I had an opportunity to see the band. That was it. They played at the old New Haven Arena, an oval-shaped ice hockey rink. I got tickets for myself and my girlfriend at the time, went to see them and - what can I say? It was just an amazing experience. They had divided the arena in half, so the stage was on the arena ice facing the entrance and

Tony DeSilvis saw *Fresh Cream* at a friend's house

exit for the heavy equipment that was used to come on and clean the ice. When the first act ended, I was looking down at the ice and I said, 'We can get down there.' And that's what we did. We went down there and got on the ice. We were in the last row of seats but we had a straight shot to the stage. And at that point everything changed. These guys came out and just levelled us. I had never experienced anything like it before.

The rumours about Clapton, Bruce and Ginger Baker were rampant at the time, so to see these guys was just an amazing experience. I understand where the name Slowhand came from for Clapton now. He just stood there and the only things moving were his hands. Jack Bruce, on the other hand, was waving that bass up and down and around and singing and just rocking the place out, and Ginger Baker was just a blur.

The crowd was going nuts.

When the band started playing everybody just put their heads down, closed their eyes and rocked with the music. I was in a little band at the time and from that point on we tried being like that but it just didn't work.

Roughly a year later, the United States had the draft going on for Vietnam. I was 19 years old so instead of going into the Army I joined the Navy. My first duty station was up in Holy Loch, Scotland and I couldn't believe it. These young guys would be walking around with jackets with things like 'Jack Bruce Rules' painted on them. You couldn't say anything bad about Jack Bruce up in Dunoon, Scotland because you would have got beat up.

OLYMPIA STADIUM
12 OCTOBER 1968, DETROIT, MICHIGAN

I WAS THERE: DENNIS BURR, AGE 15

WHEELS OF FIRE was my first Cream record, although I had heard the first two quite a lot. Cream was playing at Olympia Stadium in Detroit, so we went and waited in line for tickets and were thrilled that we got sixth row! This was my first big concert on my own and a big event for sure. The show was opened by a band called Friend and Lover, a one hit wonder ('Reach Out in the Darkness'), and I was surprised to see Jim Schwall playing guitar for them. He played a cheap acoustic with a DeArmond pickup through a Marshall, and put on a performance that rivalled Clapton's that night.

Dennis Burr got sixth row tickets

The lights came on and the roadies prepped the stage for Cream. I was seated on the centre aisle, and the crowd roared from the back of the hall as Cream walked up the aisle to the stage. It was at centre ice - Olympia was a hockey arena. Ginger Baker walked by and I stuck my hand out to him, and he slapped five with me! Many years later, I met Jack Bruce and told him about this. He laughed and said, 'He was probably angry and was knocking your hand out of his way!'

Cream came on with 'White Room' and totally killed it. I was in awe.

Clapton was playing his single pickup Firebird I, Bruce was on a Gibson EB2 bass and Baker had his silver sparkle Ludwig kit. There were three Marshall full stacks behind Clapton and Bruce - and they were LOUD! Amazingly, the sound wasn't bad. They screamed through 'Spoonful', 'Sunshine of Your Love' and a couple others before Bruce did a solo with harp and vocal on 'Traintime'. If my recollection is right, they finished with 'SWALBR', 'Tales of Brave Ulysses' and 'Crossroads'. The encore was 'I'm So Glad'.

That same evening, John Mayall was playing at the famed Grande Ballroom and we planned to go after the concert to see that last part of the show but couldn't get in. As it turned out, Clapton showed up and sat in with Mayall on Mick Taylor's guitar. It was a memorable evening and a huge influence on what turned into my musical career.

I WAS THERE: BRAD LENA

GROWING UP IN the suburbs of Detroit in the 1960s meant Motown and of course the great bassist James Jamerson. Pop and rock and roll were not all that important to me. When I discovered that the British blues-based bands that interested me were imitating black American music, I became a blues enthusiast. I found parts of *Fresh Cream* quite interesting but blues, particularly Chicago style, still ruled. It was not until *Disraeli Gears* and hearing Cream live that I became an admirer. *Wheels of Fire* simply cemented that these guys were unique. Bruce and Baker had a much large musical vocabulary than any rhythm section in that genre, adding depth and breadth to Clapton's blues. In live performance, on their good nights, it became a conversation - or an argument. Improvisational ability and inspiration are a marriage. If one isn't working together the other suffers.

Brad Lena saw Cream three times in Detroit

I saw them twice at the Grande Ballroom and once at the larger Olympia Stadium. The intimacy of the Grande was far superior, as the audience was quite close and able to observe nuances in their communication or lack thereof. Their studio recordings still sound innovative 50 years later. No small feat.

I WAS THERE: BOB BARNSTEAD, AGE 16

LIKE A MILLION other kids, I was inspired to learn the guitar during the British Invasion of the Sixties. Slowly and painfully, I learned basic chords on my $20 Wards Airline guitar. In late' 65, along with a few neighbours, we formed our first band. We were of course terrible but by 1966 we started playing friends' local parties - and anywhere they would allow us! I was drawn to British bands like the

Bob Barnstead (right) with his band The Void

Kinks, Stones, Animals, and of course The Beatles, and then in 1967 bands such as the Doors and Buffalo Springfield. But Jimi appeared and blew us all away, while another new band appeared on the scene called Cream. We spent many school lunches arguing - Jimi or Eric? As much as I loved Jimi's music, I was drawn to Cream's blues influences and superior vocals.

By 1968, my band The Void was well on the way to rock stardom, doing many local school dances and community events. Our drummer's mother worked with a former Motown recording engineer who had started a budget studio and agreed to give us a shot if we could write some decent material. At school one day, our drummer Tom said he had heard Cream was going to break up but were coming to Olympia in October to do a farewell concert. We all bought tickets. Main floor tickets were $8.50 but after seeing The Beatles there in 1966, I knew the lower bowl view was better, and tickets were only $7.50.

Come the day we piled into Tom's 1964 Ford Fairlane and headed to Olympia. I remember hoping Friend and Lover wouldn't be on long because they didn't even play instruments! Finally, the lights dimmed and we knew it wouldn't be long. The stadium erupted in cheers as the shadowy figures could vaguely be seen entering the stage. Suddenly the lights flipped on and there they were, wasting no time launching into 'Spoonful'. Unlike today's elaborate and extensive visual effects, with countess hidden backup musicians, it was just the three of them with Ginger perched between the Marshall stacks. Their second song, 'Crossroads', was the one most etched in my mind. I marvelled at the way Jack Bruce's right hand was a literal blur providing the bottom end along with Ginger, while Eric launched into his ripping solo.

Mesmerised, we sat through the next few tunes and then came 'Toad'. On cue, the spotlight singled out Ginger and both Jack and Eric put down their instruments and stepped behind the Marshall amps for a smoke and some plastic cups of whatever. We were treated to roughly 10 minutes of Ginger at his best. Again on cue, Eric and Jack reappeared and picked up their instruments and finished up to thunderous applause.

They closed out with 'Sitting on Top of the World' and departed the stage. The ovation lasted for what seemed like forever but they never reappeared, much to our disappointment. Afterwards, being musicians, we decided to push our way down to the main floor to scope out the setup they used. The roadies were hard at work and as we got closer, we were able to see one fan reach up on the stage and snatch what appeared to be a neck strap and take off running, with a screaming roadie in hot pursuit! The other roadies then surrounded the stage to prevent any similar attempts so we couldn't get as close as we wished.

The ovation lasted for what seemed like forever

On the way home I had mixed emotions. I often tell people that it was the most impressive concert I'd ever seen to this day and I will forever be glad I attended. The flip side is I was so totally crushed, as we had thought The Void were pretty good and now I understood what the big time was all about and that we definitely had a ways to go.

I WAS THERE: DAVE BOYLE
I SAW THEM at the Olympia in Detroit. They were playing *Wheels of Fire*. The opening acts were Friend and Lover, who had hit out back then, and the Siegel-Schwall Band, who may have had a bit of influence on the British growing up. Then Cream came on stage. Jack was on the left side of the stage, Eric on the right and Ginger in the middle. They each had two double stack amps and played away, Eric on his reverse Firebird and Jack on his EBO bass. That bassist had a big influence on

me growing up.

I WAS THERE: DENNIS CHESTER GRZELAK

I WAS A junior in high school, aged 16 or 17, and enjoyed going to local venues and seeing bands. I saw lots of groups - Joe Cocker, The Who, BB King, the Stones and the crazy Davies brothers in the Kinks. It was the mid-Sixties when FM radio started to become underground stations and were playing Savoy Brown, Cream, The White Album and others, music that would never be played on AM stations. And it was through these underground stations and friends that I heard about these bands. When Cream came to Detroit, we had to buy tickets. I took a friend who had never heard about them and they blew his mind. I think we paid 12 dollars.

Surprisingly, the arena was barely half full. My friends and I were blown away by how only three guys could produce such a huge sound. I followed Clapton through his whole career. I really liked Derek and the Dominos. That era opened me up to some many different types of musical styles.

I WAS THERE: JOE DIEDRICH

THE OLYMPIA STADIUM was a hockey venue. I was with my then girlfriend. There were many great songs - 'White Room' was great and Slowhand was in rare form on 'Crossroads'. The whole show was fantastic and Ginger's sticks were magic! There was a lot of weed being smoked. My girlfriend was into that big time, me not so much. But it was one of the best concerts I went to when I was young.

I WAS THERE: ROGER DELISO, AGE 15

LOOKING BACK, HOW ironic it is that although my father regularly complained about 'that loud, lousy rock and roll you and your brother listen to', he wound up taking me and my best buddy to Detroit's iconic Olympia Stadium to see my very favourite band (and guitarist) Cream. Two recently turned 15-year-old kids let loose in that vast arena, we were overwhelmed and awed by the spectacle of it all.

The Olympia Stadium, home of the Detroit Red Wings hockey team, was a 15,000 seat oblong arena with seats ringing all sides. The stage was set up directly in the middle of the covered hockey rink. Seats were sold behind the forward-facing direction of the band and their amplifiers. I wonder if it was done because the promoter didn't know if more than 7,500 tickets would sell. Well, they certainly did, and many people were seated behind the amplifiers and with no view of any kind. We sat on the front side, off the main floor, with a distant but good view.

The first band that we saw was the Siegel-Schwall Band. As a budding electric guitarist, my most vivid memory was of Corky Siegel using an acoustic guitar with with a pick up. Electric blues played in a huge area with an acoustic guitar. How cool!

Roger DeLiso's father drove Roger and his buddy to the Olympia

Eventually, the three most famous musicians in the world for British Invasion rock fans in 1968 came out. Jack Bruce so animated, with his bass-work pyrotechnics and his intense, wailing vocal style. Ginger Baker wildly and colourfully dressed, flailing and pounding and driving it all. And then, him... Eric. The tone, the precision, the passionate fluidity, but also the stoic 'I don't have to jump around, I'm just gonna stand here stock still and play and show you all why I'm the best electric guitarist in the world' stance. It was a depth of musicianship that inspired an entire generation of young guitarists, and everything I could have hoped for.

Jack Bruce must have had a very long cable to his amplifier

Jack Bruce must have had a very long cable to his amplifier, because at a couple of points he moved from facing front and went behind the amplifiers and faced those seated behind and played for them in his typically animated style. Eric did not. Another stand out memory was Ginger's 'Toad' drum solo. How could it not be? The extreme length - 15 minutes? - the energy and complexity, the double bass drums. The entire experience of Cream was a dream come true.

A final note. I was very, very close to my father. Later in life he developed Alzheimer's dementia and I took care of him for many years through the end of his long life just last July. As the decades went by, my father became very supportive of my life as a guitarist and enjoyed all kinds of music. Time changes things. Thanks for taking Dave and me, Dad... I miss you more than I can say.

I WAS THERE: KEVIN GILLESPIE, AGE 13

THIS SHOW IN Detroit was the most impactful live show I've ever been to. It's so freshly emblazoned on my noggin. At seven years old I was pulling weeds out of people's gardens so I could have the money to go buy Beach Boys records. I loved The Beatles, and still do. I have a yellow submarine tattooed on my arm. But there was something about the power of Cream that was beyond everything else I listened to. I can just close my eyes and remember being there.

Kevin Gillespie was just 13 when he saw Cream

A babysitter took my 11-year-old brother and me into Detroit and dropped us off at the Arena. It was basically a barn but the Jack Bruce bass stuff was just hitting us. It was such a visceral experience. We were huge fans to begin with but I'll never ever forget being there and seeing these three people make so much music. We never even sat in our seats. We were two little pre-teen guys who went down by the stage and stood there. We even watched Ginger Baker when he was off the stage doing stuff back stage. The live version of 'Crossroads' just gets me going crazy. That three people could make that big of a sound was terrific.

I WAS THERE: KIRK KENNEY

I HAD PREVIOUSLY seen them at the Grande Ballroom in Detroit. They were one of the best power trios I have ever seen. Ginger was fantastic on the drums, Jack Bruce was a great bass player and singer, and Slowhand was fantastic on the lead guitar.

Kirk Kenney (left) saw Cream at the Grande and the Olympia

I WAS THERE: AL RUDE, AGE 15

THE DRUMMER IN my high school band introduced me to Cream. They weren't getting a lot of airplay here in Detroit. He also introduced me to this guy Hendrix, but I got even with Jeff Beck's *Truth*. I was incredibly impressed. I loved Jack's approach to the bass. I don't play anything like him but he was definitely an influence. I still admire his ability to sing and play 'Politician'. I've been trying to do that for years and failing! 'Crossroads' was our warm up song as a band. I knew Jack's part by heart and sang it. And I loved Ginger's drumming; he was a whole orchestral percussion section back there. No other drummer at the time or since has come close.

Al Rude considered quitting music after seeing Cream play

I saw them on the *Goodbye* tour. I had to get my mother to drive me and my fellow high school band members to the show. She was our chauffeur to all our gigs till we could drive. I was in the balcony almost directly over the band. I was blown away. I'd been playing gigs at sock hops for about three years by that time. It was the first time I had the alternate feelings of 'I should either quit playing or practice more'.

I WAS THERE: TOM SKINNER

I SAW THEM many times at the Grande, sometimes on Sunday night for only $1.50. On the farewell tour I saw them at the Detroit Olympia and spent some time drinking Detroit local-brewed beer with Ginger and Jack in the dressing room before the show. I walked out to the stage with the band and sat in the first row, on the side of the stage. They were an awesome, probably the best of the era.

I WAS THERE: BOB ZACK, AGE 16

I HAD HEARD about Cream, and Eric Clapton, as they were played on 'underground radio' in Toledo, Ohio - WTTO. I got *Fresh Cream* when it came out, loved it and bought *Disraeli Gears* and *Wheels of Fire*. Several friends listened to these records over and over, so when we heard that Cream was going to be in Detroit, we got tickets. I have no idea how we did that, but come showtime four of us piled into my buddy's car and drove to Olympia Stadium in Detroit for my first ever rock concert.

Bob Zack first heard Cream on underground radio in Toledo, Ohio

The stadium was packed. We had pretty good seats off to the left side of the stage, about 20 rows up. People were smoking joints and were in a good party mood. Friends and Lover was the opening act. They played their hit 'Reach Out of the Darkness' and other songs. I thought the band's lead guitarist was pretty darn good.

Then came the main event, Cream. They had a stack of Marshall amps and a pretty big drum set. This was the phase when they all had afros as hairdos. They opened with 'Spoonful'. We were blown away! This guitar player was heads above the Friends and Lover guitar player. Cream played about 10 songs including 'Sunshine of Your Love', 'White Room', 'I'm So Glad' and 'Toad'. Suffice to say we couldn't believe what we were seeing. I think it was the first concert for all of my friends, because we couldn't stop talking about it. We all ended up going to many concerts in our lifetime, but never went together again.

I'm glad Cream was my first concert. While I think seeing The Beatles would have been a great experience, Cream was my first viewing of 'mature' music and performance. And you could actually hear the band! This show led me down a great musical path and I recall it with great fondness. Later, I got to meet Eric Clapton (1993) and Jack Bruce (2002) but never Ginger. Thanks, guys, for all the memories!

COLISEUM
13 OCTOBER 1968, CHICAGO, ILLINOIS

I WAS THERE: BILL HAWKINS, AGE 15
BEING I WAS more musically inclined than academics, in 8th Grade I would frequently cut out of school with like-minded friends and head to the local hotdog joint in downtown Arlington Heights - Snacksville - when it opened around 10am. Sat on the rotating stools near the juke box, we shoved money in there for hours playing our favourites, which at the time happened to be Cream. I'm not quite sure which side we played more, 'Sunshine of Your Love' or the flip side, 'SWLABR', but that disc got pretty scratchy from us playing it so much. I got to hear but not see Cream at the Cellar in Arlington Heights. It had an age requirement (17 years old - probably some stupid village ordinance) so we just stood outside and listened.

After that, I would frequent my friend Steve's house. He and his brother Ken were huge Cream fans. Ken was a couple of years older and had a set of drums tucked into a little side room off the basement, with double basses and a record player, which we modified with a pair of ear muffs with small speakers in each muff. Necessity is the mother of invention! I spent hours over there listening to *Wheels of Fire*, mainly 'Spoonful' and 'Toad', banging on the drums and vainly trying to convince myself I was Ginger Baker. I became very adept at air guitar and air drumming back then, and I still know every riff and beat change!

Fast forward to graduation from Junior High and the summer, when I spent an inordinate amount of time at the local park district hanging out with friends. I was talking to a girl who shared my love of The Doors and Cream. She said Cream was going to be at the Coliseum and was I interested in going? Was I? I figured out some way to scrape together the $8 or $10 and she got the tickets.

She said Cream were going to be at the Coliseum and asked was I interested in going?

I'm pretty sure we took the train downtown. I don't remember how we got to South Wabash - we probably walked. Our tickets must have been general admission because we ended up on the upper walkway on the Wabash side of the building. The place was jammed floor to ceiling with people. The accompanying act was Conqueror Worm, who I didn't know. When Cream finally took the stage, everyone on that upper level moved in behind the seated area and it was hard to see over people. I remember some older girl complaining that 'it's hot enough in here, move back'. It became a constant moving around adventure, trying to see what we were hearing. They played everything I wanted to hear and it seemed great to my young ears, but I wasn't a critic. I remember seeing the peeling paint between the trusses up above and thinking, 'It's so loud some of that's likely to drift down.'

At one point, when I couldn't get close enough to see, I wandered over to the windows and looked down onto the street. I saw all these people that didn't or couldn't get in just dancing around and jamming outside the building. It seemed like a beautiful thing that we were all enjoying this great band together.

I WAS THERE: ROBERT HARKABUS, AGE 15

I SAW THEM on the *Goodbye* tour at the Chicago Coliseum - which was an ancient dump! It was my first concert other than high school. The ticket was five dollars, and I got to go because my friend Rich from high school had an extra ticket because his girlfriend could not attend. So that worked out well for me. The sound was outstanding, apparently because they brought mountains of amps. It was the loudest sound I ever heard. 'White Room' was the star of the show, while the drum solo on 'Toad' went on way too long. 'Spoonful' was awesome. I never saw so many hippies in my life.

I WAS THERE: PETE LEKOUSIS, AGE 16

IN 1966 I was 14 years old, full of testosterone and wonder, living in my parents' small bungalow in suburban Chicago. My interests at that time were mainly about girls, doing drawings and artwork, *MAD* magazine, and the rock and roll music that was coming out of car radios and small hand held transistor radios. It was that year of high energy fuzz-box guitars and distortion, teenage excitement, but pre-psychedelics. My favourite rock band at the time was the Yardbirds. I had never been to a rock show or concert.

1967 ushered in the psychedelic era of music with The Beatles leading the way, and that aesthetic, informed by experimentation with hallucinogenic drugs and marijuana, filtered through almost every rock band's music. The invention of signal-warping guitar effects pedals helped illustrate a certain state of mind in the music; along with much longer

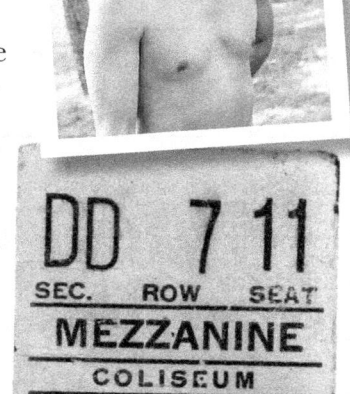

Pete Lekousis grew his hair and discovered recreational drugs in 1968

solos and song duration, which were a consequence of a shift away from radio friendly hit singles, to 33rpm record album-oriented listening. It was in this atmosphere that I first heard Cream on the radio - *Disraeli Gears*. In my teenaged mind, Cream perfectly reflected a more powerful, bluesy, psychedelic version of other bands I had loved. It is difficult to describe the excitement and power of their sound coming out of a cranked-up car radio.

By 1968 I had become acquainted with recreational drugs, grown my hair longer and fully embraced the counter-culture peace and love wave in America. The very first big venue-type show I bought a ticket for was Cream. They were playing one October afternoon at a huge old exhibition hall, located just south of downtown at the Coliseum. Designed for political conventions around 1900, the venue had simple public address system amplification and bad acoustics for music. All the sound for concerts of that era emanated from large stacks of amplifiers onstage set up behind the performers. In large venues, the sound became fainter, more distorted and had more echo, the further your seat was from the stage. I was fortunate to have a seat about 30 rows from the stage, with good sight lines, on the main floor.

The overall crowd was generally a bit older than me

The sound was very good. The overall crowd was generally a bit older than me. The Cream were nearing the end of a North American farewell tour, and mainly performed songs from *Wheels of Fire*. I had played it endlessly at home, spending hours imitating Jack Bruce's singing at the top of my lungs, staring at Martin Sharp's dynamic cover artwork and memorising every note of their inventively indulgent solos. I was completely a fan, and was utterly prepared and excited to witness this band live.

They did not disappoint. They sounded polished and confident, each song close to the recorded versions except, delightedly, during longer solos, which had the sensation of truly being improvised. This undoubtedly was true, since the band was playing a tour, and would be expected to have fun night after night, with their solos, out of a need to be creative and not be bored!

I'd describe the shared audience sensation before and during the show as electric and an almost giddy anticipation. It was great seeing Jack, Eric and Ginger in real life onstage and in person, breathing the same air, and being present in a moment that you knew was singular and special: seeing and hearing a great band, at their peak.

Ginger Baker seemed like the leader of the band, both in his central, physically commanding position on stage, but also from an almost deferential sense I got of Jack and Eric following his cues. There was a pause between songs at one point. The band stopped playing, the stage lights went down and Ginger disappeared, but Eric and Jack remained onstage. Someone in our group casually said that they had heard that

Ginger was a heroin addict and needed to be 'fixed' to continue playing, and that was why there was this pause of maybe five to seven minutes. Of course, we all nodded that it was entirely likely that our superheroes may need super drugs to be super performers, and how cool that must be. And of course, everyone knew that Ginger Baker had to be possessed, or a demon, to play like he did.

Everyone knew that Ginger Baker had to be possessed, or a demon, to play like he did

---

In reality, who knows why there was a short break. Equipment issues? Potty break? It could have been anything. After the pause he came back on stage, the lights went up and he continued. Maybe he launched into 'Toad'. He was amazing, playing passages with his feet alone, on the double bass drums. It was great fun. Of course, all their other signature tunes were wonderfully executed. 'Traintime' was a delight because it was a harmonica 'train' percussive Jack Bruce showcase. 'Politician' and 'Spoonful' featured Eric's great soloing, slow and swinging, fantastic blues.

They opened with 'White Room', which was perfect, a celebratory, psychedelic confection, as was 'Sunshine of Your Love', and memories of 1967. 'Sitting on Top of the World' and 'Crossroads' were performed like the stately, grand centrepieces of the show, satisfying in every way but not particularly inventive on the spot. Crowd pleasers, a bit rote. All in all, it was an amazing experience.

There were windows around the top of the hall and, it being an afternoon show, there was a good amount of direct, strong sunlight pouring down onto the stage and into the audience. It was an added benefit to see Jack, Eric and Ginger lit up in daylight, as opposed to artificial stage lighting. It made the experience somehow more real, less theatrical, more intimate.

I WAS THERE: LARRY D'ALESSANDRO WANGEROW

IT WAS AT the old Chicago stock yards. Chicago is a blues town. Clapton had lots of loops like Hendrix, while Ginger was always top of the list as the next one to OD. He fooled 'em all!

I WAS THERE: HANK ZEISLER

IT WAS ONE of the best concerts I've ever been to. Eric Clapton was good but it was Mr Ginger Baker that blew my mind. He did a drum solo in the middle of the song 'Traintime' that I've not heard any drummers get close to 'til this day.

Hank Zeisler remembers the Cream show as one of the best concerts he's ever been to

VETERANS AUDITORIUM
14 OCTOBER 1968, DES MOINES, IOWA

I WAS THERE: JERRY CLOUD, AGE 18

I WAS A big fan of Cream so eagerly bought a ticket when I found out they were going to be playing in Des Moines, Iowa where I was going to school at Drake University. I was exposed to music earlier than most my age through my three older brothers. I was fortunate enough to score tickets to Cream in the third row centre stage, so had a marvellous seat. What really stood out was how amazing it was that three people could produce such a full sound. I had a very clear view of Ginger Baker and was simply blown away by his talent and dedication. His hands were bandaged up and he was still bleeding through the bandages yet he put on a flawless show, never missing a beat. There was a rather large police officer standing front and centre, guarding the stage, and every so often Ginger would zing a drumstick past his head out into the audience and pull another stick into his hand never missing a beat. He did this numerous times throughout the show, much to the delight of the fans.

The stellar bass playing and awesome vocals of Jack Bruce and incomparable guitar work from Eric Clapton just made for a truly once in a lifetime experience for me. It was like a dream come true. I have seen some of the greats live, including Janis Joplin at that same venue,

Jerry Cloud was third row centre

The Doors in St Louis and The Who in Anaheim, but the Cream concert stands out as the best of them. To be that close to those three supremely talented musicians was the pinnacle of my concert going life and a memory I will always treasure.

I WAS THERE: CRAIG MOORE

AS THE BASS player in the Iowa garage band Gonn I was very influenced by the British bands of the era, in particular the Animals, Yardbirds, Rolling Stones, Kinks and Beatles, and American bands like Paul Revere and the Raiders and Jefferson Airplane. It wasn't so much technique or even the basics that drew me to the bassists in those bands as their sound. I owe my greatest debt to Chas Chandler of the Animals for showing me by example how to play bass blues and roots bass. Jack Cassidy and Paul Samwell-Smith sounded like they had blown their speakers doing aggressive, non-traditional runs, and the bass on the Raiders' records and Chris Hillman's parts on the Byrds' LPs blew my mind with their proficiency and the raw sound of it all. Al Kooper's Blues Project, whose first album came out in 1966 along with the Paul Butterfield Blues Band's debut, opened my eyes to electric blues and the blues jam aspect of those groups live.

Craig Moore was in a Cream tribute band

I knew of Eric Clapton as a former member of the Yardbirds. I wasn't aware of who had played that incredible, bombastic, dive-bomber bass part on Manfred Mann's 'Pretty Flamingo', but soon enough it all made sense. When *Fresh Cream* came out the imagery of the album cover, the experimental blues base of their unique material and Jack Bruce's rather ethereal vocals marked them as a band to watch. The creativity displayed on their second album, *Disraeli Gears*, by far surpassed that shown on the first. 'Sunshine of Your Love', 'World of Pain' and Clapton's 'woman tone' and wah-wah established them in a league of their own. The *Wheels of Fire* studio album was another giant leap beyond what now appeared the rudimentary structure of *Disraeli Gears*, but the live sides at the Fillmore blew a hole in the musical universe. I bought an EB-3 and started viewing live performance as potential anarchy. Jack's aggressive tone and nature appealed to me from somewhere very deep within.

When we heard that the owner of Des Moines Music was considering promoting a concert at Veterans Auditorium, we joined the chorus of fans lobbying for him to bring in Cream. He didn't know much about them other than the one hit on the radio, but enough of his customer base was in favour of that decision that he booked them. I bought two tickets and a poster.

I went to the show with my guitarist and good friend Slink Rand. We got to Vets Auditorium early in the afternoon, and since the stage entrance doors were unblocked, went in and made ourselves at home, with no one else in the place except the lone person on the stage apparently setting up the equipment. He was a tall and obviously strong young man with long wavy hair and a wide handlebar moustache. This person looked like many of the Cream-era pictures of Clapton I had seen and so I presumed him to be Clapton. After all, our band and almost every band I knew of set up their own gear, so why would Cream be any different?

Almost every band I knew set up their own gear, so why would Cream be any different?

The music store provided the sound system for the show, which was a standard Sunn Coliseum PA, consisting of one 2x15 speaker cabinet with a brass-grilled high frequency horn sitting on top of it, one such two-piece on each side of the stage. The amplifier/mixer was a Sun PA amp, exactly the same head as their guitar amp, except with four high impedance microphone jacks, four individual volume controls, one set of tone controls - low and high - and a master volume control. The amp sat on the stage in front of and between Ginger's bass and drums. Jack and Eric each had a high impedance Shure mic on a straight stand, and Ginger had a similar mic on a swivel stand. Limited to the four inputs on the amp, the fourth mic was on a desk stand sitting between the bass drums and pointed just slightly at an upward angle to catch the ambient sound of the kick drums along with the snare and perhaps some of the toms. There were no monitors. Eric had two stacks of Marshalls, Jack had two Marshall stacks plus two striped-front 2x15 Sunn cabinets. I didn't notice if there was a separate amp head driving those two cabinets, but there was most likely a Sunn bass head or a Kustom 200, as shown in some photos.

Several months prior I had bought my first six string guitar for $250. It was a black triple gold pick up 1957 Gibson Les Paul Custom, with an also-gold Bigsby tremelo arm. The original owner had brought it back, still in its original hard shell case. One of the guitarists in my band told me it was worth some money, so I took it with me to the Cream concert to show it to, and perhaps sell to, Clapton, since there was a picture of him playing one on the back of the *Bluesbreakers with Eric Clapton* album. As well as the guitar, I also brought along my cousin Tim's Super 8 home video camera.

Being extremely naïve and feeling somewhat entitled to roam the auditorium as a friend of the promoter, I spoke to the roadie (who disavowed my mistaken identification) after which I took the Les Paul to Cream's dressing room and left it there, sitting next to Jack's EB-3 case and Eric's guitar case, which I later learned contained a Gibson Firebird. There were no other guitars present, so I presume that Cream, at least at this show, didn't bother to carry back up instruments. We hung around all day, but Cream didn't do a sound check, or if they did it was before we got there.

I was backstage when Cream arrived that evening

I was backstage when Cream arrived that evening. Clapton was quite surprised to find a '57 Les Paul in the dressing room, and asked if I would be interested in selling him the bridge pieces (saddles) off of it. I was very disappointed that he wasn't interested in buying the guitar, and I imagine had it been a few years later he would have jumped on it. I had to decline the parts request. The show was not sold out. It was all reserved seating and most of the balcony was empty or sparsely occupied. The floor seats were probably two thirds full. I don't think Des Moines music made any money on the show and I don't think they put on any more after this experience.

I was standing in the backstage corridor when Cream came out in their stage clothes with their instruments, waiting to go on. I stood there for several minutes exchanging greetings and pleasantries. They were quite friendly and open. I was surprised that Eric was no taller - and perhaps shorter - than me, standing there exercising his fingers playing riffs on his Firebird, and Jack shorter still. Ginger towered over all three of us. He appeared friendly and smiling and at the time I had no reason to be surprised by this. I had been there all day, and as artists, staff and auditorium security came and went, they just assumed I was part of the operation. No one ever questioned me, or asked for my ticket. Slink spent the day just walking around and sitting here and there, observing what little went on around him. It was all quite laissez-faire.

As Cream made their entrance onto the stage, I ran up to the balcony overlooking the stage above Eric where Slink had gone to sit. There were no stage lights whatsoever, only overhead white spotlight auditorium lighting illuminating the entire stage in one bright circle of light from start to finish. With only the same PA system that some of the better local bands might have carried around to teen centre gigs, the only audio augmentation was a house mic hanging over the stage sending whatever it could pick up to the central overhead sports scoring/sound system used to announce basketball and other sports events held in the auditorium. There was no introduction and nothing was said by the band. I watched in awe as they opened with 'White Room', since they appeared to start without any cue, although surely Ginger counted it off in some fashion.

I watched in awe as they opened with 'White Room'

I went backstage to get my video camera and spent their entire set walking around different positions around the stage to watch Jack up close, or Eric, from whatever vantage point I wished. Eric had a stick of sweet-smelling incense stuck into one of this Marshall cabinets. A uniformed policeman working security at that end of the auditorium came over. I'd recently had my hair cut short so didn't look like the average male in the audience. 'Are they getting some sort of kick out of that stuff?' he asked, motioning towards the incense smoking from Eric's amp. I said, 'Not hardly, that's just incense. You can buy it at Kresge's and they burn it at church.' He seemed satisfied, or perhaps even embarrassed, and went back to his ordained position.

As a bass player whose life had been changed by *Wheels of Fire* and with an unencumbered close up view, I watched Jack carefully. I could never discern any real changes in his tone or volume, but he made frequent adjustments to the tone and volume controls on his bass as he played, though his incredible voice overshadowed what he was playing. They did 'Sitting on Top of the World' in the same precise arrangement as the *Wheels of Fire* studio version and quite different from the monumental landmark version that came out later on *Goodbye*. With no monitors in a huge boomy room like Vets Auditorium, I can only imagine what they were or were not hearing on stage. During a vocal on 'Crossroads', Eric got turned around on the beat, probably from the echo of the room, and was at least a full count off of what Jack and Ginger were doing. He turned towards Jack and by following the turnaround in the chord progression and Ginger's relentless 4/4 beat, he was able to get back to proper time and finish the song.

Eric simply stood off to the side of his gear, had a cigarette and waited

The audience was clearly there to listen, there was no awkward shouting or random noise from the crowd, and they roared approval after every song. They did a killer version of 'I'm So Glad'. They did 'Sunshine of Your Love', and I was taken aback by Eric's totally different solos than what was on the record. I hadn't expected him or Jack to vary their parts on such an iconic track so much. Jack's 'Traintime' was a showstopper. Eric simply stood off to the side of his gear, had a cigarette and waited.

The audience roared and applauded for an encore, but we knew that was not going to happen

During 'Toad' I again went into the balcony where Slink was sitting. Expecting at least one more song, we were surprised when it finished and we saw the tall roadie come up from behind Ginger, help him up off of his kit and, with an arm around his waist, lead him down off of the back of the stage, along with Jack and Eric, where they made a beeline for the exit doors at the back of the hall. The audience roared and applauded for an encore, but we knew that was not going to happen. Cream had left the building.

I took Slink with me backstage to retrieve my Les Paul, and I must confess to helping myself to a few of Jack's picks. Slink may have done the same with Eric's. Their cases were back there but their instruments were not, either still on the stage or in the hands of the roadie. I didn't use either of my tickets. I kept them, and the poster, until well into the Nineties, but lost them during my separation and divorce. I gave the video camera to cousin Tim to get the film developed. I never saw it. He told me that it was all red and blue lights, which would be a good trick since I never saw any such thing. Every time I see the cover of *Live Cream* I think 'I could have taken that', and many more just like it from both sides of the stage, and the front, and the back, and probably on the stage. No one would have said a word to me.

THE FORUM
18 & 19 OCTOBER 1968, LOS ANGELES, CALIFORNIA

I WAS THERE: BOB ADCOCK, CREAM'S TOUR MANAGER
DEEP PURPLE'S FIRST gig in America was supporting Cream. We were the headline act getting loads of money and they were paying to be on the bill. They turned up with six limousines, one for each of the band and one for the manager, and we turned up as headliners with a Ford station wagon.

I WAS THERE: HENRY F ROBBIE ROBINSON
HAVING LISTENED CLOSELY to *Wheels of Fire* the live performances blew me away. Seeing them play these tunes live still stands as my favourite gig of all time. I went out and bought a pearl drum kit after seeing Ginger Baker play. 20 years later I was his agent here in LA. Go figure!

I WAS THERE: TONY BEVER
I SAW THEM as a teen at the LA Forum on the *Farewell* tour. I was in high school. We had our parents drop us off at the concert as we didn't have a driver's license yet, and we got to walk behind the band tunnel to the outside afterwards. There was no security back then. This was my first ever big concert besides local park concerts. Somehow after Dylan and Vanilla Fudge we got really heavily into the Cream. The best thing about it is that Eric was a god to us then, and still is. I can still play drums on the pillows to 'Sunshine of Your Love.'

I WAS THERE: BRUCE REED

I CANNOT UNDERESTIMATE how much I was looking forward to seeing Cream for a second time since it was announced that they would be appearing at the Forum, a large enclosed sports arena holding roughly 17,000 people near LAX. Since seeing them in February 1968, they had catapulted to fame largely based on word-of-mouth and the enormous success of 'Sunshine of Your Love'.

As I entered the Forum I was pointed to my seat at the uppermost portion of the enormous facility, the nose-bleed section. I recall constantly looking back at the stage as I climbed further and further away from it, in stark contrast to the intimate surroundings of my first Cream concert. My concerns about being able to hear the music were quickly dashed as the opening act, the Mk I lineup of Deep Purple, roared to life. They played a blistering set to an appreciative audience, fuelled by the powerful drumming of Ian Paice. When they finished, I reached for the small tape recorder I had managed to bring in under my shirt and sat it on my lap.

Bruce Reed bought a Firebird on the strength of seeing Eric play one

Did I mention that my oldest son is named Eric?

Cream took the stage to enthusiastic applause. As they opened with 'White Room' the crowd went wild. As if Deep Purple weren't loud enough (they were!) the volume was edged up to yet another thunderous level. I was in awe of what I was hearing. The first thing I noticed was that Eric was playing a red Gibson 335 like Ritchie Blackmore had used earlier. After 'White Room' they played 'Politician' and then launched into the famous, fiery, extended version of 'I'm So Glad' found on *Wheels of Fire*. On the tape I can then be heard saying 'Firebird coming!' as the easily-recognisable brown Gibson was handed to Clapton. Apparently, this move was magic as Eric, Jack and Ginger launched into the hypnotic 'Sleepy Time Time'. The tape in my little recorder soon ended but the band continued to stun me and everyone else in attendance with song after song of the band's timeless music. They owned the Forum and Los Angeles that night. My life was shaped by this band in a way I cannot explain and I am so very glad I attended this concert. Did I mention that my oldest son is named Eric?

I WAS THERE: JAMES DAVIS

I SAW THE Forum show. My best friend at the time was Les Thompson, who played mandolin for the Nitty Gritty Dirt Band. He and his wife took me to a party up in Topanga Canyon that weekend and Cream were at the party along with some of Canned Heat. Ginger Baker was so drunk he would beat his drums and then throw his sticks at Clapton. He did it about three times and Eric said 'fuck this dude' and started to walk off. But everyone got Ginger to promise he wouldn't do it again. Then they started to play. I swear that when Ginger threw up he didn't miss a beat.

I WAS THERE: GEORGIA DAVEY, AGE 16

I ALWAYS LIKE the blues, because I grew up in a family where we always listened to a lot of music and my father liked blues and jazz. I started with the Stones and then I discovered the guitarists, which led me to the Yardbirds and Eric Clapton, Jeff Beck and Jimmy Page. Those three guys were my entrée into the British music scene. What I loved about Cream is that they were a blues band, not a rock band, and Ginger Baker just did it for me. He was the best drummer - sorry, Bonham, and much as I love Led Zep - and really more of a jazz drummer.

Georgia Davey waited in line to buy Wheels of Fire in Hollywood

I remember where I was the day I bought *Wheels of Fire* in Hollywood. We all stood in line to get the record. It was like this cult following, the people who I hung round with and who were into Cream and all this British music. My husband is two years younger than me and it pisses him off that I got to see Cream and he didn't! Two years made a difference in Hollywood. If you were two years younger you weren't going to concerts. And I had a girlfriend who was two years older than me and she had a car and she went to every concert I wanted to go to. My mother wouldn't have taken me to the Forum. That was a 40 minute drive from my house.

When Cream came to the Inglewood Forum in '68 I jumped on it. It was my very first concert. It was a sold out show, and the best high I ever had. People would pass drugs down the row. You never knew what you were getting.

People would pass drugs down the row - you never knew what you were getting

---

They played for something like two and a half to three hours. I remember having to call my mom saying, 'I'm gonna be late.' She thought I'd be home by 11pm and I said, 'No, it's going to be more like 12.30am.' Back in those days all the bands would play a minimum of three hours. When Ginger Baker played 'Toad' it must have gone on for 45 minutes so he had to be cranked on something. I'm sure they were all loaded. But we didn't know and we didn't care.

When they came out do the reunion in 2005, I was ready to fly my best girlfriend - the same one - to England and do a complete 360 and see the show all over again. But tickets were sold out on day one. And I was hoping they'd come out and do at least one show in LA, but that never happened. But I got the DVD so that's fine.

Ann and I could have gone backstage in '68, because we'd had the chance to meet Cream some months before, before anyone knew who they were. We had this DJ called Dave Diamond in Burbank, California, the little suburb of LA where I grew up. We used to call in the station all the time. Dave called me up one afternoon after school and said, 'Hey, what are you guys doing? I got this band here from England.' I said, 'What are their names?' Now, if he'd mentioned Eric Clapton, I would have been down there in a heartbeat but he said, 'Oh, the band name is Cream.' And I said, 'Who the hell are they?'

He said, 'I want you to take them around Hollywood, show them the sights and take them wherever they want to go.' I didn't even call Ann. She might have said, 'Yeah, let's go.' But I made the decision. I said, 'Nah, we'll pass.' And six months later, here they are - this huge supergroup that were only around for two years, dammit. And that was my one degree of separation. Eric could have been in the back seat of my car.

I WAS THERE: IRA KNOPF

I ATTENDED BOTH these shows. The set list both nights was 'White Room', 'Politician', 'I'm So Glad', 'Sitting on Top of the World', 'Sunshine of Your Love', 'Crossroads', 'Traintime', 'Toad' and 'Spoonful'. On the second night, Jack's bass amp went out during 'Sunshine' and the solo was extended by Eric and Ginger whilst the tech crew quickly changed Jack's amp head. Eric used his Firebird with one pickup for the first two songs and then switched to an ES355 both nights. On the second night Buddy Miles introduced the band, whilst George Harrison and Patti were in the audience. I didn't see them but a friend of mine who had floor seats saw them come in just as Cream were taking the stage.

Ira Knopf got Ginger to sign the photo he took in October 1968

I got to meet Ginger on 19 October 1988, 20 years after their farewell tour, at a drum seminar he was giving at Guitar Center in Hollywood. I showed him the pictures I took and he signed one from the farewell show. And I met Jack in 1997 when he was touring as part of Ringo Starr's All Starr Band tour. We talked and he signed a CD cover for me. It's not every day that one gets to meets their musical influences and talk with them about music. I felt very lucky to have been able to do so.

I WAS THERE: TOMMY CARRASCO

ERIC IS TREMENDOUS but he is not a showman like Mick Jagger or Pete Townshend. He just stands and plays. Oh, and Ginger was a beast!

I WAS THERE: LINDA K DOUGHTY, AGE 17

MY FIRST HUSBAND and I bought Cream tickets at Topanga Plaza Mall in Canoga Park, California. It was the first time we had to pay a babysitter to watch our seven month old daughter. I had a great purple velour mini dress with bell sleeves and empire waist on layaway that I was going to wear and it took me several weeks to pay it off. (I still have it, and took it with me when I saw Cream again in 2005). We drove the 50 minutes from Thousand Oaks to The Forum in Los Angeles. We were sat in the first row on the right side of the floor, about halfway back from the stage. What I remember the most was standing on our chairs singing and rocking to 'Spoonful'. The whole place was up on their feet or seats, just repeating 'spoonful, spoonful, spoonful'. It was a great concert, but I remember little else. I have saved the Cream Program for all these years, just like my purple dress, but I don't know what happened to that ticket.

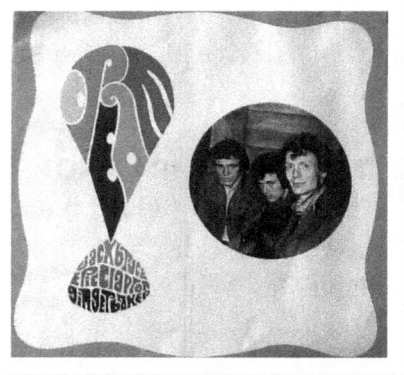

Linda Doughty was at the LA Forum

I WAS THERE: BOB HAAS, AGE 14

MY BROTHER WAS five years older than me and we did everything together. When the Cream were doing their farewell tour my parents allowed him to take me to what was my very first concert. My mind was blown away. I don't remember much, except that their last song was 'I'm So Glad'.

I WAS THERE: RICHARD A VILLANUEVA

IT WAS ONE of those concerts that you will never forget. I went out and bought *Goodbye* the day it was released. I still have it.

I WAS THERE: VICKI PLAVCHAK, AGE 19

I GREW UP in Portland, Oregon, where they only played country and western music, but attended college in Southern California, where I really got into music. I was invited on a date to see Cream's farewell concert. It was my first concert and I was totally overdressed for the occasion. Everyone was in jeans and hippie clothes. The Forum was located in Inglewood, a transitional neighbourhood south of LA. We were seated in the highest row, but I didn't care. Deep Purple came out like gangbusters. They opened with a killer version of 'Kentucky Woman' which blew my mind. They were fantastic.

After their set, there was an intermission and then the round stage went dark. When the lights came on everyone stood up. Cream started playing immediately. I think they played every song they ever recorded. We all sat down at some point. During one of the songs Ginger Baker, who was wearing a bandana on his head, plunged into a raucous drum solo. Eventually the bandana flew off and the audience jumped up and started clapping like crazy in the middle of it. Baker's curly red hair flew out all over the place and the people just kept on clapping until the end of the song. There was a rumour at the time that the band was breaking up because Baker had cancer. Everyone was caught off guard when the bandana flew off and Baker was not bald from chemo. That's why they were clapping. The group seemed to be having a good time. They did a couple of encores, including 'Sunshine of Your Love'. Then it was over. It took us an hour to get out of the parking lot and another two hours to get back to the Claremont Colleges.

Vicki Plavchak only heard C&W in Portland, Oregon

I've followed Eric Clapton since. I don't even know how many of his concerts I've been to. He seems quite temperamental, sometimes sending his friends out to do the encores. That's how I happened to see George Harrison. How lucky am I that the first concert I ever saw was the best one I ever saw? I really liked the boy who took me to the concert. We are still friends today.

I WAS THERE: STEVEN RADILOFF

LA AT THE time was the place to be for all the great bands, and The Forum was the primary venue. It seemed I was there every weekend. I knew who Clapton was from the Yardbirds and John Mayall. I didn't really know who Ginger and Bruce were, but I had just bought *Fresh Cream* and loved it. When I saw Cream would be playing at the Forum, I rushed out to buy tickets.

I grabbed a couple of buddies and we went. Right from the first note, the entire stadium

Steven Radiloff rushed out to buy Cream tickets

was blown back in their chairs. This was going to be something very powerful, and it was. Each of the three of them played like virtuosos. The depth and breadth of each song was an amazing sound from only three instruments. It filled every corner of the Forum. 'I'm So Glad', 'Spoonful', 'Toad' and 'Rollin' and Tumblin'' were my favourites. I never heard or saw anyone who soloed like Ginger. It seemed to go on forever, maybe 15 minutes altogether, and not one boring second. Everyone was on the edge of their seats and when he finished, the crowd leapt to their feet and roared with applause. The energy of the band steadily rose until the end, and the performance is emblazed in my memory.

SPORTS ARENA
20 OCTOBER 1968, SAN DIEGO, CALIFORNIA

I WAS THERE: IVY WALKER, AGE 15
THE OPENING NUMBER was 'I Feel Free' and I will remember it and their incredible performance as long as I live. The stage was entirely dark during the first part when Jack Bruce was humming and saying 'I feel free' and the stage lights came on with the first note of the guitar.

Ivy Walker thought the whole show was amazing

DALLAS MEMORIAL AUDITORIUM
25 OCTOBER 1968, DALLAS, TEXAS

I WAS THERE: ELAINE MCAFEE BENDER
MY BOYFRIEND AND I were excited to get tickets to see Cream in Dallas. He was a guitarist himself and, at the time, many guitar players idolised Eric. Clapton, along with Ginger Baker and Jack Bruce, had clearly shaken the music world. They did not disappoint that evening in concert. Ginger Baker on drums and Jack Bruce on bass were each as excellent on their instruments as Eric Clapton was on guitar. They sounded every bit as good as their studio recordings, the supreme compliment.

Apart from Baker's arms flying about on his drums, there was little flash. Clapton and Bruce were locked into their instruments and seemed almost in another world, even as they delivered vocal perfection at the microphones. How could a trio deliver such a huge, solid sound? I am not exaggerating when I say that Cream delivered an evening of music perfection.

Afterwards, we walked out to the backstage door area, hoping to get a glimpse of them leaving the auditorium. As they came out we shook hands and said hello. They nodded and waved as all three climbed into the back of a limo. I only thought to pull out my Brownie box camera as they were leaving. Their heads turned as they looked over at something and I snapped a photo. It was a great show.

Elaine Bender and her boyfriend were at the Dallas show in the fall of '68

MIAMI STADIUM
26 OCTOBER 1968, MIAMI, FLORIDA

I WAS THERE: JACKSON H BOGART III, AGE 16

MY YOUNGER SISTER was there with me. We lived in St Petersburg, Florida and drove eight hours down to Miami to see them. The opening act was a one hit wonder called Keith whose one hit was a bubble gum tune called '98.6'. How this guy got the gig I don't know. But it wasn't uncommon to have strange concert pairings. I saw Jimi Hendrix open for The Monkees!

The stage was set up so that it faced only half the stadium. They had two huge stacks of Marshall speakers on either side of the stage. I'd never seen anything like it. The promoters hadn't realised you could fill the whole stadium, or perhaps the technology wasn't up to it. Still, it was the loudest concert I had yet attended and a wall of sound just slammed into us. I don't remember how long a set they played, but they played all of their hits. The difference between hearing the live version of 'Crossroads' and 'Spoonful' on vinyl and hearing them in person was astonishing. Baker and Bruce seemed to be getting along and the musicianship was incredible. The show had no frills, just three of the best players at the top of their game. When they finished nobody wanted it to end. People were clapping and screaming for more until the lights came up and we knew they were done. One of my favourite rock memories.

I WAS THERE: DAVID KERR

THEY ENDED WITH 'Crossroads' and 'Toad' and people started to walk out. Then they did 'Spoonful', which blew everybody away. Clapton wailed - he was intricate on the high notes, with a clear tone and quality. He was regal and stood erect, while Jack Bruce hopped on one leg and then the other. Bruce played the bass like it was quick, like Bach, and Ginger Baker on those double bass drums was just awesome. I saw Hendrix, the Jeff Beck Group, The Who, Johnny Winter and Zeppelin, so I got to see the greatest guitar players of the period. Clapton was up there with the best, and Bruce and Baker were the best.

I WAS THERE: PEDRO VALDES, AGE 13

I WENT WITH two buddies. My parents dropped us off and picked us up after as they were visiting friends. By Florida standards it was a chilly night. Terry Reid opened the show and was amazing. Throughout Cream's performance the PA

Pedro Valdes (right) with Jeff Jackson & Billy Bates were there in '68 & '05

kept cutting out on them. Finally, while performing 'Sitting on Top of the World' the PA crapped out altogether. Jack stepped back from the microphone and kept singing and, unbelievable as it may sound, his voice was so powerful that we could still hear him over Ginger's drums and Jack and Eric's four Marshall amplifiers. Yes, it was faint - but quite clear.

SPECTRUM
1 NOVEMBER 1968, PHILADELPHIA, PENNSYLVANIA

I WAS THERE: MARK ROSENBAUM

I WAS LISTENING to The Beatles and the British Invasion when the music started to get heavier. An underground radio show called *The Marconi Experiment* on WMMR in Philly played albums every night between 6pm and 10pm. Nobody else was playing albums. I heard a cut from an album called *Fresh Cream*. The cut was 'I'm So Glad', immediately thought 'this is great' and went out and bought the album. And then *Disraeli Gears* came out and I just started buying the stuff up. I was so overwhelmed with the style and the smoothness of Clapton's playing. I had never heard anything like that or Baker's drumming and Jack Bruce's vocals and bass playing before.

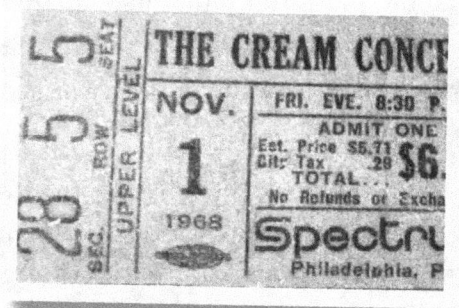

Mark Rosenbaum's Philly ticket

I started going to a place in Philly that had some live shows. I saw Canned Heat at The Trauma. Henry Vestine was the guitarist and he had a very buzzy type sound. I was sitting two feet from the stage and I was definitely buzzed away! And then I started going to the Electric Factory where all the progressive rock bands played - Vanilla Fudge, Blue Cheer, Chicago. It only held 300 or 400 people.

When I heard Cream were breaking up after only two years, I got tickets for the farewell show at the Philadelphia Spectrum. I took my girlfriend, now my wife. It was a birthday gift from me. We were born on the same day, two years apart. That show was absolutely overwhelming. Clapton even made references to it. Somebody asked them one time during an interview, 'Was there one time when you just felt everything came together and was fantastic?' And he said, 'The best time I ever had was in Phildelphia on the farewell tour.' Sadly, there isn't one recording of that night.

It was a show in the round and the stage revolved. Every time those Marshalls faced you, you were pinned to your seats and every time the stage turned and rotated a little bit, the sound was suddenly bouncing all around the place. But it didn't take away from the beauty and the intensity and the greatness of that evening.

I WAS THERE: JIM DELVECCHIO

I HAD RETURNED home from a year of being in the army in Vietnam. I was blown away by all the rock groups that had emerged. Hearing Cream, Hendrix and all the rest was like being a kid in a candy store. Like many of my age at that time, I enjoyed smoking grass and it just added to the musical enjoyment. I went with two friends to see Cream, and I have to say it was the best performance I saw - and I saw a fair amount at that time. They were on a revolving stage and I couldn't believe the amount of sound they produced for just three guys. I remember Clapton and Bruce sitting down and having a smoke and relaxing while Ginger did a half hour solo on 'Toad', pounding away on his drums with his red hair flying!

Jim DelVecchio was at the Spectrum

I WAS THERE: SANDY MCCULLOUGH, AGE 14

Sandy McCullough was just 14 when he saw Cream

DISRAELI GEARS WAS the first album I ever bought with my own money and I was pretty much hooked after that! In November 1968, four friends and I left school early and took an 80 mile bus trip from the Jersey shore to Philadelphia. This was my first major concert and I was very excited to see my favourite band. It was Ginger, Eric and Jack in the middle of the Spectrum floor on a revolving stage. The Spectrum is no longer there, replaced by a more modern arena, but I saw many concerts there after Cream and never on a revolving stage. To this day, the most amazing thing about that band is the unbelievable sound generated by just three guys. It is definitely one of the highlights of my life. I was also lucky enough to see Blind Faith at the same venue the following summer. Another great show!

I WAS THERE: JOHN DONATO, AGE 15

I WENT WITH my friend John, now deceased. We had good floor seats. BB King and Terry Reid opened. I remember Ginger Baker's 'Toad' and how skinny and sweaty he was. Word was he was a speed freak. That double bass drum was constantly beating.

John Donato was at the Spectrum

I WAS THERE: LANCE SPANO

I WAS A drummer so moved to where I could get behind Ginger. I could see that he played in thick grey wool socks, with no shoes.

I WAS THERE: LOUIE TREBINO, AGE 17

I SAW THEM at the Spectum in Philadelphia and it was a great show. A friend of mine's dad ran a ticket office and we use to get shots at tickets before they went on sale. I still have the ticket stub. The stage at the Spectrum was round and used to rotate. They played for almost four hours. They opened with 'White Room' and did four songs from *Wheels of Fire*. Cream was a band that sounded so good live and it was one of the best shows I saw. I remember Clapton wore bright red pants.

I WAS THERE: IRA STEINGOLD

LIKE MOST TEENS growing up in the Sixties, I heard all types of rock 'n' roll. The Cream were one of the first groups that attracted me. I loved Ginger Baker on the drums. I remember the Spectrum concert. I paid $7.50 for my ticket and sat on the top row. I was high on meth and had to hold onto my seat when Baker was playing because I thought I was going to be projected out of it.

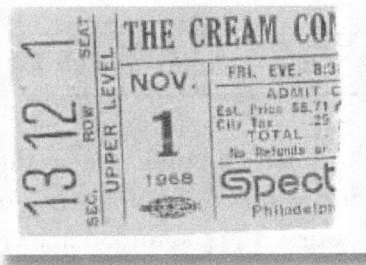

Ira Steingold saw Cream at the Spectrum

I WAS THERE: STEVE SHEPPARD, AGE 16

IT WAS MY first concert. I couldn't believe I was in the same place as them. It was surreal. I was learning to play guitar by listening to Eric Clapton, The Beatles, the Yardbirds, and everyone else who was on the radio!

I WAS THERE: BEN VAUGHN, AGE 13

MY FIRST IMPRESSION of that gig was how terrible the acoustics were. I had seen the Four Tops at a legitimate theatre only months before and was spoiled but my ears adjusted pretty quickly. The Spectrum was a brand new arena at the time and hadn't quite figured out how to present concerts. They erected a revolving stage in the middle of the floor which also provided the audience with a revolving sound mix. Sometimes all you heard was the back of the amps and the drummer. Very weird. My friend and I were up in the cheap seats and I recall the music being loud, but looking at photos of their set up that night it was probably quiet by today's standards.

The event itself was an eye-opener for me. I hadn't been around that many hippies before. I was shocked and pleased when someone passed me a joint. The night featured two openers, Terry Reid and Sweet Stavin' Chain. Terry Reid did an extended version of 'Bang Bang' by Sonny Bono with lots of screaming, which was a thing back then. Vanilla Fudge did that to pop songs too. Not my bag but Terry's guitar playing was great. Sweet Stavin' Chain were a local Philly blues band with horns and an occasional Mothers of Invention vibe. Their set was great and well received. But it was odd to watch them revolve and hear their sound change. The marijuana probably didn't hurt either.

When Cream came on the place went wild

When Cream came on the place went wild and they jumped right into it. I was only familiar with the *Disraeli Gears* album and 'White Room' so at first it just sounded like chaos to me. The mix was lousy and the band didn't appear to be listening to each other. We were all aware that this was a farewell tour so maybe this was just an obligatory performance? But then they kicked off 'Spoonful' and it all came together.

Clapton's guitar tone was truly amazing. I couldn't believe what I was hearing as it rebounded throughout the building. I don't know how long 'Spoonful' went on but I didn't want it to stop. Speaking of long, when it was time for Ginger Baker's drum solo on 'Toad', Eric Clapton and Jack Bruce left the stage. My friend was convinced they went back to the hotel to shoot up. A pretty funny thing to say but there was certainly enough time to do it. After about five minutes, I got restless and left my seat to walk around the building. Hearing the drums echo on concrete walls while observing a bunch of wasted people wander around was a priceless experience. I also met a girl, got her number and made it back to my seat in time. A magic moment. And who knows? If I hadn't lost her number 'Toad' could have been 'our song'.

MADISON SQUARE GARDEN
2 NOVEMBER 1968, NEW YORK, NEW YORK

I WAS THERE: SAL DESIANO, AGE 15

I LOVED THEM. I was in a neighbourhood band and we played a few Cream songs, like every other band in the neighbourhood. 'Sunshine of Your Love' was a must for any band. I play bass and loved Jack. I tried to play like him and even bought a Gibson EB3 bass. The concert was great except for the revolving stage. You would get blasted from all their Marshalls when they were facing you and then the music would fade a little when they had their backs to you. I never liked the large arenas. I wish I saw them at the Fillmore East. That place had the best sound system. I saw Eric there when he was sitting in with Delaney and Bonnie. Then he stole the rhythm section and started Derek and the Dominos.

Sal Desiano was in a neighbourhood band that played Cream songs

As I later learned the bass to 'Crossroads', I found out that Felix Papparlardi was the producer of a few of Cream's albums and on the *Wheels of Fire* album it said that 'Crossroads' was an edited version. The bass on that recording was completely different from any other recording of that song. Even Eric's guitar was different. I think they recorded the solos in the studio and perhaps Felix laid down the bass track, and that only Eric's singing and the applause from the audience is left from what was live. But only is Eric left to tell the truth.

I WAS THERE: PAUL AVRUTIN, AGE 14

GROWING UP IN Brooklyn, a friend's older brother turned us on to Cream, Hendrix and the like. Another older friend said he was getting tickets for Cream and asked who was in. I excitedly agreed and, being so young, had to work on convincing my parents to let the group of us go on the train by ourselves - without parents - to Madison Square Garden, full of who knows what kind of people. I worked on them for days and they finally agreed to let me go. It was only a group of four of us. We got there kind of late and I don't remember Terry Reid's set so much. But I do remember the Buddy Miles Express. It was my first experience of listening to a band with horns.

Paul Avrutin remembers Eric's amp being turned way up

This was amongst the first rock concerts to be held at Madison Square Garden. I mostly remember the show being on a revolving stage in the middle of the arena, so all the seats filled all around them and everybody could get a chance to see them from the front. Our seats were way up, but when the stage turned around to face you, it was so much louder and the big sound just hit you in the chest. The sound systems were very primitive in those days. Even though there were big speakers hanging from the top of the arena in all directions, it wasn't the rich full sound you get now.

Even though we were sitting far away when the stage revolved to face you, you could hear Clapton's Marshall directly from the amp and not the sound system. I don't remember if the amps were specifically miked up and merely picked up ambient sound from the vocal mics. They held a small ceremony in which they received a gold record for *Wheels of Fire*. There's a bootleg on YouTube of the entire set, ceremony included.

I WAS THERE: KENNY ALAN BERK, AGE 17

I REMEMBER HEARING 'Sunshine of Your Love' and just loving the whole sound. Being a young drummer, Ginger's time signature was so foreign to my ear and the sound of Eric's and Jack's guitars was mind altering. I was 17 when I saw them at Madison Square Garden in 1968 and I remember it as if were yesterday. It was absolutely life changing, as the sound was mind blowing. They were truly on fire. Jimi Hendrix at Woodstock was another life altering experience the very next year....

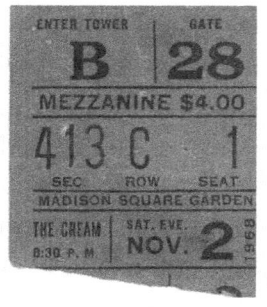

Kenny Berk was at MSG for the farewell show

Being a lifelong friend and former student of Carmine Appice many years later (in the early Nineties), Carmine, Ginger and Alan White of

Yes were doing a drum clinic in San Jose, California. It was awesome, to say the least. Carmine and Alan did their amazing solos but Ginger kept everything in 4/4. We all went out to dinner afterwards, all talking about time signatures, etc. Ginger comes out and says, 'Listen boys, it's all about finding and staying with the 4.' He then proceeded to pick up his knife and fork and lay down a groove on the table. All in all, a moment in time for me to remember, including a menu signed by all three legends.

Sam Kurshan snapped a photo of Eric at MSG

I WAS THERE: SAM KURSHAN

I WAS JUST starting getting into listening to hard rock like heavy metal and acid rock. I had a friend who was very influential upon me. I went to his house and he'd play all sorts of stuff. Back then I had also just stated to smoke pot. I'd go over to his house and we'd smoke and listen to music, and that went on for years! When I was 15, Cream came along. He had their records. One of the first rock 'n' roll albums I bought myself was *Wheels of Fire* and I was really into it.

Ginger Baker walked by me and I reached out my hand to slap him five

I heard that they were going to play at the Garden. My cousin Aaron was into public relations and he knew a lot of people. He knew Irving Felt, one of the Felt brothers who owned Madison Square Garden, and he got me the tickets. I had never been to a concert before, and I took some girl I was seeing. My mother loaned me her old Kodak Brownie box camera. It looked like a square box with no flash on it. I didn't know where the seats were going to be but they were on the floor, right at the end of the ramp that leads from the backstage onto the stage.

Buddy Miles Express came on first, and a guy named Steve Paul, who owned a rock club in New York City called Steve Paul's Scene on West 47th Street, was the MC. The stage was a round, revolving stage. Nobody had ever used that kind of stage for a concert before, and I think that was the first and last time they ever used that kind of stage at Madison Square Garden.

Cream came on. As they came out, I was sitting close enough to them that when Ginger Baker walked by me, I reached my hand out to slap him five and he slapped me five, which was kinda cool. Then they played. They played for a long time. They did lots and lots of songs from the earlier albums, *Disraeli Gears* and *Fresh Cream*, and then started doing stuff from *Wheels of Fire*. Ginger Baker did a long drum solo on 'Toad' and I took a picture of him. The shutter managed to capture it so that it looks like he's almost moving in the picture, like a blur.

About halfway through, Felix Pappalardi came on stage and received a platinum record for surpassing a million sales of *Wheels of Fire* and then they resumed the concert and it just seemed like it was going on forever. It was great. There were people smoking weed in the Garden and the whole place smelt like a big party.

I WAS THERE: VIC HARRISON, AGE 16

I WAS A pimply-faced 16-year-old living in northern New Jersey. My parents split up when I was four. On weekends, when I came of age, I would take the bus in to NYC to meet my father. We'd have dinner and walk around the city. In October of '68 I'd just heard that Cream would be performing at the 'new' Madison Square Garden. The day the MSG show was announced, my dad and I were walking past the Garden and I mentioned it to him and we found the ticket booth and promptly bought two tickets - sixth row centre. Score!

Vic Harrison was at MSG

Buddy Miles was ferocious and Terry Reid had a killer voice - he did a cool version of a Donovan song, 'Superlungs'. Cream were great and loud and I recall Clapton was mostly motionless during the show. 'Crossroads' was the magnificent highlight. What is indelibly etched into my memory banks is that the guy sitting directly in front of me at the concert was Todd Rundgren. The Nazz albums - at least the first one) - had been released by then but he had yet to go solo. He was tall but, thankfully, not also wearing a hat. As was the trend at the time, he wore a serious leather bomber jacket. He also was accompanied and flanked by two gorgeous girls. He was cool and appreciated the music.

I WAS THERE: SCOTT HASSEL, AGE 15

I GREW UP in a blue collar neighbourhood in Canarsie, Brooklyn, New York. Like most of my friends we first found rock and roll with The Beatles. It was all about British rock music from there. Back then Clapton was considered a guitar god. Ginger to this day is still my favourite drummer. It wasn't Bruce's bass but his voice that hooked me, although Winwood still has the best rock and roll voice.

Scott Hassel was at MSG in 1968 and 2005

I had to get permission from my folks to take the long ride on the subway into Manhattan alone. It was a big deal, as was the $4.50 saved from my paper route to purchase a ticket. To this day, if I close my eyes I can still see that orange ticket. They were spot on. High energy and note for note from the album. It's amazing how a musician can reproduce the same riffs and beats they play on their recordings. There wasn't any fancy technology back then.

If I close my eyes I can still see that orange ticket

When I heard they were going to play a few shows at the Garden in 2005, I was all in, as were 15 of my old neighbourhood buddies. We were all dispersed throughout the country and this was our party of a lifetime, 30 plus years later. No wives, but I did bring my younger daughter who was right around 15, the age I first saw Cream. What I remember most from the 2005 show was Ginger's long solo. I thought he was going to have a heart attack. That was amazing, for a guy who'd not taken care of himself, to play so hard and so long. The sweat was pouring off his face. Eric was seamless, making it look so simple after all those years playing those same riffs with perfect timing.

I WAS THERE: OWEN DRAPKIN, AGE 16

IT ALL STARTED for me with the song 'Sunshine of Your Love'. Every dance or party we went to, every band played it over and over way before it was released as a single. When Cream played at Madison Square

Garden, a bunch of 16-year-olds headed in to see them and they more than lived up to the hype. Terry Reid and The Buddy Miles Express opened for them but the sold out crowd just wanted Cream. They played all their songs including a couple of my favourites, 'Badge' and 'Sunshine of Your Love'. What stands out is Clapton and Bruce walking off the stage to let Baker do his solo during 'Spoonful'. For a band with three artists playing like they did, you would have thought there were five or six band members.

I WAS THERE: PATTY LOHN

I WAS IN Cream heaven. They played songs from *Disraeli Gears* which included most of my favourite Cream songs. We had great seats. I took pictures at the show which didn't come out well but it was a dream come true as we were surrounded by their sound. After they left the stage, my friend and I went up to the stage and I took a Ginger Baker drum stick that had been left behind. I saved it all these years since it had his name printed on it. I recently gave it to a drummer friend. Ginger was his idol.

Cream at MSG

Patty Lohn was in Cream heaven

I WAS THERE: RIC ARRA

WHEN CREAM CAME on, I remember some banter about Clapton's shoes before they opened with 'White Room'. Eric hardly moved compared to Jack Bruce and the bass drum sounded cool. The long middles of the songs were not boring but just filled with all kinds of sound landscapes. I wondered how long Ginger could play 'Toad' for. By the time they played 'Spoonful' I was right by the stage. I was hooked. Now, being a tribute band leader and Clapton impersonator, I know what Eric's sound is, bending notes and that singing vibrato.

CIVIC CENTER ARENA
3 NOVEMBER 1968, BALTIMORE, MARYLAND

I WAS THERE: LYNN CREEL
WHEN GINGER DID his drum solo we all stood up!

I WAS THERE: FRED SAMPSON, AGE 16
I WAS LUCKY enough to see Cream on their last tour. The opening acts were Terry Reid and the Moody Blues. Terry Reid could sing but really lacked some good songs. The Moody Blues played all the *Nights in White Satin* LP and somewhere in the middle of their set, their mellotron took a dive, and they had to stop and fix it.

Fred thought Cream were just 'phoning it in' that night in Baltimore

Cream were a powerhouse, loud with not a lot of dynamics in their show. That was reasonable, as the venue was just a big, square room and didn't have great acoustics. Clapton barely moved. He played his red Gibson ES335. Basically, it was the same show as the final Royal Albert Hall show. Ginger's solo on 'Toad' went on for at least 20 minutes, just getting louder and louder.

They seemed kind of burnt out. There was no audience interaction at all, and no interaction between each other, like they were just trying to get through the show and were kind of phoning it in. I had seen Hendrix that year and he gave an amazing show. Of course, it was different venues and different nights, but you could tell who was on the way up and who wasn't.

There was no audience interaction, or interaction with each other

I've always been a big fan of the band and of its individual members and their careers after Cream. I may have been a bit harsh in my review of the concert. In those days, we had an embarrassment of riches with so many amazing bands on the scene. And as a young man I didn't really know what I was hearing and how to properly understand what was in front of me. Ah youth!

I WAS THERE: ERIK KLINGENBERG

WHEN I WAS 16 years old, I was playing rhythm guitar and singing in what today would be called a garage band. I bought *Fresh Cream* when it was released and was immediately blown away. Cream had a sound that was innovative and new - just guitar, bass, drums and vocals. I knew when I first listened to the album that my days as a rhythm guitarist were numbered. Cream changed the sound of rock music overnight and forever.

I wore the grooves off *Disraeli Gears* when it came out. It had that psychedelic orange cover that glowed brightly under a black light. The Jack Bruce - Pete Brown songs were simply unlike anything that was being created at the time. The *Wheels of Fire* album in part captured their raw live sound. At that point, seeing them in concert was high on my list, and even more so after it became known that in May of that year that they had decided to break up.

Erik Klingenberg was at the Civic Center

Shortly after starting my university studies, my friends Randy and Denver and I bought tickets for the farewell tour concert in Baltimore, Maryland. I remember a long drive up from Virginia and arriving just as it was starting to get dark in the late afternoon. We parked the car, probably illegally on some side street, and joined the throngs of fans streaming into the venue.

The Terry Reid Group opened the evening followed by The Moody Blues. Both played good sets and people patiently sat through their performances until Cream finally took the stage and powered through a set that included 'White Room' and 'Sunshine of Your Love' and their long jam numbers like 'Crossroads', 'Spoonful' and, of course, Ginger

Baker's 'Toad'. I remember being mesmerised by the intensity of their individual playing, by the massive wall of sound that filled the Civic Center and by the energy they projected as a trio on stage. It was rock infused with what can only be described as a form of jazz improvisation.

I was mesmerised by the intensity of their individual playing

I had seen many other groups live, including The Beatles and Jimi Hendrix, but this was something else completely. As we drove back down through Virginia that night, the three of us knew we had witnessed something we would always remember, a performance of the best musicians on guitar, bass, drums and vocals at that moment in time. There will never be anything to equal the power and virtuosity of Cream.

I WAS THERE: FRANK MONTEFERRANTE, AGE 19

I WENT WITH my best friend at the time, since we were both into British music especially blues such as the Yardbirds, Cream, Rory Gallagher and the Moody Blues. The opening act was the Moodys. They were great and more hard rocking than their studio albums. The one song I distinctly remember Cream playing is 'Spoonful'. Clapton nailed it perfectly. I think they played pretty much their entire repertoire of songs. The stage sets back then were minimal so it was just three guys on stage making one hell of a sound!

Frank Monteferrante remembers 'Spoonful'

I WAS THERE: GARY MARKWOOD, AGE 16

I LOVED CREAM. I'd seen the Stones, The Beatles, Jimi and The Who, but I had a severe thing about Clapton from *Five Live Yardbirds* and his time with John Mayall. They were playing with the Moody Blues and Terry Reid. I never really dug his voice but the Moodies I knew from 'Go Now' and 'Tuesday Afternoon'. We took a Greyhound from DC. We had great floor seats. The curtains opened and Cream were playing 'White Room'. It was very dramatic. Clapton was in a lovely blue velour or soft corduroy suit and playing his Firebird. I loved seeing him, Jack and Ginger playing my favourite songs live. I loved 'Politician', which was quite different from the floating stereo leads on *Wheels of Fire*. During the solo on 'Toad' the girl across the aisle started weeping, not hysterically but (I guess) moved by love for Ginger. Afterwards, a friend's father picked us up in DC at the station. I got in so much trouble, getting home so late. My old man made me get my hair cut - every two weeks! - for a while. He'd already freaked from dropping me and my friend at a Monkees show at the Civic Center in the summer of '67, them being hippies and all. I saw them again at MSG in 2005. I thought they were fabulous.

I WAS THERE: JIM BAYLIFF

IT WAS THE last show they did in the US and the first band I saw. Terry Reid (the rocker, not the country Terry) started the show. Then the Moody Blues came on. I sat next to the Baltimore Symphony Orchestra to see them. Cream opened up with 'White Room' when the curtain got stuck. For 20 seconds we just saw them from the knees down. Ginger Baker did a half hour drum solo that was fantastic. All for 10 dollars. Those were the days!

Jim Bayliff saw the last Cream show in the United States

I WAS THERE: MATT LAROSE, AGE 14

I SAW THEM at their last concert in Baltimore, which was their second to last in the States, and then again at Madison Square Garden in 2005. It was my first date with Donna Zgorski. I was amazed I paid so much for tickets at $10 each. The Terry Reid Group opened with 'Season of the Witch', and the Moody Blues were on second. Frustration led one of them to kick over a mic stand, which was drama for this 14-year-old. Then the curtains parted to 'White Room'. 'Ladies and gentlemen… THE Cream.' It was still 'The' Cream in those days. It was a life-changing experience for me. Ginger Baker was a god to me, and still is.

I WAS THERE: JOHN MALAY

I SAW THEM at the Baltimore Civic Center while I was in college in Pennsylvania, their next-to-last US gig before they went back to the

UK and did the break up performance at the Royal Albert Hall. It was an exciting show but plagued by technical glitches; poor sound, dead mics, etc. Jack Bruce went to do 'Traintime' and his mic quit, so he knocked the stand to the floor and walked and used Clapton's. Typical for that era.

RHODE ISLAND AUDITORIUM
4 NOVEMBER 1968
PROVIDENCE, RHODE ISLAND

I WAS THERE: NORM GAUDREAU

I saw them on their so-called farewell tour at the Rhode Island Auditorium in Providence, Rhode Island, an indoor arena that held 5,300 people. Initially a sports venue, the auditorium also hosted concerts and religious events. It was billed as 'positively the last ever appearance by the incredible Cream'. The first show was set for 6.30pm and sold out quickly so the promoter added a second show at 9.30pm. The second show was cut short due to a city-imposed noise curfew. I was at the 6.30pm show.

Terry Reid was the opening act. The stage was in the round and about 6,000 people were in attendance. I remember paying $4.50 for a ticket and there being a mountain of amps on stage. I could not believe that three people could be so loud. I also remember a fan in front of me so stoned

Ad for Baltimore Civic Center

Poster for the last ever US show... until 2005

he was screaming at the top of his lungs. Ginger Baker was supposedly dying. He was probably the greatest drummer I ever saw. I don't remember much more, but I know I saw something special. Their set list was 'White Room', 'Politician', 'I'm So Glad', 'Crossroads' and 'Toad'.

I WAS THERE: JIM CENTRACCHIO

THE AUDITORIUM WAS better known as a hockey rink as The Rhode Island Reds hosted hockey games there. There were two shows booked for that gig. My friend, Bruce Bates (bass guitarist in our band, The Stonehenge Circus) and I had tickets for the 6.30pm show. It was a sell-out crowd so the promoter even booked a second Cream appearance for a 9.30pm, trying to squeeze as much profit out of the occasion as possible. We were sad that the band was breaking up and that this was their next to last gig in the United States, the last being the 9.30pm show, before their final performance at Royal Albert Hall in the UK.

We had seats high up in the bleachers with the stage and band below us and to our right. Jack Bruce stood on the left side of the stage from the audience's point of view, with Ginger Baker in the centre and Eric Clapton to the right. Although the Auditorium was known as a cavernous place, the band had stacks of Marshall amps that had no problem filling the venue with a heavy and full measure of their playing. The sound level was high and the effect certainly mimicked the feel of all the live numbers on their album.

They opened with 'White Room' and followed that up with 'Politician'. Both these numbers our band would play at gigs! They then did 'I'm So Glad' and 'Crossroads', which was very similar to what is presented on the *Wheels of Fire* album. The intensity of the music really spread through the auditorium that night. The final number was 'Toad' with Ginger doing a great extended drum solo climaxing with Jack and Eric coming back in for the conclusion of the song and the concert.

Because a second concert was in the works that night, there was no encore with concentration put on emptying the venue in order to clear the seating and get cars out of the parking lot and nearby streets to have places for ticket holders for the second show to park nearby. It was a good thing we were able to get tickets for the original 6.30pm show, because with the delay between the shows, the second show had to be cut short after just 30 minutes of 'Spoonful' and 'Toad', as Providence had a noise ordinance that went into effect at 11pm.

The bad memory of that night for me was getting back to my car which was parked on a side street right next to the auditorium and finding that someone had stolen my Epiphone Casino guitar and a Fender reverb head while we were at the concert. As naive as I was at the time, silly me thought having the doors locked would keep thieves out. I made out a report to the Providence Police Department, even having serial numbers for the equipment, but those items were never recovered.

So it was a bittersweet memory of Cream. The show was great and it's amazing to look back at those days and see how inexpensive ticket prices were back in the day. That concert and many others were priced at under $10 a ticket. Special effects back then might include a light show similar to what came out of San Francisco, with overhead projectors shining images from a sheet of plastic placed over some coloured liquid or oil and moved around to make bubble and amoeba-like images bounce around on the large screen behind the bands.

I WAS THERE: ALAN BARTA, AGE 16
I FOLLOWED THE Yardbirds, so was naturally interested in Cream. I played guitar in an unnamed band, so looked to famous heroes for inspiration. Cream was not a very tight band, more of a jam band with lots of improvisation, but then so were the Grateful Dead and a lot of other groups that caught my interest. The recordings seemed so perfect, though live was often a disappointment. I was impressed by Baker's kit with the double bass and stacks of brasses. He had a way of mimicking guitar licks in percussion. I was not very sophisticated in my musical analysis and I can only say that they bumped, thumped and wailed.

Alan Barta admits his musical analysis at 16 was unsophisticated

I WAS THERE: ED MACE
I HAD JOINED a local rock trio with drums, lead guitar and myself on rhythm guitar. We were playing lots of Cream and Jimi Hendrix. Along the way I broke my high E string and the B string. The guitarist told me, 'Why don't you just play bass on those four strings?' I did! Eventually I purchased a $99 violin-shaped electric bass. We were huge Cream fans and when we

Ed Mace witnessed a truncated Cream show due to a local noise ordinance

heard they were coming to Rhode Island for their final concert, we had to see them!

They had already played a first set and by the time they came on for the 9.30pm show, they only played two songs, 'Spoonful' and 'Toad'. We were in our glory watching these masters at work. We found out later that there was a local noise ordinance so they really had to tone down the volume. I remember having a clear view of Eric Clapton, just a partial view of Jack Bruce and a great view of Ginger Baker, whose fiery red ponytail was flipping back-and-forth wildly during his playing and especially during his 'Toad' solo! The sold out crowd were loving it. By the end of their short set, each member was supplied with whipped cream pies that were tossed at each other on stage to mark their one of many 'final' concerts. They then quickly exited the stage and passed by right in front of me, as I reached out and touched Ginger's left shoulder. It was this young teen's brush with greatness and something I'll never forget. I followed and saw Jack in West Bruce and Laing and two versions of his Jack Bruce and Friends band. I still listen to the magnificence of Cream and can hear Jack's wonderful influence on my own bass playing to this day.

I WAS THERE: STEPHEN MARTIN

I SAW THEM at Rhode Island Auditorium in Providence, Rhode Island. The opening act was Terry Reid, who I believe was considered for the job of singer in Led Zeppelin.

Ginger Baker (left) and Eric Clapton in action at Rhode Island Auditorium

Following the completion of the American tour, Cream returned to the UK for two final farewell shows at London's Royal Albert Hall.

ROYAL ALBERT HALL
26 NOVEMBER 1968, LONDON, UK

I WAS THERE: BOB ADCOCK, CREAM'S TOUR MANAGER
THERE WASN'T ANY security in those days. We had people getting on stage who shouldn't. But we never had anybody getting on stage who was threatening. There's a difference between threatening you and being enthusiastic. We would never be tough with them. There might only have been three of us but all three could handle ourselves. They play 'Sunshine of Your Love' at the start of the *Farewell Concert* film and at the end of 'Sunshine' about a dozen fans at the Albert Hall rushed the stage. If you look carefully, you'll see somebody in a bright yellow top, which was me. And all 12 of them went off stage in less than a second. All 12 of them were just disposed of straight away.

I WAS THERE: GEOFF BARKER
LIKE MANY MUSIC-mad teenagers in the early Sixties, I became obsessed with the new rhythm and blues music being played by the cooler UK bands of the day. I saw the Stones at the Station Hotel and the Crawdaddy Club in Richmond and distinctly remember their final gig there, where Mick announced they would be replaced by a new band called the Yardbirds. I had no idea who they were, but soon found out about them... especially their guitarist! I followed Eric's career changes from them to John Mayall and then the announcement in 1966 of a 'supergroup' - Cream. I passed on 'Anyone for Tennis' (I just didn't get it) but bought *Fresh Cream* and of course the incredible piece of work that was *Disraeli Gears* (how did you pronounce 'SWLABR'?) which was on permanent play in our house. Then the stunning double set *Wheels of Fire* with that wonderful silver gatefold sleeve and the live Fillmore tracks.

For various reasons (including marriage and a family) we didn't get to a Cream gig until it was nearly all over; I worked near the Royal Albert Hall and as soon as their farewell concert was announced I walked up to the box office to get tickets for me and my wife Ann. No way were we going to miss this. I remember on the day the excitement rippling through everyone as we queued outside. I've often seen film of the doors being opened but haven't ever spotted us!

We had pretty good seats, off the floor and about half way up the first raised section, but most importantly, almost directly facing the stage. (I've also tried to spot us there and failed again!) On came Eric, Jack and Ginger and the place went nuts. I remember thinking, 'Blimey, Eric's wearing a Country and Western shirt!' Then they were off and running. It seemed incredibly loud in hindsight, although there are probably pub bands with bigger gear today. I can't remember what they started with - was it 'White Room'? But they performed an astonishing powerhouse set, with all our favourites. I'm sure they ended with 'Sunshine of Your Love' which was followed by a mini stage-invasion. I watched, mesmerised by Eric's playing with his amazing improvisation adding to all those familiar songs. But they were all great... truly great.

On came Eric, Jack and Ginger and the place went nuts

I'm glad we witnessed it live as Tony Palmer's film of it is unwatchable. All those pretentious camera techniques with constant zooms in and out and those close ups of Jack's teeth fillings, Ginger's left ear and Eric's picking finger, plus the fan headbanging the stage and more close ups of hippies idiot dancing. We just wanted to see the band, dummy! I wonder why it didn't cross his mind to simply show them - all three of them - in one long shot, just playing? And don't get me going on the appalling movie sound. Did he record that on cassette? It's a celluloid dog's breakfast and ruined the only record of one of the most historic rock concerts ever by one of its greatest bands. But as the saying goes, 'you had to be there'. In this case, most definitely. 'I'm so glad' we were... to see and hear it how it really was on that amazing night in London all those years ago.

I WAS THERE: HENRY ETTINGER

I LOVED THE blues. I saw The Beatles' Christmas Show with the Yardbirds. That's where I first discovered Eric Clapton. I liked Clapton from when he was in Mayall, and followed his career right the way through. Cream's music appealed because it was new, and different to everything else at the time.

I WAS THERE: ROGER HINSHELWOOD

WHEN CREAM'S FINAL concert at the Royal Albert Hall was confirmed, I tried phoning for tickets but couldn't get through. There was a post option which I tried and just managed to get three tickets for the last of the two concerts that night. The second (earlier) concert was added at a late stage due to unprecedented demand. Our tickets were for the orchestra stalls, to the left of the stage and higher up. Me and two fellow fans and friends, Steve Goode and Ron Attree, duly set off for London from Birmingham by train. Ron, being a little scatterbrained, was asked frequently whether he'd still got his ticket, his response a consistent 'yes'.

We arrived a touch early and eventually reached the ticket kiosk to show our tickets. Ron was going frantic, 'I can't find my ticket!' Ron and Steve had both came to my house that morning and I had given them their tickets before we left for the station. We were now in a blind panic but quickly realised that Ron's ticket was the middle one of the three, which made it a little easier with Royal Albert Hall staff. I phoned my dad at home and he confirmed that the ticket was lying on the coffee table, so he rang the Royal Albert Hall as we waited. Panic over, we all got in and took our seats a few feet above the stage behind and to the right of Jack's back. Not ideal seats but we got totally uninterrupted Cream as the band easily drowned out any audience noise.

Rory Gallagher and Taste, plus Yes, were the support acts but although they were both very good no one was interested in anything other than Cream. The noise when they came on stage was unbelievable and I think the band were shocked at how well they were received.

I'd seen them once before in 1967 at the Swan Hotel, Yardley

I'd seen them once before in 1967 at the Swan Hotel, Yardley in Birmingham, and also Eric when he was with the Bluesbreakers. Both were mind-blowing occasions.
To be honest Cream were not brilliant this night. Their hearts weren't in it. But they still played a lot better than any of the hundreds of other bands I'd seen. Eric appeared confused when at the end shouts of more echoed around the hall getting louder and louder. We had two encores, finishing with 'Sunshine'. Then that was it.

Although we left the Royal Albert Hall to find a bar and then a curry house before catching the milk train back to Birmingham, none of us spoke a word to each other until we met up again a few days later. We had been literally stunned into silence.

I WAS THERE: NICK HAIRS

MY FINAL CREAM gig was their farewell gig at the Albert Hall. I had poor seats here on the stage behind the band. Why they used to do this I don't know. It was a good gig, I suppose, with the excitement of seeing them and it being the last time and all that. Taste were great by the way!

I WAS THERE: BRIAN HORTON, AGE 19

Brian and Diane Horton were at the Royal Albert Hall in 1968

WHEN I SAW the news that they were splitting, I tried for seats at the Albert Hall for the last night. This was pre-internet booking, where all the seats go in seconds, but living outside London I still was only able to get two seats up in the last row before the arches, where people stand. Luckily, as we had those last rows we could also stand and dance all the set. In the end these were great seats, as the sheer roar of the audience, the drums, bass and Clapton's guitar merged into one.

I took my then fiancée Di (we are soon to celebrate our 49th anniversary). She was not a rock fan when she went in but she was when we left! I have the concert on tape and the sound and visual quality does not do justice to the sheer power of the performance. Jack Bruce was exceptional, laying such a strong bass line, and Ginger Baker just seemed in another world, sweating like a pig. Eric was very controlled at the beginning, but built into a stunning performance. My favourite tracks that night were 'White Room' and 'Sunshine of Your Love'. It was uplifting but so sad to think it was the last time we might see them in their prime. But this was the one to tell your grandkids about!

I WAS THERE: KEVIN HIGGINS, AGE 14

IN LATE 1966, a school friend had a copy of 'Wrapping Paper', which I thought was odd and not very good. However, 'Cat's Squirrel' on the

B side was a revelation. I was aware of the Yardbirds and Clapton, but knew little or nothing about Baker or Bruce. There was no internet and no real way of researching anything about Baker, Bruce or Clapton, other than by word of mouth. This led to John Mayall and Graham Bond's bands. Again, school friends had a couple of their albums.

I bought *Fresh Cream* purely on the strength of 'Cat's Squirrel' and was hooked. 'NSU' and 'I'm So Glad' were the stand out tracks, 'I'm So Glad' for the wailing guitar solo which just about summed up Cream. I remember jovial discussions with friends about what made a 'supergroup' and a rivalry over Motown or progressive rock. I have to admit I liked both! *Disraeli Gears* was a must buy when it was released. It was a Christmas present from my Mum and Dad (from memory, it cost 27s 6d). The cover art fascinated me and I can remember attempting to create the cover of *Disraeli Gears* and *Wheels of Fire* on assorted school exercise books. Stand out tracks were 'We're Going Wrong' and 'Outside Woman Blues'.

Little did I know that Cream were even louder!

As I was only 13 in 1967, I wasn't allowed to go to any form of gig and there were no progressive bands on TV, and only occasionally on Radio Luxembourg. Therefore, my news mainly came from Melody Maker, which was read from cover to cover several times. I was pretty upset at the news they were breaking up. I managed to convince my parents that it would be safe to go to the farewell concert as it was in the Royal Albert Hall. Obviously, any other venue would have been unsafe for a 14-year-old! Off I went down to the local travel agent - Andrews on Denmark Hill, Camberwell, South London - to see if I could get a ticket before they sold out. I went with a friend with the aim of buying two tickets, but when the man from Andrews phoned the Albert Hall he was told there was only one ticket, which I immediately claimed as mine.

I arrived at the Albert Hall very early and had to kick my heels outside for what seemed an age. This was my first gig and I was fascinated by the sights and the characters milling around the hall. My ticket was directly opposite the stage and high up in the gods. The support band was Taste, which included Rory Gallagher as the lead guitarist. I couldn't believe how loud they were. Little did I know that Cream were even louder! I have very few memories of the actual concert other than they were loud and it didn't seem to last for very long before it was all over.

I went home on the 45 bus to Camberwell with my ears buzzing and with a mixture of happiness at having seen the band and sadness that I would never see them again. I certainly didn't pay an arm and a leg to see the final, final farewell concert. I was a Clapton fan until the likes of *461 Ocean Boulevard* and by then my musical tastes had moved on anyway.

I WAS THERE: NIGEL LANNING

I WAS AT the first of Cream's final concerts at the Albert Hall on 26th November 1968. The date is etched in my mind. I had to rush home from school, change and then get the bus down to Kensington. I should have been doing my homework. As the records show, Yes and Taste were on with them. I was also at one of the 2005 concerts when I guess 'Slowhand' was financially helping out Ginger Baker and Jack Bruce.

I WAS THERE: CHRIS MILLER

Chris Miller remembers blistering solos from Eric

THE FIRST (AND last) time I saw Cream was at the Royal Albert Hall for the farewell concert. The concert itself was everything a Cream fan could have wished for. Eric was superb with blistering solos, Jack was playing his usual full bass lines and Ginger was driving it all along in his inimitable style. I was up high in the cheap seats, but I did take some pictures of them on stage. Getting cameras into a gig back then was problematic. Nowadays, every man and his dog has a phone, so they've largely given up trying to control it!

I WAS THERE: DAVID MORTON

I WAS AT the farewell concert of Cream at the Royal Albert Hall. A company that I worked for had a box there. I also saw Janis Joplin and Yes amongst many others from that time. I played drums in a band called Tramps and played support to quite a few bands of the period. Indeed, I was invited to ditch my band and go with some friends' band, which I declined in order to stay with Tramps. That band was Free who went on to become Bad Company. The rest is history but Simon Kirke did a great job for them and we stayed mates. I've always considered Ginger Baker as the best drummer that I've heard and that includes some big names. I saw Eric in Harrods about 18 months ago and he has aged lots. I guess that's understandable.

I WAS THERE: PAUL MANN, AGE 19

I HAD FOLLOWED a lot of blues-based bands and seen a lot of John Mayall. I'm not sure if I saw him with Eric. I sent a cheque to the Royal Albert Hall and asked for any seat. I got two seats in a box, about as far away from the stage as it could be. I went with my girlfriend Christine and we didn't know anyone else and found it rather awkward. Cream came on and Ginger had his hair tied back. John Peel introduced them and they ripped into 'White Room'. The concert didn't last long but I was so excited I got the wrong train home! In 2005 I was working in Germany, phoned the Albert Hall and got a ticket for the first night in Row 11 in the stalls. They started with 'I'm So Glad' and were so tight and rehearsed. I knew this was it and soaked up every number. There were a lot of Americans in the audience.

Paul Mann saw Cream at the Royal Albert Hall in 1968 and 2005

I WAS THERE: RICHARD PILCH

OF THE 10 times that I saw Cream, the one that will live forever in my memory is the farewell at the Royal Albert Hall in 1968. They played two shows on the same evening. Also on the bill were Yes, Taste and compere John Peel. The cost was a now unbelievable £1.50 in today's money. I took the day off work and went with my girlfriend at the time. We had brilliant seats in the arena and if you look carefully at the recording of the concert you can see me a few times in the audience. After Yes and Taste (with the unknown to many Rory Gallagher on lead guitar and vocals) had done their sets, John Peel came out and said, 'Tomorrow they will be Eric Clapton, Jack Bruce and Ginger Baker but tonight for the very last time they are Cream.'

They were magnificent. We were at the second performance but had to leave to catch the last train home from Liverpool Street just as they were doing an encore of 'Stepping Out', which usually lasted for at least 15 minutes. But what a night. On the way out I bought the big poster for Goodbye with them all in their sparkly suits. It stayed on my bedroom wall for years. Having seen Cream 10 times, it was a pleasure and an honour to have seen them on their very last gig.

John Peel came out and said, 'Tomorrow they will be Eric Clapton, Jack Bruce and Ginger Baker but tonight for the very last time they are Cream'

I WAS THERE: JOHN BUTT

I LOVE BLUES music and when I first heard Cream it was a sound I had to hear more of. I remembered Clapton from the Bluesbreakers and that was confirmation they were going places. I only saw them once and that was at the Albert Hall for their farewell concert. I thought that was the last time I would see them. As luck had it they had a reunion at the Albert Hall so I got to see them once again.

I WAS THERE: ALLAN AINSWORTH, AGE 16

I WAS AT the last Cream performance and quite frankly it actually changed my life. Whilst I was in the sixth year at school my lifestyle was pretty basic, being a Mod with short hair, parka and scooter and listening to Motown and soul. Two older boys were already getting into heavy blues bands and their influence started to rub off.

I was at the last Cream performance and it actually changed my life

One of them suggested the Cream's last concert. I had never heard of them and went along more for the experience than anything and - wow, was I blown away? I hung on every song played, every riff and every solo taken in turns by each of the three masters. Years later I watched the televised version and - shock, horror! - when the cameras panned at the end they stopped on this short-haired 16-year-old kid that was me. I acquired the Cream LPs, grew my hair and started to attend concert after concert. I went to Hyde Park to see Blind Faith, saw Led Zeppelin at Bath and saw many other great bands including The Who and Free, the highlight being camping on 'the Hill' for the 1970 Isle of Wight Pop Festival and seeing Hendrix shortly before he died. I have followed many heavy metal and blues bands since, but look back fondly on those heady, crazy days of long hair with turned up collars on our long RAF coats (even in summer) and trying to look super cool and of travelling into London to the Marquee and popping up to Primrose Hill and Camden Town. I still today greet the sweet smell of patchouli oil with a memory of some very happy times. All started by three amazing musicians who were so talented yet so flighty they couldn't go on playing together, denying the world a unique talent and sound never really to be recreated.

I WAS THERE: JOHN BLACKLEY

AFTER WALLINGTON PUBLIC Hall I saw them in Spalding in '67, along with Jimi Hendrix, etc. That was an amazing experience, very hot and sweaty. They seemed to create music on a different level to anyone else at that time, including Jimi. And then, almost in a flash, it was over. I was lucky to get a ticket to their farewell in '68. As John Peel announced at the beginning, 'Tomorrow they'll be Eric, Jack and Ginger, but tonight they're CREAM!'

I played drums in a band in the Sixties and took my sticks again in the Nineties, in a band called The IV Remnants. We're still going, playing covers including 'Crossroads', 'Sunshine of Your Love', 'Strange Brew' and 'White Room'!

I WAS THERE: ANNIE BURTON, AGE 15

IT WAS THE first proper music concert I had been to, and of course I was completely blown away by their performance. I had only recently been introduced to their music by a school pal and they immediately touched something in me. I felt very privileged to see and hear them but was also desperately sad that they were splitting up just as I had discovered them. We were on the very top tier at the Albert Hall. It might have been standing rather than sitting. I remember walking around but there could be another reason for that memory as I also remember that my excitement unfortunately affected my bowels and I had to pay several visits to the loo!

I WAS THERE: FROG GODDARD
THE LAST TIME was at the farewell at the Royal Albert Hall. I told my foreman I needed the day off to see Cream's last performance. He said, 'What if I say you can't have it?' I said, 'then I will leave the job. There is no way I'm missing the last chance to see Cream!' By the way, Jack Bruce lived in my area and would often be seen in the local pubs and sometimes jammed with local bands.

Jane (pictured right) and her friend Joan followed Cream from the start

I WAS THERE: JANE DYER
I SAW CREAM'S farewell concert at the Royal Albert Hall in 1968. My girlfriend Joan and I had followed Cream right from the start, as both of us liked the Yardbirds and had seen them several times. There was no internet then so you had to go in person to the box office or send a cheque or postal order, but tickets for the first concert had all sold out by the time we got there. Then they announced a second concert, so off we went to London again by bus. This time we were successful.

On the night of the concert, we had to leave school early and get permission to change out of uniform. We got the Green Line Bus from Slough up to London. I can still remember the warm up groups - Yes and Taste - who were okay, but we really wanted to see Cream. The show was great - we were right up at the back, in the gods, but the atmosphere was electric. My most vivid memory was the way Jack and Eric went off the stage and left Ginger drumming away for about 15 minutes on 'Toad'. The crowds were so well behaved, no manic screaming like the pop concerts we had been to before, just pure music fans. It was a great evening!

I WAS THERE: HERVÉ FRANÇOISE, AGE 22
IT WAS THEIR *Goodbye* tour. It was my first time in London. I was on my own. There was a big line outside the Royal Albert Hall and I bought a ticket from a gentleman who could not attend. At the time, I was living in northern France and listening to Radio Caroline and Radio London a lot. That's how I discovered Cream. However, I was quite familiar with Eric Clapton from when he was with John Mayall. I was totally stunned by their music, which is always so much better when it's live.

They played loud and I loved it. Also, I was extremely impressed by the professionalism and the obvious talent of the trio. The atmosphere at the Royal Albert Hall was delightful. I still think about that sublime concert once in a while... it was absolutely unforgettable!

I WAS THERE: JOHN HOLMES

I ALSO WENT to the farewell concert. Tickets went on sale at the Albert Hall and you needed to be there very early to secure any. You could also apply by post but I can't imagine too many of those being successful as they would sell to personal applicants first. Unfortunately, I didn't get there early enough, but when they announced a second, early show I made sure I was outside at soon after 6am. That was early enough, and I still have my ticket stub. I saw quite a few of the Marquee regulars at the show (I was one of them), and I think the two shows are pretty well documented, even though my memories of the event are hazy now. We did consider trying to stay in for the second show, but there was no chance of that!

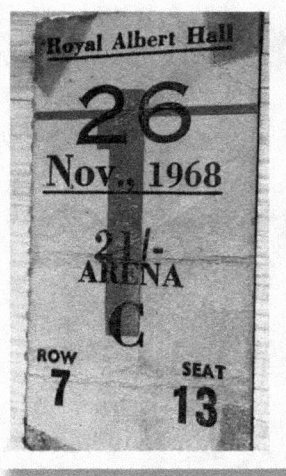

John Holmes still has his ticket stub from the farewell show

I reckon I saw every one of the great acts of the Sixties, but no one blew me away like Cream did - and that includes Hendrix. The funny thing is, listening to a lot of that live stuff now, eg. the *Farewell Tour* box set, it's quite hard to sit through an entire album of mainly long improvisations. At times it becomes disjointed, and there are certainly a good few bum notes! However, it was obviously being there 'in the moment' that captured the excitement of it all. I can fully understand why David Gilmour spent weeks correcting all the bum notes and duff bits before Pink Floyd released *Pulse*.

I WAS THERE: TOM O'BRIEN, AGE 17

AT THE VERY beginning of 1968 my mother, recently widowed, took me with her when she moved from a small town in Ireland to London, where a relative went to some trouble to get me enrolled in a Jesuit school called St Ignatius College in Enfield, though I'm sorry to say I didn't stay there too long. But while I was there, I had some classmates who were dedicated Cream fans. I think I'd probably heard of them before that but just in passing, because of the singles they'd already released. I don't remember which of their albums I listened to first but I bought the *Wheels of Fire* double album when it came out that summer. By then I was working in an import/export office near the Strand. I bought my concert ticket from a booking agency near where I worked and I remember the suited guy behind the counter saying archly, 'The Queen's Farewell Concert? Is Her Majesty leaving us?' Or perhaps he really did have trouble with my accent.

There were two concerts on the same day. I went to the earlier one. I was up in one of the balcony seats looking down on the stage. I have a strong visual memory of how the group looked. Eric Clapton was in a kind of cowboy shirt, Jack Bruce in a blue velvet (or corduroy) suit and Ginger Baker with a bandana on his head. But my memory of the actual music later became somewhat mixed up with the music of the Tony Palmer film of the concerts, which I watched when it was later shown on TV. There were two support bands, Yes and Taste. John Peel was the MC and I remember him, as he introduced the latter, saying something like, 'And now for some fugitives from the Emerald Isle.' Words which would have had a certain resonance for me.

I WAS THERE: JOHN WELLS

I FOLLOWED JOHN Mayall's Bluesbreakers and the Graham Bond Organisation. That led me to follow Cream. About that time I listened to the Yardbirds and even Captain Beefheart - well, *Safe as Milk* anyway. I used to visit Cook's Ferry and may have seen Peter Green there, and I used to go to the Cambridge on Sunday nights. The live music was always blues or rock which jarred with the Tamla Motown stuff they played at the break on a monster mono speaker to the right of the stage. I also visited the Warwick in East Barnet regularly. The overwhelming influence was The Beatles, who I saw at the Finsbury Park Astoria in '63. Being born in 1950, I 'owned' the era that was the greatest music generation ever.

I WAS THERE: JEFF RICHARDS

AFTER SEEING THEM in 1966 at the Windsor Festival, I bought their albums and played them over and over. Being at boarding school was very frustrating when Cream played concerts I could have gone to, but I managed to see them again in May 1967 at the Speakeasy in London. Oh my god, the music was transcendental.

Cut to the farewell concerts at the Royal Albert Hall. We'd managed to get tickets for the last matinee - couldn't get them for the very last show, dammit. Sad and uplifted, we left after the matinee and as we walked away, a woman came up to us and asked if we wanted tickets for the evening. She sold them to us at cost price! There'd been some illness, and she had three tickets and there were three of us. Unbelievable, and very lucky that one of us (not me) was well-off, and had the cash.

Back we go. John Peel was the presenter, and he told the same joke in both sets: the Pope had recently given a ruling that Catholics were not allowed contraceptives, and John said the carol for Christmas was 'Don't come all ye faithful'.

That last set... I recall a head banger six rows in front of me. He must have had a headache next day as he never stopped. We kept them there as long as we could, and here's a memory that I've never been able to check: they asked, after some encores, 'What do you want us to play?' One wag suggested 'Anyone for Tennis', which got a laugh, but me and two guys nearby yelled for 'Stepping Out', which is something they played when they jammed. Did they play that? Old age has removed the memory....

Going home on the Tube, the wealthy friend played his reel-to-reel tape recording of the concert. He was asked to turn it off by Major Respectable, and three fans further down the carriage told him to piss off. The BBC showed the concert later in the year, and I had to go to my sister's to watch it as I had no TV in the digs I was in.

The reunion concert? I tried everything to get tickets, but didn't want to pay touts so no joy. I can't imagine the number of 'fans' there who weren't even born when Cream were playing!

I WAS THERE: JOHN WILKES

I WAS IN the gods at the Albert Hall for the final concert. Ginger playing 'Toad' for over 30 minutes was unbelievable. I'd first heard Eric when he was in the Yardbirds as I was very into the guitar greats - Berry, Diddley, Leadbelly, John Lee Hooker and even T-Bone Walker. His playing with Yardbirds was a little twee for my taste but I recognised his talent.

John Wilkes saw the final show at London's Royal Albert Hall

However, I was completely blown away when he played with John Mayall's Bluesbreakers. The Bluesbreakers turned my musical tastes upside down as I had never heard the type of riffs he was producing. It was a natural progression to listening to Cream. I knew of Jack Bruce but I was never a great fan of jazz. Ginger had begun to put out long solos with Graham Bond and when the three came together there no one to match Cream's pure exuberance.

Seeing them at the last Albert Hall concert was both a happy and sad occasion, seeing as they only spent three years as a band. I had high hopes of Blind Faith but they proved somewhat disappointing. That was all of 50 years ago but I maintain that popular music peaked with Cream and nothing since has surpassed their genius. Music will never hear their likes again.

I WAS THERE: STEVE COBHAM

THE SECOND TIME I saw them was the last concert, at the Royal Albert Hall. My friend Willie's older sister worked as a librarian at the British Library or the British Museum and she queued up and got tickets for us. They were up in the gods and cost 7/6 or something ridiculous. Willie and I went down to London, bought a copy of *Oz* (which was difficult to get hold of in Bletchley) and probably a copy of *IT* as well, queued up outside the Albert Hall and went in and got into the gods. The warm up acts were Taste and Yes. I didn't like Yes at all - not enough guitar for me - but I really enjoyed Taste. And then Cream came on and I was completely amazed that Eric was playing an ES-335. I didn't realise he'd ever played that with Cream, and I think that might be the only occasion when he did.

I was completely amazed that Eric was playing an ES-335

The concert film shot by Tony Palmer was rubbish. It jumped about all over the place and also cut between the first house and the second house, because the clothes were totally different. There was a pause and I remember shouting out 'god, it's god!' Probably nobody ever heard it apart from me but it was just my little contribution to the last Cream show. I didn't get any sense at the time of 'oh dear, this is the last Cream gig' because it was just so exciting to be there. The acoustics were terrible.

I think this was before the flying saucers they fitted up in the roof to try and act as baffles. I've got loads of bootlegs of Cream and the Albert Hall bootlegs don't sound very good. You can hear that there were problems. On the last song the place just completely erupted. It was amazing.

I wasn't interested in the reformation. It just wasn't like Cream. I just loved the Les Paul through the Marshalls sound. I'd rather have Clapton with Mayall, but Cream were good! When Cream were on, they were really on.

I WAS THERE: DEREK WITHEY, AGE 22

I WAS AT the second farewell concert at the Albert Hall. I remember the date very well as on the same day the Australian Embassy approved my application to emigrate to Australia, and I sailed off the following March. I was introduced to Cream by a college friend in December 1966 and purchased all their albums. I also watched all their TV spots. I saw them with a work colleague called Eric and a friend of his whose name might have been Peter. Eric had the tickets and we met at the venue. As I was living in Kilburn, I'm pretty sure I went there on the Tube. My memories of the concert are somewhat vague but I thought their performance was rather lacklustre compared with their albums and TV gigs. It was as if they were going through the motions. However, I have since discovered that the relationship between Ginger Baker and Jack Bruce was then very poor. 'Badge' is still one of my favourite songs.

I WAS THERE: JOHN PINFOLD

I HAD TICKETS for both of the *Farewell* concerts but had to give the early show tickets away. I was there for the last one though. My story actually starts a few years before. I lived in Wimbledon and was friends with Terry Brennan and also knew Tom McGuiness, both of whom lived close to me. Terry was for me the best blues singer in the UK and he formed the Roosters with Tom and Eric Clapton. They had a great line up with drums, piano, Tom and Eric on guitar plus Terry singing and harmonica. The drummer was Robin Mason and the pianist Ben Palmer. I was an avid record buyer and sometimes Eric, Tom and Terry would come to my parents' house to listen to music. It's a long time ago but I am sure they were electric, doing Lightnin' Hopkins, Lightnin' Slim, Lazy Lester, Slim Harpo and a few other bluesmen numbers. They were unique because they didn't have a bass player, just two guitars.

Unfortunately the Roosters didn't last long - Terry told me years later that Eric was upset because Terry was getting married and it wasn't the right thing for the image. Tom joined Manfred Mann, Eric the Yardbirds and Terry eventually the Muleskinners. My friends and I used to go to the Star at Croydon and the Crawdaddy at Richmond to see the Yardbirds most weeks. The Muleskinners took up a residency in Balham (I think they took over from the Moody Blues) and we went there, but I couldn't stand Paul Jones' voice so we didn't bother to see Manfred Mann often. I got married in 1966 and didn't see Eric again until the farewell concert. An incredible night and forever in my memory.

THE BREAK UP

I WAS THERE: BOB ADCOCK, CREAM'S ROAD MANAGER
PEOPLE ALWAYS REFER to Cream burning out due to the number of gigs. That's true, but that really isn't the reason. When Cream formed, all three of them had been on the road for years. We're not talking music virgins here. We're talking hard, grizzled touring musicians who were well used to the rigours of the road. We did a lot of gigs. There was a huge touring schedule. But that wasn't the reason that the band burned out. It's so hard to detail the difference between modern touring and touring in the Sixties. I've done both, so I know what's involved. In the Sixties it was a piece of piss. You could get a huge foolscap sheet of paper and work in every day. And it looks difficult because of the number of gigs. But it's no different to the way modern bands like Iron Maiden and AC/DC work. They work far harder than Cream ever did. And the difference between touring now and touring then is that Cream didn't very often do soundchecks. They didn't turn up to the gig until 7 o'clock at night, and there were no press conferences, no media meetings, no reporters to talk to, no radio stations to visit, no meet and greet sessions, no VIP areas. There was none of that. It didn't exist. That's the pressure that makes touring today difficult, because you don't get any time to yourself. Whereas we had loads of time to ourselves, even though the number of gigs were the same as a band touring today. And also we flew everywhere first class. We stayed in the best hotels. We never did a bus tour. And that really knocks it out of you. You want to get tired on a tour? Do a bus tour.

The main reason Cream split up was because of a group called The Band. When Eric heard The Band's *Music from Big Pink*, he decided that he was going in the wrong direction musically. That had a big, big effect on him, listening to that album. It wasn't just the songs and the melodies and the guitars. It was the very fact that The Band were a band. They'd grown up together. They were friends as well as being in the same band. Cream were never friends. At the end of the gig, everyone went their own way until we met up to leave for the next show. Everyone had their own individual lives. Whereas The Band were a group of friends. And this more than anything is what moved Eric to leave Cream and form his own group. He said to me, 'One of my biggest regrets is not growing up with a band that I put together at the age of 15 and became successful with.' And this clearly played on his mind. The Band had all that. They had all that integration that he sorely missed. I get it. It's some sort of family replacement.

We flew everywhere first class. We stayed in the best hotels. We never did a bus tour

I WAS THERE: CHRIS HOLLEBONE

THE SPLIT WAS an accident waiting to happen. We all knew that they were three quite volatile personalities, and that particularly Jack and Ginger had a history of falling out with each other from back in the Graham Bond days. I used to read *Melody Maker* religiously in those days, and there were signs of things getting a bit fractious and obviously drugs and alcohol were also creeping in, so it was no huge surprise that it came to an end. But they managed to hold it together. That last concert was a pretty spectacular gig. It was a good way to go out. They definitely hadn't lost it all along the way.

They were a trendsetting band in many ways. I think it's very difficult to compare them with someone like The Beatles because the musical styles are so very different. A large percentage of what The Beatles did was brilliant songwriting. But the type of music they were finally putting out was very different to what you used to get with Cream. There were some good songs written, mainly with Pete Brown and Jack, but there was also a lot of harking back to the old blues standards, interpreting them in a new way and presenting them in a way that had never been done before. That was certainly a big factor in me being interested in what they were doing.

Hendrix was an exceptional guitar player but I did feel that the Experience were rather coming on the coat tails of Cream and that it was very similar approach to things, albeit the music might have been a bit different. It definitely took a heavy influence from Cream and I can't imagine the Experience being formatted the way they were if Cream hadn't been there before them.

> *If Eric was wearing a military jacket, we were wearing a military jacket. They were horrible!*

Like many in the Sixties, we were followers of fashion. If Eric was wearing a silk shirt we were wearing a silk shirt. If he was wearing a military jacket, we were wearing a military jacket from the Portobello Road. But a guardsman's jacket was an impossibly impractical thing to wear. Whenever I see an event like Trooping The Colour, I think, 'You poor bastards.' They were horrible.

TOAD'S PLACE
29 DECEMBER 1980, YALE, NEW HAVEN, CONNECTICUT

I HEARD THEM: MARK PESCE

I SAW JACK Bruce play this bar in New Haven, Connecticut. Just before my wife and I were ready to leave, I went back into the house and grabbed an LP, *Early Cream*. We got to Toad's and, as we were standing in line waiting to go in, a guy came up to me and asked, 'Why did you bring an LP with you? Were you really coked up?' And then he said the magic words: 'Do you guys want to meet Jack?'

After the show, this guy showed up and says 'follow me'. We walked downstairs. There was a line to see Jack, and we were fourth or fifth in line. After about 20 minutes, I just wanted to go home as I was starting to crash because of coke, so we started walking down the hallway to the exit. As my wife got to the first step, our guy stuck his head out the door, looked at the line and yelled 'where were those two in line?' We ran down the hallway and entered Jack's dressing room.

When I stood before Jack, I was speechless. He was a god to me, like Michael Jackson or McCartney are to other people. He was sweating, asking questions of his band and obviously still full of adrenaline after the show. I just stood frozen and he said, 'So mate, how are you?' My mouth couldn't move and he said, 'You wanted to see me - why?'

I said, 'Could you sign this LP?' He looked at it, said 'I don't remember this one' and signed it (I still have it). Then he said, 'Is that it?'

At that point I heard 'the voice' inside my head telling me 'ASK him!' 'Jack, I've been a Cream fanatic all these years. Do you think you'll ever reunite with Eric and Ginger?'

He started laughing and said, 'Why did you like us?' I said 'the jam'. He said, 'Mark, I'll tell you what I tell anybody asks, and I get asked that a lot. As long as we're alive, anything can happen.'

A NIGHTCLUB
1982, SOMEWHERE IN NEW JERSEY

I WAS THERE: RJ ROTONDO

I NEVER SAW Eric, Jack and Ginger play together but I actually played three songs with Jack Bruce in a New Jersey club. During my band's sound check a guy from the club was pulling on my pant leg (it was rather high stage for a club) so I said, 'Yes, what can I do for you?' He said, 'The club owner is friends with Jack Bruce and he may show up tonight.' My response was pretty much 'yeah, right, OK, sure'.

Fast forward to the end of the night and it's the same guy tugging on my pant leg. 'Yeah, what is it?' 'He's here.' 'Who's here?' 'Jack is here.' I look out. I can't see much, the place is packed, the lights are in my eyes, etc. The guy says 'dedicate a song to him' so I made an announcement, 'Folks, listen. Jack Bruce is in the house and we'd like to send this out to him.'

The only Cream song we knew was 'Crossroads' and we launched into it. About a third of the way through, the crowd parted like the Red Sea and this little fella came running up and leapt up onto the very high stage. He took one look at me, the front man, and realised that both I and my microphone stand were about a foot taller than him. He raced up the drum riser and perched himself on the drummer's shoulder to sing into his microphone. I was fairly in shock at this point but I continued playing!

We finished, the crowd went wild and Jack just pulled out a harmonica from his shirt pocket and started playing. He never said a word of direction as to what key, etc., so I figured it was in G and told the band and we proceeded to do a 12 bar slow blues.

That's when I realised Jack was drunker than drunk

The song finished and the pant-pulling fellow was saying, 'Last song, we gotta finish up.' In my head I was thinking, 'OK, I got super bass player Jack Bruce up here. Let's get him on bass,' and I motioned for him to come down off the riser. That's when I realised he was drunker than drunk. We strapped the Fender bass on him and I said, 'Jack, how about 'Sunshine of Your Love'?' He said, 'No 'Sunshine'.' 'OK, what do you wanna do?' 'Anything,' he said, and so we launched into 'Roll Over Beethoven' to keep it simple. We finished up. I put my guitar on its stand. As I turned back towards Jack his two friends were on stage and dragging him right by me - passed out!

RODEO DRIVE
1988, BEVERLEY HILLS, USA

I WAS THERE: DARYL GENIS

I WAS AT the Beverley Hills Rodeo Drive Versace to pick up an evening gown for my then wife. Eric was there too. We were the only two people in this very small store, and the store employee had gone up to the second floor in the elevator to get Eric's order. There was this uncomfortable, pregnant silence and in the end I said, 'Excuse me, can I ask you something?' and he said 'yeah, sure' and I said, 'Other than Alpine Valley, do you have any plans to any blues nights here in the States? I'd love to see something like the Albert Hall shows here.' Eric said, 'My people have considered it and they say that it doesn't pencil out in America.'

I said, 'Eric, you may not want to hear this but I am a friend of about 5,000 people that trade live recordings of your shows. When you go to the Forum 5,000 of those seats are people that I know that will go every show that you put out. If you were to book the Forum for as many nights as they would give it to you, and never touch an electric guitar, you would fill the house every night just playing an acoustic guitar.' He said, 'Really? That's an interesting point of view.'

After a few minutes I said, 'Can I say something else? If I wanted to listen to Stevie Winwood, I would have bought *Back in the High Life* back in the Seventies. Apart from one song, *August* was total crap. Don't put shit like that out for your fans.' Eric didn't get mad or anything. He just smiled and said, 'Really? Which song did you like?' I told him I liked 'Holy Mother'. I said, 'If I could take a guitar and lock myself in a soundproof room and make one note sound like you make any note sound, I'd die a happy man.' And he put his hand on my shoulder and he said, 'Keep playing. Keep trying. That's what it's all about.'

TRANCAS MARKET
APRIL 1990, MALIBU, CALIFORNIA

I WAS THERE: DARYL GENIS

CREAM RELEASED A box set of *Disraeli Gears*. When you opened it up it had a CD and a booklet with a bunch of pictures in it, and a certificate that said it was a limited edition box set. I had gone to England and had Eric sign it. And when Jack Bruce played a club in Redondo Beach called Annabelle's, I was on vacation and had my girlfriend's sister take the box set to this club and get Jack to sign it. Ginger used to teach drums at Trancas Market in Malibu, California. When I found that out, I drove up and during a recess in the drum lessons I walked up to Ginger with the box set and he was like, 'Wow, what's this? I didn't even know they released this.' I shook his hand and said, 'Can I tell you I think you're the greatest drummer ever?' And he laughed as he was holding my hand shaking it, and he said: 'We have a lot in common then, because I do too!'

I said, 'I think you're the greatest drummer ever' and Ginger said, 'We have a lot in common then!'

CENTURY PLAZA HOTEL
1993, LOS ANGELES, CALIFORNIA

I WAS THERE: HAROLD SHERRICK
CREAM WERE BEING inducted into the Rock and Roll Hall of Fame. I was asked to photograph the event and arrived at around three in the afternoon. When I entered the hotel, I could hear music from two floors down and I knew this was Cream doing their soundcheck. With my camera gear on my shoulder, I immediately started running to the escalator. As the music got louder, I knew for sure it was Cream doing 'Sunshine of Your Love'. When I reached the bottom, I ran to the doors and flung them open. Security came from every direction! I just yelled, 'I just want to listen!' I've been a Cream fan since 1967 and that was one of the highlights of that event.

The rehearsals were magic. It was like the 25 years had not gone by. But at the actual thing, we had to listen to a lot of bozos making extraordinarily mundane speeches. **Ginger, talking to** *Forbes* **magazine**

I WAS THERE: DARYL GENIS
THE FIRST THING I tried to do when I got out of law school was to reunite Cream. I had a letter from Jack Bruce's agent saying that he'd do the show with a $100,000 guarantee up front. I had a letter from Ginger Baker's management saying they would be willing to participate without any contingencies. And I got a really nice 'FU' letter from Roger Forrester that basically said, 'Eric considers himself to be an artist and artists like to move forward and reuniting with Cream would be seen as a step backward, but thank you for the offer.' My career as a concert promoter was a one and done failure. I kept that letter in my guitar case for many, many years.

I was absolutely mesmerised by the Fool guitar. As a kid I bought some psychedelic glow in the dark paints and attempted to paint my acoustic guitar. But it was nothing like the Fool because I don't really have a lot of artistic talent. One of the things that always bothered me was the story that Eric loaned the guitar to Jackie Lomax when they met at Apple, and Jackie kept the guitar without Eric's permission and ultimately sold it to

Todd Rungren for money to buy drugs. Eric asked Todd for the guitar back and Todd told apparently gave him a punch list of things that Eric needed to do to get the guitar back. Eric said 'fuck it' and walked away from the guitar. Todd ended up selling the guitar at auction because he owed the IRS a couple hundred thousand dollars. I think he sold it for $250,000 to a Japanese businessman and donated $25,000 to Crossroads and that kept Todd out of jail.

Around 1984 I bought a vintage 1964 Gibson SG with patent applied for humbuckers, the exact same guitar that was the basis for the Fool, from Norman's Rare Guitars in the San Fernando Valley. My wife was going to paint it for me but when she saw the beautiful cherrywood finish said, 'No, the guitar's too pretty, I don't want to damage it.' Getting accurate pictures of the whole back side of the Fool was the trick because all the photos in the public domain pre internet were pictures of Eric playing the guitar. I made a deal with Lee Dickson, Eric's guitar tech, that he'd provide accurate photos of the front and back of the original guitar and I'd make two replicas, one for me to keep and one for me to give to Eric. At one point I'd become a cocaine addict and checked myself into a live-in hospital. Eric's music was one of the only things that gave me any satisfaction. The guitar was a way of giving something back to him.

I made a deal with Lee Dickson that I'd make an exact replica of The Fool for Eric

I went on vacation and left the guitar with John Carruthers at a guitar shop in Venice Beach, California. He broke the guitar down and gave the body and neck to Tom, a local artist who was going to do the paint job. When I came back, I heard Cream was being inducted into the Hall of Fame. I wanted to give the guitar to Eric so that he could play it at the ceremony so Cream could actually go backwards in time. John said, 'I can't put your guitar back together right now' but gave me the name of a guitar tech at Voltage Guitars in Hollywood. John said, 'This guy knows Eric's guitars. He'll be able to set it up exactly the way Eric likes it.' I drove up to Voltage and gave this guy the guitar. Next day I picked it up and drove to the rehearsals, taking place in a ballroom in the basement of the Century City hotel.

There was no security. A Mr Baum came over. He rented vintage amps to bands travelling through LA. Then Lee Dickson came over. The deal I had with Lee was that I would give the guitar to Eric myself. I said, 'I just want to give him the guitar myself and to tell him personally that his music has really given me a lot of joy at some very low points in my life.' But Lee and I got into this big argument and both started tugging on the guitar case as he tried to take it out of my hands.

Baum was like the United Nations, 'Hey, hang on a second. How about I take the guitar over to Eric, and point to you while you're over here at the door? I'll tell him you've brought the guitar and you want to give it to him, and we'll let him decide what he would like to do.' So Mr Baum walked the guitar over to Eric. Eric took it out of the case, went up on the stage with the guitar and plugged it in. Albert King had died just a few days before and Eric started to play 'Born Under a Bad Sign'. He played a minute and a half of the song through the amplifier unaccompanied, then unplugged it, walked over to the case, put it in the case, walked back to me, handed me the case and said, 'It's a very lovely instrument. It's as beautiful as the original. But it's too extravagant of a gift.' He put his free hand on my shoulder, reached towards me and said, 'You keep it and enjoy it,' patted me on the shoulder and walked away.

I still have the guitar. If Eric would play it again and then sell it in auction, I'd be willing to let him keep 50 per cent of whatever they get for it for Crossroads and send the other 50 per cent to the IRS to pay down my tax bill. A vintage SG which has not been repainted or refinished is worth about $18,000. A refinished SG is worth less, while a perfectly duplicated Fool right down to the year, make and model is maybe worth between $25,000 and $50,000. But if Eric were to take the guitar and play it again and then offer to sell it, it would literally be worth anywhere from $100,000 to half a million dollars, especially if he would play it in a show.

ROYAL ALBERT HALL
2, 3, 5 & 6 MAY 2005, LONDON, UK

I WAS THERE: ED TRACEY

AFTER 37 YEARS I had a chance to fulfill a boyhood dream. It was worth the wait. I grew up in West Hempstead on New York's Long Island before we moved further east in 1969. As an 11-year-old, I remember seeing an ad in the paper for a 1968 concert by the rock band that had quickly become my favourite - Cream. Alas, my father thought I was too young. As it turned out, the show at that barn-like dump of a venue was faulty and only lasted 30 minutes. Cream broke up later that year. I thought I'd never have another chance to see the three of them together.

But by late 2004, stirrings were being reported that perhaps there was a chance that a reunion could take place. Enough time had passed to allow for old wounds to heal. Eric had parted ways with his manager Roger Forrester and was seeking new challenges, while bassist Jack Bruce had undergone a liver transplant, which had initially not gone well. This gave an impetus to them to discuss getting back together… while they still could.

Ed Tracey was too young to be allowed to see Cream on Long Island and had to wait until 2005

When the news finally came, many headlines included the words 'I'm So Glad', a reference to the song by bluesman Nehemiah 'Skip' James that was a part of the band's repertoire. When they recorded the song, they made sure that Skip got his royalties, something that wasn't often done in those days, which paid for his medical bills. The band received a letter of gratitude from his widow after his death in 1969.

Ed Tracey was amongst those at the first Cream reunion show - photo Ed Tracey

Ed Tracey's ticket for the Royal Albert Hall

Four shows were scheduled for May 2005 at the 5,200 seat Royal Albert Hall, the same venue Cream had last performed at. These shows were so well received that they later added three shows at New York's

Madison Square Garden that October. Had the New York shows been part of the plan from the start I might have concentrated on attending a show there instead, because my friends were not interested in travelling to London for a concert. But I could not let this chance slip by.

My friends weren't interested in going to London; I couldn't let this chance slip by

Tickets went on sale at 9am London time (4am Eastern time) on a Monday morning via telephone and the internet. The phone was terminally busy and the internet never completed. The Albert Hall website did not have a 'best seat available' option so I kept choosing a section and row and clicking 'purchase' only to have it come back as 'sold out'. I seldom use expletives but that morning 'rat bastards' were the *cleanest* words I uttered. After an hour, I went to sleep in frustration.

When I got to work that day, the tickets I had tried in vain to buy were now for sale on eBay and ticket broker sites at premium prices. I vowed not to reward these extortionists. But this band meant that much to me that I finally gave in. I wound up paying seven and a half times face value for an upper level seat at the first show. The broker said they'd deliver it on the day of the show to wherever I was staying.

They just walked on stage, picked up their gear and counted into 'I'm So Glad'

In London the day before the show, I looked up the address of the ticket broker and went to pick up my ticket early. They checked their inventory of single tickets and offered me a free upgrade to a choir seat, way above and behind the band but close and - best of all - in the overhang row. I was now paying just two and a half times face value for an excellent seat, rather than seven and a half times face value for an average one.

I met up with Grant Scale and Dennis Lawrenson, two Australians I knew from a Jack Bruce fan site, and the night before the first reunion show, the three of us went to see Cream's lyricist Pete Brown perform at the Bull's Head in Barnes and we got to talk to him for a while.

At the Royal Albert Hall the band came out at 8.07pm. No

announcement, no flashpots, no strobes - they just walked on stage, picked up their gear and counted into 'I'm So Glad'. No one knew what they'd play but it was basically the old songbook plus they added 'Stormy Monday'. And they only briefly spoke to everyone. Talk about old school. Their voices were a bit worn and a line or two was flubbed, but they were great. And as well as the first reunion show in London, I got to see the last show in New York, this time paying face value for the ticket and with my brother and close friends. The MSG set lists were identical to the Royal Albert Hall except that they added 'Tales of Brave Ulysses'.

Ed Tracey met up with two Australian Cream fans who flew in for the show

I WAS THERE: PATRICK SMITH

I BOUGHT A floor ticket online for a ridiculously high sum of money. It being hard to choose between the four different dates I thought, 'The first night might have some flaws after 38 years not playing a full concert together, but emotionally it must be a big moment when they hit the stage.' And it certainly was. For the first minutes there were standing ovations that seemed they would never stop. During 'We're Going Wrong', I actually burst into tears. It was so beautiful and I felt I was taken in a time machine back to the Sixties, even though I was only five years old when they split in 1968. It was almost like a religious experience. They played wonderfully all night and it still amazes me how they could perform about 20 songs and not sound repetitive at any point. Each song had its own character both in harmony, performance and feeling. I never ever will regret the sum I paid for that ticket.

I WAS THERE: MARK ROSENBAUM

I ALWAYS SAID that if they ever got back together, no matter where it was, I had two wishes. To see The Beatles, and to see Cream. When I heard that Cream were getting back together I went online the day the tickets went on sale and scored two tickets. It took a lot of begging my wife for her to say 'yes, let's do this', but we went to London for three days and stayed at a hotel within two blocks of the Royal Albert Hall. We were there for the opening night and when they came out on the stage the crowd was completely overwhelmed. I was almost in tears and so were a lot of people around me. Eric was almost speechless. He had a hard time addressing the crowd. And then the show went off. The DVDs they released afterwards didn't show a lot from the opening night. They later said that they were a little bit rusty. We would never have known.

Mark Rosenbaum was at the Royal Albert Hall in 2005

I WAS THERE: CHRIS JOHNSTON

ERIC INSPIRED ME to play the guitar and Cream is my favourite of all the bands he's been in. I grew up listening to Chuck Berry and rock'n'roll and a bit of country and western through my parents. I've been a fan of Eric since I was 10 years old and discovered my dad's tape of *August*. When *The Cream of Eric Clapton* came out in 1987, I bought it as a present for my dad and ended up listening to it more than he did. I then got an interest in playing and dug into Eric's past.

In 2005 the tickets were going for thousands and I'd never have been able to afford one. But on the Tuesday, I got a call about two o'clock in the afternoon from a friend. He knew the sound guy who had managed to get us two complimentary tickets on the proviso that we didn't mind being in the engineer's booth. I said, 'I don't care if I'm in the gods standing up, as long as I'm in there!' It was like we'd won the lottery. We were in the best spot in the whole place for sound. Just thinking about it now gives me goosebumps.

They came on and started playing and it was just a magical experience. I remember Eric taking solos and when the engineer was reaching over to put the slider up this massive wall of sound filled the hall. It was a real one-off experience. There was loads of hype around it at the time, because no one knew how it was going to end up and whether they were going to argue, but they pulled it off. I'm glad I saw it there,

Chris Johnston on his Strat

because the Madison Square Gardens gigs weren't as good. There was a little bit of tension by then. And there was a bit of trepidation about what gear to use. 'Do we go back and use our Marshalls and our Gibsons?' I think they played a little bit safe and went with what they knew and what they'd evolved with. I've seen Eric 30 odd times now, starting in 1994 with what was his hundredth concert at the Albert Hall, but that Cream concert is up there as one of the best.

Chris Johnston got to see the show from the engineer's booth

How Eric feels about Cream depends on how he feels on the day he's asked. Sometimes in interviews he'll say that the music was crap and other times he'll say, 'I love the guys' and 'I miss Ginger and Jack'. As he said at the time, it was good that they could all do it because they were all fit and able to do it. And now that Ginger and Jack are no longer with us, he probably feels grateful that he did do it. I went to the Ginger Baker memorial concert in March 2020 and that was a humbling experience. There was a big picture of Ginger at the back of the stage. Looking at Eric looking back at Ginger while all this music was playing was quite an emotional thing to see.

My go to Cream track is 'Sunshine of your Love'. The lick is so iconic. You can ask any guitar player or bass player to play it. And even the drumming, because it's off the beat. It's almost reversed. It's their signature song, while 'Crossroads' is a bit like 'Layla'. It's become almost an Eric staple. He plays it at every gig. The songs they produced are iconic. They've stood the test of time and will carry on.

I WAS THERE: DAVID MACLEAN

CREAM PLAYED THE Hermitage Ballroom in Hitchin, Hertfordshire on 16 September 1966. I wasn't there but the week before my band - The Countdowns - played the same venue. But it was clear that Cream were going places and that we weren't, although our lead guitarist, Alan Painter, went on to back Roy Orbison and our drummer, Alan Eden, became a highly successful session musician and businessman. I became a huge Cream fan and caught up with them at the Alert Hall reunion concerts. Their performance was stunning. Ginger Baker was awesome,

Eric was cool and collected and Jack sang beautifully. Having dashed across London straight from work, I think I was the only person in the audience wearing a suit amongst a sea of unreconstructed hippies!

I WAS THERE: J DAVID SPURLOCK

David MacLean caught up with Cream 49 years later

I SAW ALL seven Cream reunion shows and partied with the band after the last one, in New York. Though they were toying with the idea of adding dates in LA and Japan, as the backstage pass-like invites hinted, that ultra-exclusive affair turned out to really be the Goodbye Cream Party. Backtrack some months to the first gig: the night before flying, I often have a lot of work to do plus packing and don't get any sleep and that's how it was prior to flying to London for the Royal Albert Hall shows. So the night before the first gig, I was already running on no sleep and then I flew all night, arriving in London in the morning, so that was my second night with no sleep. After checking into my hotel, I walked down to the Albert Hall to get the lay of the land. I then got something to eat and went back to the hotel to freshen up but still no time to sleep prior to the show.

I got to the show and there were people everywhere. I was looking for my friends Larry Yellen and Scooter Weintraub, who worked with Eric. Scooter was by the mobile recording unit and he told me Larry was around somewhere. I got in line to get in and started chatting with others. They were a bit surprised that I flew over from the States and that I was able to get a ticket for all four nights. I was briefly interviewed for a radio show I seem to recall being named *I've Been Waiting So Long*, very apropos and just like the lyric to Cream's 'Sunshine of Your Love'. There was also a brief interview for the BBC 2 TV show *Grumpy Old Men*. Perhaps that was apropos for Ginger.

I told some in line that I hadn't slept in two days. They were surprise I was still on my feet. As I told them, every now and then my legs would get weak but as soon as I thought of Eric, Jack and Ginger stepping onto a public stage together for the first time in 37 years, I was ready to rock! At some point we heard a commotion. It turned out to be Geezer Butler from Black Sabbath. He was at the ticket window trying to get a ticket for the gig which had sold out instantly a month or so prior. 'Do yew know hoo I am? I'm Geezer Fucking Butler!' he insisted, but it didn't help.

I then saw Cream lyricist Pete Brown walking by me. We had not met prior but I called out 'Pete!' and he turned and we started to chat. I told him I was a friend of Jack's and that I published a Jack Bruce newsletter. He had heard of the newsletter and we stuck together to get inside. The security was very tight. Everyone had to have both photo ID and the exact credit card the tickets were purchased with. Scalpers were selling tickets for record prices but with those security measures, I'm not sure how people got in with scalped tickets.

I then saw Cream lyricist Pete Brown walking by me

Pete and I saw the whole opening night show together. It was such an emotional, once-in-a-lifetime rush as the band came on stage. They were all lucky to be alive considering the lives they had led, but particularly Jack who had been near death and in a coma not long before. Pete agreed they were very good. My first thought was, 'This is the best medicine Jack could possibly have.'

The show was great and well rehearsed, although the first night was a bit rushed. I could tell the band was a bit nervous not knowing how the ancient tunes would be received - possibly more so by the press than the die-hard audience - so many years later. But the crowd loved every minute and in my 50 years of concert going I have never witnessed so many standing ovations in a single show as at those Royal Albert Hall Cream reunion shows.

Celebrities in attendance that week included Paul McCartney, Ringo Starr, Olivia Harrison, Jimmy Page, Roger Waters, Sheryl Crow, Bill Wyman, Pete Townshend, Roger Daltrey, Steve Winwood, Alice Cooper, Bryan Adams and Brian May. Prime Minister Tony Blair had tickets for the last night but word was that the election that night kept him unavoidably detained. The only thing missing seemed to be 'Tales of Brave Ulysses' and 'I Feel Free', especially as there was a promo card in most seats for a new Cream CD collection named *I Feel Free*. I don't think anyone held out hope for 'SWLABR'. One highlight every night was 'We're Going Wrong', particularly as few people ever got to hear that live in the old days or on record.

The notoriously critical London press also loved the concert. Almost all of the reviews were for the opening night and amazingly (as they are notoriously tough), they were all good. I recall one headline: 'One of the Best Bands of the '60s is Now One of the Best Bands in Their 60s'. What the press didn't know was that every night was a bit different but generally they got better every night.

I WAS THERE: DAVID KLEIN

I NEVER SAW Cream back in the day but always regarded them as fantastic musicians who created music that generated an emotional response from me. When I saw Blind Faith in 1969, I was more in awe of them. I remembered being bored with Delaney and Bonnie (even though Clapton played with them) and I was baffled that their support act Free got booed off the stage. I guess that the fans were just impatient.

In 2005, when we heard news of the Cream reunion, we entered all of our secretaries in the lottery and I and two other guys from the firm scored tickets. We ended up trading tickets so that we could go to three of the four shows in London. It was a real party as we joined up with several of our other friends who also got tickets. It was during a brief six months period when mushrooms were legal in England so we were all flying high for the shows. Jack was ill (I think he just had a liver transplant) and was seated for most

David Klein saw three of the four Albert Hall shows

of the show. He was, however, playing unbelievably well. My favourite songs were probably 'White Room', 'Toad' and 'Sunshine of Your Love'. I also enjoyed 'Rollin' and Tumblin''. They played the same set every night but the songs sounded just a little different, each time. They were all very relaxed and the music didn't seem quite as intense. Maybe it was their age. Perhaps the most relaxed was Ginger, although his solo on 'Toad' was thunderous. It was an unforgettable experience and, all in all, a great time.

I WAS THERE: HOWARD JOHNSTON

I WAS TOO young to see them first time around. However, it was simply wonderful to see them together again and I thank them all from the bottom of my heart for the privilege. I went to three of the four London Royal Albert Hall gigs (only missing Tuesday 3rd May) and flew over to the United States for all of the MSG gigs. Six out of seven ain't bad!

That first night at the Albert Hall - with no compere introductions - the three of them wandered on stage and the place erupted. The standing ovation lasted several minutes and had them stunned. I looked around and grown men were in tears. I have never seen anything like that at any gig, before or since. It was a momentous coming together of the gods and the faithful and a truly moving experience. It is hard to explain, but I will never forget it, and I am not exaggerating. I think we all felt proud to be a part of the brotherhood (and sisterhood). People who dug real music played by real people. Music played by exceptional talents that has more than stood the test of time.

I WAS THERE: DARYL GENIS

I DIDN'T WANT to fly all the way to England and not have seats. I had the money, so I found a place selling third row centre seats for $5,000 apiece and bought two tickets. But we had young kids at home and my then wife didn't want to go with me so I ended up going to England by myself. I wound up with tickets for three nights. I went to the Royal Albert Hall and was scoping out the scene, trying to sell the spare ticket I'd paid $5,000 for. I realised I wasn't going to get anywhere near five grand for it - the touts were selling good tickets for just hundreds of dollars. All the touts were trying to get my ticket and one of them offered me $200. I said, 'I'd rather just keep the ticket than sell it that cheap.' Having a whole, untorn ticket would be something significant.

I had one foot in the door of the Albert Hall when one of the touts came over and said, 'I might have somebody who's interested in your ticket.' He introduced me to a gentleman and his son who had flown over from New York and who didn't have tickets. I said, 'I have a third row centre seat.' He said, 'What do you want for it?' I said, 'I'm into it for $5,000. What do you have?' 'All I have is $800 and I brought my son because I wanted him to see Cream.' And I said, 'Well if you paid me $800 for this ticket, who would use it?' 'My son. I'll just go back to my hotel.' And I said, 'You know what? Use your $800 to buy another ticket and I'll take your son as my date. He'll sit with me in the third row and you can go get yourself a good ticket.' So I took his kid as my guest. The kid was awestruck. The satisfaction saw on his face as he was watching Cream was worth the five grand.

If you paid me $800 for this ticket, who would use it?

I also saw the New York shows and bought a bunch of tickets on Ticketron to try and sell them and recoup some of my costs and give me something to do while I was there. While I was trying to sell tickets one night, this couple came up to me. I said how much I was looking for and they said 'we can't afford that'. The girl was 18 or 19 years old. She said, 'My dad turned me onto Cream. I grew up listening to Cream with him.' And I said, 'Are you guys students? Are you working?' They were minimum wage workers and I took two tickets for really good seats that I was trying to sell and said, 'That's a great story. You deserve these tickets.' I gave them to her.

I WAS THERE: TOM THATCHER
A MIRACLE HAPPENED in 2005. Cream announced that they were to reform for four dates at the Albert Hall. The excitement was universal, and the questions were all much along the same lines. Had they still got it? Were Jack and Ginger able to get on well enough to play? They had sold out in three hours but I managed to buy two tickets on the black market for an incredible amount of money so off we went. Rarely have I been so excited.

The audience was extremely well behaved. I think we were probably the only British people in our row. It seemed that everybody except us had flown in from America, or Canada, or South America, or Japan - indeed, from everywhere. The average age of the punters suggested that they could not have been born when Cream broke up, so had never experienced the firestorm of Cream in full cry.

The concert was absolutely fantastic. A weakened Jack Bruce, recovering from surgery, a half-crippled Ginger Baker and a very together Eric Clapton, but suffering from a stinking cold, played like gods. Every song was a highlight, but for me, 'We're Going Wrong' and 'Toad' summed up the band - an extraordinary mixture of hard blues, angular yet fluent and fluid playing, great singing and harmonies, a rhythm section that was a lead section and a guitar that sounded like three guitars. My son described Ginger's solo in 'Toad' as 'the best five minutes in rock I've ever seen' and I won't disagree. Just now and then, Jack's extraordinary bass would catch fire, Ginger would pick up on it, and off they'd go - the firestorm was still there, not too far below the surface. Listen to the version of 'Stormy Monday' and you'll see what I mean. My one regret is that Eric chose Fender over Gibson - but who's counting?

On their day Cream were a force of nature. It was impossible to separate the musicians in full flight because they become one mighty volcanic eruption.

I WAS THERE: JOE SALAMONE

I FLEW THERE with my wife and two daughters, and enjoyed the live concert immensely. I came to the United States at the age of 15 and I started to listen to them and their music as soon as I got here. They are my favourite trio and I love their music and the lyrics. It saddens me that Jack Bruce and Ginger Baker have passed away. I love Eric Clapton. I've seen him live many times. My mythological hero is Ulysses. Of course, they wrote 'Tales of Brave Ulysses for me.

I WAS THERE: PETER BENNETT

I GREW UP at a boarding school in Abingdon, near Oxford. My family was not especially rich and when many of my chums bought the latest LPs, such as The Beatles or the Stones, I taped them. As a reward for winning a scholarship, my parents bought me a Ferguson reel-to-reel tape recorder. It was a great machine and I got many shocks taking it apart! In the sixth form there were fewer rules. We lived in our own house and music suddenly became exciting. Amongst the classics I was given or bought were *Fresh Cream* and *Disraeli Gears*. The latter with its freaky flower power sleeve was a revelation, completely different from anything else - and for me more exciting than the current Beatles issues. And I was fascinated by Jack Bruce's deep rumbling bass.

Peter Bennett was getting regular electric shocks from his tape recorder

Cream's farewell concert at the Albert Hall in 1968 was beyond the reach of a 16-year-old schoolboy but saw many fine Jack Bruce concerts, including one at a club in Hampstead, while Eric Clapton's appearance with Delaney and Bonnie at the Albert Hall in December 1969 was the third concert I ever went to. And I'd managed to catch Blind Faith's debut in Hyde Park, but it was hugely disappointing.

By 2005, I was living and working (in a bank) in Norway, there being no jobs in Mrs Thatcher's England in the Seventies. Cream had announced a new 'farewell concert' - at the Albert Hall of course - and this time I was certainly going to go! Eric had decided that it was now or never, as Jack Bruce had liver cancer. They had all matured and become friends!

Annoyingly, I was on a training course the day tickets went on sale, but I said to the course leader before we began, 'You are planning to take a break at 10am, aren't you, because that's when tickets go on sale!' He was sympathetic and, amazingly, I secured two tickets. Eureka! 40 years of music was coming to a climax.

I flew to London for the May 5th concert, which it turned out was the most used for the ensuing CD and DVD. I went with my almost as fanatical brother and we took our places high up in the balconies. But hey, this was Cream. Who cared?

The concert was low key: no Rolling Stones busty women or Pink Floyd flying pig

The concert was actually fairly low key: no big screen or stage, no Rolling Stones busty women or Pink Floyd flying pig. There was simply a backdrop onto which they projected the classic Sixties psychedelic bubbles. All three of them walked on very soberly dressed - Eric in jeans, Ginger in a Cream t-shirt (which he advertised after 'Pressed Rat and Warthog'!) and Jack the most in costume in a colourful coat that he could have worn 37 years ago. And they play everything, from 'I'm So Glad' through to 'Badge' and 'Crossroads', a Clapton favourite he still almost always plays. The music was good - more a smile than a scream - we have all got older, Cream too.

Jack was in amazing form considering he was seriously ill, but his voice was as strong as it was in 1968. Ginger was wry and hard working and Eric was as always a gentleman, giving credit to all. The music - they played it all - was great to listen to. It wasn't a case of the earth moving, more a warm sunset. But we were happy that that phase of our musical life was complete. I've been to greater concerts but Cream was the most satisfying. They did it because they wanted to. They were friends, and we could buy the DVD and smile with them whenever we wanted to. May 5th 2005 was our 'crossroads'!

I WAS THERE: CHRIS EGAN
I ONLY SAW them at the Royal Albert Hall reunion shows. I thought I'd be watching Clapton closely but I was mesmerised by the brilliance of Jack Bruce.

I WAS THERE: JERRY CRUISE
'GO TO THE back of the Albert Hall, look for the fountain and the blonde with the leather pants.' Click. He hung up on me. Well, I didn't find a fountain but I did find a walled off statue and there sat, to my amazement, a beautiful blonde girl in leather pants. 'Are you Jerry?', she asked. 'Yes.' 'Here's your ticket, maybe I'll see you there,' and away she walked, all smiles and carefree confidence. As I looked around the crowd, I was amazed to see so many familiar faces. One foot to my right was Keith Urban, who struck up a conversation after I asked several people in the crowd to stop sticking phones in his face for a picture. To my left was Eric Idle, to my right Sheryl Crow and Lance Armstrong. Behind me were Jimmy Page and Tony Banks from Genesis, in his private box. I watched him, arms crossed, as he watched the show. By the end, he was on his feet cheering as a fan just like the rest of us. Tom Hanks, in town for the filming of *The DaVinci Code*, and I had a conversation in the washrooms, ending with 'isn't this amazing?' He laughed and said, 'No, this is fucking amazing, and thanks for not bugging me!'

Jerry Cruise picked up VIP tickets from a mystery blonde

My friend Boris Jaeggi was back in Switzerland nursing the stomach flu. I'm forever grateful to him for VIP tickets to the show of a lifetime.

I WAS THERE: ROGER PEEK

I TURNED MY son onto the music of Cream when he was 15 and said to him more than once, 'If those three guys ever get together on a stage again, I will go anywhere on the planet to hear them play.' One day, with the appropriately cryptic sense of occasion, he simply informed me, 'Father, the time has come.' Thus, we set about making a reality out of the tyranny of distance. For me this involved over 60 hours of air travel in five days to make a return trip to London from Christchurch, New Zealand. On learning of our travels, the genial Englishman seated next to us in Row T in the circle at the Royal Albert Hall said, 'Goodness. I drove down from Norwich and thought that was a long way.'

First impressions of the venue included the stage set with Ginger's kit sporting two bass drums. Despite the intervening years, we were perhaps still to be treated to the thunderous coda to 'Sunshine of Your Love'. But my favourite trivial 'georock' question - 'Where are the Marshall Mountains?' 'At the back of any stage Cream are performing on' - was no longer relevant.

They sacrificed a lot of the improvisation but none of the energy

To describe the reception as rapturous when the three emerged from the wings after such a long hiatus of paid performance would be an understatement. Past disagreements, artistic differences and the regrettably short time this unit spent at the pinnacle of their craft were forgotten in that euphoric moment. And not a note had been played. Some well-chosen (if partly tongue-in-cheek) words from the bass player followed and without any introduction the setlist began its inexorable roll into rock history with 'I'm So Glad'. I was reminded of the possibly apocryphal but heartwarming story tale of Jack Bruce exiting the stage after a West, Bruce and Laing gig to find Skip James's widow waiting to express her appreciation for the income that had enabled the old bluesman's healthcare in his final years as a result of Cream's insistence on paying him the royalties due.

'Sweet Wine' and 'Spoonful' were the most anticipated 15 plus minute epics. The 2005 versions were pared back to about half that length. They sacrificed a lot of the improvisation but none of the energy. Jack Bruce had explained that recreating the original live performance standard through massive stacks was never a realistic prospect for the reunion.

'Badge' was touted as the 'first time played live, ever'. Eric had, of course, performed it numerous times. But from the unmistakable bass intro to the roar from the crowd to summon the trademark guitar lick in the bridge, the original rhythm section ensured the status of 'first time played live, ever, by the Band that always mattered most.'

'Stormy Monday' came as a surprise to my knowledge it had never appeared on a Cream setlist before. As a vehicle for Eric's innate blues guitarmanship, it certainly served its purpose. 'Deserted Cities of the Heart' and 'We're Going Wrong' complemented Jack's trademark class bass playing right across the concert. My only regret was the omission of 'Tales of Brave Ulysses' with the lazy slaps of Baker's thunder interwoven by Clapton's relentless wah-wah guitar phrasing. 'Sunshine Of Your Love' was an absurdly obvious pick for the encore, and I'm not sure I shall ever forget the primal roar that rose from every throat in the place when that 'world beating riff' (to quote Jack in a less-than-modest moment) again resounded throughout the Royal Albert Hall.

It was an absolute privilege to have been there

I WAS THERE: MICHAEL STANSFIELD

IN 1969 I was in the third year at grammar school. My mate, the drummer in a band we're going to form called Blitzkrieg, introduces me to an album with three blokes with long hair, wearing shiny silvery evening suits and with daft smiles on their faces. Then he plays me a track called 'I'm So Glad'. I'd never heard anything like it! Up to that point I thought the zenith of 'progressive underground music' was 'Witch's Promise' by Jethro Tull. Boy, was I about to get one hell of a life changing shock! 'I'm So Glad' blew my mind. It took me a while to get my head around the tonal cadence

Michael Stansfield had to wait 36 years to see Cream

and structure of what Cream's art was about but I was then enrolled in a form of musical artistic appreciation as would give me profound pleasure for a lifetime. What Bill Haley and Elvis were to rock and roll, what The Beatles were to pop, Cream were to rock and blues - the big bang, setting the benchmark for others to follow.

When in January 2005 it was announced that there would be a second coming of Cream at the Royal Albert Hall, only death itself was going to prevent me from attending. And I did, with a long-time friend and fellow Cream addict. The two plus hours we witnessed were worth every penny of the £925 I spent on two £125 tickets. The boys still had it - and were better in some ways - and yours truly can now die with a smile on his face. Thank you Eric, thank you Jack and thank you Ginger, for giving my eyes that night the best thing I'd ever seen on Planet Earth. Musical gods.

I WAS THERE: MICKEY MODERN TURNER

IT WAS ALWAYS about Clapton for me. His playing was and is the foundation and his presence is the front of house. They were brilliant that night, aided by a wave of nostalgia from a packed house. I was in a box directly opposite the stage, and had a brilliant view. Back in the day I was more of a Mod, a soul boy liking Tamla and blues, but I did like Cream's hit singles, especially 'White Room'. I rate them highly. I always go to the Royal Albert Hall to see Clapton. It's become a family get together, as my brother-in-law promotes Clapton.

I WAS THERE: MIKE J SAMPIER

A FAN SINCE the age of 12 and the release of *Fresh Cream*, they never played my hometown of Portland, Oregon. The closest I got was in August 1969 when I saw the mighty but short-lived Blind Faith. I had to wait over 36 years after Cream's demise to see my favourite band. On the first day of ticket sales, I struck out, but tried again the second day. At that point only VIP tickets were available. I bought one for £350. It was worth every penny. I only had to travel a short distance to get to London, from Galway. I joined other people in the VIP section who had travelled from as far away as Australia and the USA. To help pass the time, I asked fellow fans to predict the show's opener. There were many suggestions but mine was the one that turned out to accurate.

We dedicated fans made our three master musicians wait as our welcome back applause delayed Eric's opening notes of 'I'm So Glad'. Witnessing that moment when Ginger, Jack and Eric didn't have the nerve to stop our heartfelt cheering, and they probably comprehended what their music meant to us fans, still gives me such a warm feeling inside all these years later. While sadly Jack and Ginger have left us, thankfully their glorious music rolls on so gladly.

I WAS THERE: PETER SMITH

THIS WAS A big gig for me. I'd watched the Cream farewell concert on TV in the late Sixties and was just mesmerised by Clapton. His hair, the psychedelic-painted SG, the woman tone he described in the film, all seemed just sensational to me as a kid. I so wished I'd had the chance to see Cream. I remember older boys at school talking about seeing them at a gig in Newcastle and how great they were. I was so jealous of them. I bought *Goodbye Cream* and played it again and again.

I saw Clapton many times in the Seventies and Eighties, plus Jack Bruce and Ginger Baker with their solo projects. But to see Cream was a great dream, an ambition. When the rumours of a reunion came to fruition and it was announced that the three legends would come together for a series of shows in London I was determined to go. I was nervous about getting tickets and stressed about it for days before they went on sale. That morning, I had two phones and a computer to hand and got straight through to the Albert Hall box office on one of the phones, managing, to my joy, to buy tickets only ten rows from the front of the stage. I then waited in anticipation for the gig. Would it be as good as I hoped?

Marie came with me, and we both thoroughly enjoyed the experience. Judging by the American accents in evidence, the Albert Hall was full of fans who had travelled a long way for the honour of seeing this legendary band play for one more time. The atmosphere was strange, everyone was quiet in anticipation. It was as if the crowd couldn't believe what they were seeing. Quiet,

Peter Smith was there on 6 May 2005

almost religious. The set covered everything I could have wished for, with a selection from all of the albums. As Richard English wrote in a review for *Rock's Back Pages*, 'For a while we were transported back to the late Sixties, to the sublime expression of the first supergroup.'

> *Clapton was god again, Jack sang beautifully and Ginger pounded away on his drums*

Clapton was god again, Jack sang beautifully and Ginger pounded away on his drums. The crowd stayed in their seats until almost the end. For 'Sunshine of Your Love', which was the encore, we were all up and we managed to get right to the front. Marie was leaning on the stage directly in front of Jack Bruce and I was just behind her. You can even see us on the DVD if you look closely. Towards the end of the set, Eric said 'we were cut off in our prime' and Ginger replied 'this is our prime!' It was a night I will remember forever. Sometimes your dreams do come true, and sometimes they are as good as you dreamt they would be.

I WAS THERE: STEVE ELLIOTT

WHEN BANDS FROM the British Blues Boom of the Sixties were discussed, two names that always came up were the Yardbirds and Cream. Reading the *NME Encyclopedia of Rock* by Nick Logan and Bob Woffinden, its front cover proudly hailing it as 'the standard rock reference book', I discovered that Clapton had been in the Yardbirds and Cream but also John Mayall's Bluesbreakers and - briefly - the Plastic Ono Band. As a massive Beatles fan, I needed to hear some of this stuff.

On a Saturday morning visit to a secondhand record stall on Oldham Market, I spotted an original stereo copy of Cream's *Disraeli Gears* for the princely sum of £2.20. Parting with half my weekly pocket money seemed a bit extreme but something inside my head said I had to do it. I wasn't disappointed. I hadn't heard anything as good as this in ages. It had a simplicity about it, but sounded exciting and contemporary.

A week later the same record stall had a copy of *Best of Cream* which not only opened my eyes but with 'Crossroads' totally blew my mind. Eric's second solo was the first time a record had made the hairs on the back of my neck stand up. I raved about this amazing music I'd discovered to the guys at school. My friend Andy Buckley lent me a couple of Yardbirds 45s and I was hooked.

In October 1980, BBC2 broadcast *Cream's Last Concert*, a 30 minute compilation of five songs from the Royal Albert Hall show in November 1968. That was it for me. Almost every week, I'd go to as many local record shops as I could and buy vintage vinyl by anyone and everyone involved in late Sixties music. And every so often I'd dig out my old Cream, Bluesbreakers, Blind Faith and Pink Floyd LPs and mourn the fact that the music of today was... well, complete shit compared to these wonderful acts!

Parting with half my weekly pocket money to buy Disraeli Gears *seemed a bit extreme*

When in 2005 it was announced that Cream were to reform and play four nights at the Royal Albert Hall, I applied for a ticket not holding out much hope but was delighted to receive one and looked forward to the big day. I hoped they'd sound like the Cream of 1968, or at least Clapton with a better backing band than usual. In the event, it was like a cross between the two. I'm still not convinced the mixing on the official CD and DVD totally did justice to what was coming from the audience towards the band that I heard from the seventh row that night. I'd seen Eric in concert twice before, in '87 and '90, and frankly found some of his newer stuff to be a bit anaemic and boring, but from the start of 'I'm So Glad' I knew this was something special.

All three members were in cracking form and although I'd never been a fan of drum solos, Ginger's showpiece 'Toad' was an unexpected highlight. Jack Bruce was in great voice, having had a lifesaving liver transplant a couple of years previously. Those two hours went by too fast. I count myself lucky to have seen those three incredible musicians giving their all to a British audience for what turned out to be the very last time. They were the most influential British band after The Beatles, paving the way for a musical revolution that still continues to produce great rock bands.

MADISON SQUARE GARDEN
24 - 26 OCTOBER 1005, NEW YORK, NEW YORK

I WAS THERE: MARK ROSENBAUM

WORD GOT OUT that they were going to do a few shows in New York. My wife almost killed me: 'You could have seen them in New York!' I made sure I got tickets. My neighbour and my two of my three kids - my oldest was in China teaching English - came with me and took a train up to New York. It took me 37 years to see them a second time, and then I saw them twice within a few months. I thank God that they were able to get it back together. I was sitting close enough at MSG to see a little friction between Jack Bruce and Ginger. It wasn't evident at the Royal Albert Hall shows, where I think they were so thrilled that they were actually able to do it and to get back together.

Clapton was a blues purist. That's why he left the band he was in, because he didn't want to go for the commercial stuff, and the others were jazz musicians. Jack was classically trained, which over the years he said was a waste of his time, but I'm sure it had a lot to do with how he approached what he did. It was the purest of the blues and Jack and Ginger's jazz influence. Ginger always said it was not a rock band but a jazz ensemble. Of course, you could say that all day and the fans wouldn't believe you. It was a mixture of the direction of the three musicians who were all incredible in their own right. Until Cream came along, there wasn't a band that did all those long improvisational solos. And I think it opened up a lot of minds and a lot of musicians to the fact that there was more than just a song to be played.

I'm glad they got back together while they still could

I'm glad they got back together while they still could. Jack had just come off of liver transplant a few months earlier and Eric said that they were lucky that they were still around and could still do it, whereas other bands had already lost people. If you watch Eric's acceptance speech at the Rock 'n' Roll Hall of Fame you can see that he was really touched that they got back together for that. I think he really felt something very, very deep that night.

I WAS THERE: PAUL BASTKOWSKI

DISRAELI GEARS WAS given to me by my Aunt Karen, who was seven years older than me, when her mother (my grandmother) told her to 'get rid of that music.' I went with a friend of mine, Jimmy, and a boyhood friend of his who subsequently became my concert-going bud. Jimmy turned to me before the Cream hit the stage and said, 'I've never seen Clapton before.' After I picked my jaw up off the floor, because I thought I'd seen everybody, I looked at him and said, 'Well, this is as great a place as any to start.' I remember distinctly thinking, 'There's no way Ginger is gonna pull this off' but he absolutely did. You know, Baker was not one to practice. Ging just went at it!

I WAS THERE: HOWARD JOHNSTON

IN NEW YORK Monday was great and Wednesday was greater but Tuesday was the night that they really blazed as of old. That is in no small part due to the energy that Eric possessed, which possibly left him sapped for the following night. I had a ball at all three gigs, sitting in different parts of the Garden each night. The Cream were and are a mighty powerful unit of three equal parts. If anybody particularly shone throughout, for me it was Jack Bruce who rose to the occasion every night and quite clearly did not want to stop after 'Sunshine'. Ginger was splendid, and it was his job to bind this explosive chemistry together which he did with great flair and bombast, whilst the restless fireworks of lead guitar, harmonica and lead bass threatened to explode in every direction.

At Madison Square Garden there was a distinct lack of the genuine warmth and real affection - evidenced by the absence of any hugging, back slapping and chit chat between Eric, Jack and Ginger - which had been the hallmark of the Royal Albert Hall gigs. Eric himself, who had been so verbal in London, hardly said a thing to the midtown audience. It was largely left to Jack.

Many Americans thought that the band were better in New York. They were certainly louder at MSG, which is three times the capacity of the Royal Albert Hall, but each of the seven gigs had its highlights. Some numbers blazed in Manhattan more than in Kensington six months before. The inclusion of 'Tales of Brave Ulysses' was worth the price of admission alone, and the whole crowd - me included - went crazy for it. However, there was a different vibe about the New York gigs.

Some Americans had told me they hated the Garden as a venue. I assumed - since this place is part of rock 'n' roll history - that it was acoustics that they poured cold water on. But so many fans (including many Americans) felt the atmosphere in London was better. People were toe-tapping, thigh-slapping and handclapping in their seats just as appreciatively as they would have been on their feet. The audiences at the Royal Albert Hall back in May were totally into what they were witnessing. You could feel genuine love for these three guys back in London in May.

So many fans, Americans included, felt the atmosphere in London was better

---

Each night in New York, enormous numbers of people were constantly up and down from their seats, going to talk to people and heading to the bars all the bloody time. It was highly irritating. I also saw many trendy, spoilt little-rich-kid, young Ivy League types who were far more interested in waving to friends, ordering drinks from the endless succession of eager waiters all over the place or messing with mobile phones.

Most insultingly to Eric, Jack and Ginger, they were also talking at length and at volume throughout. This was annoying but particularly unforgivable during the quieter passages in 'We're Going Wrong' and 'Stormy Monday'. These idiots only applauded after tracks like 'Badge' and 'White Room'. Many people complained about it afterwards in the bars, including Americans themselves who felt ashamed and embarrassed by their fellow countrymen. One guy told me that Eric in particular gets pissed off with all these throngs of people coming and going to the exits. If Eric's attention was wandering, one reason may have been the apathy he witnessed from sections of the crowd. If he appeared keen to beat a hasty exit on Wednesday night, perhaps it was because he was looking forward towards playing at Albert's place again where people really listen, and drink and talk before and after the gig - but not during it!

I WAS THERE: JOE BIRISH

I SAW THE second of the three shows at Madison Square Garden. It was a very similar set to the Royal Albert Hall reunion shows but they added 'Tales of Brave Ulysses'. I had seats pretty high up on the right side of the stage. The crowd loved the band as soon as they took the stage and started into 'I'm So Glad'. Ginger Baker had a headset mic and sang along with Eric and Jack in the chorus, and his voice came through as he sang in a lower octave. From a jamming perspective, my favourite song was 'Sweet Wine'. They all played with real abandon and fire. 'Toad' was the last song before the encores and Ginger was at his best. I found recordings online of all three MSG shows and Ginger played the longest drum solo of all three nights the night I saw. He seemed in a good mood too!

Joe Birish got the longest of Ginger's drum solos at the 2005 MSG shows

I WAS THERE: DAVE DUNLAP

I GREW UP in New Jersey. I was in a gang of about 15 of us. We were the youngest boys of very large families. My family had four. All my friends came from families of six, seven or eight kids. Our older brothers and sisters bought us these four albums, because we were only listening to Elvis and they said, 'You have to listen to better music.' They bought us *Disraeli Gears* and *Live Cream Volume II*, and *Beggars Banquet* and *Get Yer Ya-Ya's Out* by the Rolling Stones. The first time I heard *Disraeli Gears* I was absolutely shocked at how good it was, and I've been in love with Cream ever since.

I saw the first night of the reunion tour at the Garden. It was a huge deal for me. When I first heard about it, I was shocked. I tried to get tickets for me and my brother and I failed. But, unbeknownst to me, my wife also tried to get us tickets. She succeeded, and it was really a great surprise. I was very, very happy that I was going to see Cream. My brother and I decided that we were going to take the bus and the tubes in, like we always did for Manhattan. I can take the bus to Jones Square, Jersey City and then the PATH train takes us right to the Garden. It was a rainy cold night. I said, 'Sonofabitch, it's too cold to even drink.' Normally we'd have a few beers before a concert but on this occasion we didn't. My brother said, 'No, let's not drink. You don't want to forget anything.' There were people trying to hawk tickets from us, people trying to rob you, people trying to mug you to get your tickets.

We got in and the seats were not that bad, on one of the upper levels, right above Clapton, slightly to the left. It was a great show. We saw people from all over the world. We were sitting next to people from Israel, and people from England and there was a bunch of kids from France. When Cream first came on, a lot of the adults of my age and older were crying. I was crying. I don't think Eric Clapton realised how big of a thing Cream was. I think he thought it was just a maturation through his musical life and I think he was very fortunate to have those two playing with him because they were absolute geniuses. And, as time went on, I think he realised that and knew that they both needed help and were not well and needed money and I guess it was his way of trying to make things right.

When Cream came on, me and a lot of the adults of my age and older were crying

I don't think he broke up the band. I think they all did that. But looking back he must have realised, 'Wow, this band's really good.' Their stuff is incredible. That '68 tour was incredible. I've seen over 200 shows by different bands. I've seen everybody and that stuff is incredible. It's jazz.

The first couple of songs - 'I'm So Glad' and 'Spoonful' - they were a little slow. But once they got to 'Pressed Rat' they started picking it up and you could see that they were looking at each other and they were happy and that they were really getting into it and thinking 'this is a good show'. They didn't disappoint. They burst into 'Tales of Brave Ulysses', which was an incredible rendition of that song. 'Badge', I never liked. And 'Politician' was great, and might have been the best song of the night, because Jack finally started feeling comfortable with singing. He was very weak because of the surgery and you could see that he finally got into his groove. The rest of the songs they just blasted out. They were tight. You could tell that they had rehearsed. It's one of the five best shows I've ever been to.

I WAS THERE: JOE BRENDER
I WAS FIFTH row from the stage, with Clapton to my left side. I thought I'd died and gone to heaven. Baker was at his best, telling the audience not to buy merchandise from the streets!

I WAS THERE WITH TIM MILLER: RICHARD B KELLEY

BEST OF CREAM was the third album I ever bought with my grass-cutting money. Aged 12 when they split, I was much too young to witness the band even if they'd come to my secondary market Midwestern town (they never did). When the Royal Albert Hall reunion shows were announced, I was plenty old enough to go, but London was still too far away and prohibitively expensive for a guy with two young sons and an ailing father. Then Cream announced a three night stand at Madison Square Garden. I had a college buddy who knew his way around New York City so I wondered if he'd like to meet up for Cream should I be able to procure tickets? He replied 'go for it' and so I did.

Richard Kelley's friend Timothy Miller was with Richard in the press box

Richard Kelley was at MSG for the 2005 reunion

The morning tickets went on sale, I had my American Express all paid up and ready to go with Ticketmaster. A few seconds after 10am, I entered the 'Cream at MSG' ticket portal and started hammering for two, anywhere in the building. My first few tries came up empty as though the show had already sold out, which was not beyond the realm of comprehension. On the fifth or sixth pull I came up with two tickets but their location wasn't described very well, if at all. 'The hell with it,' said I and bought them. I'd find out their location on the night of the show. The Hotel Pennsylvania, literally across the street from Madison Square Garden, was the cheapest hotel room I could find.

The day of the show, a mini-hurricane had stalled over Newark and our flight from Dulles International Airport near DC kept getting delayed. I thought we might miss the show. A flight to JFK was called and we decided to see if we could get on that one - same terminal, same airline. The lady at the counter asked if we had checked baggage. When we replied that we didn't, she printed us a couple of boarding passes and directed us down the entryway. The flight from DC to NYC barely lasted a half an hour and then we were on a shuttle to Penn Station.

The lobby of the Hotel Pennsylvania was gorgeous and modern. The room was anything but, and the curtains were little more than rags. But the view beyond them was Madison Square Garden and 'CREAM' was emblazoned on the marquee! inner was procured at Lindys, across from MSG. The restaurant was full of old rock 'n' rollers and we were delighted to see Leslie West seated at the table adjacent to ours. I wondered why he wasn't in the Cream green room, given his work with Jack Bruce and Felix Pappalardi.

From the hotel we saw 'CREAM' emblazoned on the MSG marquee

We made our way into the Garden. An usher directed us up to level two and another usher led us to a sequestered area at centre court at the bottom of level two. We were in the press box! We had regular chairs and only a built-in desk in front of us, and were high enough that no one could stand and block our view. We had a place to comfortably watch the show and a surface to put our beers on.

A Cream show in the Sixties starting well after midnight or lasting until dawn would have had my parents banning me from such future outings. That night the crowd *was* our parents, or in many cases our grandparents, and the show started just a polite few minutes past 8 pm. The lights went down and you could see Jack Bruce entering from the stage left wings, guided by a roadie with a flashlight on the darkened floorboards. He carried his bass on stage with him and merely assumed his position, stage right. In the background one could see the long, lanky silhouette of Ginger Baker climbing the drum riser from the rear and settling into his seat. At the same time, though still in the dark, the handsomest man to ever wield a Fender Stratocaster nonchalantly strolled to his position.

Before the cheers of the crowd could become too deafening, Clapton gently strummed the first chords of the inspired opener, 'I'm So Glad'. He played them again as Jack Bruce fell in with him and on the third time Ginger joined in as Jack and Eric began to sing the refrain. Twenty thousand old hippies with a lump in their throat and many (like me) trying to choke back tears. My god, this was Cream!

'I'm So Glad' proved to an excellent rave-up to start the show but the real fireworks didn't come until about four minutes into the follow up, 'Spoonful', when Clapton began a stunning solo lasting well over four minutes and so hot it must surely have melted his guitar's strings. Surely, audience minds were being melted.

'Outside Woman Blues' came next and found Clapton in fine vocal form, as well as effortlessly peeling off blues licks. Next up came Ginger's vocal turn on the weird psychedelic pop chestnut, 'Pressed Rat and Wart Hog'. Like the Albert Hall record, Ginger informed the audience that 'Pressed Rat and Wart Hog' had reopened their shop and were selling hats and t-shirts in the lobby. He also gruffly noted that there were bootlegs being sold 'all over the place'. I never saw any.

Another quasi-Sixties pop song followed in the form of 'Sleepy Time Time'. It sort of lived up to its name but here was Cream playing songs that had all but been forgotten as they'd entered the final months of their original existence. Like the concert stages of old, the presentation was pretty spartan. A few spot lights highlighted the band members at appropriate times but the main effect was a long, low video screen behind the band which would change colours and visual effects to match the mood of the songs. It wasn't tall enough to block anyone's view so tickets could be sold behind the stage.

Ginger said that 'Pressed Rat and Wart Hog' were selling hats & t-shirts in the lobby

---

The set list had followed that of the Albert Hall shows exactly so those in-the-know assumed that 'NSU' would follow. In the first (of two) surprises of the night, Clapton activated his wah-wah pedal and the opening riff of the epic 'Tales of Brave Ulysses' washed over the Garden. At two minutes 30 he replayed one of his most memorable solos, drawing the biggest applause of the night thus far. 'NSU' did indeed follow and provided a showcase for the first real jam of the evening as each member seemed to meander off on his own until Jack resumed the vocals, snapping the well-rehearsed trio immediately back into line. Ginger's drumming was almost military-like on this one, and demonstrated a depth of musical knowledge that I do not understand and certainly can't explain.

The opening bass line to the beloved 'Badge' began and I was immediately 13 and back in my childhood bedroom, blasting *Best of Cream* on the portable stereo my great aunt left me in her will. At one minute 15 seconds, the band slightly extended the pause that precedes another of Clapton's most famous riffs and solos and the excitement was palpable. Orgasmic even.

Ginger's drumming was almost military-like on this one

Cream '05 immediately transitioned into 'Politician' and Jack discreetly leaned or sat on a tall stool for the first time that night. Or maybe it was the first time I had noticed. He would return to this bracing position throughout the evening. 'Politician' was played pretty straight and didn't contain the overwrought and lengthy jamming of the live, late Sixties versions. Indeed, most of the songs played thus far had been in the realm of four to five minutes, with only 'Spoonful' approaching the ten minute mark.

'Sweet Wine' followed, containing a healthy dose of brilliant but meandering jamming that never got out of control like Cream were wont to do in their heyday. A lesser song, but the instrumentation expertly delivered with a terrific sense of adventure.

To change things up a bit, Jack sat in his 'comfy chair' and started blasting the riff to 'Rollin' and Tumblin'' on a harmonica. Like the world's greatest front porch musicians, Eric (with a slide in hand) and Ginger fell in behind him, giving him plenty of room to blow his horn for several minutes. Many such harp solos run out of ideas, but this one just kept building until Jack brought it back to the top. The band ended this bit of traditional Delta blues on a downbeat and Jack thanked 'the best audience in the world'.

Eric began a seven minute nod to his solo career with a blistering version of 'Stormy Monday'. It was at this point I realised he had been playing his beloved Stratocaster, Blackie, for over an hour and I'd never once seen him tune the damned thing. With every sonorous note he played you knew you were listening to Eric Clapton and absolutely no one else on earth. That tone, that attack. 'Eric Clapton on guitar and vocals,' announced Jack as the song ended. The world had heard that line a few million times on radio and record in the previous decades.

'Deserted Cities of the Heart' followed and once again I was slapped with the genius of these three musicians doing what only they could. On 'Born Under a Bad Sign', I realised our heroes might be getting a tad winded as it wasn't quite filled with the fire and fury of the decades-earlier versions. 'We're Going Wrong' contained yet another trademark Clapton delivery but was apparently placed in the set as a restroom and beer break. As a Midwestern tourist, I wanted my bragging rights to paying $10 for a beer.

Beginning with a downbeat from Ginger not heard on the original (or maybe edited out), 'Crossroads' wasn't played at the breakneck pace of the *Wheels of Fire* version. Faster and more swinging than Eric's solo versions, it was delivered in less than three and a half minutes, 40 seconds less than the version played millions of times on FM radio and in dorm rooms throughout the universe. Much like Eric's solo shows, another slow blues came in the form of 'Sitting on Top of the World', now featuring Jack back on harp. This one wasn't played at the Albert Hall but another slow blues took the air out of the room... until Eric stepped on his wah-wah pedal again.

A slow blues took the air out of the room... until Eric stepped on his wah-wah pedal

---

'White Room' brought the crowd to life. The show was now essentially over except for the obligatory drum solo and I still hadn't seen Eric tune his black Strat. I could never figure out why Cream and others what finish a 45-minute set with a 15 minute drum solo. Tonight would recapture those glory days. 'Toad' began with a bit of improvisation by all three members which included a tease of 'My Country Tis of Thee', musically alluded to by Jack and Eric both and then 10 minutes of Ginger on drums. The band fell back in and ended 'Toad' as Eric shouted 'Ginger Baker! Jack Bruce! Thank you!' Jack responded with 'Eric Clapton! Thank you very much! You're beautiful! You're lovely!'

After a five minute wait, Jack Bruce strode back to the stage and began noodling on his bass as Eric joined in playing a white Stratocaster for the first time all evening. The staccato attack of the 'Sunshine of Your Love' riff suddenly cut through the Garden as Ginger joined in. The old hippies were roused from their exhausted stupor once more (and for the last time that night). Like 'Crossroads', 'Sunshine' was played slightly slower than the original but the arrangement remained the same until the trio decided to stretch it out at about the four minutes 30 mark. Two and a half minutes later they ended the song and the evening's show, leaving the stage with hand waves but otherwise not engaging the crowd. We were left to reflect on having witnessed two hours (almost to the second) of one of the greatest bands of all time.

Later in 2005, an excellent official reunion website was launched. It featured a fan discussion forum. The general consensus was that the October 25 show was the best of the three in New York. Some enterprising individual had posted MP3 files of an exceptional near professional sounding audience recording of the entire show. I downloaded them. The next day I returned to the website to see if anyone had posted recordings from either of the other nights. Clicking on the fan forum link I found the October 25 recording was gone, as was the fan forum. Somebody at Cream Inc didn't have a sense of humour.

I WAS THERE: ALAN LEFTON

CREAM ARE MY all-time favourite band. Not having seen them in their heyday, I had to see at least one of these shows. Luckily, a friend had an extra ticket and VIP seats for the Albert Hall and I went into work the next day and told them I would be out of the office and going to London - I didn't ask! The entire experience was incredible and when I saw all three members of Cream walking out on stage at the Royal Albert Hall together, it honestly felt like a dream. I had seen Clapton five or six times and Jack - my all-time favourite musician - 12 times or more. This was the first time I'd seen Ginger live.

Being critical of my favourite band was a bit tough. I was not all that crazy about Clapton's guitar tone. You cannot get the same sound or punch from a Strat and a Fender amp as you will with a Gibson and a Marshall. Sorry but it just doesn't work that way. Jack was the same for me. He used a vintage Gibson EB-1 with one pickup instead of the Gibson EB-3 he basically made

Alan Lefton, pictured here with Jack Bruce in 1999, was at MSG with his son Mike

famous using the back treble pickup. He did not get the same tone either; he couldn't. They should have reunited years before. Jack almost died the previous year and he was still frail for the show. However, when he sang 'We're Going Wrong' my heart stopped. That was the highlight song of the show for me.

But I loved the show and can relive it on the DVD, and it was so great to see them jam again. I honestly thought that Ginger was the most true to form. In some ways his playing had improved. He wasn't as wild and hard, but more precise and rhythmic.

I honestly thought that Ginger was the most true to form

I went to all three NYC shows and took my son Mike to the October 25th show, where we had second row seats. He even got one of Clapton's guitar picks. The shows were not as good as the Albert Hall (Cream thought so too) and there was friction between Jack and Ginger. I was close enough to see that in the first show. But I thought Clapton played better in the NYC shows and all-in-all the shows were a wonderful, magical and memorable experience. If I could go back in time I would definitely relive it.

I WAS THERE: MIKE LEFTON

I BECAME A huge Cream fan at age 13 in 2004; perfectly ripe for reunion time. Being from New Jersey, the Royal Albert Hall in London was a bit too far for a 13-year-old too travel, so I had to experience the reunion first through bootleg recordings and then the official concert film. When it was announced that they would be returning to NYC for three more concerts, I knew I had to go. My dad was lucky enough to get us second row seats directly in front of Eric Clapton. No other event that year would be anywhere near as exciting.

I remember walking down 7th Avenue towards Madison Square Garden and out of the darkness appeared a glowing light from the marquee… 'CREAM'. Pure elation came flooding over me as the lights dimmed and Jack Bruce, Ginger Baker and Eric Clapton all walked out onto that stage for what would be my only chance to see Cream together in my lifetime. I can honestly say I don't remember much about the performance itself as I was so focused on watching my heroes jam together and taking in the feeling of being in that moment. I do, however, remember being so close to catching one of Ginger Baker's drumsticks after 'Toad', but it went one or two rows directly behind me. This was made up for by the fact that after the show, we waited around the stage and one of Eric's guitar techs gave me one of his guitar picks.

It wasn't until I heard the bootleg recordings from that night that I realised their playing wasn't quite on a par with the London shows, but that didn't matter. I had the once in a lifetime experience of seeing Cream perform live for one of the last times ever. Too much has been said to critique their sound, instrument choice and lack of energy when compared to the Sixties, but that this reunion ever happened at all is nothing short of a miracle. I will always be grateful to have been a part of the experience.

I WAS THERE: JIM CHIRONNA

BEING A HALF-ASSED guitar player who wasn't enough to see the original Cream, I was ecstatic to get a chance to see Clapton, Bruce and Baker on the same stage jamming together again. I never thought I'd get the chance. Sitting in my seat before the show started I was filled with anticipation and struck up a conversation with a guy next to me about how lucky we were to be there. He said, 'Yeah we're lucky, but it's not gonna sound like the Cream we remember, because Clapton is playing a Fender Strat and in the Cream days he played a Gibson SG or Les Paul. So his tone won't be 'on'.' My response was, 'You're shitting me, right? It's not good enough that these legendary musicians are gonna jam for us tonight, I think Eric Clapton knows how to get the tone he needs and wants for this show out of his guitar.'

I think Eric Clapton knows how to get the tone he needs and wants out of his guitar

Needless to say, it was an amazing performance. Clapton hit all the tones and his playing was virtuoso balls-out guitar. Bruce was ripping the bass lines and his singing was powerful and inspired. Ginger Baker was an absolute madman on the drum kit, just like I had always heard, and I finally got to see Cream just kill it. And the know-it-all dickhead who was next to me whining about Clapton playing a Strat instead of a Gibson couldn't say shit except that it was one of the best shows he ever saw. RIP, Jack and Ginger. The music world sorely misses your greatness.

I WAS THERE: BILL LEVY

1968 SAW THEM on the same bill with Richie Havens, The Soul Survivors and Terry Reid at the Village Theater. I was 18. I'd first heard *Fresh Cream* at my high school buddy's apartment in Astoria, Queens. We played in a band together at high school and to say I was blown away by their sound would be an understatement. Like clockwork, 37 years later, I saw them again at Madison Square Garden. Jack Bruce playing bass guitar pretty much influenced me to want to go home and burn mine.

I WAS THERE: PACO PRIOR

I WAS AN 11-year-old kid with impeccable musical taste. I was into them from *Fresh Cream*. *Disraeli Gears* put me over the top. I was an aspiring drummer, and Ginger Baker was 'the goods'. I learned to play drums by daily playing along to Cream's records. My poor five younger brothers and sisters.

Flash forward to the announcement that they were going to do three reunion shows at Madison Square Garden. Absolutely nothing was going to prevent me from seeing one of those concerts, and the fact that I lived less than an hour away from NYC sealed the deal. I went with my best friend and bass player for my band, Saul, who was equally into the group. Fuelled by a stellar Chinese meal from a place across from the Garden, we were more than ready. It was everything I could have hoped for, and beyond. We had excellent seats, maybe 25 rows from the stage. The lights gleaming off Ginger's beautiful green kit was almost blinding. And then the opening notes of 'I'm So Glad' signalled the beginning of an absolutely phenomenal show. You'd never know these guys hadn't really played together in years or that there was ever any antagonism or bad blood between them. The whole show was brilliant; every song you could have wished for was played, right down to 'Pressed Rat and Warthog' with Ginger's croaky lead 'vocal'.

Paco Prior learned to drum by playing along to Cream records

40 years after playing along with their

records, I was in hog heaven. The interplay between Jack and Ginger was even more of a revelation in person. They completed each other's musical thoughts on every song. I was so focused on seeing Ginger in person I almost ignored what Eric was doing. Of course, he was equally brilliant. Through the magic of YouTube, anyone can see these amazing MSG shows. I'd like to think the night I attended was the finest. All I know is, had I not gone and then I'd seen those MSG videos, I'd have been kicking myself until I drew my last breath.

I WAS THERE: LANA MARIKO SOFER

CREAM BROKE UP soon after I discovered them in sixth grade. I was devastated. When I found out they were having a reunion I was elated, but crushed - there was no way I was able to go to the Royal Albert Hall in May 2005. Then I found a two-page colour ad in the *LA Times* announcing the Madison Square Garden shows. I showed the ad to my son who was in his senior year in high school. 'Do you think you can take two days off from school?' He said, 'I think so.' Thanks to a good musical education from me, my son was a big fan of great music and appreciated a lot of Sixties stuff. My husband grew up in New York, had seen Cream twice in the Sixties and gave me his blessing to take our son to NY.

A floor ticket was $350. I have never paid that much for a single concert, but this was a once in a lifetime opportunity. The day the tickets went on sale, I had two Ticketmaster accounts ready, one on each computer. Starting a few minutes before, I nervously got on the site and constantly clicked the refresh buttons on each computer even though I knew it didn't matter until the site went live. Success! I was able to secure two opening night seventh row tickets on the floor. The gig was Monday. My son, who was in two bands at the time, had a charity gig for tsunami victims on the Sunday, so we had to take the red eye, arriving at JFK around 6am on Monday morning. My girlfriend picked us up at the airport and we checked into a hotel located across from MSG. My son went straight to bed.

That evening, we headed to MSG. At this point, we did not have the tickets in hand. In order to prevent unlawful resale, the promoter didn't send floor tickets beforehand. I was kind of nervous and kept logging into my Ticketmaster account. We stood in line to pick our tickets. Those who picked up their tickets were so excited, pumping their fists as if they won a lottery. The average age of the audience was somewhere between 50 and 60 years old, but they were all acting like little kids on a Christmas morning. Nobody could contain the excitement. I was one of them.

When the band came out and began to play 'I'm So Glad', I was so overwhelmed I started to cry. But after the initial teary moment I think I had a big grin the entire time. I'd never thought it was possible to see them live. Not only that, my son was next to me. What a fantastic feeling that was.

When the band started to play 'I'm So Glad' I was so overwhelmed I began to cry

---

My friend's friend was supposedly backstage with them that night. When he asked Eric, 'How are you doing?' Eric supposedly responded, 'I am nervous.' Their playing was really matured by the different experiences each of them had had in life and music. They brought what they learned during the absence. The rough edge they used to have was gone, but that did not mean they didn't have power. It was softened with maturity and became rich Cream. Maybe due to his liver transplant two years earlier, Jack appeared to have aged quite a bit since I last saw him, four years earlier, and his voice sounded older and lacking the punch it once had. But he still sang with power. Ginger looked younger and healthier than before.

As soon as they started to play, we realised this was not a 'let's get together and play the hit songs' nostalgia-type reunion. In a way they were tighter than before. Maybe due to his arthritis and having to accept the limits on his movement, Ginger played more compact and with no waste.

Eric solo often seems to play as if he's obliged to go through a certain routine. With Cream that night, that wasn't the case, although he seemed a little stiff. Perhaps he was indeed nervous. 'Stormy Monday' changed everything. Suddenly he was relaxed, totally immersed in the music and playing freely. It really brought him out of himself. His guitar solo was more soulful than I'd seen before. After that, everything went up a notch. Jack looked very happy to be playing with Eric. And Ginger smiled at Jack.

The second half's performance was beyond my expectation. I appreciated and respected that they took this reunion seriously and put their effort to put an amazing show. There was just one encore, 'Sunshine of Your Love', and of course I could have listened forever. But because the whole thing was so satisfying, I didn't feel deprived to have just only one encore. Having such rich Cream, I was comfortably full!

Being able to experience the show with my son was great. My son's classmates told his teachers he'd gone to New York. The teachers assumed he'd gone to check out colleges. When he returned to school wearing a 'Cream at MSG' t-shirt, one of the teachers was so upset. 'You didn't go there to look at colleges. You went there for Cream!' She was just jealous. I would be too, if I'd missed the chance to see Cream live.

I WAS THERE: CHRIS SZELIGA

I WAS THERE Tuesday night at Madison Square Garden. This was not rock 'n' roll time. They walked on at the stroke of 8.30pm nad for two hours I was 15 again, listening to *Disraeli Gears* until the needle wore through the groove. I heard all of the grumbling about how the jams didn't turn into the old 'street fights' of the Sixties. But I liked it. They played as an ensemble rather than three guys trying to outdo each other. It was great music.

I WAS THERE: SHAWN ROSVOLD

MY DAD WORKED at a radio station in Sydney, Nova Scotia, Canada that didn't play 'that' music. The record companies sent them records anyway and my dad brought them home to me. *Fresh Cream* had several songs on it I really liked, including 'Sleepy Time Time' and especially 'I'm So Glad'. *Disraeli Gears* came out just after I turned 16, dropped out of school and discovered drugs. My favourite tracks were 'Blue Condition', 'Take It Back', 'SWLABR' and 'Sunshine of Your Love'.

Wheels of Fire marked a couple of major milestones in my life. I finally had sex with a real live woman, and then met my first girlfriend. By the time we had sex I was 17, it was winter time, we both lived with our parents and getting together was very difficult. But my girlfriend had a girlfriend whose boyfriend had a car. Back seat make out sessions blossomed into full all-nighters when we discovered unlocked summer cabins with beds and blankets. It seemed 'Badge' was always playing on one of the New York radio stations as we headed home at dawn, hung over and satiated.

Living in a small Nova Scotia town meant we only got to see local bands play concerts and I was devastated when Cream broke up because I knew I would never get to see them live. Fast forward to 2005 and Cream announced a reunion tour. I was working in New York City radio, so this was my chance to finally see them. Tickets were purchased as a birthday present for my old friend and music super fan, John Whidden. The show we saw almost defies description. To this day I marvel that just three people could put out that sound. And, best of all, this small town boy's dream of seeing one of the best and most important bands in history finally came true.

I WAS THERE: JOHN WHIDDEN

IT WAS THE concert I never thought I would see. It was the concert I'll never forget.

Because of Cream I started buying and listening to albums, not just singles. Before Cream I was basically a singles guy. *Disraeli Gears* was the first album I bought, based solely on the strength of 'Sunshine of Your Love'. I debated buying it. What if 'Sunshine' was the only good song on it? But there wasn't a weak track on the album. The high point was 'Tales of Brave Ulysses'. It was and still is my favourite Cream song. At Madison Square Garden, like most everyone else there I wanted to hear 'Sunshine' and 'White Room', but it was really 'Tales of Brave Ulysses' I was cracking to hear.

It was the concert I never thought I'd see

Second up was 'Badge'. I was not disappointed. With Bruce putting in one of the strongest vocal performances I've heard and Baker driving the song while also holding it steady, Clapton weaved in and out as our tour guide, punctuating every highlight along the way. For a few minutes Cream did live what they had done for years on record…took me sailing with brave Ulysses on his journey. It was a short sojourn, but amazing! Three lads from Britain mixing Greek literature with blues, plus some help from a Beatle on 'Badge' (the other highlight of the night for me).

All three made it look effortless. It was a big, full sound, but not thunderous. All three brought out the best in each other. Outside, it was pouring with rain but the electricity inside was drying everyone off, as if anyone actually cared they were wet and cold.

What struck me most about the show was how tight the band sounded. It was as if they had been playing together, without a break, for years. They also looked to be having a blast, which was surprising with all the stories over the years about friction between Baker and Bruce. They also made it look so easy. Their musicianship has never been in question, but to pick up decades later, except for some shows in London, and sound as if they had never stopped playing together was remarkable. That enjoyment seeped into my soul and the soul of the audience.

I did read later that there was some animosity between Ginger and Jack and that Clapton wasn't pleased with the sound. I love you Eric, but sorry, I disagree with you. I thought the October 24th show was incredible in every way. It was also more memorable because it was a 50th birthday present from my wife Mary and my friend Shawn Rosvold, who lived in New York at the time. They, along with Cream, came together and took me on a wonderful adventure that even Ulysses would have been envious of.

I WAS THERE: TOM VANNORTWICK

I WAS THERE for the opening night at Madison Square Garden. I borrowed $800, bought two tickets on eBay and drove to New York from Virginia. It was the most important show I've ever seen. Eric was great and Jack's voice was beautiful. Ginger was good, but occasionally he sounded as if he hadn't listened to the songs since rehearsals in May as he missed a few little parts here and there. I had bought the DVD a few weeks before seeing them and was blown away by them adding 'Tales of Brave Ulysses'. All in all, I wouldn't trade seeing them for any other concert I've ever seen. They are my favourite band ever.

I WAS THERE: MIKE MCGARRY

MY GRANDMOTHER LIVED with my aunt, uncle and their two sons, Ron (called Kavie, their last name was Kavanaugh) and Patrick. I was the last born of the cousins and I worshipped Kavie and Patrick. They were the brothers I never had and I always thought they were so much more sophisticated. I imitated everything they did, including their taste in music. They got me hooked on The Beach Boys, the Righteous Brothers, Sam and Dave, Tom Jones, Marty Robbins and many others. They were off to college and I was visiting my grandmother for a weekend and was looking through some of their albums when I noticed one with a shiny cover and a picture of three men. The title was *Disraeli Gears* so I decided to play it on the console stereo in the living room while Gram was cooking in the kitchen. The first track was 'Strange Brew' and that got the hook in. The second track was 'Sunshine of Your Love' and the hook was set. I played that album through three times that day. It was the fall of 1968. I was 10 years old.

When they came to MSG in 2005, we had seats in the mezzanine level behind the stage. Since they were using a surround sound system, we didn't miss out on anything. I was looking over Ginger Baker's right shoulder all night, and watching the drum solo for 'Toad' was awesome! I couldn't believe he was 67 years old.

Mike McGarry was at MSG

I WAS THERE: ROB CARPENTIER

I'M A BIG Clapton fan and scoring tickets was a huge coup. I hadn't heard of any recent activity from Bruce or Baker and I thought 'they'll sound a bit stale as they've aged somewhat'. But they were simply amazing, as tight as ever and vocally superb. 'I'm So Glad' sounded better than the original. 'NSU' had perfect harmonies. 'Stormy Monday' was a testimony to Clapton's genius when it comes to the blues. And 'Toad' showed that Ginger Baker is like a fine wine, he got better with age. It was definitely one of the top three concerts I've ever been to, and I've been to a hundred of them since the mid-Seventies.

I first heard Cream's 'White Room' at the age of 13 and bought the *Wheels of Fire* album and started following them. I bought two more albums and was disappointed when they broke up. I then heard this music at a party and was told it was Blind Faith, with Clapton and Baker in it. I remember going out and buying the album the next day. That album is in my top five favourite albums of all time. I followed Clapton into Derek and the Dominos as I was becoming more focused on lead guitarists. I discovered that three of my favourite guitarists - Clapton, Jimmy Page and Jeff Beck - had all once been in the Yardbirds, but not all three together. (My favourite guitarist of all time is Hendrix). I saw that Clapton's career was much more visible than Bruce's or Baker's, and bought just about every record he made, starting with *461 Ocean Boulevard*. I'm still a huge fan and listen to him as often as I can.

I WAS THERE: RALPH CONFREDO

I STARTED PLAYING music aged seven when I saw The Beatles on *The Ed Sullivan Show* in 1964. When I reached my teens, deep into music, I decided to play rock 'n' roll rather than concert band music or the old Italian standards my parents preferred. Bass became my first rock instrument due to the mistaken idea that it was strung the same as mandolin, the instrument I started with back in '64. Jack Bruce was my first musical influence, and in my naivety and desire to be as good as him, I figured if I could play 'Spoonful' for as long as Cream did on *Wheels of Fire* then, dammit, I was a bass player! My second bass, and my first good one, was a Gibson EB3 like Jack's. I remain a dedicated musician and my love for Cream, especially Jack with his musical spirit of adventure, has never faded.

When I heard Cream was reuniting for a series of shows at the Royal Albert Hall, I intended to bankroll a trip to England by selling my prized Hofner 500/1 Beatle bass but could not convince my wife of the logic. Fortunately, Cream announced plans to perform at Madison Square Garden in New York, a place old and familiar to me - growing up near the city, as a teenager I would take the bus to Manhattan to see the Knicks and Rangers play as well as going to the circus, boxing matches… and rock concerts! I was able to purchase tickets for the second, middle show at the Garden.

I remember being surrounded by people like me - older, mostly male, with many, many musicians in the audience. On stage, there were no dancers, there was no production - just a somewhat psychedelic backdrop, and certainly not the old school liquid light show I hoped for. There were Fender Vibro-Kings on stage for Eric with a Marshall micro-stack on top to playfully satisfy the old heads who wanted amplification from the old days. And a chair on stage for Jack as he struggled with his health issues.

When they came out, you could tell the applause was not so much in anticipation of the music that was about to happen as it was in appreciation of careers, musicianship and cultural impact. I'm willing to wager there were many in the audience whose lives were changed by the band and the music. They opened with 'I'm So Glad' and my eyes filled with tears. The sound was better than I expected or remembered from past concerts I attended at the Garden. Ginger benefited most from modern technology; I thought he sounded like thunder!

I was most pleased to hear 'Tales of Brave Ulysses', one they skipped during the Royal Albert Hall shows. It was interesting to see Eric as a band member in a trio format and not as the frontman in a larger group, as he'd been for decades. Jack's playing was not nearly as reckless and inventive as it was in the old days; my only disappointment regarding the show was Jack not being the musical provocateur he was as a younger man.

Ginger benefited most from modern technology; I thought he sounded like thunder!

I cried like a baby when Jack died and tried to understand why. Cream represented many things for me. They were around at a critical point in my musical life both as a listener and as a musician. They represented dedication and virtuosity at a time when I was just beginning to aspire to musical competence. They were nicely psychedelicised at a time when I was exploring alternate philosophies. I could see my own mortality in those old(er) men. As the heroes of my youth fade, I feel my own youth recede into memory. The Cream reunion show was more than just a concert; it reunited me with my younger self.

I WAS THERE: MIKE DOCAMPO

THE STANDING OVATION as they walked out was the most amazing one I've ever witnessed. It took a long time before they could start playing. Many people were looking for the wrong thing and were disappointed by the show. Their expectations were mixed with the soundtrack of their youth and their memories of the live recordings, expecting the Gibson/Marshall crunch and the sonics echoing in cavernous halls. Here, Eric was using his signature Strat through tweed twins and the PA was crystal clear. I'm a long-time player who gleaned his skills from this group. Whatever these gentlemen played together was Cream music and I loved it for what it was, and not for what I thought I wanted it to be. Sure, they weren't as

Mike DoCampo remembers an amazing standing ovation

aggressive. But they weren't just decades older (and wiser). They weren't under the influence of the drugs that made them so aggressive back then. I still love the old recordings and revere them to the point that, when playing certain music, I go for that tone and attitude. But I can enjoy the artistry of the reunion show.

I WAS THERE: BOB GARRARD

I WAS BORN in South London, part of a family with a bit of a musical heritage. Mum was a singer and two uncles were good piano players and jazz musicians. My mum took me to see Joe Brown and his Bruvvers in concert in Tooting in 1962. From that point on I was hooked on guitars, and I got my first guitar for Christmas in 1963. The Beatles were my first love and I remember my older sister telling me about a super group called Cream while I was busy listening to *Sgt. Pepper*. She bought *Disraeli Gears* and I listened intently. The one track that stood out then and still does was 'Sunshine of Your Love'.

I worked in IT for many years and eventually ended up in NYC. One of my big clients was, like me, a guitarist and a big Clapton fan. We both agreed that when Eric did the old Cream songs live, they were a bit over produced and lacking the raw energy and drive of the original three man line up in the movie of the farewell concert. When they announced the reunion gig in NYC, I managed to get four tickets via our corporate entertainment group. The day of the concert, one of the client team backed out as he had a family emergency. Left with a free ticket, and unable to find anyone else at short notice, my 18-year-old musician daughter drove home from university in Pennsylvania to come to the show with me.

For her it was a musical education. For me, I was 14 again and listening to the magic sounds these three guys produced. They all worked so hard on stage - Clapton

Bob Garrard went from south London to NYC

working harder than his solo gigs as the sole guitarist and Jack Bruce (as I later found out) playing in considerable pain. My daughter was taken with Ginger Baker - she had never seen anything like Ginger's drum solo on 'Toad' before and she loved 'Pressed Rat and Warthog'. The highlight of my evening was 'Badge' and 'Sunshine of Your Love'. It was a unique night and one that has stayed with us both.

A year or so ago l got tickets to a Sheryl Crow concert, and by making a donation to her charity, got a meet and greet and invitation to her sound check. I was wearing my Cream reunion t-shirt. Sheryl asked whether I went and I replied 'yes'. She asked me about a few questions about the concert. I think she went to one of the Albert Hall concerts. My daughter is a big Sheryl fan and was knocked out that Sheryl would ask for my opinion.

I WAS THERE: AL LIEBSON

I DISCOVERED CREAM in the late Sixties when my old pal Stan played the raunchy 'Sunshine of Your Love' single for me. At some point I saw the *Farewell Concert* on TV and heard a song that sounded very familiar. I said to my sister, 'I didn't know Cream did that song,' and she said, 'What? 'White Room'? Are you kidding me?' I went out the next day and I bought the *Best of Cream*. I've been listening to and loving Cream all these decades, and when my buddies and I found out that they were coming to New York in 2005, we knew we had to go. It was one of the great nights of my life. We were sitting way on top, but it didn't matter - they were fantastic. Unlike a lot of these other bands that reform, they didn't need an extra guitarist or keyboard player, they didn't need a horn section or a group of female background vocalists - any of that would have been awful. I feel blessed to have been able to see Cream after all those years. RIP Jack and Ginger.

Al Liebson discovered Cream in the Sixties

I WAS THERE: DANIEL MEDINA

LIVING IN BRAZIL in the mid-Eighties didn't make for a particularly thrilling musical experience. On the radio, hair metal and Brazilian music were the main offerings. Being 16 at the time, I wasn't particularly enamoured with neither. But there was one classic rock radio station that had very intriguing music from the 1960s and 1970s. Late one night, the main riff of 'Sunshine of Your Love' by Cream came on and my ears were absolutely in love with that heavy but classy sound. It really spoke to me and I instantly became a fan. As they'd broken up in 1968 and the chances of them reuniting for the longest of time seemed to be around zero, seeing the band live was simply too fantastic a notion to entertain.

When they announced the Royal Albert Hall shows, I nearly had a heart attack. Here was a chance to see this incredible band live and I was prepared to pay almost any sum to do so. But, alas, I couldn't get tickets. But to my delight, they announced more shows in New York that fall. And, for all the gods, I was definitely going to be there. I got a seat at Madison Square Garden. Now I just had to fly from Brazil to New York. That should have been the easy part. I had to connect through Miami which normally is not a major problem, except that this was hurricane season....

I arrived at Miami on time. But soon it became clear that Hurricane Wilma was about four hours away from hitting the airport. After so many expectations and such excitement at seeing my idols play in front of me, there was a very real possibility of, instead, just having to find shelter. Finally, the gods of rock smiled on me and I boarded the plane to New York just a couple of hours before they closed the airport.

As long as the band played well, I'd be able to tell my grandchildren that I had seen Eric Clapton, Jack Bruce and Ginger Baker live. But when the band took the stage, they sounded as if they never broke up. While their performance had a maturity to it that represented how much the musicians had grown over the past 40 years, they had retained that incredible ability to improvise over several songs, all of them pushing each other into new territories. Their sound wasn't as loud or raw as in the Sixties but it had a newfound finesse that only musicians of that calibre could summon up and make work in a band situation. Watching Cream live in 2005 stands as one of the best things I ever did in my life. I can now proudly say, 'I watched Cream play live in front of me. The gods of rock must be smiling.'

I WAS THERE: AVRIL MARIE

I SAW THEM live at the Garden back in the Sixties. I remember there being a revolving stage in the middle of the venue, and Mr Baker did a 40 minute drum solo that in my opinion was far too short! I came out of the concert feeling that I had heard the best band in the world. I am a huge Beatles fan but Cream, as it usually does, rises to the top! I also saw them three times at the Garden on the reunion. I never get tired of listening to them; each musician is a maestro in their own right.

Avril Marie was at MSG in 2005

Mr Baker did a 40 minute drum solo that in my opinion was far too short!

I WAS THERE: HOWARD WOLF

WE SAT IN the first row of section 115, right next to the stage. The show was fantastic. It was everything that I expected. Jack Bruce was incredible! It was a great night in the Big Apple.

I WAS THERE: DONNA QUINN

I DIDN'T SEE them until 2005 at Madison Square Garden in New York. All I smelt in the whole arena was marijuana.

I WAS THERE: PERRY RUSSELL

IT WAS LIKE walking into a cathedral. The audience was up there in age (I was 57). I brought my son who was 14. I was impressed by the reverence the audience had. Everyone there knew they were seeing something special. And Cream didn't disappoint. I didn't even realise Ginger Baker was still alive. I always thought he was the best drummer in rock and he didn't disappoint. He made it look easy. Cream were a very special band. My friends and I used to play air guitar to the *Wheels of Fire* album, especially 'Spoonful', 'Traintime' and 'Crossroads'. My favourite member was always Jack Bruce, and though he was physically ailing it didn't seem to affect his singing or playing. Their set was pretty solid. I thought the highlight was a cover of 'Stormy Monday', as pure of a blues as I have heard. I think the Allman Brothers' version on *At Fillmore East* is the standard, and Cream met it. The audience got to see true classic rock legends. They didn't disappoint. I think we all felt honoured to be present at this show.

The audience got to see true classic rock legends

EXTENDED PLAY

Here are some more Cream-related memories from the Sixties and Seventies.

WOODLANDS YOUTH CENTRE
17 FEBRUARY 1967, BASILDON, ESSEX

I WAS THERE: PETER STEVENS
I SAW THEM at Woodlands School in Basildon, Essex. Clapton got quite upset with the audience because some people were shouting out for John Mayall's Bluesbreakers. He played the rest of the gig with his back to us all. Jack Bruce's singing, bass playing and harp were outstanding as was Ginger's very dynamic drumming. I seem to remember one of his specialities was a drum roll on the two bass drums. Before the gig we saw them all having a drink just down the road in a pub called the Owl and Pussycat. It was amazing, but perfectly justified, to think that a couple of years later they were taking the USA by storm and packing out places like the Fillmore.

THE UPPER CUT
1 JULY 1967, STRATFORD, LONDON, UK

I WAS THERE: RITVA KUNOSSON
I WAS WORKING in Stratford and my best friend, a Swedish girl called Febe, used to chum around with Ginger Baker. When I broke my arm I got Eric to sign the cast. It never dawned on me that they were famous. They were just friends to us.

CITY HALL
17 NOVEMBER 1967, SHEFFIELD, UK

I WAS THERE: PAUL REDFERN

CREAM WERE ON tour with the Jimi Hendrix Experience. I can't find the ticket unfortunately so I can't tell you what the actual date was but I think it was in the autumn. It was the first gig I had a ticket for and I had to miss night school to go. In those days, they were still doing those package tours, so there were no less than seven bands on in one night. No one was on stage for longer than 30 minutes!

Cream were actually playing a show in Sweden, where a reviewer commented, 'Cream would benefit, like most other pop groups, by playing at a more subdued volume.'

MARITIME HOTEL
DATE UNKNOWN, BELFAST, UK

I WAS THERE: ELIZABETH MURRAY

I SAW THEM in the mid-Sixties in Belfast, at a place called the Maritime which was a club in a small hotel. It's been knocked down now.

There is no verified record of Cream having performed at the Maritime.

TRADE UNION HALL
DATE UNKNOWN, WATFORD, UK

I WAS THERE: LINDA WALKER

I SAW CREAM at the Trade Union Hall in Watford. They were brilliant, and of course Clapton was terrific.

There is no verified record of Cream having performed at the Trade.

LYCEUM
DATE UNKNOWN, EDINBURGH, UK

I WAS THERE: NICKI ANDERSON
I THINK IT was just after *Disraeli Gears* came out so they played a lot from that album. Eric Clapton was playing with them and the music was amazing. I never kept photos or tickets and stuff. We all got pretty stoned in those days!

There is no verified record of Cream having performed at the Lyceum.

LADS CLUB
DATE UNKNOWN, NORWICH, UK

I WAS THERE: SHEILA JOHNSTONE
I SAW THEM at Norwich Lads Club on King Street in either '67 or '68. Ginger Baker's drum roll was fantastic and went on forever.

There is no verified record of Cream having performed at the Lads Club. Derek and the Dominos (with Eric, not Ginger) played there on 3 October 1970.

HYDE PARK
7 JUNE 1969, LONDON, UK

I WAS THERE: PAUL SMITH
I WAS WITH a group of friends that went to see Blind Faith. Nice day out, but we were so far away it would have been better to stay at home and play records!

SALT PALACE
22 AUGUST 1969, SALT LAKE CITY, UTAH

I WAS THERE: CHRIS WHEELER
I SAW BLIND Faith in Salt Lake City. I'll never forget seeing Ginger's

collection of milk containers around his kit after the show. It was thrilling to hear one of the best drummers ever!

HAWAII INTERNATIONAL CENTER ARENA
24 AUGUST 1969, HONOLULU, HAWAII

I WAS THERE: JUDITH JONES
I WENT WITH a group of kids, including my brother, to see Blind Faith. I remember seeing them on stage, hearing the drums and the music. It all went right through me. It's something I will always remember. It was a blast.

CIVIC AUDITORIUM
1 NOVEMBER 1970, JACKSONVILLE, FLORIDA

I WAS THERE: FREDA JOHNSON COBB
I SAW DEREK and the Dominos with Eric. You paid $5 to get in and everyone walked around and stood at the stage. It was a small stage too. I went with a few girlfriends, and I met my ex-husband there. The band was awesome. They played some slow and some fast songs. But I was interested in the band and Eric was so cute. I leaned up against the stage in front of him and watched him most of the time they played. They took a break and came back and played some more. I can still hear the words 'in a white room with black curtains…' and I was hooked from the very beginning.

ESSEX UNIVERSITY
6 NOVEMBER 1971, COLCHESTER, UK

I WAS THERE: GRAHAM DAY
I FIRST BECAME aware of Cream when 'Wrapping Paper' entered the lower reaches of the *New Musical Express* chart. I found it a strange and quirky number which nevertheless stimulated my interest in the band. During 1967 a favourite album was *Disraeli Gears*, with its luminous psychedelic cover, somewhere upon which was pictured Ginger Baker running along through an autumnal-leaved street scene, hunched, with his

shirt tail hanging down beneath his jacket! I loved 'Sunshine of Your Love' and 'Strange Brew', both of which are still played at full volume when the opportunity presents itself. Unfortunately, in my rural idyll in Suffolk there were not many opportunities to see top flight bands perform. I thought I had cracked it with the Cream reunion concerts at the Royal Albert Hall in 2005 but, being very ill at the time, I was unable to go.

But I did see Jack Bruce perform at Essex University. It was a foggy winter's night and I went with my friends Dave and Kevin. We were in our early twenties and Essex University LCR was the 'go to' place to see the more underground bands. The entrance was down some very steep steps and, it being a cold night, we hurried inside and found a place to sit cross-legged on the floor, as was the norm in those days. Soon Jack Bruce and his band arrived on the stage. His band consisted of Graham Bond, Chris Spedding and drummer John Marshall, who later replaced Robert Wyatt in Soft Machine. Dave's mum described Pink Floyd as 'a nice row' and Soft Machine as 'an awful one'!

The musicianship was tight, showcasing Jack's earlier jazz roots

Dave had bought Jack's *Songs for a Tailor*, a well-constructed, thoughtful and very enjoyable album. Many of the audience were not so impressed. However, the musicianship was tight, showcasing Jack's earlier jazz roots, and his band were the perfect support for his vocals. The audience disaffection for the set was demonstrated when the traditional 'encore' rang out at the end. It was not loud or boisterous enough for Jack and the band to be persuaded to return to the stage.

We were still seated when a roadie came back onto the stage and switched the amplifiers off. 'That's it, then,' we said to each other. That was the end of that. Jack was obviously unimpressed!

I LOVE 'I FEEL FREE': SHAWN MARGARET COHEN

MY PARENTS WENT out of town and I had a 16th birthday party. My ex-boyfriend at the time was not invited but

Shawn Margaret Cohen's ex-boyfriend gatecrashed her 16th birthday party

most of his friends were and my teenage girlfriends and I were all having a great time. I went upstairs for a moment to my bedroom, put some lipstick on and as I came downstairs wearing a pretty sexy jumpsuit and platform heels (this was 1972), there he stood, my very first boyfriend, Glen, who I was still madly in love with! He watched me descend those stairs like a Ziegfeld Folly girl. On the stereo came the song 'I Feel Free' by Cream and he took my hand, kissed me and asked me to dance to it, which we did. The song is all about how this man feels wonderful and free being with his girlfriend, so there was a beautiful reconciliation.

Many years later, Glen died in a tragic accident while riding a bicycle, but every time this song comes on the radio, I just know Glen is saying hello from heaven. Just this year, it came on the radio in my kitchen on the morning of my birthday and I just danced to it, and I was sure Glen was there in spirit, dancing away to it with me. His sister recently had her birthday. She lives in California and what came on the radio as I was writing to her on Facebook, wishing her a happy birthday? You guessed it - 'I Feel Free' by Cream. I told her this story and she was thrilled to think her brother was sending his love via this song.

I LOVE CREAM: ANDREW J NEWBY

I AM A huge Clapton fan. I started teaching myself his style at around 15 years old. Cream gave me 'Crossroads', the key to the blues, which took me right back to Robert Johnson, including that impossible flick in rhythm of a 4 bar. Clapton is quoted as not liking his solo at the farewell gig when he played 'Crossroads'. Nevertheless, it was indicative of his eventual style, emulating electric blues players from Chicago and the Delta blues. The best guitar break there is is in the song 'Badge', with the delicious chorus and pedal-enhanced guitar break of about 15 seconds after each verse. It's beautiful and enlivens the song and the listener. Also, the impeccable use of the wah-wah in 'White Room' is total proof of Clapton's god given talent. As a person who values Clapton as a father figure, his influence on me has been essential in exploring music and life itself even. His story stopped me drinking alcohol and I've managed eight years so far, despite a recent three month blip. Sobriety is the best.

Cream gave me 'Crossroads', the key to the blues, which took me right back to Robert Johnson

---

AFTERWORD

HOW DO YOU define Cream's legacy? Through the critical reverence shown to albums such as *Disraeli Gears*, which was only named the 87th greatest album of all time by VH1 in 2001? Or by totalling up their career album sales? *Wheels of Fire* was the world's first platinum-selling double album, but 15 million albums sold pales in comparison with the 75 million sales racked up by Oasis more than a quarter of a century later. And yet few people would argue that Oasis should be ranked higher in the pantheon than Cream.

Somehow, the numbers don't really stack up when it comes to trying to place a value on Cream's worth. Perhaps the acclaim is measured in the proportion of the contributors to this book, who can only represent a small sample of Cream fans around the world, who describe seeing one of their concerts more than 50 years ago as the greatest they ever saw.

Cream fused jazz, rock and blues in a way that had never been done before, and developed the concept of the extended solo, allowing Eric, Jack and Ginger to showcase their individual talents on stage, even if an unfortunate by product of this was so many rock acts of the Seventies feeling the need to unsuccessfully mimic Ginger Baker's 10, or 20, or 30 or 40, minute drum solos. Jack Bruce never achieved as much artistically as a solo artist as he did with Cream, and similarly Eric Clapton has rarely received the accolades post-Cream he got when he was part of the ultimate rock three piece. No matter.

Cream made an indelible mark on music history and, more than half a century later, their music - and the memories of them performing it - live on.

ABOUT THE AUTHOR

RICHARD HOUGHTON LIVES in Manchester with his fiancée Kate and pomapoo Sid. The author of more than a dozen fan histories on classic rock acts, Richard is presently working on books on Queen, Jethro Tull, Thin Lizzy, Slade and Neil Young.

If you've seen Cream - or any other classic rock act - and would like to share your memories with Richard for possible inclusion in a future book, please get in touch at *iwasatthatgig@gmail.com*.

www.ingramcontent.com/pod-product-compliance
Lightning Source LLC
Chambersburg PA
CBHW050207130526
44590CB00043B/3029